Making
It So

Making It So

A MEMOIR

PATRICK STEWART

GALLERY BOOKS

New York   London   Toronto   Sydney   New Delhi

G

Gallery Books
An Imprint of Simon & Schuster, Inc.
1230 Avenue of the Americas
New York, NY 10020

First Gallery Books hardcover edition October 2023

GALLERY BOOKS and colophon are registered trademarks
of Simon & Schuster, Inc.

For information about special discounts for bulk purchases,
please contact Simon & Schuster Special Sales at 1-866-506-1949
or business@simonandschuster.com.

The Simon & Schuster Speakers Bureau can bring authors
to your live event. For more information or to book an event,
contact the Simon & Schuster Speakers Bureau at 1-866-248-3049
or visit our website at www.simonspeakers.com.

Interior design by Davina Mock-Maniscalco

Manufactured in the United States of America

10 9 8 7 6 5 4 3 2 1

Library of Congress Cataloging-in-Publication Data has been applied for.

ISBN 978-1-9821-6773-8
ISBN 978-1-9821-6775-2 (ebook)

To the memory of Ruth Wynn Owen and Cecil Dormand:
inspirational teachers not only of English literature,
but also of acting and the meaning of theater

The web of our life is of a mingled yarn, good and ill together: our virtues would be proud, if our faults whippt them not: and our crimes would despair, if they were not cherisht by our virtues.

—William Shakespeare, *All's Well That Ends Well*

Contents

Chapter One   1

Chapter Two   29

Chapter Three   59

Chapter Four   85

Chapter Five   109

Chapter Six   131

Chapter Seven   153

Chapter Eight   173

Chapter Nine   195

Chapter Ten   217

Chapter Eleven   231

Chapter Twelve   249

Chapter Thirteen   257

Chapter Fourteen   273

Chapter Fifteen   293

Chapter Sixteen   305

Chapter Seventeen   317

Chapter Eighteen 333

Chapter Nineteen 349

Chapter Twenty 369

Chapter Twenty-One 385

Chapter Twenty-Two 393

Chapter Twenty-Three 403

Chapter Twenty-Four 423

Chapter Twenty-Five 439

Acknowledgments 445

Index 447

Chapter One

We called it t'bottom field, never wondering where, in relation to "t'bottom," t'middle field and t'top field might be. Reflections of this kind were pointless in our working-class corner of Northern England—not just to us kids, but to the whole community. They led you nowhere, and had you been foolish enough to articulate them aloud, you'd have been given a belt round the ear and a lecture: "Who the bloody hell does tha think tha art, asking stupid bloody questions like that? Ya want to get a grip, lad."

All of us lads lived either on Camm Lane or the street with which it intersected, Towngate. Enough mystery in those names alone to attract several ear-belts. What the heck did "Camm" mean? I had no idea then, but I have since learned that the word is English of Norman ancestry: a habitational name for someone from the French city of Caen. "Habitational." The mere utterance of such a mildly erudite word would have gotten me kicked off to bed without any supper.

And what about "Towngate"? There was no proper town or gate to be seen anywhere. It was a little cobbled lane with a short row of houses and, behind them, a triangular lot with houses on two sides. Like the dwellings on Camm Lane, these houses were small and austere, mostly "one up, one down." Those of us privileged to live on Camm Lane looked down upon the Towngate kids because, compared to us, they appeared slovenly and their environment coarser—there always seemed to be a lot of yelling coming from that direction. Nevertheless, two of my friends lived there. My pal Fred's family was so hard up that he wore Wellington boots to school, without socks, every season of the year.

Mirfield, my hometown, sits in what was known as the West Riding of Yorkshire: the westernmost subdivision of Yorkshire, the United Kingdom's largest county. People who know me from my stage work or as *Star Trek*'s Captain Jean-Luc Picard are often surprised to learn that I come from the North of England. The North, as we call it, is analogous to the industrial Rust Belt in the United States: blue-collar and tough, with cultures and attitudes distinct from the snootier South, and London in particular.

During my childhood, Mirfield had a population of around nine thousand. Along the river stood several weaving sheds, a humble term for what were, in fact, textile mills that rose four or five stories high. My mother, Gladys, worked in one of them. The rest of our local economy was agricultural, with farms that grew corn, wheat, brussels sprouts, and kale. This kale was not destined for fancy salads. It was grown solely to feed livestock, which must have been why the Mirfield cows always looked so healthy. Their milk was delivered not in cartons or bottles but in large pails on a rickety cart drawn by an old horse. The dairyman ladled the milk by hand into my mother's large kitchen jug. It was often still a little warm when it arrived, and it was delicious. I don't believe pasteurization was a part of the process.

T'bottom field, my refuge, was one of several fields in the area that were left unplanted, reserved for occasional use by grazing cattle and sheep. This field was also the site of parish church festivals, summer bring-and-buy sales, brass band concerts, and football and cricket matches. In September 1945, when I was five years old, it was where the town's adults held a V-E (Victory in Europe) picnic celebration for us children.

In certain corners of t'bottom field, the grass grew tall. One of my private pleasures was to lie on my back among this grass and watch the clouds drift across the sky. At times they formed recognizable shapes: animals, castles, sailing ships, mountains. These were a marvelous tickler of my imagination and afternoon dreams.

I had many flying dreams. I loved them. All I had to do to get airborne was gently flap my arms up and down. I would rise slowly and vertically, higher and higher, never fearful, until I reached a point where I maneuvered myself into a horizontal position. From there I would swoop down, leveling out and flying fast, just above the ground. Then I'd suddenly lift my head and climb back up again until I was flying between the clouds. For some reason, I never went above the clouds in these dreams. Maybe this was because Mirfield boys like me weren't expected to have lofty ambitions. Certainly none that would ever take me into outer space.

I was born on July 13, 1940, on a Saturday afternoon around five o'clock. My father was away at war. My arrival was slightly delayed because my mother's midwife, having examined my mother that morning, decided that I was not yet ready to appear and declared that she was going to a movie matinee at the Vale Cinema, half a mile away in the center of Mirfield.

But not long after the midwife's departure, my mother's water broke and I was on my way. I suspect that, having heard the midwife say that she was going to the pictures, I had decided that I wanted to know what movie she was seeing, who was in it, and who directed it. A neighbor of my mam's volunteered to go to the cinema to fetch the midwife. But my mother, a kindly soul who loved the movies, refused this offer, saying that she could hang on until the midwife got back.

So, there I was, eager to get out but delayed by my mother's determination to let the midwife enjoy her movie until the end. I like to think that it was then, patiently waiting in the birth canal, that I came to understand that movies are important, and that acting was to be the main purpose of my life—that is, as soon as it could get started. In any event, my mother and I held on. The midwife arrived in due time and out I came: not exactly camera-ready, but after a slap on the bottom and a quick hosing-down, I was ready for my close-up.

I was named after my father, sort of. Though his given name was Alfred, his army buddies called him Pat. This was because he had a temper, and where I grew up, "throwing a Paddy" was slang (and an anti-Irish slur) for pitching a fit. On account of my father being English rather than Irish, "Paddy" got Anglicized to "Pat." He embraced the nickname. Before he went away to war in 1939, he instructed my pregnant mother to name me Patricia if I was a girl and Patrick if I was a boy.

Though he was a stranger to me in my early life, I learned that my father was a fierce, formidable man. In the 1920s and '30s he served in India as a member of the King's Own Yorkshire Light Infantry: the KOYLIs, as they were known. He rose in rank from private to sergeant, earning a row of ribbons that he wore proudly on his chest. By the time of Britain's entry into World War II, he was already in his forties but nonetheless an eager founding member of the British Army's esteemed Parachute Regiment.

Though he was arguably too old to be jumping out of airplanes, the regiment used my father's age to their advantage as a recruiting tool. He had a small, defiant mustache and, like all the men in my family, a prematurely bald head. The recruiting officer would have Dad stand beside him. At a crucial moment in his recruiting speech, he would nod at Dad, who then whipped off his red beret to reveal his hairless pate. The officer scornfully addressed the young soldiers, yelling at them, "What's wrong with you lot? If an old man like this can jump out of planes, shouldn't you be doing it as well? Or are you all too lily-livered?" It worked; the conscripts queued up to become clones of my father, Sergeant Stewart.

Years later, my father explained to me why the soldiers in the Airborne Divisions were such outstanding fighters. Twice during the war, he had jumped, under fire, into German-held territory. Every soldier who boarded the transport plane was initially fearful, he said. But once they survived the experience of jumping out and their parachutes opening, they became utterly fearless. Dad said he had heard men singing and whistling, playfully calling out to their fellow parachutists as they floated through the air. And those who made it safely to the earth, freeing themselves of their parachutes without getting shot, became unstoppable warriors.

Well, after hearing this, I promised myself that I would also become a parachutist. Like my father, I, too, would boldly see the clouds from above! The only difference was that I would never have to worry about being shot at as I floated down. I was downright impatient for this experience as a boy. But somehow, it . . . just hasn't happened. Not long ago I read a news story about an eighty-year-old grandmother who jumped out of a plane while tethered to an experienced parachutist. She landed safely on the ground and had the time of her life. Good for her—but what I've come to realize is that I prefer to live in my dreams.

My father did not live long enough to see me become Captain Jean-Luc Picard. I have often wondered what he would have made of *Star Trek: The Next Generation*—the spectacle of his son, who strongly resembled him and was forty-six years old when cast, commanding an interplanetary spacecraft. Would he have been proud? Would he have wanted to have been aboard the starship *Enterprise*, standing over my shoulder, nudging me when the moment came for Captain Picard to say "Engage"?

In fact, he was very much with me. But it would take me years to comprehend this.

My wife, Sunny, loves to tell friends that I had a Victorian childhood. In many respects, she is right. One of my earliest memories is of sitting atop the steps that led to the yard in front of our house, 17 Camm Lane, and watching the lamplighter light the gas lamps along our street. He came around every day at dusk. With one pole he opened the hinged pane on the lamp. Then he turned on the gas, and with another pole lit the flame. I used to shout "'ello!" to this man, and he would respond

with either "Ay oop!" ("Look out!") or "Ow do?" ("How are you?").
How much more Dickensian can you get?

We spoke with heavy Northern accents, in a Yorkshire dialect
nearly incomprehensible to Londoners, let alone Americans. "Hello"
was rendered in our tongue as "ow do." "Nothing" was "nowt." "The
window" was "t'winder." "Leave me alone" was "Geroff!" If I wanted
to ask a pal to come out to play, I would say to him, "Ata laykin aht?"
"Ata," descended from "art thou," meant "are you." "Laykin" is a very
old word for playing; in Shakespeare's day, actors were sometimes
called lakers. "Aht" is "out."

Our house, and four others just like it, were arranged around an
elevated yard set back from the street. It was eight steps to the top, a
number I clearly remember from a game my pals and I played, hopping
up and down the steps while counting. I should explain what I mean
by "yard." It was a big rectangle of crushed cinders and dirt bordered
by large slabs of stone in front of each house. In front of each door was
a boot scraper to help you get the cinders off the soles of your shoes
before you entered the house. I am still unaccustomed to the American
usage of the word "yard." Our house in Los Angeles has both a front
and a back yard, but these, to me, are more like lovely gardens.

Just to the right of my childhood home were two air-raid shelters
known as Anderson shelters. They must have been put in place right
around the time I was born. They were made of corrugated steel and
half-buried in the ground, with curved roofs. These shelters were
meant to serve all five houses in the yard, but I don't recall them ever
being used. When the sirens went off, which was a rare occurrence,
we hurried across the road in our pajamas and dressing gowns to the
big stone cellar of my Auntie Annie's house.

The only function the Andersons ever served for me was as a private spot for an innocuous age-nine kiss and cuddle with a girl. But
not quite private enough: One afternoon, as I was taking shelter, as it
were, with my female friend, our moment of intimacy was interrupted by our next-door neighbor, Lizzie Dixon. Lizzie was an otherwise kind woman who, like my mother, worked in the weaving sheds,
as did her husband, Gilbert. She just happened to poke her head

through the shelter's opening at an inopportune moment. When she caught sight of what this girl and I were up to, Lizzie told us off in no uncertain terms. To her credit, she never ratted us out to our parents.

17 Camm Lane, as I have said, was a classic "one up, one down." The ground floor had a front door—there were no others—that opened straight into the living room. This room was square, with a large window to the left of the front door that looked out onto the cinder yard. Upon entering, you came upon two stone steps with another door above them, which opened to a flight of steps, also stone, leading to the upper floor. Below this staircase was another door and another flight of stairs, leading downward to the cellar.

Let's start there, in the cellar. Everything was bare stone or brick. Against one wall, and attached to it, was a stone table. On that stood what my parents called the "safe." Its contents were not precious valuables but food: fresh meat, bacon, vegetables, and milk. The safe's door was covered in mesh so that the cellar's cold air could penetrate it, but not the bugs. I remember Sunny's shock when she asked me how we kept things cold, and I told her that I grew up with no refrigeration of any kind.

The cellar was divided in half by a brick wall, and behind this wall was a coal chute coming down from the yard outside. Our coal arrived in bags carried on the backs of deliverymen, who dumped them next to an iron lid in the stone pavement in front of our house. These bags were then tipped over so that the coal could empty into the cellar. This process created a lot of coal dust that the mesh in the safe couldn't keep out, so every item of food that was brought up from the cellar had to be washed.

In the center of the ground-floor living room stood a large wooden table with four wooden chairs around it. There was no upholstery on these chairs. There was a sideboard where cutlery, plates, and glasses were kept, as well as my jigsaw puzzles and board games.

Well, I say "games," but there was only one, Monopoly, which I loved to play.

It's strange now to reflect on a game about money and property being the primary source of entertainment in a household as poor as ours. I loved owning Mayfair and Park Lane, though I had no idea what those names represented except wealth. I also loved owning the railway stations, all four if possible, which doubled the fines of other players landing on them. If I was playing with pals, I always insisted on being the banker, but if I played with my brothers or parents, I was considered unqualified for the job.

I still have this Monopoly set. The original box is long gone, but the cash, cards, and game board, while faded and dog-eared, have survived from my youth. Occasionally, when I visit the homes of friends these days, I will see a Monopoly box sitting on a shelf, and the urge to play almost overwhelms me.

The floor of our living room was covered in ancient and cracked linoleum, with a smallish handmade rag rug set down in front of the fireplace. Ah, the *fireplace*. It was the centerpiece of our house. It was made entirely of black iron, but my mother cared for it as if it were made of marble. She polished it every week with a paste she called "blacking," and when she was done, it shone.

In wintertime, you would find me sprawled on the living-room rug in front of this fireplace, usually in the company of our family dog, a handsome Border Collie named Rover. I firmly believe that Rover recognized me to be the youngest Stewart and took it upon himself to cosset and cuddle me. I was only ten when he passed away, and I missed him dearly thereafter.

In the fireplace's center was a grate in which we burned the coal from the cellar, or, if times were hard, coke. I loved this fire, though I was never allowed to touch it. The first and only time I picked up the poker to have a go, my father, who happened to be home at the time, grabbed it from my hand and said firmly, "*Never* touch another man's fire." I have passed on this lesson to my children and grandchildren.

To the right of the grate was a hot plate, heated by the coals underneath, on which it was possible to boil water or heat up soup or broth. To the left of the grate, also heated by the coals, was the oven, in which my mother cooked joints of meat. But the fire's main function was to heat the room, which it did beautifully. For years, that fire was the only source of heat in the house, though by the time I was in my early teens, a small fan heater had been purchased.

To the left of the fireplace was a shallow stone sink with a cold-water tap above it. That was it for us—no running hot water. To the side of the sink was a small gas ring burner, where water could be boiled if there was no fire.

Up the stone steps was a small landing with a door into my parents' bedroom. To the left of their door was a narrower, flimsier door behind which was a double bed that I shared with my brother Trevor, five years older than me. I suppose that this would have made our home, technically, a "two up, one down." But in name only—the bed took up almost all the space in the room. There was barely enough clearance to open the door, and behind the door stood a very small wardrobe where our few clothes were kept. The wall that separated the two bedrooms was very thin, and sounds in one room could be clearly heard in the other, which led to some uncomfortable though intriguing noises.

Above one side of our shared bed was a double-paned window. Throughout the winter or in wet weather, it was kept closed. But on summer evenings, after I had been put to bed, I opened the bottom pane, and the sill was exactly level with the bed. I could hear the voices of my parents and our neighbors as they sat on their doorsteps gossiping and passing the time of day. They kept their voices quiet, as there were several other children's bedrooms overlooking the yard. But occasionally my ears could make out a laugh, or the sound of a match being struck to light a cigarette. I loved those warm evenings and friendly, reassuring sounds. I felt safe and protected by all the adults down below.

This was our home.

"Hang on a minute," I hear you say. "What about . . . the facilities?" Here I must make a confession: The future twenty-fourth-century commander of the *Enterprise* grew up with neither a toilet nor a bathroom in his house.

Around the side of 17 Camm Lane stood a squat brick building that had two toilets at one end and two more at the other. In between were the dustbins. Each toilet was assigned to a specific house. (The fifth house in our row, I believe, had an indoor toilet. Ah, luxury!) These toilets had their own individual stalls and doors, but no electric light, heat, or sinks for washing one's hands. No toilet roll, either—just old newspapers. At least they had rudimentary plumbing: a water tank mounted above, equipped with a pull cord for flushing.

Lurking in every bedroom, however, was a chamber pot known as a "gazunder," because that's how Northerners described something that "goes under" a bed. The gazunder was strictly for peeing. If you had to go "number two," you were compelled to hold it in 'til sunrise.

The Stewart family toilet served a separate function for me as my reading room. When there is only one social room in your house, where else might you go for a little bit of peace and quiet with your novel or comic book? Not the upstairs bedroom. For some reason—don't ask me why—it was considered out of bounds by my parents until bedtime. And while we had no TV or record player, the radio was always on, which made concentration tough. I spent hours in that toilet. In the depths of winter, I would wear an overcoat and a woolly hat. There was no lighting inside, so I took a candle with me, which provided illumination and warmth to my fingertips.

And I read and read. We had barely any books in our house—just a big medical directory, some war-related books, and a Bible. But the Mirfield public library had a very good children's section, and as I got older, the library's selection of American literature became my obsession. Hemingway, Fitzgerald, Steinbeck, Raymond Chandler's Philip Marlowe detective novels—I read them all. You could only take out two books at a time, so I spent part of every Saturday morning at the library. There were often references and actions that I didn't understand, being way outside of my life experiences, but that didn't matter, except for me desperately wanting to understand them. Yet the narratives kept me going. It was then and there, at the local library, that my love of storytelling began.

So that explains the lavatory setup. Now, to complete the picture of my early home life is—ta-dah!—bath night. This occurred but once a week, always on Friday. Because we had to boil the water for baths, there was a tightly scripted schedule that could not be messed with. My father, when he was home with us, always took the first bath because Friday evening marked the beginning of his weekend rounds of the local pubs and workingmen's clubs.

First our gas boiler, which stood between the sink and the fireplace, had to be filled with water, several gallons' worth. This was done by attaching a hose to the cold-water tap. Then the gas was lit beneath. While the boiler was heating, my father lathered up his brush with soap and shaved with hot water from the kettle. He used an old-fashioned straight razor, and I was always the one Dad called upon to shave the back of his neck. I became very good at it, largely because I was terrified of what he would do if I cut him. When I was a little older, I sometimes (for reasons you will soon understand) had to overcome the urge to move the razor to the front of his throat.

This was a perilous and scary job, given his short temper and insistence on looking immaculate when he left to meet comrades and drink the evening away. But in time I became very proficient at it and speedy, which I know he respected. I was paid threepence ("thruppunce," in Yorkshire) for this work, which was, in time, increased to sixpence (a "tanner," probably named for John Sigismund Tanner, the eighteenth-century chief engraver of the Royal Mint).

Hopefully the bathwater would be hot by the time Dad had finished shaving. Trevor and I were tasked with carrying up our old zinc bathtub from the cellar. It was positioned near the boiler's tap, which, once the coal dust had been cleared out, we opened to fill the tub. At this, we were all sent upstairs so that Dad could undress and bathe in peace. He never took long, and soon he would come up the stairs to dress for his night out. This was the cue for

Trevor to take his turn and go downstairs to bathe in the same water that my father had used. (Immediately upon being emptied, the gas boiler was refilled to heat up water for my mother's bath and mine.)

My father was out the door at 7:30 p.m., dressed in gray flannels, a white shirt, his Parachute Regiment tie, and a blazer accessorized with his KOYLI badge on the breast pocket. He looked magnificent.

Trevor was a fast bather, and as soon as he had dried himself off and dressed, he, too, was out the door to meet up with his pals. But before he left, he was duty-bound to empty the bath. This involved bringing up a rubber tube from the cellar, putting one end of it in the bathwater, and then sucking hard on the other end to coax the water up the tube, whereupon it was emptied into the old stone sink. This was not a pleasant job, and Trevor always cleaned his teeth afterward. Trevor joined the Royal Air Force when he was eighteen, so I inherited the task of emptying the bath. I don't recall ever swallowing any bathwater by accident, but the process filled my mouth with an awful taste, simultaneously soapy and dirty. Needless to say, I followed my brother's custom of always cleaning my teeth.

Next came my bath. Mam would find some nice music on the radio. I changed into a dressing gown, a hand-me-down from Trevor, and passed the time reading until the boiler was ready and it was time to fill the tub again. I loved climbing into the bath and lowering myself chin-deep into the warm water. I just had to be careful to keep away from the side of the tub nearest the fireplace, as it got a lot hotter than the water in the tub. At different times, we all got nasty burns from touching the rim of the bath.

My mam always had a towel warming for me before the fire. When I was done, she wrapped me up in it and dried me off, which I always enjoyed. Then I climbed into my pajamas—also, at one time, Trevor's. Finally, it was my mother's turn to bathe. I kept her company, my head buried in a comic book in order to afford her some privacy. After a while, she got into the habit of asking me to scrub her back with a flannel. This did not in any way make me uncomfortable. I loved my mother so much, and helping her wash seemed to bring her so much comfort and contentment: feelings that, alas, she all too rarely experienced.

For the first five years of my life, with Dad off to war, my mother was my only parent, and she was a happier person then, though I recognized this only in retrospect.

Life was mostly bliss for me in those very early years. My parents' bed was a large double that took up a lot of space, but there was room beside it for a small cot. That was where I usually slept. Having my mother always so close—when I fell asleep and when I woke up— made me feel so reassuringly *safe*. She had a soft, round, pretty face that shone like the sun.

The guardrail on the side of my cot could be pushed down, and one of my earliest recollections is of rolling out of the cot onto my mother's mattress. As soon as I was in place beside her, she would throw the covers over us both, and I found myself in a cotton cave warmed by my mother's body. I would tickle her and she me, and we would laugh and laugh, until, exhausted, I would collapse into her arms, with my head buried into her neck, her hair around my face.

We sometimes played this same game of snuggling and laughing in an armchair, or on the rug, or even when the rent collector came. As noted, times were hard, and often my mother didn't have the rent. So when we heard the knock on the door, we always knew who it was, and we hid underneath the big table, where the rent collector couldn't see us through the window. He would knock repeatedly and shout, "Come on, Mrs. Stewart, I know you're in there! Open the door!" I would giggle, and my mother would hush me with her finger on my lips. Then, when we knew the man was gone, we rolled out from under the table, hysterical with laughter.

It was a serious situation, but my mother never let me feel the gravity of it. It was all just fun and games to me. What this was costing her psychologically, I never knew. But surely there must have been a price.

My parents had a complicated relationship well before I entered the picture. Trevor and I had a much older brother named Geoffrey who was, despite being born out of wedlock, our full brother. My unmarried mother gave birth to him in September 1923. My father quickly acknowledged the baby as his. But shortly after Geoffrey's birth, Dad joined the army, went into training, and was shipped off with his fellow KOYLIs to India.

Geoffrey had a ribald sense of humor, and in his adult years, he derived pleasure from introducing himself to my young girlfriends by saying, "Hello, I'm Geoffrey, and I'm a bastard." Every time I heard Geoffrey say this, I laughed. You have to understand how funny it sounded in a Northern accent, though I suppose I should have been more sensitive to the shock that my girlfriends expressed. I never really understood why Geoffrey did this, but if it was his frank and direct way of saying, *My dear, I want you to know everything about Patrick's family*, that was fine by me.

I have often wondered where Geoffrey's conception might have occurred. Certainly not in my mother Gladys's home, as she lived with her parents, Freedom and Mary Barrowclough, and her sister, my Auntie Annie. And probably not in my father Alfred's home, because he was still living with his mother, Mary Stewart. I can't imagine that my parents splurged on a hotel room, because they couldn't have afforded it. When I asked Geoffrey where he thought it happened, he replied, with characteristic tartness, "In a ditch behind a hedge."

Geoffrey also harbored a theory that my father, whom he loathed, was not his biological father. It is true that Trevor and I bore little resemblance to Geoffrey. And Geoffrey's surname was not Stewart but my mother's maiden name, Barrowclough. When Mam died in 1977, Geoffrey, only half in jest, suggested that our dad had murdered her, smothering her with a pillow in the council house in Mirfield where they lived out their later years together.

Highly unlikely. What is true is that Geoffrey was disinclined to like my father from the very beginning of his life. When Alfred Stewart joined the army, my maternal grandfather went to the county court with my mother to seek a judgment compelling Dad to pay for child support. Gladys won her case—I have seen the pertinent court files—and Dad sent along the money, though it didn't amount to much. Geoffrey and my mother lived with my Barrowclough grandparents, who, though they were of modest means, provided a cozy and secure home.

Freedom Barrowclough was, by all accounts, remarkable. He was a short, stocky Yorkshireman with a bald head—I get it from both sides—and a large mustache, who served as an elected councilor for his district in Mirfield and, in time, was elected in a unanimous vote to be the Mirfield Town Council leader. He was much loved by his neighbors and constituents for championing the rights and needs of the working people.

My mother had fond memories of growing up as a Barrowclough. When her father came home on a Friday or Saturday night from his local workingmen's club, he often brought a few friends with him, all in high spirits. Freedom would come up to her bedroom, Mam said, scoop her up, and carry her downstairs. My grandparents had an old upright piano, and my mother was a proficient self-taught pianist. Sometimes, Freedom would ask her to play something for the gathered men. Other times, he would sit her atop the piano, and Mam happily led the party in singing songs.

The most interesting aspect of Freedom's life, to me, is a position he held outside his duties as a councilor. Adjacent to t'bottom field was a pie-and-pea shop that he ran for a time, serving classic Northern takeaway: savory meat pies accompanied by mushy peas and gravy, all prepared by Freedom himself. My mam sometimes assisted her father in the shop, and she told me that the food was "right good." My grandfather was generous of spirit, and if a local family was struggling with health or money problems, he personally delivered pies and peas to them, never asking for payment. Freedom died in 1937, three years before I was born. I so wish that I had known him. My son, Daniel, carries the middle name Freedom in tribute to his great-grandfather.

In 1935, my father's service in India came to an end, and so did my mother's days as a Barrowclough. He came home and immediately married her, and shortly thereafter, she became pregnant with Trevor.

Was this the climax of a passionate, years-long love affair that finally became permissible in society? Did Alfred joyfully reunite with Gladys with hopes for a blissful future? Was he hiding from some other relationship? Was he simply ready to disappear into a conventional life as a working-class family man? I cannot bring myself to believe any of these things about my dad. All I know is that I could play him well in the movie version.

And what of sweet Gladys Barrowclough? Why she said "Yes" to Alf Stewart more than a decade after he had dumped her is incomprehensible to me. Did she genuinely pine for him all those years that he was away? Did she feel that, as a woman in her thirties, the clock was ticking, and that Alfred was the best that she could do? Did she no longer wish to live with her parents? Did she feel that Geoffrey needed a father figure? I am skeptical on that last count because Geoffrey had the kind, loving Freedom Barrowclough to look up to.

In any event, my parents were married and moved into what was then called a "low decker," essentially a bungalow, near the pie-and-pea shop. I never lived in this place, and even as a child, when my mother pointed it out to me, I was shocked at how tiny it was and how small its windows were. It must have been horrendous for Geoffrey, as they all would have had to share a bedroom, which itself might have been just a corner of the living room. At some point, my immediate family moved to 17 Camm Lane, and Geoffrey moved back to his original childhood home, that of my grandparents. Upon their passing in the late 1930s, he continued to live in that house with its new occupants, our Auntie Annie and her husband, Arnold Cartwright. This entire arrangement was also something that was never discussed.

I liked Uncle Arnold. He was private and shy, but he had a gentle, engaging sense of humor. My father, however, had only contempt for him, which grew into hatred when 1939 came around and Great

Britain declared war on Germany. Arnold did not join the military. I do not know the reason for this—if he was a pacifist, or if there were health reasons, or if he held some sort of essential wartime job that exempted him from service. But his not putting on a uniform made him, in my father's eyes, a coward. Appallingly, Dad referred to Arnold as "she."

Dad surprised the family when he reenlisted in 1939; he was old enough and had served long enough to be exempted from further military duty. I suspect that he had quickly tired of family life with Gladys and Trevor, and soon there would be another kid to deal with. A note on that: Decades later, I was reading a play I had been sent that was set during World War II, and there was a scene in which a soldier bids goodbye to his wife. The penny dropped. I was born less than a year after Britain's entry into the war. Might I have been conceived the night before my father left to serve his country? I have looked at the dates and it seems probable. Do I have Adolf Hitler, of all people, to thank for my being in the world?

I know little of my paternal background. Sometime during his youth, my father moved with his mother and three siblings to the West Riding of Yorkshire from Tyneside, in North East England. Because of Tyneside's proximity to Scotland and my surname, Stewart, I like to think that somewhere in the mists of time, I had Scottish ancestors. I enjoy the idea of coming from people who lived in a picturesque Highland glen or alongside a scenic loch.

But my research into this side of my family has yielded scant results. One detail stands out to me: On the marriage certificate of a great-grandmother named Elizabeth, the space for her signature is marked with an X. She was illiterate. This makes me quite sad. What must her life have been like? What hardships did she endure? Did she dream of a different life? What would she have made of my life? My time on the *Enterprise* sometimes makes me envious of the character I play, Jean-Luc Picard. How I wish I had his ability to travel through time and to be teleported into faraway places via the ship's transporter. However, the truth is that all I want to do is revisit the past.

Perhaps I could have made things happier.

Yorkshire was also coal country, and when he was fourteen years old, my father left school to work "down the mines." But he wasn't a miner. His job was to open the heavy rubber or leather swing doors that separated different chambers of the mine. He would sit on the floor and pull the doors open to let a horse- or donkey-drawn wagon of coal pass through. That's all he did. I don't know if his job qualified him for a miner's lamp, but we had one on a shelf in our house on Camm Lane when I was growing up, and I presumed it to be his.

This job did not last long. His mother loathed him doing such dangerous, unhealthy work and urged him to find other employment. This included working at a glassblowers', working for the LMS (London, Midland and Scottish) Railway as a painter, and doing odd jobs at the local railway-engine sheds. I asked my father once what it was like toiling underground, but the only response I got was a frown and a long exhalation of breath. That was all I needed to know that I shouldn't inquire further.

Another taboo subject was my paternal grandfather, William Stewart. I never met the man, and he was seldom spoken of. The mere mention of his name made my father angry, so I knew better than to bring up such questions. The only grandparent I ever knew personally was William's wife, Mary, who cut an intimidating figure. In my childhood I visited her just a few times, and what I registered was that she rarely spoke, and when she did, everyone had to listen—and what she had to say was never pleasant. Grandma Mary was quite tall and thin, her mouth perpetually turned down at the corners, her hair always severely pulled back from her face, which was set in Northern granite. She was well put-together in a drab way: a blouse, a cardigan, "sensible" shoes.

There was one meeting with Grandma, however, that was quite different. If you'll permit this diversion into my future, it occurred in 1960, when I was twenty years old. I was about to embark on a life-changing two-year world tour with the Old Vic Theatre Company, headlined by none other than Vivien Leigh, a double Oscar winner for her portrayals of Scarlett O'Hara in *Gone with the Wind* and Blanche DuBois in *A Streetcar Named Desire*. More on that adventure later.

But news of this pending trip reached my grandmother, and not long before my departure, a letter from her arrived, requesting that I come visit her at her home. Grandma lived in Blackpool, a resort town on the Lancashire Coast known for its long, brightly lit promenade and noisy amusements. Blackpool served the working class, and I had spent many joyful summer holidays there. Mary's letter, though, was not so much an invitation as it was a summons—and it wasn't to spend a holiday, but to take an audience with her.

My instinct was to decline the invitation, but after a family discussion, it was agreed that a command from Mary Stewart was so unusual and unprecedented that I should honor it, if only to satisfy everyone's curiosity. My mother offered to accompany me. I think she actually rather liked Mary, perhaps because it gave her pleasure to see someone who could control and emotionally manipulate my father.

Mam and I ate prepared sandwiches on the train to Blackpool, because Grandma had made plain in her letter that she would not be giving us lunch. When we arrived, we were given a cup of tea by Grandma's live-in companion, whom we'll call Dorothy.

My mother and I tried to make small talk over tea, but this was not a feature of Grandma's approach to communication. It was unmistakable that something was up. When the tea was done and quickly cleared away, my grandmother told Dorothy that it was time for her to do some household shopping and that she should take my mother along with her. *Oh, God help me, Grandma Mary and I are going to be left alone.* My intimidation turned into serious unease. And let's be clear, I wasn't a little kid—I was twenty.

Once we were alone, we sat across from each other in armchairs, and Grandma began to talk . . . about her mysterious, long-absent husband and my father's father, William. The familiar rigidity of her face dissipated and an unexpected softness appeared. She told me how much she had loved William, how hardworking a man he was, and how much he had cared about his four children, which, of course, included my father. And then she mentioned how much he had loved his job in the theater.

What?! Stop, wait. Theater! WHAT theater???

The theater in Jarrow, she said. She was referring to a town in Tyneside near where Mary and William made their home in Hebburn. I knew that my father had been born and spent his early life in that region, but nothing about *his* father ever having had anything to do with the theater.

William was a stage carpenter, my grandmother said. He made the scenery and some of the furniture for the plays. He also worked as a handyman in all parts of the building, not just backstage. One day—Grandma didn't know how it happened exactly—William was pushed onto the stage as a performer when an actor failed to show up. He didn't have much to say, just a few lines, and after he uttered them, he just stood there until another actor pushed him off into the wings. But that was all it took—he was hooked, and he asked the theater manager if he could be given other parts. He didn't expect to be paid, as he would continue his job as the in-house carpenter. Of course the manager agreed: They were getting a new company member at a cost of nothing. I have the impression that the business of theater was much more informal in those days.

Well, Grandma continued, they started giving my grandfather more and more acting work even as he kept his day job. And then this part-time hobby developed into something else. Perhaps it is best described, simply, as ambition.

Grandma's story got a little confusing at this point, and I could see that she was becoming upset as she recounted the details. Her husband wanted to stop being a carpenter and seek out more acting roles. That meant only one thing: London. He left Hebburn and his family to pursue a life in show business. I couldn't follow all the details that my grandmother was relating to me, but the upshot was this: His new career took off, and he was consistently getting work in the West End. He never returned to Hebburn.

Grandma and the four children had been deserted. Looking back, I think it's possible that my father, saddled with his own abandonment issues, was an apple who did not fall far from the tree.

Somehow, my grandmother had connections in the West Riding of Yorkshire, and that's where the five of them went to live, and how my father ended up a Yorkshireman. Mary Stewart didn't have a penny to her name. She took in laundry, which allowed her to work at home and care for her children, and they all crammed into a little rented stone cottage. Those must have been very hard times. Britain was walloped by a severe economic slump in the aftermath of the First World War, and the North was particularly ravaged by poverty and hunger. Jarrow, where my grandfather discovered his love of the theater, became the epicenter of worker anger and frustration. In 1936, two hundred unemployed men, most of them veterans of the local shipyards, staged a protest in which they walked on foot for nearly a month all the way down to London, a procession that came to be known, famously, as the Jarrow March.

I wish that I had asked my grandmother more questions about how she and her children survived these times, but I didn't want to pry. It was amazing enough that she was telling me all this to begin with. Dad had two brothers, William and Clifford, and a sister, Doris, who I knew in later years as my Auntie Dolly. Grandma told me one lighthearted story about them. One December, she was busy doing her pre-Christmas baking, which included four loaves of fruitcake, a Northern specialty that I love to this day. In my part of England, these cakes were made early so that they could be stored in a dark place and left to "mature." In Grandma's house, there was a lockable sideboard. Being able to lock up the cakes was essential, she said, because her children were always hungry, and there would be no treats for Christmas if they got into that sideboard.

Clearly, she underestimated their determination. When their mother was out one day, the Stewart children, led by the eldest, William, got hold of a screwdriver and undid the back of the cupboard, bypassing the locked front. They took out the fruitcake loaves, carefully cut off a slice of each at the end, and then, with a long-handled spoon, scooped out the center of each loaf, eating up the contents on the spot. When they were done, and no doubt full, they put back the end slices they had cut off so that the loaves looked as if they were still whole. Then they put them back in the cupboard and screwed the back panel into place again.

Weeks went by and Christmas Eve arrived. The sideboard was unlocked and the loaves were taken out. Of course they immediately fell apart. I asked Grandma how she responded. She told me that she chased the children around the kitchen with long wooden tongs normally used to pull laundry out of hot water. Finally, she admitted, she sat down in a chair and wept.

Later on, Auntie Dolly told me a story that filled me in regarding the last time my Stewart grandfather was ever heard about. A magistrates' court in the West Riding had charged the elder William Stewart with desertion and sentenced him to pay a weekly sum of money to his family. He did send payments for a time, but then they stopped.

The police in London then went looking for William and learned that he was appearing in a play at the Elephant and Castle Theatre, south of the River Thames. The play was already underway when the police arrived. A stage manager showed the officers into the wings, where my grandfather was about to make an entrance. They told him that he was under arrest and that he must come with them to the station at once. William assured them that he would, but he pleaded to be allowed to make his next entrance and do the scene, which was his last in the play anyway. Otherwise, my grandfather said considerately, it would ruin the evening for the audience.

The police assented to William's modest demand. He went onstage and played his scene. But when it was over, he quickly exited on the other side of the stage and made his daring escape. According to my grandmother, he was never seen or heard from again, though she later learned that he had found his way to America, where he continued his career as an actor.

I first landed on the shores of the United States near the end of my world tour with the Old Vic Theatre Company, in the early weeks of 1962. It occurs to me that it's just barely possible, given our ages and chronologies, that Granddad William and Grandson Patrick stood on American soil at the same time.

My grandmother never explicitly gave me a reason why she invited me to Blackpool that day. I suppose that she wanted me to know that my interest in the theater was not without family precedent. Perhaps she was even somehow still proud of her runaway husband and still felt love for him. But the timing of her summons proved prescient. At some point during that same world tour, I received a letter from my mam telling me Grandma Stewart had died. Our memorable tête-à-tête marked the last time I ever saw her.

I remember going for a long walk after taking in this sad news. I reflected upon the life that I was living, thousands of miles from home, and the life that Mary Stewart had lived. She had only ever experienced gray Northern streets, and sometimes, for an hour or two at a time, the Blackpool promenade. My mother's horizons weren't much wider. She never left England, and, for that matter, saw very little of her home country. My parents traveled once to Stratford-upon-Avon to see me play Shakespeare. That's as far flung as her life got, apart from when she came with her sister, my Auntie Annie, to a Saturday afternoon matinee of a show I was doing at the Library Theatre in Manchester. It was a modern play with a lot of cursing and naughty language, most of it spoken by my character. After one of my tirades, there was a long silence onstage, which was interrupted from the seats by my auntie's unmistakable voice, saying, "Eee! That's niver our Patrick."

World-conquering ambition was not part of the makeup of Northerners—at least not the ones in my family. When I was around ten years old, my outrageous dream was to be a long-distance lorry driver. In Mirfield, most of the boys went straight from school into heavy industry or the coal mines. Most of the girls went into the weaving sheds. And a handful of my peers ended up in reform school and, inevitably, a few years later, prison.

During summer-holiday road trips to the North Sea Coast, we crossed the A1, the main road from London to Edinburgh. We stopped at this junction for drinks and ice cream. I loved to stand in the car park and simply watch the traffic speed by. But it was the lorries, rather than the cars, that I drooled over.

In similar fashion, I loved trains, and railway engines in particular. You've heard of the peculiar English term "trainspotting"? I was an avid spotter. My friend Bryan and I liked to position ourselves at the side of an embankment in Mirfield. Most of the engines had numbers on the curving plates above the main driving wheel. But a small number of them, thrillingly, had *names* on their plates. Down the line from our spot was a small footbridge where other pals staked out their spotting spot. This meant that they often saw the oncoming engine before we did. When we heard them cry out "It's a namer!" we were nearly overcome with anticipation.

Most of the time, the oncoming engine was one we had seen many times before. But when it wasn't, the yells turned into screams and we knew it was something special. I vividly remember the day when the screams escalated into all-out hysteria. Open-mouthed and pop-eyed, we watched the *Sir Nigel Gresley* hurtle past, roaring magnificently, a plume of white smoke rising from its funnel. I had read the name of that engine in books but never expected to *see* it with my own eyes. An unforgettable moment.

One more trainspotting escapade. When I was eleven, our church choir was invited to participate in Evensong at the Festival Church, on the roundabout at the end of London's Waterloo Bridge. This was during the 1951 Festival of Britain, a sort of UK-only world's fair that celebrated our country's achievements and cathartically broke through the postwar gloom. I had never before been down to London, and we would be traveling by rail—quite a leap from trainspotting. We were there for only two nights, but we visited all the famous sights and, of course, the futuristic highlights of the festival itself, the Dome of Discovery and the Skylon.

When I got home, the first thing my mother asked was, "What did you like best, Patrick?" I cried out, "Mam, I touched the *Mallard*!"

It was not at all what she had expected, and she looked confused. Trevor, who also sang in the choir and had been on the trip, said, "Mam, he is such a twerp. *Mallard* is a railway engine." I admit that both of Trevor's assertions were correct. BUT: *Mallard* at that time held the world speed record for a steam engine, 126 miles per hour, and it had achieved that accomplishment on our turf, on a stretch of track somewhere north of York. When our train arrived at King's Cross station, there, idling on the other side of the platform, was *Mallard*, freshly in from Edinburgh.

Our group walked past it. Well, some of our party did, but not me. I stood and stared reverently at the name etched into its boiler: MALLARD. I could hear Trevor shouting out my name down the platform, but there was no way that was I going to waste this moment. I stood on tiptoe and reached up, leaning over the edge of the platform, and I . . . just . . . barely . . . touched . . . the nameplate. Yes, I could have very easily fallen onto the tracks and injured myself, but I didn't. I touched *Mallard*'s nameplate.

This experience ranks alongside the time that Kirk Douglas came to greet me backstage after a performance in Los Angeles as an all-time highlight of my life. But it also illustrates the context in which I was raised: Lorries and namers were as exhilarating as life ever got.

I was five years old when World War II ended and my father was finally "demobbed"—army-speak for demobilized and officially released from the military. My childhood was never again the same.

In fairness to my father, his demobbing must have been a very depressing experience. He left the British Army as an RSM, regimental sergeant major, of the Parachute Regiment—a superstar among the noncommissioned ranks. But back in Mirfield, he was a nobody, except perhaps to the handful of other local demobbed men who had served under him.

I learned later in life from my brother Geoffrey that there was another potential reason for his dark moods. Before my father left the army, he took a meeting with his commanding officer, a colonel, who asked him what his civilian plans were. My father had no ideas as such. The colonel then asked Dad if he had heard of the Dorchester hotel in London. When my father said he had not, the colonel explained that the Dorchester was one of London's five-star luxury hotels, and there was an assistant doorman position open that could be held for him. The sweetener to this offer was that, in a couple of years, the head doorman was due to retire; my father, if he performed his duties well, would inherit the job. The wage was not great, but the gratuities were significant, especially upon ascending to the position of head doorman, which also came with lodgings in the actual hotel. On top of that, the colonel told Dad that if Mrs. Stewart was also interested in a hotel job, one could be found for her.

My father was excited at this prospect and told the colonel that he appreciated the offer but needed to discuss the matter with his wife first . . . and apparently, as soon as Dad relayed this extraordinary news to Mam on Camm Lane, she shot the idea down without a second thought. She didn't care about the accommodations and the income. She simply wanted to stay in Mirfield, and that was that.

I have reflected upon her decision often and concluded that she was fearful of leaving the security of the only place she had ever lived. But the most astonishing aspect of this story is that my father assented and agreed to turn the job down. He had just spent the last five years living away from my mother and had done spectacularly well for himself. In London, his life would have been full of promise and security. I have no doubt that he could have managed an arrangement of living without my mother and sending his wages north to his family, if that could have been agreed upon. In Mirfield, by contrast, his future was totally unstable.

For five years on Camm Lane, it had been two children with a loving mother and an auntie and uncle living just across the road. I have no recollection of when, specifically, the atmosphere in our home began to change. It's taken me decades of analysis, beginning in the late 1980s, to understand and cope with the impact of the violence, fear, shame, and guilt I experienced as a child. The first and most important step was to acknowledge to myself that these things had happened at all. Nevertheless, I have never arrived at a place where I can say, "It was that Saturday night, that month, that year." That is still buried. All I know is that when I was five, I was very happy. By the time I was seven, I no longer was.

Chapter Two

One day, something happened at t'bottom field that left me shaken. A few of us had been kicking a ball around when I spotted a squirrel darting up the branch of a tree. We all stopped and stood in wonder, observing this creature with delight, because squirrels were rare where we lived. Then there was a shout from an older boy who was walking toward us. He wanted to know what we were looking at, and we pointed to the little creature in the tree. It was then that I saw he was carrying an air rifle, which he lifted and pointed. I yelled "No!" but it was too late—he had pulled the trigger. The squirrel was hit and began sliding down the tree's trunk. It dug its claws into the bark and temporarily broke its fall. But it couldn't hold on. Scratching desperately at the trunk, it slipped farther and farther down, until it fell with a gentle thump onto the grass and lay still.

I turned and ran frantically away from the scene, over the wall and up Camm Lane to our house. Crashing through the door, I encountered my mam, just home from the mill, looking at me with alarm. I threw my arms round her and howled. Eventually, after I'd calmed down a bit, I told her what I had witnessed. It was the first time I had ever seen a living creature die. Mam held me tight and calmed me, wiping away my tears.

But I was not a softy as a boy. I couldn't afford to be. Where I came from, if you weren't tough on the playground, you became a target for bullying. At times, *I* was one of the bullies, which I regret to this day. There was a lad in our class who had a deformed hand: a small lump of skin and bone with tiny stubs for fingers, and only three of them. We would surround him and threaten him with violence if he didn't hammer his hand against the stone wall until it was bloody, just for our cruel amusement. When he obliged and we were all satisfied, we would give him a shove onto the cobbles and run off laughing. I look back upon this behavior with deep shame.

But the squirrel incident must have spoken to a more empathetic side of me. As I reflect upon it now, I realize that it was not the squirrel's death that elicited my tears but its desperation as it scrabbled to cling to the tree. I sensed the terror the poor creature was feeling, and this induced terror in me. I suspect that it's exactly this identification with others' fears and feelings that led me, eventually, into wanting to act.

This empathy would soon come into play with regard to my consoler in the squirrel incident, my mother. I do not have a specific memory of my father's homecoming, but suddenly Dad was among us in 17 Camm Lane, and it was clear to my brother Trevor and me that he was not happy to be there.

Finding a new job, the right job, was not easy for him. There was nothing available that could possibly have made up for the status he'd held in the army as a figure of immense responsibility and respect. When he first got home, he was basically an itinerant laborer: digging trenches, mixing cement, unloading lorries. Taking orders rather than giving them. Later on, he worked as a painter at the massive Imperial Chemical Industries plant on Leeds Road in nearby Huddersfield. I am convinced his health suffered from whatever he was inhaling at this workplace. His lungs had already been weakened by two bouts of malaria in India, and he smelled vile when he came home from work, before he peeled off his overalls.

By contrast, my mother took immense pride in her work at the weaving sheds. I only visited her there once, and I was made uneasy by the loud, clanking machinery and the smell of dyes and exhaust. But I saw how brightly Mam went about her day in that not-bright place, wearing a long gray cotton coat, her hair pinned up and wrapped in a turban-like covering. It wasn't just the satisfaction of an honest day's work; it was also the camaraderie, the pleasure she and her female coworkers took in each other's company. After the army, Dad simply never knew that feeling.

My father only struck me once. It didn't really hurt, but it was humiliating enough to leave a lasting impression. Soon after he had been demobbed, we went as a family on holiday to Blackpool. One day we were walking along the promenade when my father spotted a fruit-and-vegetable shop. He said, "There's something I need to pick up there, but you go on walking. I'll catch up." Soon enough he returned to us, holding something in his hands behind his back. "Patrick, close your eyes and hold your hands out," he said.

I did what I was told. What I felt was something alien and strange in texture, fuzzy and slightly soft. It could have been some kind of little creature. I yanked my hands away and the object fell to the ground. I opened my eyes. It was something I had never before seen: a peach. Only now, it was on the pavement, smashed to bits on impact.

My father had been stationed in warm-weather countries and knew all about the delights of a fresh peach. Had I followed his script, I would have regarded the fruit quizzically, asking, "Dad, what's this?" and he would have said, "Why, it's a peach, Patrick. Enjoy!" Then I would have taken a bite and smiled in rapturous gratitude. That was what he was looking forward to. But I had gone and fucked it up.

My father was furious. With an open hand, he delivered a heavy slap to my head. The promenade was busy, and many people saw him strike me. No one intervened, though Dad received some scornful looks. As for me, I was fine physically but mortified inside—both at disappointing my father and at having all of those strangers' eyes upon me.

Life with Dad wasn't all bad. He could be a playful, entertaining man whose company I enjoyed, most particularly when he shared his stories with me of jumping out of airplanes and being in the army stationed in India. He always took me to the services that were held on Remembrance Day in our town park, for which he dressed in a blazer, a white shirt, and a regimental tie, and wore his service medals, which numbered around eight. I loved looking at these awards and cherished the moments when he allowed me to hold them. One of his ribbons had a tiny bronze oak leaf pinned to it. Dad explained that he had received this in recognition of having been "mentioned in dispatches," meaning that his commanding officer had singled out something my father had done in his report after the action.

In July 1945, when I was a week away from turning five, the United Kingdom held its first postwar election, in which the Labour leader Clement Attlee emerged triumphant, displacing Winston Churchill from 10 Downing Street. Dad had been a fervent Labour supporter all his life. He took me with him to the local polling site, which happened to be my first place of learning, the Lee Green Infants School. My father gave me an assignment. While he was inside voting, I was to march up and down the pavement carrying a placard he had made by nailing a cardboard sign to an old broom handle. On the sign he had inscribed the slogan VOTE FOR MR. PALLING—LABOUR. Mr. Palling was his preferred candidate in the local election. The night before, Dad drilled me in the chant I was to recite while marching: "Vote, vote, vote for Mr. Palling / You couldn't vote for a better man / Mr. Palling is our man and we'll have him if we can / If he'll only keep his shoulder to the wheel." A somewhat paradoxical series of sentiments, I realize now, but it seemed to make sense at the time.

I dutifully marched and chanted, holding the placard high above my head. Suddenly, I turned around to discover an irritated policeman standing in my way. "What the bloody hell does thou think th'art doing?" he shouted. "Here, give me that." He tried to grab the broom handle, but I pulled it away and said, "You can't have that, it's mine! My dad made it for me."

"Thou cheeky little bugger, I'll show thee!" he replied, raising his hand to smack me on the head, as policemen were allowed to do with impunity in those days. At that very moment, my father emerged from the school and saw what was going on. He had dressed up for the occasion in his regimental sergeant major's uniform and looked utterly magnificent. The copper lowered his hand. Under his breath, he said to me, "Tha'd better watch thee fucking self." Then he released me to my father, to whom he offered a crisp salute.

Many years later, shortly after my father died, I was having a drink in one of the local Mirfield pubs, the Plough. An old man I didn't know came up to me and asked if he could buy me a drink, saying: "You see, I knew your dad and I know that he recently passed away. I served with him during the war and he was a very impressive man. Nobody took any liberties with him. He was very respected. And I'll tell you what, when he walked onto the parade ground, the birds in the trees stopped singing."

The trappings of the military offered my father consolation and nostalgia, but not a contented postwar existence. At some point, he became what is known as a "weekend alcoholic." During the working week he never touched a drop, and the evenings of Monday through Thursday passed with relative normalcy in our house. But on Fridays, Saturdays, and Sundays . . . look out.

After his bath and my customary neck work, he was off to the pub or workingmen's club. In those places, he reminisced with his pals and played snooker, darts, and dominoes. And he got very drunk. Ale was his poison—he was not into the hard stuff—but oh, it made him appallingly cruel.

Trevor and I were always in bed by the time he came home, but never asleep. We were keeping an ear out for his return. He often sang as he approached the house. If it was a romantic ballad, like "I'll Take You Home Again, Kathleen," that was a good sign—he was in a sentimental mood and not looking for trouble. But if he was singing army songs, he was bound to enter the house in a foul temper, looking for a fight. Some nights, he had already been in one—at least one local pub banned him from the premises because of his behavior.

Mam always waited up for him. That was smart of her. If she had been asleep in bed when he came home, that would have meant immediate trouble. Awake and ready to receive him, she was at least prepared to neutralize his rage with a snack and a pot of tea. But on some nights, there was no pleasing him. He would manufacture a trivial reason to get angry: Something was out of place on a sideboard, a chair had been moved, the food was no good. My mother was never much of a cook, but that wasn't the point. He was frustrated with his lot in life, the ale lubricated this frustration, and he unloaded it all on Mam.

Often, the abuse was verbal, which was bad enough. But when my mother, at her wit's end, argued back, that's when things turned physical. Trevor and I had a system for monitoring these situations. We crept down the stairs and sat quietly behind the door that led into the living room. These steps, by the way, were made of cold, bare stone. I remember one of my father's punishments, when my brother had done something to displease him, was to make Trevor drill holes in the steps to prepare them for the installation of treaders—not with an electric drill, mind you, but a hand drill, which took months of tedious, arduous work.

Perched together on the steps, Trevor and I hugged each other close, girding ourselves for the sound we dreaded: Dad hitting Mam. Sometimes it was with an open hand, other times with a closed fist. Always, he aimed for her head.

I still envision these scenes with disbelief. How could anyone be violent toward my mam, of all people? And how could this violence be committed by my dad, of all people? In these moments, I hated him. I wished he didn't live with us. I wished he could somehow be gone, that I would wake up someday to the news that he had died.

After hearing and witnessing one too many of these Friday night episodes, becoming familiar with their rhythms, Trevor and I became our mother's protectors. When we knew that Dad's moment of violence was approaching, we would run into the sitting room, pleading, "No, no, don't hit Mam! Don't hit Mam!" Trevor inserted himself bodily between the two of them, sometimes as my father's fist was raised in the air, locked and loaded.

And the strangest thing would happen during these interventions. Dad, as if a spell had been broken, slowly lowered his arm. Then he turned away and started to undress, silently and deliberately. He would take off his trousers, fold them carefully along the creases, and place them gently on a metal hanger. Off came his blazer, which he meticulously smoothed out and hung up in the closet. It was as if he was imposing military discipline upon himself to right the situation. Meanwhile, I embraced Mam, who wept as she wrapped her arms around me.

When Trevor left home to join the Royal Air Force at eighteen—no doubt fueled by a desire to get the hell away from Dad—I became my mother's sole protector, assuming Trevor's job of standing between my parents. Fortunately for me, Trevor was still living with us when the worst of these violent episodes occurred. Once, Dad hit Mam hard in the head with a pint mug, knocking her to the floor. When Trevor and I bolted in, she was bleeding heavily and barely conscious. Trevor ran next door to the Dixons for help, and Lizzie Dixon hurried to the house of a neighbor who had a telephone. They called an ambulance, and must have also called the police, because an officer turned up at our place.

Dad started his ritual of slowly folding his clothes as the officer watched him with incredulity. But he was not on our side, I soon learned. As the medics revived Mam and treated her injuries, the policeman implored *her*, rather than my father, to keep things in check. "Mrs. Stewart, you must have done something to provoke him," he said. "It takes two to make an argument, you know." No charges were ever brought against my father—a situation that was all too common in those days before society took domestic abuse seriously.

I must take a moment to pay tribute to Lizzie Dixon. Yes, she was the lady who gave me a good talking-to when she caught me with a girl in the air-raid shelter, but above all, she was a strong, principled, and compassionate person. A millworker like Mam, Mrs. Dixon knew what it was like to scrape by, and she was angered by my father's reckless spending on drink. Beer was cheap, perhaps a shilling a glass, but these were precious shillings we couldn't afford to spend.

But what really pushed Mrs. Dixon over the edge was the physical violence to which she became privy. The wall that separated our houses was quite thin. One night, she overheard my father instigating yet another row and decided that she could take it no more. She burst through our door as Dad was about to hit Mam. A fierce and physically formidable woman, Mrs. Dixon pushed up her sleeve and held a fist right under Dad's nose. Speaking softly but firmly, she said, "Come on, Alf Stewart, try it on me. Let's see what happens." Dad looked at her, turned on his heel, and headed out into the yard. Mrs. Dixon put a consoling arm around Mam and said, "Gladys, next time he has a go, you just call out for me. Good night, love."

My parents never split up. Over time, my father's rage dissipated and the violence stopped. It couldn't have hurt that I had matured into a tough kid, big for my age and a good boxer. I only boxed for a year, in my mid-teens, but I never lost a fight. My father, in turn, had boxed for the army when he was in India. I suspect that there was a part of me that, despite everything, wanted to emulate him. My final fight came in a tournament in which I found myself matched against a friend, Fred, who was even bigger than me. We were equals in terms of skill, though, and I caught him with a right uppercut. There was an instant gush of blood from his nose, which splashed all over both of us and the floor of the ring. The referee examined Fred's nose and determined that it wasn't broken, but he instantly stopped the fight.

I never fought again, much to the dismay of my gym teacher, who had high hopes for me. I think that all that blood on the floor was too vivid a reminder of the last time I had seen such a sight at home.

Later that day, Dad was eager to hear how I had done. I told him that the ref had stopped the fight because of Fred's bloody nose and that I was done with boxing. Simple as that. His reaction was unexpected. His face softened and he placed a hand on my shoulder, a rare gesture for him. Though he said nothing, he clearly understood my choice and accepted it.

Recalling this moment makes me melancholy. Not because I stopped boxing, but because I realize that some form of sincere communication had passed between the two of us, and I wish now that there could have been more. There were opportunities for us to talk, man-to-man, in the years before his death in 1980, but I never seized upon them. Would he have been receptive? I shall never know.

It has taken me decades to process my feelings toward my father. I was well into my sixties before I was able to acknowledge publicly what I had witnessed and endured as a child. When I finally did, I used my platform to raise awareness of domestic violence and direct money and attention to Refuge, a UK organization devoted to women and children who experience such horrific environments.

I never once heard my father say the words "I love you," even casually at the end of a visit or a phone call. I reflect upon this now because only recently, I was doing press for *Picard*, the latest in what is now a long line of *Star Trek* series, with Michael Dorn, who plays the Klingon officer Worf. Michael is six-foot-three and imposingly muscular, but in real life he is sweet and playful, the opposite of his taciturn, militaristic character. I have known him dearly for more than thirty-five years. As we wrapped up our interviews, I stood up on my tippy toes to hug Michael, and I said to him, "Michael, I love you." Softly, Michael replied, "I love *you*, Patrick."

I'm not one to use that phrase lightly, but it came so naturally to me in this instance. It was also the same with my mother—I always told her that I loved her. But in postwar England, men did not openly say this to each other, and where my father was concerned, love might not have been the applicable word anyway.

It doesn't take an advanced degree in psychology to figure out the appeal of acting to someone who grew up in a household as troubled as mine. The stage would prove to be a safe space, a refuge from real life in which I could inhabit another person, living in another place and time.

But before I even dreamed of such a calling, I was just a poor English kid in love with music and the movies, particularly anything that came from America. My father listened to boxing matches on the radio, some of which took place in New York at a grand-sounding venue called Madison Square Garden. Trevor and I listened to these matches from our bed through a little speaker that was connected to the radio downstairs. Joe Louis was my favorite American boxer and Bruce Woodcock my favorite British one. We Stewart brothers would playact these fights and did voice impressions of the radio commentators.

On Saturday mornings, Trevor and I eagerly listened to a BBC music program called *Children's Choice*. It came on at five past nine, after the news. On weekdays, the program was called *Housewives' Choice*, playing song requests sent in by female listeners. The housewives got five days a week; we kids got one. We never had a record player in our house, so Trevor and I had no means of playing music of our choice. We cherished those Saturday mornings, staying in our pajamas and running back upstairs after breakfast to listen to the show on our little speaker.

Children's Choice had a fairly limited repertoire, and many songs were repeatedly requested, which meant that Trevor and I were able to learn them by heart. We were especially taken by cowboy songs, which conjured visions of an American Old West that seemed like the most romantic, fun place in the world. "I'm an Old Cowhand

(From the Rio Grande)," "Streets of Laredo," "(Ghost) Riders in the
Sky," "Whoopie Ti Yi Yo"—these are songs that, to this day, I can
sing from memory.

The movies, though—now, *they* were introduced to me by my mother.
She loved going to the cinema, which was something of an affordable luxury for people of our class. Mirfield itself had two theaters,
the Vale and the Regal Pavilion, within a twenty-minute walk from
home, and farther afield, the town of Dewsbury had five cinemas and
the town of Huddersfield three, all a short bus ride away.

Our first mother-son outing to the movies, though, was a disaster. I remember the film being called *The Hand*, though it is listed in
reference guides as *The Beast with Five Fingers*. Even the more innocent title should have served as a warning, but my mother was not
too intuitive or questioning a person, and she happily led me into the
theater to see what turned out to be a horror film starring Peter Lorre
as a man tormented by a hand that had been chopped off of somebody and taken on a life of its own. It scuttled around and strangled
people as scary music played. Neither Mam nor I could take it, and
we left before the film was over.

But we got over that unexpected fright and kept on going to
movies together: Walt Disney films, Doris Day musicals, Randolph
Scott Westerns. From American pictures, I caught a glimpse of how
people lived outside of my little corner of England, even if it was an
idealized portrayal. I saw lush green lawns that stretched down to the
road, so different from our cinder-covered yards. I wanted desperately to be one of those paperboys who rode a bicycle along a foot-
path, tossing newspapers from his bag onto driveways where shiny
new American cars were parked.

Those cars alone were mesmerizing to a future gearhead like
me. My parents never learned how to drive, let alone owned a vehicle. On my street, only one family had an automobile, an impressive

1930s-era Jaguar four-seater. I'd see the mother driving it around. Her husband held some kind of important job, and she ran her own hairdressers' named Maison Valerie. I knew the car to be big and roomy because, although I never rode in it, I did once have a cuddle in its back seat with the salon's namesake, the couple's beautiful daughter, Valerie.

As my cinema tastes started getting more sophisticated, I started seeing films on my own, multiple times. In those days, that was the only way to familiarize yourself with a movie you really liked. To afford this, I took little jobs here and there. I had no shame about knocking on neighbors' doors and saying, "Is there any errand I could run for you, any odd job that needs doing?" During holidays, when I had more time, I invented a proto–Uber Eats job for myself: On Friday mornings, I took every household's order for fish and chips. Later in the day, I'd stand in the queue of the fish-and-chip shop, where the sight of me was always met with groans, since they knew I had a high volume of orders. I'd return to my neighborhood with everyone's evening meals, collecting a modest service fee for purchase and delivery.

The film that compelled repeated viewings was *On the Waterfront*, which came out when I was fourteen. I first saw it on a Monday night by myself. My friends and I had a system for getting in when we weren't accompanied by a parent: We would approach a couple or a single person in the queue, offer them money to purchase a child's-rate ticket, and walk into the theater with them, whereupon we'd separate from these strangers. It's a miracle that we got away with this without someone ever trying to take advantage of us.

Initially, I was disappointed to discover that *On the Waterfront* was in black-and-white. I loved 1950s Technicolor and thought that's where the movies were headed. But I hung on, and I'm glad that I did: *On the Waterfront* blew my mind. Until I saw it, I had never experienced a film about people like me and my family. We weren't in Brooklyn, we weren't longshoremen, and we didn't have a waterfront, but there were aspects of the characters and their situations that hinted at my own life. They lived in shabby apartments and they didn't have much. They struggled to get by, lining up every morning at the docks, hoping for work that wasn't always there.

The last line of that film, with the foreman saying, "Awright, let's go to work," has stayed with me all these years. Marlon Brando's character, an ex-boxer, overcomes the machinations of Lee J. Cobb's mobbed-up union boss, and the reward at the end of the film is simply that everybody gets a job, a payday. I understood that.

I went back to see *On the Waterfront* that Wednesday and again on Friday—three times in a week. I couldn't get enough of that famous scene in the back seat of a cab, where Brando complains to Rod Steiger, who plays his morally compromised brother, that he "coulda been a contender." To me, the most stunning part of the scene is when Steiger pulls a gun on Brando, only for Brando to push it away, gently, calmly, shaking his head in pity. The naturalism and emotional power of that moment hit me in ways I couldn't fully comprehend. I was not yet thinking like an actor, or even thinking about becoming an actor, but I knew that I was seeing something special. You can imagine how I felt when, twenty years later, working on my first feature film, a thriller called *Hennessy*, I played a scene opposite Steiger—in the back of a car, no less, where I pulled a gun on him.

But before acting, there was school. The Lee Green Infants School (named for an actual green and not a person) was a ten-minute walk from our house. For my first year, Mam took the trouble to take me to school and pick me up afterward. But this meant that she had to give up her job at the mill, a luxury our family couldn't afford. She also missed the companionship of her female coworkers. So at the age of six, I started traveling to and from school by myself, and I loved it.

Often, I left home earlier than I needed to just so I could dawdle. There was a butcher's shop along the way, and I was fascinated by the hunks of meat on display in the window, particularly those that could be identified as coming from a certain part of the animal.

I loved looking at ribs, running my fingers along my own as I did. Then there were the hooves and knee joints—for boiling down into stock—and kidneys, livers, and hearts. But the most fascinating items were the pigs' and sheep's heads, their dead eyes staring right through the window at me.

Sometimes I imagined they could talk to me, and I invented conversations we might have: *What's it like to be a pig? Can you still grunt or baaaa?* Then I'd grunt or baaaa at them myself, banging on the window, cracking myself up. This would attract the glare of the unamused butcher, who routinely chased me away shouting, "Eh! Bugger off, thee!"

I wasn't scared by the sight of pigs' heads because my father considered them a delicacy, and three or four times a year, my mother splurged on one for him. She brought it home in a bucket and simmered it over the fire for hours in a huge cast-iron pot. Then she served it to Dad, just as it was, on a plate. He picked up his big army-issued knife and fork and started in on the unconventional meal. In one of the strange rituals unique to our household, Trevor, Mam, and I would take this as our cue to go out for a walk, giving Dad privacy until he finished eating. I never once saw him put a forkful of pig's head into his mouth. But when we came back in, there was guaranteed to be very little left of it on the plate.

There was a rewarding byproduct to this ritual. When my father had gotten up from the table, my mother used a large spoon to skim off the fat floating on top of the liquid in the pot. She transferred this fat to a clean basin, which was then left in the cellar to set. The resulting spread, sprinkled with a little salt, was delicious on toast. We called this open-faced sandwich a "lardy."

A side note on toast: I still love a slice of it in the morning, dark almost to the point of burned, with coarse-cut Oxford marmalade. Nowadays, I use a toaster, of course, but during my childhood days, it was not so simple. We could only make toast if there was a fire. So when we had one going, I would cut a nice, thick slice, find the toasting fork—it looked like a trident made out of heavy-duty wire—and then crouch over the flames, turning the bread carefully to ensure even browning on both sides. It's still the best toast I've ever enjoyed.

I ate with the zeal of a hungry soldier. Table manners were not a point of emphasis in our household. The only rule that Trevor and I were expected to observe was that everything we were served *had* to be consumed, no questions asked. I obliged this command with vigor, though with little regard for neatness. Decades later, when I was a headlining actor in *Star Trek: The Next Generation* and various Hollywood films, my American colleagues were taken aback by the savagery of my eating habits, so unbefitting a Shakespearean actor. You can take the boy out of Mirfield, but . . .

Just past the butcher's shop was a long, high stone wall. I stood on tippy-toe every morning to look over it. Why? Because over the wall was a wide, sloping meadow with, at the bottom of it, a "ha-ha." That's an old term for a low, partially sunken stone wall that protects a grand house and its grounds from the livestock grazing in the meadow. (I later learned this word origin from my first acting teacher, Ruth Wynn Owen, who lived in a house guarded by such a ha-ha.) The house I encountered on my walks to school was like no other in the area where I lived. It was large and built of stone, three stories high, with a huge porch and expensive cars parked in the driveway: a Wolseley, a Jaguar, a Sunbeam-Talbot. I fantasized about living there, all of that space for just one family. I didn't know who resided in that house, but I was somehow aware that the children were away at boarding school.

Just before I reached my school, I passed a small building where a man made and sold boiled sweets and, at certain times of the year, toffee apples. I saved my pennies during toffee-apple season until I could afford to buy one as I walked home from school. I made every treat last, slowly licking the sticky toffee coating until, when it was thin enough, I could bite through into the apple itself, usually a delicious green-skinned Granny Smith.

I went to the Lee Green school for three years, until I was eight. It was a Church of England establishment, so every day started with prayers, a hymn, and a reading from the Bible. I was never chosen to read in front of the class. I'm not sure why; perhaps they knew that my father was an atheist.

I do, however, remember one "performance" of sorts that marked my first understanding of how organized humiliation can be turned into entertainment. Our teacher was reading aloud to us and I was bored. My mother always gave me a clean white handkerchief every Monday, which was to last the whole week. I took out my hankie and started idly gnawing on it, passing the time. The teacher caught me at it.

"Come out here, Patrick Stewart, what do you think you were doing?" she said. I was too embarrassed to speak. "Come on, Patrick," she ordered, "tell us." Softly, under my breath, I muttered, "I was eating my handkerchief."

"You were eating your handkerchief," the teacher announced, "but if you're not going to tell everyone out loud, show us." Reluctantly, I tucked a corner of the handkerchief into my mouth. Then, very slowly, bit by bit, I started to feed the whole thing in. My classmates began to titter. As they did, I saw an opportunity to turn my embarrassment into comedy.

The other kids started chanting, "Eat it all! Eat it all!" I felt my eyes bulging, my cheeks protruding, and my face turning scarlet as I completed the task. Then, taking in a big breath through my nostrils, I belched loudly and spat out the wet hankie, which landed on someone's desk. This was greeted with wild applause. Even my very severe teacher couldn't help but grin at my antics.

Retrieving my handkerchief, I made my way back to my desk. But before I sat down, I took a bow as my classmates continued to applaud. Yes, my very first curtain call.

At the age of eight, I moved on to the rough-and-tumble Crowlees Boys' School. I use that description because our teachers lived in fear of us. One of them, Mr. Ward, had the temerity to call out a boy in my class for his misbehavior. The kid simply laughed in his face. Mr. Ward, without hesitation, slapped the boy on the cheek. My classmate yelped and ran out of the room, returning a minute later with his older, larger brother, who immediately grabbed the teacher by the lapels of his coat and spat in his face. The younger boy got behind and began punching him in the back.

Mr. Ward shouted out for help. All of us were by now on our feet, wild-eyed, but we did nothing to rescue our teacher. The older brother took hold of Mr. Ward by his throat and pushed him backwards over a desk. The teacher was going purple in the face when, finally, the headmaster, Mr. Haigh, charged in and pulled the older boy off him. The big brother was sent back to his classroom. Our classmate simply returned to his desk, grinning, very pleased with himself. So far as I recall, there was no further action taken against the siblings, who remained in the school.

During my time at Crowlees, I learned of the existence of the Quarry Theatre in Mirfield. It was an amazing open-air venue set in what had been an actual quarry. A previously subterranean wall of stone now served as a backdrop, in front of which a platform had been built. This was the stage. The audience sat situated within the big chomped-out hole where a hunk of earth and stone had been excavated, in curved, rising rows of seats like those in a coliseum.

This theater was on the grounds of the Community of the Resurrection, an Anglican monastic order. I saw the brothers around town a fair bit. They dressed in black, ankle-length cassocks with buttons down the front and black belts at the waist. They were scholarly, kind men, and, in their social work, akin to the Jesuits in the Catholic Church. But of paramount importance to me, the Community of the

Resurrection provided the venue in which I enjoyed my very first acting experience.

In 1949, Mirfield decided to celebrate itself by presenting a pageant devoted to the town's history. I should note that Mirfield had a large pool of amateur acting talent because we had many churches and chapels, and these places of worship regularly hosted plays and, at Christmas, pantomimes—the traditional English holiday revues of music and comedy. By English custom, the Prince Charming character was always played by a young woman, and the elder, comic "Dame" character by a man in drag. The barrier to participating in the pageant was low—one simply had to volunteer, which I did. My small part came early in the script, such as it was, in a medieval-times scene where yours truly got to play a lively character called Tom o' Towngate.

I loved everything about the pageant experience: the rehearsals, the dress rehearsals, and the performance, of which there was only one, at five p.m. I have no memory of who directed, but I recall being given orders and carrying them out as best as I could. I did not understand why some of the other young actors were so nervous and shy during rehearsals—and, right before the actual performance, fully scared.

Stage fright is an affliction I've been blessed not to have. If I may digress: In the entirety of my acting career, I have only felt a twinge of fear three times. The first was when I stood on a pitch-black stage waiting for a spotlight to hit my face and cue my first line, "To begin at the beginning." This was in my second year of studying at the Bristol Old Vic Theatre School, when I had been entrusted with the role of the narrator in Dylan Thomas's masterpiece *Under Milk Wood*.

The second time was in the Hollywood Bowl in 1998, as I stood behind a music stand while the symphony orchestra played the rousing overture to Stephen Sondheim's brilliant *Sweeney Todd*. I was playing the title role in an edited concert version of the show, with Lynn Redgrave as Mrs. Lovett. It was just the two of us onstage, and as the orchestra pounded out the introductory chords of Sweeney's entrance, my heart pounded just as fast.

The third time was in 2009, as I waited in the wings of the Malvern Theatre in England for the lights to fade up on the set for Samuel Beckett's *Waiting for Godot*, and then watched my dear friend Ian McKellen, as Estragon, climb over the wall of the set, stumble to the center of the stage, sit down on the floor, take off one of his boots, and say the line that was my cue: "Nothing to be done."

Only now have I figured out the one thing that links all three of these experiences: Except for a few seconds in *Godot*, I never left the stage in any of them.

But no such worries came over me during the Mirfield town pageant. When its single performance was over, I was so sad that I was nearly tearful. Something had happened to me: I wanted to feel what I had experienced on that stage in the Quarry Theatre again and again. Soon thereafter, another opportunity presented itself: Our local parish church was putting on a pantomime at Christmastime. So when my brother signed up, I did, too.

The pantomime's organizers were sure they wanted Trevor, less so about me. My sibling was a better singer, a better actor, and much better-looking than me. The only thing I had ever done, acting-wise, was the town pageant. Somehow, though, Trevor talked them into taking me. I was cast as John Bull, the invented iconic Englishman, akin to Uncle Sam in the US but chubbier and usually dressed in a Union Jack waistcoat—a bit of a stretch for a slim nine-year-old boy. I had only a couple of lines to speak, but, as with the pageant, I loved every moment, and this time, we did a whopping *three* performances. I was on my way.

Soon after the Christmas pantomime, I auditioned for our church choir. My brother had been a member for a few years and had excelled, getting selected as leader of one of the two sections of the choir, which was divided as such because we sat in two sets of stalls on either side of the altar, known as the decani and the cantoris. Our parish church, Saint Mary the Virgin, was big, almost cathedral-like in scale, quite an anomaly for a town the size of Mirfield. Our distinguished choirmaster, Mr. Allott, ensured that it had a choir as magnificent as its building. In fact, we were judged one of the twelve best

church choirs in England, which was why, at eleven, I ended up singing in London as part of the 1951 Festival of Britain.

Unlike Trevor, I was not a notable chorister. Indeed, I was something of an embarrassment to my big brother. Still, I had a ball. I
loved Christmastime especially, when we sang pieces from Handel's
Messiah—I really gave it my all on the "Hallelujah" chorus. We also
had an indoctrination ceremony I rather enjoyed. On the edge of the
graveyard, behind the church, was a gnarled, ancient oak that we
called the Devil Tree. The trunk was split open near its base, leaving
a crevice that we boys could maneuver through with some contor-
tion and effort, entering one side and exiting the other. When a new
boy joined the choir, after his first Tuesday evening practice, the rest
of us grabbed him, tied his hands behind his back, and, using poles
with nails sticking out of them, prodded the inductee through the
hole in the tree. We warned him that if he yelled, we would prod him
harder. I actually found this experience fun. One or two boys, however, did not. They complained to their parents, and one Tuesday
evening, Mr. Allott announced to us that this custom had to end.

Not long after the London trip, my youthful voice began to break.
Mr. Allott advised me to stop singing until it became clear which section I would graduate to, tenor, baritone, or bass. In truth, I think he
just wanted me to stop singing. I never returned to the choir, and I
have no doubt he was glad to see me go.

My mother loved going to our parish church, especially with
two of her sons in the choir. Which is why it pains me to recall
what a dreadful snob and un-Christian person our vicar, Reverend
Hall, was. He and his family lived in a huge house opposite the
church, and I believe he was Oxbridge-educated. After every service, he stationed himself at the church door, where he greeted
congregants as they exited. But as I observed repeatedly, to my dismay, he only gave the time of day to parishioners who were well-off
or socially prominent. On more than one occasion, my mother
held out her hand to him and said, "Thank you, Vicar." He completely ignored her—or, sometimes, recoiled at her advance, as if
he might catch something from shaking the hand of a lowly mill-

worker. I only wish that we choirboys could have prodded *him* through the Devil Tree.

In my final year at Crowlees, I was scheduled to take what was known in England as the eleven-plus exam. This was a grueling all-day affair that played a large part in determining the future of many a British child. The exam was effectively a sorting system, determining which pupils demonstrated the academic aptitude to attend a grammar school. Next to the private boarding schools to which the rich sent their children, grammar schools were the most selective of English secondary schools. The other categories were the secondary modern school, to which most kids were shuffled off, and the technical school, for nonacademic kids to learn a trade.

I did not pass my eleven-plus.

The circumstances under which this occurred are a matter of family debate. Trevor's version of the story is that I took the test and failed. But he's wrong. I have a vivid memory of my eleven-plus experience. Here's what really happened.

It was a lovely spring day in May. Since the exam was to take the entire day, Mam packed a lunch for me before she left for the mill. Dad had already gone off to whatever job he held at the time. Soon after my mother departed, I began the ten-minute walk to my school.

Just before Crowlees Boys' came into view, there was a T-junction. Fifty yards to the right was the entrance to my school's playground. To the left, a quiet local road continued gently downhill for half a mile before reaching the busy main road that ran alongside the River Calder, from Dewsbury to Huddersfield.

On this day, on a whim, I chose to go left.

I crossed the main road and proceeded down another hill, through a railway underpass, and then along the river. I passed a riverside pub, took another left turn, and climbed up to the south side of the valley. There I caught a view of the Mirfield Golf Club, a snooty place, closed to the likes of us Stewarts, and a couple of big stone houses, and, finally, the Bluebell Wood. This patch of land was aptly named: a real wood that, in spring, was thick with bluebells. I loved this place and had been there many times: alone, with my family, and with school chums. In a few years' time, I would bring girlfriends there.

The Bluebell Wood offered panoramic views of Mirfield, the whole town spread out to the north and west. I could see the roof of my school, and even the boys in the playground. The weather was May-perfect, and for a couple of hours I walked my favorite paths before sitting down, leaning against a stone wall, and eating my packed lunch while thoroughly enjoying the view. I even took a little nap. I look on this day as one of the happiest of my childhood, as if I had given myself a wonderful gift.

However, I knew that I had to carefully plot my path back to Camm Lane. I did not want to run into any of my classmates or, worse, my teachers. I took a long, circuitous route home that was blessedly free of chance encounters with people I knew. When I opened our front door, Mam was already home. She immediately asked, "Well, love, how did it go?" As offhandedly as I could, I replied, "Oh, it were all right. What's for tea?" And that was that.

Remarkably, there were few repercussions for my going AWOL. When I got to school the next day, my form master questioned me about my whereabouts the day before. I made my excuses, and he accompanied me back home that afternoon to discuss with my parents and me what had happened. There was talk of the possibility of me sitting the exam the following school day. But in the end, my parents didn't force me to, and I simply never took the exam. Nor was I punished for my avoidance of academic duty.

My parents were not particularly interested in education. I don't think it mattered to them whether or not I went to the grammar school. Indeed, they might have been secretly relieved, because there was literally a price to pay for passing the eleven-plus. The out-of-pocket expenses for the required uniform, competitive-sports uniforms, exercise clothes, books, and satchel were considerable, and we didn't have the money. (Side note: My fellow actor and near contemporary Tom Courtenay is also a Yorkshireman of modest background. Unlike me, he passed the eleven-plus and went to grammar school. In his wonderful memoir, *Dear Tom*, he notes that his family could afford only the cap that went with his school uniform, while his auntie sprang for the school scarf.)

The question I still ponder today is: Why did I cunningly and truly walk away from an opportunity for advancement, something that might have impacted my future in a positive way? What was my problem?

Maybe it was fear—of having to face and live with empirical proof that I wasn't good enough. Maybe I was trying to protect myself, psychologically, from the axe of failure that was going to lop off my head. On the other hand, I was certain that I did not want a future like the present in which I lived. I did not want to live in a world that would pass me by, without my having left some kind of impact on it.

These mixed-up feelings, which stayed with me through the first two decades of my professional acting career, were not entirely a bad thing. They imparted a certain discipline and determination. Yes, sometimes my fear of failure inhibited me and kept me from taking chances. But at other times, it motivated me and kept me hungry. My father, through hard work and dedication, had transformed himself from a nonentity into a regimental sergeant major. It would take similar determination for me to haul myself up the career ladder and become a working, in-demand actor.

As for grammar school, the one nearest me was a short walk from Camm Lane, an easy commute. But if that was the best recommendation for going there, it was not enough. Looking back, I realize I was rather intimidated. I'd had a fair amount of exposure to that school. Its playing fields and running tracks were just over the wall from the Crowlees Boys' School playground. The students there seemed different, snooty—a perception verified by my encounters with them on the streets. More than once, I was ganged up on, as were others from Crowlees, and the grammar school boys ridiculed those of us not privileged to attend the academy. Only once did I ever set foot on their campus, for a play they were putting on. I was stared at and pointed at, and I could see boys whispering remarks to each other.

No one confronted me and literally said, "What are you doing here? Go back where you came from!" but I felt it in the air. None of us who lived on Camm Lane attended the grammar school. Theirs was a community that I wanted no part of, I realized.

I must also admit that I would have struggled there. I was well-read but not academic, and my life in the classrooms would have been one of low marks and constant failure—except, perhaps, where sports were concerned. In my early teens, I was a good enough athlete to represent my district in a countywide tournament known as the Yorkshire School Sports, as a sprinter and hurdler. That Saturday, in the town of Beverley, I not only held my own against the grammar school boys in their fancy uniforms but beat them out, finishing first in every heat and quarterfinal.

What happened next, in the semis, hinted strongly at the turn my life was soon to take. I had not stopped acting. Indeed, at the time of the track meet, I had spent the previous two nights in a school production of the John Dighton farce *The Happiest Days of Your Life*. Given that the athletic event was on a Saturday, I faced a quandary— if I reached the finals, I would not have enough time to get back to Mirfield to be in that night's performance.

So I threw the next two races. I deliberately came in fourth in each one, therefore not qualifying for the semis and finals. The moment the second race was over, I ran to the changing rooms to get into my street clothes and head back to Mirfield. I was almost dressed when my track coach charged through the door. He was fuming. "Stewart, I know what you just did and I know why you did it! You are a disgrace to Kirklees!" he said, alluding to our district. "I never want to see you at one of my coaching sessions again!"

I am not proud of what I did, and I know I let people down, but I had this compulsion to act, and I respected that more.

In September 1951, I started the next phase of my education at Mirfield Secondary Modern School. I was excited, as a number of my pals from Crowlees would be joining me, and my daily walk took me past the house of my father's brother Clifford, who lived in a brand-new council estate that bordered the school's playing fields.

Uncle Clifford was, in fact, the principal caretaker of the school, which right away afforded me a certain status. On cold, wet days I visited him in the underground boiler room, which was a blessing, as the school, a recently repurposed Ministry of Defence warehouse, didn't yet have much of a heating system. Clifford was a wise soul with a keen sense of irony, a kinder man than his brother Alfred. His wife, like Mam, was named Gladys, and she and my mother got on really well.

Clifford and Gladys's youngest son, Tony, was in my grade, and we became good friends. He was also my introduction to classical music. Tony loved Haydn and Mozart and had a terrific record collection, which we listened to in his front room for hours—a luxury unavailable to me in my own house. I suppose the friendships we make when we're young say a lot about how our unconscious tastes develop. Tony was much smarter than the rest of our peer group, and very quickly it was obvious that he belonged in the grammar school—and that is exactly where he ended up. He took a late entrance exam and was accepted, so at the end of our first year together, we parted. I was happy for him, but missed him terribly.

The secondary modern school was a long, sprawling building with a large lawn on either side. Its main hall served as the school's assembly room, dining room, and theater. For several years now, it has been officially known as Stewart Hall. How I wish my parents could have lived to see that.

On one wall, just before a flight of four steps that led up to the hall, hung a print of a painting that fascinated me. I looked at it every day when we queued up first thing in the morning for assembly. It was a portrait of an old man in armor wearing a beautiful gold helmet embossed with an elaborate pattern and accessorized with a plume of feathers. He had a mustache and an air of confidence and determination. For four years, I constantly stared at him, thrilled by how his image made me feel.

I bring this up because not too many years ago, I traveled to Berlin to promote *Logan*, a film in the *X-Men* series, and while I was there, my wife, Sunny, and I paid a visit to the city's great art museum, the Gemäldegalerie. We were walking through its rooms devoted to the Dutch Golden Age when, suddenly, I stopped cold. There it was, way on the other side of the room—my painting, the man in the gold helmet, only it was the *original*. I was overcome with emotion and, according to Sunny, quite pale. Concerned, she asked me what was wrong. I wordlessly led her across the room to the artwork, staring at it just as I had at its reproduction more than sixty years earlier.

The museum label to the side revealed its name: *The Man with the Golden Helmet*, attributed to "The School of Rembrandt van Rijn." (This means that the painting, once attributed to Rembrandt himself, is now believed to be by one of his contemporaries.) I was transfixed, the child of eleven once more, back in that school hallway. The child who had minimal expectations of a worthwhile future. And now here I stood, still full of wonderment at this figure in the golden helmet, but in the body of a grown man who was in Berlin because he was a leading actor in a Hollywood movie screening at a film festival. Were he and I now of the same status? Never doubt the capacity of art to bring about moments of profound emotion and reflection.

I have been looking at the painting again, on my computer, and I am struck by something: The face of the man in the golden helmet is strikingly like mine as it appears now. Has this been at the heart of my fascination—that, as a child, I subconsciously recognized it as some kind of premonition?

The Mirfield Secondary Modern School wasn't as academic as the grammar one, but it offered an entirely different experience from my two previous schools. For a start, the curriculum was much more extensive: English, math, history, geography, science, music. We also had extended sessions, once a week, in metalwork, woodwork, art, and domestic science. I loved the first two subjects and the opportunity they presented for me to use my hands and work with drills and saws. I made a brass letter opener and a rather accomplished drinks trolley that I designed especially for my eldest brother, Geoffrey, and his wife, Alma, whom I adored. Geoffrey and Alma have since passed, and to be honest, I kind of want that trolley back. Would it be uncouth of me to ask their three sons which one of them has it, and if I may reclaim it?

The year I arrived at the secondary modern, the art master, Philip Haycock, persuaded the school to buy a potter's wheel and a small kiln. This became my passion. Every part of the process suited me: preparing the clay, kneading it, getting it pliable, and then smacking it down on the wheel and cupping my hands round it; molding and shaping the clay; getting the project wrong and turning it back into a lump of clay, sprinkling a little water on top, and trying again. So sensual, so sexy, even at that age. At my current flat in London, there are two pots I made years earlier at school. They sit on a shelf alongside some Inuit pottery, of which I am a collector. My works pale in comparison to those of the Inuit, but when Sunny first saw them and learned of their Mirfield provenance, she fell in love with them and insisted that they go on display. Mr. Haycock would be thrilled.

Domestic science was what Americans would call home economics: cookery class, basically. Ours being a coed school in a blue-collar town, the expectation was that the girls would be more into cooking than the boys. But our teacher, the wonderfully named Mrs. Collymossie, was ahead of her time, making no distinctions concerning gender. She was determined to turn us *all* into great cooks. She lectured us about the history of cooking and the science of how ingredients interacted with each other. We cooked and fried and baked and boiled, and at the end of the class, we gleefully ate our work. I have never met another Englishman of my age and background who was offered a class like this. My firm belief is that the kindly Mrs. Collymossie knew that among her students were children who did not get much of anything to eat at home, so she saw to it that we all got one good meal a week.

The subject that most captivated me, though, was English literature. In my second year, I was assigned to the Eng-lit class of Cecil Dormand, who was also my form master. He was to have a transformational impact on my life.

Mr. Dormand was tall and handsome, with an informal manner that put us kids at ease. He wasn't *too* informal with us—if he caught a pupil glazing over with an inattentive stare, he wouldn't hesitate to nail this pupil in the head with a piece of chalk. We actually loved him for this. If you somehow managed to think fast enough to catch the piece of chalk he'd aimed your way, you received a "Bravo!" from Mr. Dormand and a round of applause from the rest of the class.

But the real reason I became devoted to Mr. Dormand was that he was the man who introduced me to the works of William Shakespeare. One day, early in the term, he placed a copy of *The Merchant of Venice* on every desk. At the time, I did not know that Mr. Dormand was also an amateur actor and director. Nor did I have any idea what the hell *The Merchant of Venice* was.

Mr. Dormand told us to open the play to Act IV, Scene 1. He went through the list of characters in the scene and attached a pupil's name to each role. Just when I thought I was going to get away with not having a role, he ended by saying, "Stewart: Shylock."

The name meant nothing to me. I had no idea that I'd been cast in the most challenging, complex role in the play.

"All right," said Mr. D, "start reading." We all bent our heads over the strange-looking columns of print and started reading. Silently. A moment passed before Mr. D erupted: "Not to yourselves, you idiots, out loud! This is a play, it's action, it's drama, it's *life*. Start again."

We did, and we were dreadful. None of us could make sense of what we were reading, what the story was, or what most of the words meant. "Adversary"? "Void"? "Dram"? "Obdurate"? Nobody in our world used words like that.

As I listened to my classmates struggle, desperate to comprehend what was going on, I suddenly saw the name Shylock hurtling toward me on the page. I had just enough time to see that immediately following the name was a huge speech. *Oh, hell*, I thought, *I'm buggered.* I took a deep breath. As I exhaled, a classmate read my cue line: "We all expect a gentle answer, Jew."

Jew? Hey, I actually knew that word! In the open-air Dewsbury Market was a big stall run by a lively, loud, comical individual who theatrically auctioned off his multitudinous wares, usually starting with "Two quid. Who'll give me two quid?" Then he'd follow up with "Nobody? Right, who'll give me one? Ten bob? Five? All right then, two. SOLD to the lovely lady here in front." Above this man's stall hung a sign: LOU THE JEW—EVERY SATURDAY.

This man, Lou, was the sum total of my knowledge of Jewish people. There were none I knew of in Mirfield. I must have heard the word countless times while sitting in the choir stalls or listening to the BBC Radio news. But if I did, I didn't register any understanding of it. To me, a Jew was Lou, and I liked him.

So, given Shylock's ethnic background, I made an instant choice to read him in the way Lou would have said it:

"I 'ave possessed yer grace of wut I perpose."

There, it had happened, I had done it: spoken out loud, for the first time in my life, the words of William Shakespeare. In the moment, it was no big deal. Shakespeare, up to that point, had held no meaning to me. But writing these words now, I feel a thrill. *Here is where and when it all started.*

The actual line in the play reads, "I have possessed your grace of what I purpose." That's Shylock in the climactic trial scene, the first line of a long speech. I know it well now. I have played him four times: once in repertory in Bristol, twice for the Royal Shakespeare Company in two radically different productions, and once in a one-man show at the Leeds Playhouse that I created around the character.

But as a young newcomer to Shakespeare, I was lost. "I have possessed your grace." What the hell did that mean? "Of what I purpose." "Purpose" as a verb? *What?* I had no idea what I was saying. After that day, we never returned to *The Merchant of Venice* in Mr. Dormand's class.

Still, I did not say that I *disliked* reading Shakespeare's words out loud. They fired my curiosity. There was color in his language. I saw pictures being painted. Cecil Dormand remained my English teacher for the rest of my three years at Mirfield Secondary Modern, further cultivating my interest in literature and drama. He unlocked something in me. I think he intuited that I enjoyed escaping into the world of fiction, away from my dull, uncomfortable, and sometimes frightening home environment. Through literature and language, he gave me a new life.

Chapter Three

Not only did Mr. Dormand bring Shakespeare into my life, but he also cast me in my first significant role: as Joseph in a Christmas nativity play. This development excited me for one simple reason: I had a big crush on the girl who played Mary. Stanislavski would have approved of this deeply personal psychological approach, but it didn't end up serving me well. In rehearsals, I tried really hard to be a seductive Joseph, but my attempts were completely undone by Mr. D's decision to put me in a long, gray, phony-looking beard that made everybody laugh, Mary, Mother of Jesus, included.

Reflecting on this now—first Shylock, then Joseph—I think that Mr. Dormand sensed potential in me as an actor and was keen to present me with serious acting challenges (as opposed to fun romantic opportunities). There was little that was conventionally academic in his style of teaching, which suited me well, and he was himself passionate about theater; I think that in his youth, he had harbored hopes of becoming a professional actor himself. Mr. D was the first person to suggest the very idea of an acting career to me. Perhaps he saw in me a chance to vicariously live the experience that had passed him by. I also suspect that he saw something meaningful in the pleasure I took in letting go of Patrick Stewart of

Camm Lane and inhabiting someone totally different; he was definitely aware of the dynamics of my home life.

Mr. Dormand was the architect of another, far more significant development in the making of Patrick Stewart, Actor. Early in the spring term of 1953, I was summoned to the headmaster's office at Mirfield Secondary Modern. *Oh, what the bloody hell have I done*, I thought. The headmaster was Frank Bassett, and the name suited him perfectly: In Yorkshirese, "bassett" is pronounced more like "bastard." Eventually you'll learn what backed up this assessment.

With Mr. Bassett in his office were Mr. Dormand and a man I had never before met. I was introduced to Gerald Tyler. Right away, this set off alarms. I had been reading more Shakespeare since Mr. D had turned me on to it, and "Tyler" sounded to me like a Shakespearean henchman: Tybalt, Tyrrell, Tyler . . . you do the math. Mr. Dormand explained that Mr. Tyler was the director of drama for the West Riding County Council's Department of Education, and he had a proposal for me. Somehow, this sounded ominous to me rather than promising.

But when Mr. Tyler spoke, his voice was soft and pleasant, with a slight and reassuring Yorkshire accent. He explained that the council was organizing an eight-day "residential drama course" during the coming spring bank holidays, to provide coaching and instruction for local individuals, young and old, who were enthusiastic about amateur dramatics, or "am-drams," as we call them in England. Everyone involved in this course, from lighting and sound techs to actors and directors, would receive tutelage in the ways of the theater, and the eight days would conclude with an evening presentation before a live audience. The instructors would all be theater professionals.

Mr. Tyler let me know that Mr. Bassett and Mr. Dormand had suggested me as a suitable candidate for this program. The only problem was that the minimum age was fourteen and I was still only twelve. Therefore, he explained, they would "adjust"—in other words, falsify—my paperwork so that I was, in their records, fourteen. I was to tell anyone who asked that that was my age, which wouldn't be awkward, as I was big for twelve and looked older than my classmates.

"So, Patrick, what do you think?"

I didn't know what to say. I'd never before been presented with such an offer, and I was out of my depth. I asked if "residential" meant I wouldn't be living at home. Correct, I was told. Everything—classes, meals, accommodations—would be provided by the council. The program was to take place in the Pennines, the mountain range that runs through the middle of the North of England, at the Calder Vale High School in a small village called Mytholmroyd.

I was in a conflicted state—excited by the offer but terrified by the likelihood that such a program would expose my significant ignorance of acting, theater, and the wider world. Mr. D saved me by saying that he, too, was going to be a student on the course and would gladly keep an eye on me. That was all I needed to hear. I immediately said yes.

It wasn't until I got home and notified my parents of this exciting development that the subject of cost came up. Dad, straight to the point, said, "How much?" I told him I wasn't certain what "provided by the council" meant. Dad instructed me to find out.

The next morning, during a break, I asked Mr. Dormand about such costs, and he said that they would all be taken care of, everything except my bus fare to get there and back. This delightful news satisfied my parents, and I was in.

In the six weeks that led up to the course, it was all I could think about. I was so nervous. I was going to be surrounded by people older than me: grammar school pupils, university students, adults with jobs and income. The lecturers and coaches, I learned, were from prestigious universities and drama schools. Some of my soon-to-be fellow students were already preparing to become professional actors. What had I gotten myself into?

I told none of my friends about my pending stretch as a theater trainee, as they would have made fun of me. So I just told them that I was going off to stay with a friend. I worried inordinately about what I should wear—not that there was much choice. I had very few articles of clothing. In school, I asked Mr. D about the dress code, and he reassured me that it was entirely casual. He did, however, advise me to bring workout gear, as each day would start with a movement class and other physical exercises. I packed my school gym clothes: soccer shorts, a T-shirt, and trainers (sneakers, to you Americans). They turned out to be just right. The program was to take place in May, when even in the Pennines the days were sometimes warm.

I met Mr. Dormand at the bus station in the town of Halifax. His fiancée, Mary, had come to see him off, and she was so beautiful and kind that I felt even better about having an ally in Mr. D. We chatted the whole way on the bus, and Mr. Dormand was so relaxed and friendly that I had to keep reminding myself that he was my teacher. Another Dickensian touch to the story of my life: the poor kid plucked from a life of dreariness by an out-of-nowhere benefactor.

After the bus dropped us off in Mytholmroyd, we ascended a steep road on foot. Mr. Dormand pointed to a large, imposing building: Calder Vale High School. When we got there, people were saying their hellos and goodbyes in the parking lot. It seemed to me that everyone knew everyone else except me. Fortunately, a familiar face, that of Gerald Tyler, the county council's drama director, soon greeted us.

The school's classrooms had been temporarily converted into dormitories. I was shown to a classroom outfitted with six camp beds. A spartan setting for each pupil: a pillow, a sheet, and a blanket. No cabinets or dressers for clothes, not even blinds on the windows. But I didn't care. I was accustomed to cramming into my tiny bedroom with Trevor, and this was thrillingly new, sharing sleeping quarters with strangers.

I had just put my suitcase on the assigned bed when in walked an imposing, very tall lad, three or four years older than me, who immediately grabbed my hand and gave it a hearty shake. His name, he said, was Norman, Norman Lambert. He was from Darton, a mining community just north of Barnsley. He had won a scholarship to Wakefield Grammar School, which momentarily made him suspect in my eyes, but then he told me that his father and brother were both miners and they lived in a council house; he came from my kind of people. Plus, he loved acting. Norman and I would become lifelong friends (though I am sorry to say that he was only in his sixties when he died, after a productive career not in acting but in aeronautics; he ended up living in America and working for McDonnell Douglas).

The classroom gradually filled up with our other roommates, but one bed remained unclaimed, heightening the air of mystery surrounding its future occupant. Then, suddenly, the door crashed open and into the room strode a human hurricane—a sturdy, confident fellow who greeted everyone with great cheer and a ferocious hug. He was almost four years older than me. He introduced himself to me as Brian Blessed. He was not yet the globally renowned actor, mountaineer, adventurer, and star of TV shows, stage musicals, and movies as disparate as *Blackadder*, *Cats*, *Flash Gordon*, and *I, Claudius*. But I could tell instantly that he was a one-off; they broke the mold when they made Brian. Like Norman and me, he, too, was of humble origin, from the South Yorkshire mining town of Mexborough. I was beginning to feel more comfortable by the minute.

We all migrated to the dining room, where Mr. Tyler laid out the schedule for the next seven days and introduced us to the men and women who would be our guides, advisers, and inspirers. Right away, I was struck by an extraordinary-looking man, quite short with olive skin, a prominent nose, and thick black hair combed straight back from his forehead. He spoke in a thick middle-European accent and wore beautiful pleated trousers, soft slip-on shoes, and a rather eccentric long jacket. Raphael Shelley, better known by his nickname, Rudi, was introduced to us as the renowned "head of movement" at the prestigious Bristol Old Vic Theatre School. I had never considered movement as a discipline, and I could never have anticipated the influence that this man—a Prussian Jew who had fled from the Nazis, I later learned—was to have on me.

I was drawn also to a petite, poised middle-aged woman with short, dark hair and a beautiful smile. She was introduced to us as our voice teacher, Ruth Wynn Owen.

Our classes started first thing the next morning. We began with all the actors spread out on a large hall floor, where Rudi Shelley walked among us, talking about posture, balance, and stillness. He was riveting, though his thick accent at times made him a little difficult to understand. Then Rudi had us line up and walk in a circle along the perimeter of the room. I felt extremely self-conscious. At one moment I found myself walking unnaturally and comically, swinging my left arm in sync with my left leg, then the same on my right. Rudi urged us to quicken the pace and keep calm and balanced.

It was all rather solemn and studious until Rudi suddenly shouted out, "Oh my God, stop, stop! You all walk like pregnant fairies!" A riot of laughter ensued, which put us all at ease and instantly changed the tenor of the class. The hour passed quickly but exhilaratingly. I was drenched with sweat but truly warmed up. Every day would start with Rudi's exercises, and I found myself eagerly awaiting his class when I awakened.

Five or six different scripts were circulated among the students, prep work for the showcase performance we would put on come Saturday night, which was an anthology of these various pieces. I found myself cast in a traditional commedia dell'arte romance, playing the comic servant Harlequin. We sat in a circle and read through the script, and when we were done, Ruth told us that we would find out our roles in the coming Saturday night's production the following morning.

I was enthusiastic about the afternoon demonstration of stage fighting, complete with staves and swords, by a professional fight choreographer. I offered myself up to be one of the first to be coached. I took to stage fighting naturally, and early in my professional career, I relished any chance I had to do battle—until I discovered how scarily erratic some actors are with swords and daggers in their hands.

At dinner, we sat together on long benches, getting to know each other, laughing and making a ruckus, as theater people are wont to do. After the meal, some of the adults went down to the pub in the village. We younger students stayed behind and continued our conversations. By day's end, the intimidation factor with which I had started this adventure was no more.

I loved how everyone treated me as an equal, as if I were much older than I actually was. There was also, I must add, a lot of flirting and healthy sexual tension, thrilling for a newly pubescent boy like me. The program was populated with so many clever, fun, lovely young women. One in particular, Barbara Dyson from the town of Brighouse, which sits five miles west of Mirfield, caught my eye with her delightful face and laugh. She was good company. We were chatting on the terrace after dinner, and I was so relaxed that when she asked me how old I was, I forgot about my solemn pact with Messrs. Dormand and Tyler and told her the truth. A look of shock and dismay crossed her face. But we survived that wobble and became good friends.

I also quickly became close with Brian Blessed. Most of the time, he talked and I listened. He seemed to know so much about life and creativity, and he had the most colorful vocabulary I had ever encountered. His tales of woe, peril, and sexual conquest were peppered with curse words, idiomatic expressions, and eroticism. I was simultaneously titillated and thrilled, though not so naive that I didn't see through his exaggerations and embellishments. But I didn't care: His imagination was as great as his storytelling.

The week passed too quickly. I didn't want it to end. At long last, I had found myself in the company of people who shared my interests, people with whom I fit in. Yes, the rest of them were older and generally smarter than me, but I liked that—I could *learn* from them. And we shared a common objective: to give a live audience the best entertainment we could, having fun in the process.

When Saturday night came around and our performance was imminent, I was not in the slightest bit nervous. I was so keen to just *get out there*, in front of an audience. My mam even made the journey to the school with a friend and afterward told me she had enjoyed every single moment. I wanted her to stay and meet everyone— my new family, as I thought of them—but Mam had to catch a late bus home. I walked her and her friend down to Mytholmroyd to see them off, and then I raced back up the hill. I didn't want to miss a moment with these marvelous people. I never even went to sleep that final night; we talked and laughed all the way to dawn.

At breakfast, after packing my bag, I said my goodbyes. Never in my life had I been sadder to leave a place and a group of people. But everyone was saying, "See you next year." We had heard a rumor that the plan was to repeat the course at the same time in the same place for 1954. Mr. Dormand confirmed this on our bus ride home, which offered me solace in my state of longing.

He also told me that Gerald Tyler was so pleased with my work that he wanted me to join the Brighouse Children's Theatre, of which Mr. Tyler and his wife were directors. I had heard of this group, given Brighouse's proximity to Mirfield. They had their own dedicated theater and regularly performed stage classics in addition to their kid-friendly repertoire. Their work was well-known throughout South Yorkshire and the West Riding.

This was a big step up: a chance to work with experienced actors, even though they were amateurs. It didn't hurt that the beguiling Barbara Dyson happened to be a member of the BCT, which meant that I would get to see her again. Over the course of our week together at Calder Vale High School, our age difference seemed less of an issue. We kissed a few times, but that's as far as it got.

The other relationship that developed significantly during that week was with Ruth Wynn Owen. When I went to bid her goodbye, she hugged me and told me that I had promise. She also wondered if

I might like to continue to work with her. *Would I ever!* I asked Ruth what this would entail. She also lived in South Yorkshire, she explained. If I could manage to get to her house during weekends, she could continue her acting tutelage. She gave me her address and telephone number, and when I got home, I made inquiries about the public transport possibilities.

They existed, but it wasn't an easy trip. I would have to take one bus from Mirfield to Dewsbury and another from Dewsbury to a town north of Sheffield called Hoyland. From there, it was a mile-and-a-half walk to her house, which sat in the wilds of the country. In total, it was a three-hour trip each way, and I had just enough pocket money for the bus fares—a true haul, but one I was up for. Ruth suggested making a start after the summer holidays, which would give her the chance to contact some of the others who had been in the program with me and to see if they, too, could join in on our sessions, for which, generously, she charged no fee. She asked if I could do Sunday afternoons, which was perfect— my days in the parish church choir were over, to my relief. Even better, I soon learned that my two best friends from the course, Norman Lambert and Brian Blessed, would also be attending.

The summer of 1953, during which I turned thirteen, was particularly warm and sunny. My pal Bryan Holdsworth invited me to join him and his parents for a week in Filey, a small seaside resort in northeast Yorkshire on the North Sea. Under prior circumstances, in my pre-acting life, this would have been an experience to relish: a holiday in a pretty town, away from the strife in my household. But while it was indeed a pleasant vacation, I found myself getting antsy—all I could think about was working with Ruth Wynn Owen and seeing Norman and Brian again. These people, in their kindness and willingness to share their knowledge, were changing my life. I felt less alone in their presence because we had a common passion.

I desperately wanted to be around them all the time. By comparison, the amusements of Filey seemed rather dull.

Returning to school was also a colossal bore, just more of the same, though on the first day, a significant honor was bestowed upon me. I had been made a prefect, one of the leaders of the student body, even though I was only in my third year at Mirfield Secondary Modern. A few days later, however, something ghastly happened that made me certain this honor would be rescinded.

It had been a normal school day. My pal Brian Cooke and I were on a break, horsing around in an entryway with two girls from our year. It was entirely innocent: laughing, teasing, some playful pushing. Dividing us from the yard outside was a pair of doors with diffused-glass windows that blurred whatever was on the other side of them. Suddenly, these doors violently burst open, revealing a scarlet-faced headmaster, Mr. Bassett. "I saw you!" he yelled. "I saw what you were doing, messing with these girls. It's disgusting. Go and wait outside my office!"

We all protested, the girls included, but Mr. Bassett was unmoved, commanding us, "Do as I say. And you two girls, go and see Miss Lockwood," referring to the deputy headmistress.

Mr. Bassett stormed off to his office, with Brian and me following him down the corridor. We were kept waiting in the hallway a long time, until a teacher with whom Mr. Bassett had a meeting left the office. My name was called. I wasn't nervous because I knew that nothing untoward had happened and that it could all be explained.

But I quickly discovered that I would not be allowed to speak, period. Mr. Bassett went over to a hat rack in the corner of the room, pulled out a long bamboo cane, and told me to hold out my hand, palm up. Disbelieving that this was happening, I did so. The headmaster raised the cane above his head and then brought it down harshly, with an audible swish, onto my open hand. It hurt like hell. And he wasn't done. He did it three more times and then told me to hold out my other hand, which also received four lashes. Finally, he lowered the cane. With tears pouring down my face, I cried out, "We didn't do anything!" Big mistake. Mr. Bassett looked at me, grabbed my right hand, and gave me a further two lashes.

"Now get out and send your friend in!" he bellowed, breathing heavily. I'd tucked my hands under my armpits and was incapable of opening the door. With a grunt, the headmaster pushed past me, threw the door open, and yelled for Brian to come in. Brian stared at me as he walked past. He looked terrified, and not only because he had overheard what had happened to me.

I knew Brian had a skin condition that affected him particularly in his hands; even a rough handshake could make his hand swell up alarmingly. I was about to yell a warning about this to Mr. Bassett, but before I could, the beating had already started. I heard only four swishes through the door before they suddenly stopped. Mr. Bassett must have noticed Brian's condition. There was silence from the room and then some muttering. The door opened and Brian walked out. What a lad. He, too, had tears on his cheeks, but he was holding his maimed hand high in the air, with a huge grin on his face. He put his good hand on my shoulder, holding the horrendous beaten hand in front of my face.

"Now we've got him," he said. "We've fucking got him."

Brian left the building right away, went straight home, and told his father what had happened. His father came to the school immediately to confront Mr. Bassett. A few days later, Brian's father wrote to the local education authority, lodging an official complaint.

Two terms went by with seemingly no consequences for the headmaster. Then, quite unexpectedly at a morning assembly, Mr. Bassett announced that he would be retiring at the end of the summer term. At first, this news was met with total silence. Then, at the back of the hall, a fourth-former (the equivalent of a high school senior in the US) whistled in celebration. Instantly, the hall erupted in laughing and cheering.

Miss Lockwood eventually managed to get the hall back under control, but Mr. Bassett was furious and scarlet, exactly as he was the day he abused me and Brian. The beauty of it was that now he could do nothing about it. Good riddance.

When the autumn term began, we found ourselves with a new head-master: Charles Besley, a youthful, pleasant-looking man. He came to Mirfield Secondary Modern from a private boarding school in Scotland called Gordonstoun, which was known for its rigor and physically demanding outdoor activities. A few years later, Gordonstoun would become famous as the school to which the Queen and Prince Philip sent Prince Charles—a surprise, given that Eton or Harrow would have been the predictable choices.

As for me, I was impressed that a senior teacher from such an esteemed private school would choose to run a secondary modern school in a mill town in West Yorkshire. I liked the figure that Mr. Besley cut. After he was introduced to us by the chairman of the school council, he made a delightful speech: modest, funny, and, in an endearing way, grateful. It was received with heavy applause.

After that, Miss Lockwood got up to deliver the usual start-of-term announcements. First she introduced the school's new teachers. Then she came to what everyone was waiting to hear: the names of the new head boy and head girl, the leaders of the entire student body, and the names of the house heads, the leaders of Mirfield Secondary Modern's four student units.

"Head boy: Patrick Stewart."

When I heard my name called, I was flabbergasted yet somehow unsurprised. I had never coveted the job or fantasized about being "HB," as we called it. The very notion was simply unthinkable: not the sort of thing that happened to lads like me from families like mine. But as the badge was pinned on my lapel—by then I had acquired a proper school blazer—it felt logical. I was up to it. I absolutely knew that being head boy was a task that I could confidently undertake. This was the best of Alfred Stewart presenting himself in me. I've since felt this version of him turning up many times in my life and career, not least when I first took the bridge of the USS *Enterprise*.

I was about to leave the stage when Miss Lockwood took me by the arm and said, "We are not done with you." She proceeded to announce the new heads of each of the school's four houses.

"Head of Bury House: Patrick Stewart." I found myself standing there as another badge was pinned on my lapel.

This time, I considered the honor over-the-top. There were plenty of pupils in Bury House who were more than qualified to be a great head of house. When, later that day, I had a private meeting with Mr. Besley to discuss my duties, I raised the matter with him, suggesting that the Bury House honor go to one of my classmates.

He smiled and nodded. I thought I had gotten my way. Then he said, "And that is exactly why you are the person to be head boy and head of house." I didn't really understand, but something in his manner made me feel that I should shut up and get on with the formidable jobs I had just been given.

Why was I being so honored, given my lack of outstanding academic achievement? A clue lay in the reaction of my father that night when the news of my "promotions" reached his ears. He said nothing. He just smiled and nodded his head, as if it all made sense to him, as if he had been preparing for this day. No, I wasn't put in charge of a regiment of soldiers, but I was tasked with the leadership of two dozen boys my own age and an entire school of younger lads. Dad, for all his many flaws, had imbued in me a natural grasp of leadership. Indeed, I felt no unease about the actual work of being head boy and head of house. And one fringe benefit of these honors was that my classroom marks went up. With this public recognition of my leadership skills came a boost in my intellectual self-confidence.

Among the privileges and responsibilities that came with being head boy were being onstage at morning assembly, occasionally making announcements about matters of discipline and student behavior, and heralding the academic and athletic achievements of fellow students. Usually the head girl with piercing, intelligent eyes (yes, another crush) stood beside me and made similar announcements pertaining to the girls of the student body. We also sometimes read passages of literature that we got to choose ourselves. One Monday morning, I took the stage with the weekend edition of the local newspaper and read stories with a funny or feel-good angle. This last task I particularly relished. I felt I had taken my peers out of school for a moment and into the outside world.

I also held meetings with the prefects about school discipline and event programming, chairing them in rotation with the head girl. My favorite meetings were those with the teachers and staff, with the headmaster presiding. I loved being in a room with adults and being treated like I was one of them. It assured me that I was on a path to leaving behind that burdensome period of life called childhood.

These meetings fed my confidence, and I sensed that my father noticed this. Indeed, my designation as head boy spoke to his love of hierarchy and regimentation, and here I was, at the top of the ladder. Dad, to my surprise and slight dismay, became active in my school's parent-teacher association. I later found out that he did so at the urging of my foremost champion, Mr. Dormand. Soon enough, Dad worked his way up to the position of PTA chairman. The role gave him some importance and, I think, helped restore some of the dignity he had lost since leaving the army.

The eventful first days of this school year momentarily distracted me from my eager anticipation of working with Ruth Wynn Owen at her home. But the night before our first Sunday meeting, I could barely sleep from excitement.

I set off the next morning on the bus, almost beside myself. In Barnsley, the bus stopped to pick up and discharge passengers, and to my delight, Norman Lambert came on board. We talked without pause until we left our second bus and set off on the hike to Ruth's home. A mile in, we turned off the paved road and followed an unpaved track for a quarter of a mile, finally arriving at some big gates with a long drive leading to a large house that stood a couple of hundred yards away. It must have been two hundred years old, with a raised terrace along the front and beautiful green lawns leading down to a ha-ha and the grazing fields beyond. It was a lovely late-summer day, and I could hardly believe that I was going to spend several hours as a guest in a place like this.

Eagerly, I pushed the doorbell. Norman and I heard ringing deep inside the house, but no one came to the door right away. After a bit of a wait, we heard deliberate, dainty footsteps coming down what sounded like a very long hallway. The door opened and we were met by a thin, tall, elderly woman who regarded us suspiciously and finally said, "You had better come in." Given her impact on us, she might as well have said, *You had better go away.* Her face was closed and mirthless, and her manner of speaking was unlike any I had ever heard: a very upper-class drawl, with the lips hardly moving.

We later learned that this woman's name, in yet another case of life imitating Dickens, was Miss Stella Pettiward. Perfect. I eventually worked out that she was some kind of relation or family friend of Ruth's who had lived with the family for decades. Miss Pettiward silently led us down a tiled corridor to the kitchen, where we found Ruth, who greeted Norman and me with big hugs.

Also in the kitchen was an absolutely beautiful girl of fifteen or sixteen. She had voluminous ginger hair that fell to her shoulders and a face I found almost too pretty to bear, her perfect pale skin delicately tinted pink at the cheeks. Her name was Meg. She lived in the house and Ruth treated her like a daughter, but Meg was not related. She was born Margaret Shuttleworth in Lancashire in North West England—I wouldn't know this until years later—and her mother was a friend of Ruth's. Meg had come to live with Ruth and her husband, Ian, whose surname, confusingly, was neither Wynn nor Owen but Danby. He was some kind of higher-up on the Yorkshire Coal Board. They had two friendly daughters, Ann and Sally, and Meg lived with them as a de facto sister and an acting protégée of Ruth's. Meg Shuttleworth had already taken the stage name Meg Wynn Owen in tribute to her mentor. If that name rings a bell, it might be because Meg later starred in the popular TV series *Upstairs, Down-*

stairs and played the stern secretary who discovers Hugh Grant's prime minister unselfconsciously dancing in *Love Actually.*

Soon the other students arrived: Brian Blessed, to my delight, and another boy, Roy Semley, who had been in the one-week acting course. What work we undertook that day I cannot remember, but as the months and years went by, it all began to fall into a rhythm—"routine" being too dull a word to describe what took place during our time under Ruth's tutelage. First of all, there was the location. Our sessions usually took place in the family's gorgeous sitting room, which was furnished with ancient but comfortable armchairs and sofas, the walls hung with old paintings and mirrors. Outside, there were lovely gardens to spend time in when the weather was nice. In summer, we sometimes sat on the lawn and did our work there. And what was our work? Ruth had been a professional actress and she loved language. That was the focus of everything we did. Like Mr. Dormand, she immersed us in Shakespeare, having frequently served as the understudy for her good friend Dame Peggy Ashcroft, performing, for example, Portia in *The Merchant of Venice.* Unlike Mr. Dormand, Ruth took a more visceral, less cerebral approach to Shakespeare's language, and to language in general. She talked about the power that words have in their very sound and in how they relate to the words that precede and follow them. She told us that it's a mistake to believe that words come only from the brain—that they emanate from and speak for the whole body. Words were everything to Ruth—it was from her that I learned "onomatopoeia," one of my favorites ever since.

Ruth proved to be the first in a series of great vocal coaches, all women, who helped connect me profoundly with the lines I spoke: Cicely Berry, Patsy Rodenburg, and Kristin Linklater, a Scotswoman, who was particularly inventive. Kristin urged her actors to brood on words in silence and let them soak into every pore of the body before speaking them aloud. She had a monthlong residency with the Royal Shakespeare Company when I was there, and in one exercise, she had everyone lie on the floor and whisper to a fellow actor a word or a line of verse that was inaudible to the other people in the room. And so we lay there, the room still and silent, letting our semisecret words percolate through our systems. Then the moment inevitably arrived when these words demanded release. Sometimes this happened quietly, without movement, a still-prone actor softly speaking the words into the air. Others leapt onto their feet, speaking loudly with arms outstretched. It sounds gimmicky in theory, but it was a thrilling exercise, because the moment an actor spoke his words, it ignited something in another actor, and then another— not a knee-jerk or jokey reaction but the deep, genuine need to communicate something. Out of that, suddenly there was a scene taking place, human interaction without artifice. My weekend work with Ruth was where it all began, though: the invaluable instruction I needed to study a role, inhabit it, and bring it to life on the stage. I had some bad habits that she broke. I was by nature a fidgeter, and she taught me the importance of stillness, poise, and calm. Ruth also observed that there were times when I simply forgot to breathe when I was speaking my lines. She explained how the audience picks up on this—that if you're holding your breath or laboring to get through a sentence, it creates a tension that inhibits acting and takes viewers out of the moment. Breathing properly, she taught me, is as important a part of speech as the words are.

Another thing Ruth addressed was my accent. Over time, our Sunday session ranks were filled out by other boys and girls from the region, and most of us "spoke Yorkshire," betraying our humble roots. Ruth was insistent that if we were serious about acting, we needed to learn "received pronunciation," or "RP" as they called it in the business. RP was basically the way that BBC newsreaders spoke. People sometimes assume that it's simply a posh aristocratic accent, but that's not quite right, as aristocrats have their own peculiar, phonetically bizarre accent. (For example, the men of the British royal family don't wear trousers but "trizers." Most certainly *not* RP.) Since that time, by the way, the BBC has changed policy; nowadays, newsreaders are encouraged to speak in their natural, regional accents. It's so much truer to British life, and I love it.

Nevertheless, Ruth eradicated my accent so successfully that my Yorkshire relations insist that, even when I deliberately try, I can no longer speak broad Yorkshire. Sunny, however, tells me that she can always tell when I am speaking to one of my family members on the phone, because my RP accent shifts noticeably northwards.

With Ruth, we didn't read exclusively from Shakespeare. She exposed our provincial minds to *No Exit*, by Jean-Paul Sartre, the existentialist play from which the aphorism "Hell is other people" is drawn. It is a brilliant, though savage, piece, and it was a joy to read. But the Shakespeare speeches that she assigned us to practice in advance were the ones I liked best. My favorites were Hamlet's soliloquies, the future King Richard's opening speech in *Richard III*, and Henry's speeches from *Henry V*. The girls performed speeches by *The Merchant of Venice*'s Portia, *Antony and Cleopatra*'s Cleopatra, *As You Like It*'s Rosalind, and *Twelfth Night*'s Viola.

To sit in a comfortable chair in a beautiful house in the country for a few hours on a Sunday afternoon, listening to dear friends speaking Shakespeare's texts and then listening to Ruth analyze them, was heaven on a stick. We had loads of riotous fun, especially when Brian Blessed was around, but we also created an environment of profound mutual respect. The silences in that room were as electrifying as the noisy moments of applause and laughter—mysterious moments of awe and contemplation.

I was still only in my early teens, and these days in Ruth's sitting room were my first experience of being truly, blissfully lost in acting, in a glorious world of sounds, faces, words, and joy. I have never forgotten this feeling, and ever since, whether in a rehearsal room or on a soundstage, I have tried to manifest that magical environment of shared mission. It can be done, but only if all the participants want it to happen.

When I got a little older, Ruth invited me to come visit earlier, on Saturdays, and stay overnight. These weekend-long stays only enhanced the pleasure I took in our sessions. However, there was one unsettling aspect to sleeping over at Ruth's.

From the very first time I walked into the sitting room, I had been struck by one of the paintings in it, a full-length portrait of a handsome woman dressed in what I perceived to be seventeenth-century clothes. I might have been seeing things, but every time I looked in the direction of this painting, it appeared to be enshrouded in a very subtle haze. In the guest bedroom where I slept, there was another old painting of a woman in a similar period dress, and it, too, seemed surrounded by an unexplainable mist. After dark, it got more intense: The mist turned into a soft glow.

This scared me, fundamentally. The bedroom had no bedside light, only an overhead one whose switch was by the door, so reading in bed was out of the question. I couldn't bear to look at the spooky glow for long, so I developed a routine: I stood in my pajamas, took a last look at the painting and the mist, and then flicked off the light, dove into bed, and immediately pulled the covers over my head. There I stayed until morning.

Finally, at the risk of coming off as insane, I decided to tell Ruth about "the glow" I had seen around her paintings. She smiled. "Oh, you've noticed it," she said. Her voice was cheerful, but I wasn't reassured—it was even spookier to have my paranormal visions confirmed. "Yes, it's always there," Ruth continued. "It was with us when we and the paintings lived in another house. The mist has followed us around."

The topic was dropped because we had to move on to the day's voice lesson. But later on, when Ruth and I were alone, she said, "I have decided I want to tell you about our house and family, if you would like to hear."

Well, of course I did.

She told me that her family and the houses they had lived in were frequently visited by spirits. There was one house where members of the family heard all manner of unexplained noises: chatter in empty rooms, footsteps on staircases no one was climbing, doors banging shut though nobody had pushed them. Most remarkable of all was the figure of a little girl who appeared to Ruth in the night, standing at her bedside. When Ruth smiled at this girl, she told me, the girl smiled back and then faded away.

When the family moved to their current home, Ruth said, the little girl had moved with them. But her appearances were different. Ruth's bedroom did not have an en suite bathroom, so if she needed to use one, she had to walk down a long hallway. Often, when she opened the door, there the little girl stood, waiting for her. She took Ruth's hand and escorted her down the corridor. Upon reaching the bathroom, the girl smiled and vanished.

Ruth informed me that I was among the very few whose eyes had picked up the mist around the paintings. She was curious to know if I had experienced other phenomena of this nature, but I hadn't . . . yet. That said, if you are impatient for more Patrick Stewart ghost stories, skip ahead to my early days on *Star Trek: The Next Generation*, when I was living in a house on Moreno Drive in the Los Angeles neighborhood of Silver Lake. I just can't seem to shake these visiting spirits.

My experiences with Ruth and her other young acolytes were heady stuff. Though I was only thirteen, I was self-aware enough to take measure of my life and recognize that it was changing because a series of authority figures—Ruth, Mr. Dormand, and Mr. Besley— had demonstrated great confidence in a lad from an ordinary family. Their confidence proved contagious. Back home in Mirfield, I started putting myself forward to the town's various amateur theater groups, who seemed happy to have me.

Recently, at the bottom of a drawer, I came across a Letts School-Boys Diary of 1954. The week beginning Sunday, April 4, reads like this:

Sunday: *Should have met Frances but her bike broke down. Went to the church, but did not see her.*

Monday: *Went to the pictures with Gerald. Elizabeth Blakely came and sat next to me. I had not seen her for a month.*

Tuesday: *Talked to Jean. I think she is very nice.*

Wednesday: *Went to Harrison's with the form and Mr Mitchell. (?)*

Thursday: *Drama Club. Mr Dormand did not get a play, so it only lasted ten minutes. (?)*

Friday: *Went to the fair with Gerald. I saw Frances. I did not walk her home.*

Saturday: *Went to the Pavilion (cinema) with Frances. Went to the fair at night. I walked her home.*

Not a bad life, eh? And I was only thirteen.

As small as Mirfield was, it had at least seven active drama societies. Television was still in its infancy, and our resourceful community was industrious in making its own amusements. Even my mother belonged to such a society, the all-female Old Bank Methodist church drama group. The plays they put on included male roles, which proved no hindrance—there were two or maybe three women in the company who specialized in playing men. As with the Christmas pantomimes, no one thought it was odd that women played the male roles. The audiences never laughed at the sight of women playing men, and these performances were considered perfectly acceptable. (Perfectly acceptable, that is, as long as the gender nonconformity stayed on the stage.)

Mam had difficulty memorizing lines, so she played only small roles, usually servants and maids and, once, a butler. Nevertheless, I attended every show she was in and I loved watching them. But one night, something awkward happened: The play was underway when my mother made an entrance, dressed as a maid, carrying a tray. She spoke the line "Enter Mary with kippers." The audience howled with laughter, but her entrance wasn't meant to be funny. I quickly intuited what had happened. Because my mother had trouble learning her lines, she kept her script in the wings, consulting it immediately before going on. "Enter Mary with kippers" wasn't dialogue, but the stage direction for her character. Still, I loved Mam's delivery of it: very avant-garde, very Brechtian. But unfortunately, the laughter confused my poor mother, who hurried offstage without ever having said her correct line.

It didn't take long, though, for Mam to see the humor in the situation. Thereafter in our family, whenever someone had something uncomfortable to discuss, he or she would first utter Mam's errant line, "Enter Mary with kippers," to disarm everyone involved. It always worked.

My participation in amateur dramatics, or "am-drams," was more substantial. In my mid-teens, I sometimes found myself working for up to four different drama companies at the same time. It was a good thing we were assigned very little homework in my secondary school because I didn't have time to do any more than the bare minimum. Yet for all the enthusiasm I had for acting, for all the joy it gave me, it didn't strike me as a viable career. Acting to me was just fun. Maybe that's why I couldn't envision being a professional actor. I had seen what work looked like through my parents' eyes, and work wasn't supposed to be pleasurable.

When I was still not quite fifteen, my time at Mirfield Secondary Modern was drawing to a close and I had to consider my future. There had been talk in my household of my taking an exam to get into technical college, as Trevor had. But tech stuff didn't interest me, and nor, frankly, did any further time in school. I was tired of being bound by rules and discipline, of being compelled to study and do things I didn't care about. Even my roles as head boy and head of Bury House were losing their appeal.

One late afternoon I was on dinner duty at school, stacking tables and chairs at the end of the day, and Mr. Dormand happened by. "You know, Patrick," he said, "being head boy, you don't have to do that." I explained that I enjoyed the work and thought I was setting a good example for the younger pupils. "And what are you going to do, Patrick?" said Mr. D. "In three months' time, there will be no more school for you."

I confessed that I had no idea what was next. Mr. Dormand took a thoughtful pause. Then he spoke. "Have you thought about acting?"

I didn't follow what he meant. "I *am* acting," I said, "and I am really enjoying it."

"Well, then," said Mr. D, "why not make a career of it? Go to drama school in two years' time. You'll be ready then. Keep doing the weekend work I know you do with Ruth, and I will put you in plays, even when you have left school. And we'll talk more about Shakespeare."

I was initially speechless. Then I shook my head and explained my rationale. "Sorry, I can't do that," I said. "Nobody I know has ever done that. That job is not for people like me."

"That's where you are wrong," retorted Mr. Dormand. "People 'like you' are starting to attract attention as actors. One or two are having a lot of success."

"Like who?" I said.

"Oh, Albert Finney, Stanley Baker, Richard Harris," he replied. "The theater is changing."

But these encouraging words, even coming from my benefactor, Cecil Dormand, failed to persuade me. I told him it just wasn't realistic.

Several days after this discussion, I was summoned to the headmaster's study. Mr. Besley wanted a word. He told me that he had heard that I had rebuffed Mr. Dormand's acting-school suggestion. Was this correct? I assured him that it was.

"Well, Patrick, something else has come up that I feel might be more to your liking. I have been talking with Henry Wilson, the editor of the *Dewsbury and District Reporter*"—our local newspaper—"and he has suggested that I put to you the following offer. There is a place on his reporting staff for a trainee reporter."

As had been the case with the weeklong drama program three years earlier, I was underage, but special allowances would be made for me. Mr. Besley explained, the candidates for these positions were usually seventeen or eighteen and had gone to a grammar school. They had more impressive exam results and academic track records than mine.

"Nevertheless," Mr. Besley said, "I talked at length about your abilities and your time as head boy and the clear success it has been. You are a hard worker, and, furthermore, you are a local boy, born and bred in Mirfield. As you are aware, there is a Mirfield edition of the paper, which makes you, in that sense, very suitable. Your father had a distinguished war service, and Henry has great respect for that. You could start the day after you say goodbye to us. What do you think?"

I am certain that I must have looked dumbfounded, if not downright stupid, at that moment. I was as confused as I was flattered. A reporter at a local newspaper! Nothing had been further from my thoughts and ambitions, such as they were. Sure, I read the satirical *Punch* magazine every week and enjoyed the articles, reviews, and humor. I had privately mused that maybe, someday, I would be clever enough to write like that. But writing as a day job? Absurd. I couldn't even muster a response.

Mr. Besley filled the silence. "Look, I have discussed this with Mr. Dormand and he is in full support, as are other members of staff I have spoken with. Furthermore, you would be a fine feather in the cap of Mirfield Secondary Modern School. Nobody has left here to take a job like this. Please, will you think hard about it?"

I nodded, indicating that I would. I left the office, noting the huge grin on Mr. Besley's face.

That evening, I told my parents about the newspaper offer. I discovered that Mr. Besley had already discussed the matter with my father, who, after all, was the chairman of the parent-teacher association. My father admired success and respectability. He read the

Mirfield Reporter, a sister paper of the Dewsbury publication, every Friday. It was no surprise that he enthusiastically argued for me to accept the offer. My mother gazed upon me with fondness and pride. I knew that taking the newspaper job was something that would bring her happiness. And that's all I really wanted for her.

So it was decreed. Bye-bye, acting, and hello, journalism.

Chapter Four

I was utterly unprepared for the job I was about to take on—intellectually and practically. Mr. Besley had asked me if I could type or write in shorthand. I could do neither. So he found someone who could give me evening classes in both, which I started right away. The dear man also gave me a farewell present, a portable Wrighton typewriter that had been in his family for years. I proudly set it up on our table at home.

I was also underqualified in the wardrobe department. I had no "adult" clothes befitting a reporter. My school blazer and gray flannel trousers had seen me through my last three years of school. I didn't yet own a suit. In fact, when I finally got one, I wore it only once. This was a few years later, when Trevor was getting married. For that occasion, my father took me to the Dewsbury Cooperative Society tailors, the cheapest around. He had my measurements taken and chose a blue woolen material that I disliked. He instructed the tailor to make the suit for someone bigger than me, as I would "grow into it" and it would therefore serve me for years. As the wedding photos from that day illustrate, my hands were invisible, swallowed up by overlong sleeves. I had already reached my adult height of five feet, ten inches, and had no more growing left to do. Needless to say, I gave that suit away as soon as I could.

So, what was I going to wear to my first proper job? In this instance, my parents sprang for an off-the-peg sport coat. And with some of my own savings, I bought myself a pair of fawn corduroy trousers. In those days, corduroy was considered bohemian, and my rationale was that even if I wasn't qualified to be a writer, I could at least *look* like a writer: a new costume for my latest performance. Later on, under the influence of my best pal and role model at the paper, Barry Parkin—a worldly old soul of eighteen—I bought a meerschaum smoking pipe to complete the look.

The *Dewsbury and District Reporter* occupied a triangular building that in retrospect looked like a miniature version of Manhattan's Flatiron Building. From the time I landed the job to my first day at the office, I read the paper religiously from front to back. But I just couldn't see myself fitting in—not because I was dazzled and intimidated by the writing (I wasn't) but because most of the paper's content was dull and provincial. There was never anything in the *Reporter* that interested me at all. I had been reading the novels of John Steinbeck and Raymond Chandler, the plays of George Bernard Shaw, and the witty columns in *Punch*. Here the paper was all district council meetings, road closures, and tributes to retiring businessmen. Criminally boring.

I tried my best to find ways to make my job more interesting. After weeks of lobbying, I persuaded the newspaper's subeditor, a man with the magnificent name of Charlie Pickles, to let me write a review of an amateur theatrical production being performed in a church hall. The play and the performances were not bad, and, having enjoyed it, I gave it a good review. The following morning, I handed in my typed copy to Charlie.

Charlie was a gaunt, weary man who communicated primarily in groans. I hadn't even made it back to my seat before I heard him going on in particularly emphatic fashion. He called out my name, not pleasantly. Everybody in the newsroom stopped what they were doing and looked my way—I was in trouble. Apprehensively, I went over to Charlie's desk. He began to read my review aloud, stopping dead after reading a phrase I was rather proud of, in which I stated that the show was "perfect for this intimate little theater."

"'Intimate'? Do you know what that means?" Charlie said.

"Yes," I answered, "it means—"

"Intimate!" yelled Charlie, silencing me. "We can't have words like that in this paper!" There were giggles and sniggers all around the newsroom. Standing behind Charlie, I pulled a shocked face and put my hand in front of my mouth. That, too, got a laugh—such a big one, in fact, that Charlie spun round in his chair to see what was going on. I'd gone back to a straight face, but now he thought I had disrespected him.

In my remaining months at the *Reporter*, I was never allowed to forget that morning and the shameful, scandalous word I had attempted to slip into a family newspaper. Almost every time I came back from a council meeting or a local court, someone would ask if I had witnessed any "intimacy" that morning. I actually enjoyed this ribbing, as it imputed to me a status I had previously lacked.

The paper, a weekly, published three different editions for the local markets. The flagship paper served Dewsbury, while there were also a *Mirfield Reporter* and a *Batley Reporter*. These editions all carried the same content apart from their front and back pages. We had about eight reporters on staff, averaging on the young side. Most of my colleagues were using their time in Dewsbury to get qualifications for a bigger and better job somewhere else—perhaps at the daily *Yorkshire Post*, published in Leeds, and then onward to the big national dailies.

Still, I recognized that I was fortunate to be exactly where I was. On my first day at the paper, there was another new boy, a Cambridge graduate six years my senior who seemed a zillion times smarter than me. He made friendly fellow-new-boy small talk with me, asking me questions about my family and background—and what school I had gone to. To my relief, he didn't act condescending when I told him the truth. Within months, he had moved on anyway to whatever bright future awaited him.

The aforementioned Barry Parkin, three years my senior, quickly became my good friend. To him I owe my thanks for any claim to having been a cool 1950s dude. He helped get me into the Saturday night dances at the town hall, where there was an age minimum of seventeen, once more compelling me to lie about my age. These dances—that's where the girls were. Barry knew all the latest steps, and whenever we got a few hours away from the paper, he gave me dance lessons. The fact that he always led and I played the girl didn't bother me at all, because it made me realize what kind of moves would make the girls happy.

The realio, trulio, coolio guys at these dances were the Teddy Boys, so named because they wore knee-length Edwardian jackets with velvet collars. The "Teds" embodied the height of teen rockabilly fashion: skinny drainpipe trousers, string ties, thick-soled shoes, and big, greasy hairdos swept up in a quiff and then parted in the back—the latter feature known as a DA, or duck's arse. Everybody gave the Teds a wide berth, though I secretly longed to be one of them. They danced in front of the right-hand corner of the town hall stage, nowhere else, and nobody ever dared venture into their space—they were known to carry knives. The Teddy Boys were faithful to their female dance partners, so their moves were well practiced and fabulous. I borrowed their moves with some success, attracting the girls sitting on the benches against the walls. My dance style has not really evolved since then.

Generally, though, life as a six-pound-a-week junior journalist was not particularly thrilling. Mostly I enjoyed watching the seasoned pros go about their jobs. I was assigned to work as an assistant for one of the few female staff members, a middle-aged woman named Margaret Court, who was responsible for the *Mirfield Reporter*'s front page, a senior position. Margaret drove a nice Hillman Minx car and I went on ride-alongs with her, during which she explained what we were after, story-wise, and how she would get the goods. I saw her smooth-talk reluctant interview subjects into spilling what they knew, usually by flattering them and making them feel important. She knew when to introduce a provocative phrase and pivot the conversation in the direction she wanted.

Shrewd reporter that she was, Margaret quickly cottoned on to my not really being that interested in journalism. She got me to admit to her, before I'd fully admitted it to myself, that acting was what I really wanted to do for a living. She questioned me about what it was like being onstage, and I was delighted to prattle away.

After a few weeks of being Margaret's number two, she sat me down and described what my role in covering Mirfield would be like. I was relieved to learn that I no longer needed to bus it to Dewsbury every morning. Rather, I would spend much of the day astride my bike, making a series of calls on various figures in town who would be expecting me. They ranged from the chairwoman of the Mirfield bridge club to the proprietor of a certain butcher's shop who was known to be the biggest gossip in town. Given my experience with my father eating pigs' heads, I was at ease with the butcher and his craft. He told lots of jokes, and I particularly enjoyed the weird contrast of how his delivery of a punch line coincided with his swift decapitation of a sheep.

Elsewhere on my rounds, there was a clerk in the local council office who didn't like his job and spilled all sorts of secrets that were so grudge-related and unverifiable that I couldn't write about them. I visited the police station, the firehouse, the undertaker's office, and the Salvation Army, picking up tidbits here and there. The bartender at the Black Bull pub regaled me with tales of alcohol-fueled indignities, but again, they were not fit for publication.

I ducked my head into several churches and rectories, too. I never got much out of the High Anglican vicar of the Hopton parish church. I think he looked down upon me because I'd told him I had been a choirboy at the decidedly un-High Mirfield parish church. But also in

Hopton was the secretary of another church, the Wesleyan Chapel, an older woman who lived in a large Tudor house—an authentic one from the sixteenth century—and in her sitting room she always served me coffee poured out of a beautiful silver pot.

One morning, two months into our routine of daily chitchat, she lowered her voice and said in hushed tones, "Are you aware that you have an aura?"

I told her that I had no idea what she meant.

"It's quite rare," she said. "I have only seen it once before, around a minister who came to preach one Sunday evening. It is pale blue and it surrounds you." I looked over my shoulder. "No, no, Patrick," she said, "you can't see it. Only certain people can. But it is all around you and it is beautiful. It tells me you are a very good person."

I was flustered and speechless—the paranormal following me around again, without my doing anything to solicit its presence. "It's all right," the church secretary said, topping up my coffee. "Of *course* it is a little unsettling for you. But please, never forget what I have told you. Whatever your life brings you, this light will always shine."

I conveyed this story to only two people: Mam, who like me had no idea what to make of it, and my acting coach Ruth Wynn Owen, with whom I had previously discussed ghosts and the glowing mist around her old paintings. Ruth took this news in stride.

"Oh, yes, I saw it the first time I met you at Mytholmroyd and I see it now," she said. "You must not be afraid. Your friend was right: It is beautiful. But I didn't see it when you were acting. I wonder why. Perhaps we should work with that in mind. It could be a very important asset to you when you are onstage."

Hmm. Never before had it occurred to me that what these people were detecting in me was, potentially, an indication of my own gift. I had to take their word for it because I couldn't figure it out myself. That said, I have sensed emanations coming from certain performers onstage—notably, the actors Judi Dench, Juliet Stevenson, Harriet Walter, Ian Holm, and Ian McKellen—that speak to more than their skill, as if each is enrobed in an invisible cloak of truth that elevates their always stellar performances.

Every Wednesday morning at eleven a.m., I parked my bike against the wall of the rectory at the Community of the Resurrection, the local Anglican monastic order known colloquially as the CR. The Father Prior, the senior-most brother of the CR, always had a pot of coffee going and a big tub of biscuits. I was never in his office for less than an hour because the Father Prior loved to talk and I was the perfect audience. Best of all, he loved the theater. He went to London often, seeing three or four shows per trip.

The Father Prior not only described the performances he had seen but also re-created them for me, impersonating Dame Peggy Ashcroft, Dame Sybil Thorndike, Alastair Sim, Sir Donald Wolfit, Sir Ralph Richardson, and, his favorite of them all, Sir Laurence Olivier. The time whizzed by, and always, once or twice during these visits, there came a knock on the door by a concerned brother who was wondering what all the noise was about.

The CR campus was also the location of my one legitimate scoop as a reporter. Its brotherhood was committed to social justice, and one CR brother, Father Trevor Huddleston, was sent down to South Africa to oversee the order's mission in Rosettenville, a suburb of Johannesburg. In this capacity, he teamed up with a young member of the African National Congress named Nelson Mandela to protest the apartheid government's decision to bulldoze the Black suburb known as Sophiatown and forcibly eject its residents. For his efforts, the ANC awarded Father Huddleston its highest honor, the Isithwalandwe Medal, recognizing "those who have made an outstanding contribution and sacrifice to the liberation struggle."

However, Father Huddleston's work had placed him in conflict with South Africa's ruling National Party, whose segregationist leaders made threats against him. Fearing for his safety, the CR secretly recalled Father Huddleston to England in December 1955, the media and public being none the wiser. That is, until cub reporter

Stewart, while putting on his cycling clips after his customary Wednesday morning call on the theater-loving Father Prior, noticed a very tall, thin man briskly walking across the frozen lawn in a long black topcoat, his breath steaming into the cold air. I recognized him at once as Father Huddleston. But . . . he was believed to be in South Africa.

My first reaction was to stare open-mouthed with excitement, and that excitement prompted me to call out his name. He stopped and looked in my direction, and I hurried toward him. As I got close, he volunteered a cautious "Hello." Politely, if a little breathlessly, I said, "Father Huddleston, my name is Patrick Stewart and I work for the *Dewsbury Reporter*. This is a surprise seeing you here, as I understood you were still in South Africa."

There was a silence while he looked me over. After all, I was only fifteen. Again with the utmost politeness, I apologized for disturbing him and asked if he could answer a couple of questions. Another silence. Then he broke into a warm, delightful grin. "I suppose such an encounter should not be a surprise, Mr. Stewart," he said. "What can I do for you?"

We spoke for only a few minutes, and I didn't pull out my notebook. When we were done, I thanked him, hopped on my bike, pedaled back home, and then caught the next bus to Dewsbury. My early, flush-faced arrival surprised everyone in the newsroom. Charlie Pickles asked me what I was up to. I told him that I needed to type up something quickly, as I had just had an important encounter and not taken notes.

There were only a few sentences of copy when I pulled the page out of the typewriter; I'd decided that I could fill in the background after my editors knew the bare bones of the story. I delivered my single piece of paper to Charlie's desk. He read it through twice. Without moving, he groaned the word "Christ." But then, suddenly, he was animatedly grabbing me by the elbow and pulling me down the corridor. "We have to talk to Henry," he said, meaning Henry Wilson, the editor in chief. He didn't knock on Mr. Wilson's door. We just hurtled in and Charlie banged my piece of paper on the boss's desk. Mr. Wilson read it once, quickly, and said, "Right, I'm calling the *Post*, there's still time. I'm going to deal with this. Charlie, get more details from Stewart here. This is a world scoop!"

And lo, the piece, with quite a lot more background filled in, appeared in the widely circulated *Yorkshire Post* that evening. Before that happened, I asked Charlie if I was going to get a byline. He shot me a dismissive look that could only mean *fuck off*.

Still, I look back on that episode with pride. I had behaved sensitively while also getting the story. I had the right instincts to be a journalist, should I have chosen to follow that path. The problem was that I knew, even at that high-water mark, that journalism wasn't where I belonged.

I think that what wore on me most was writing obituaries— or, rather, reporting them. These were not of anyone famous, but of ordinary, working-class Mirfield folk who lived in houses like the one I'd grown up in. Usually, these write-ups were a single paragraph long. I would be given the name and address of the deceased, along with the name of a surviving relative. At some point between the death and the funeral, I would knock on the deceased's door and announce who I was and why I was there, which always led to me being invited in.

Without exception, the husband, wife, or other loved one would offer me a chair and a cup of tea. The curtains were usually drawn, lending a certain gloom and solemnity to the proceedings, but a light was considerately left on so that I could take my notes. Margaret Court had advised me to start by gently offering my condolences before asking my questions. And though Ruth Wynn Owen had successfully taught me how to speak in received pronunciation, I reverted to a friendly Yorkshire accent for these visits, which put the interviewee at ease.

The interviews never took more than fifteen or twenty minutes. I'd finish my cup of tea and close up my notebook. But then came the moment I dreaded. With a tenderness and a strange pang of need came the inquiry, "Would you like to see him/her, love? He/she looks real grand."

I had only one feeble response: "Well, I don't want to trouble or upset you." Remember, I had been dismantled not so many years earlier by the death of a squirrel. But the response to my gentle demurral was always, *always*, "Eee, it's no trouble a'tall, Patrick. Come on, love." Then I would be led into another room or upstairs to a bedroom, where, lying in an open coffin, was the deceased, the delicate traces of the undertaker's work still evident in the face.

I stood respectfully, my hands folded in front, and my head slightly bowed, as Margaret had taught me. After a minute of silence, I raised my head, sighed deeply, and said, "Yes. Yes indeed, he/she looks grand." This was the cue for the corpse to receive a tearful kiss from the wife or husband, and for me to say "Thank you" and get shown out.

One busy morning, I was shown three dead bodies one after the other. I returned to the office feeling ashen. One of the older reporters asked me what was up, and when I informed him, he looked at me in horror. "Patrick, hasn't Margaret told you? You don't have to go through that. Here's what you do. When you're asked to see the body, you say, 'Thank you so much, but I have just had a death in my own family and I think I'm still too upset to do what you ask. I hope you will forgive me.'"

He was right. I confess that this ploy left me feeling a bit of a faker, but I never had to look at a dead body again until my parents passed on, decades later.

The final, far bigger barrier to my development as a journalist was . . . am-drams. Charlie Pickles was beginning to believe in me, which translated into me being sent out on evening assignments. But by the end of 1955, I was also involved in four or five different theatrical productions, and in good parts, no less. They all held rehearsals on weekday evenings, though, and if I couldn't attend rehearsals,

I was no use to any of the drama groups. So, I made deals with Barry and other amenable reporters to cover for me when I was rehearsing, and I did the same for them when they were otherwise occupied. I also established a network of contacts who agreed to phone me with details of the events I was meant to be covering. Sometimes, when I was confident in my information, in the folly of youth, I made up copy. None of the paper's readers knew the difference, but I still didn't feel good about such a fundamental breach of journalistic ethics.

Then, one evening when I was assigned to attend a council meeting, a huge fire broke out in a mill at the center of town. Mr. Pickles phoned around to find someone free to cover the fire. He was told that I was at the council house, practically next door, so I was the man for the job.

You know where this is going. I was, in fact, in rehearsal in a different town, and even when I got to the office the following morning, I knew absolutely nothing about the fire. Charlie was waiting for me, glowering. "Where were you, you bugger?!" he demanded. I said nothing. An hour later, I was summoned to the office of the editor in chief.

Mr. Wilson showed great restraint. First he asked me for an explanation. I told him the truth: that I was rehearsing a play and had arranged for a colleague to get me details of the council meeting. I thought I would be fired right then and there, but Mr. Wilson was more measured. "Your behavior, Stewart, is unacceptable and I will not tolerate one more day of it," he said. "But I am letting you stay on the job, provided that you give up all these stupid amateur theatricals."

He'd put me on the spot. An ultimatum, decision time. It didn't take long for me to muster my answer.

"Mr. Wilson, thank you for your offer," I said, "but I am going to try and make a career in the theater."

"Then you can pack up your typewriter and get off my paper, right now," he said, rising from his desk. "Good morning."

I shakily returned to the reporters' room and told Barry what had happened. "Don't go, don't go, you're making a huge mistake," he said. "You'll never find a better job than this. Apologize to Mr. Wilson, he'll let you stay on."

But I was resolute. Barry knew there would be no changing my mind, and offered me a hug. "I think you're a fucking idiot," he said, "but it takes my breath away that you have the conviction to do this."

I packed up my Wrighton typewriter and made my way around the office, saying my goodbyes. Margaret wept, which made me feel bad. But the biggest surprise was Charlie Pickles. The scowly subeditor took me into his bony arms and actually hugged me, saying, "Ahm goon' to miss thee, Stewart." It was a moment that I can characterize only as . . . intimate.

That night at supper, I told my parents my news. Mam looked anxious and a bit frightened. To my relief, Dad stayed calm. He nodded and said, "All right, son. So . . . what are you going to do?"

I told him that I had no immediate answer, but that I would look for a new job and continue doing my bit for the household; I was already giving them a third of my wage. I added that I intended to apply to drama schools in a year or two, when I was of the age to do so.

I was surprised to see both of my parents bob their heads, as if they knew this announcement was coming. "It's your life to do as you like," Dad said. And that was it.

A few days later, I arranged to meet up with my cousin Tony in a pub. He was my Uncle Clifford's son, the one who went to the grammar school. He was excited by my plan to become a professional actor and offered me an employment lead. He had been working part-time in a furniture store in Dewsbury but was about to give up the job. We arranged for me to show up at the store the day Tony offered his resignation so that he could propose me to the manager as his full-time replacement.

Credit Tony for his foresight: A few days later, I was the new salesboy at Hudson's Furniture, the most high-class shop of its kind for miles around, occupying four floors and catering to the area's more moneyed folk. I was at the bottom of the shop's hierarchy, which began with Mr. Derek Hudson, the owner, followed by the manager, the assistant manager, the first salesman, the second salesman, then finally yours truly.

My days began in the basement, where I filled the kettle and boiled water for the mugs of strong tea that I was expected to bring to the rest of the sales staff. I swept the area around the front door, turned on the window lights and then all the lighting on the upper floors. There was a customers' lavatory on the second floor that I was charged with keeping tidy and inoffensive, which sometimes entailed opening a window.

On Tuesdays and Thursdays, I washed the outside front windows. On Saturdays, the big day for sales, I washed them on both the outside and inside. Mr. Hudson himself liked to preside over the Saturday hubbub. As soon as he appeared in the shop, I shot out the door to get him a cappuccino from the fancy new café around the corner. Then I hustled down to the basement to remove my drab, gray, week-worn smock coat and put on a jacket and tie—on Saturdays I was officially a salesman, albeit the lowly "third."

Here is how the day went. The doorbell jingled. In walked a customer. The manager immediately got up from behind his desk and welcomed the guest and took them off for a tour of Hudson's splendid goods. If the bell clamored again while the manager was occupied, the assistant manager presented himself to the new customer. And so it went, down the pecking order. It was, in a sense, a kind of lottery: You never knew what kind of customer you might have on your hands. Someone might come in eager to furnish an entire house—this did actually happen once while I worked there—or turn out to be a lookie-loo who had no intention of buying a damn thing.

I was a very good furniture salesman, if I do say so. On Saturdays I did a lot of hanging around, but when I recognized that circumstances were breaking my way, I prepared myself, regarding my new customer(s) rapidly but carefully. How old were they? What were they wearing? What did their voices sound like? And critically, what kind of salesman would they most feel comfortable buying furniture from? And, at once, I became that very person. It was like one of my acting exercises with Ruth Wynn Owen, but far easier. It comes down to this: If any of us want to do business, we'd rather do it with someone with whom we feel comfortable. So sometimes I greeted my customers with a broad Yorkshire accent: "Eh, yup. 'Ow yer doin'?" And sometimes I used my neutral RP voice: "Good morning, how can I help you?" I enjoyed the challenge. It was a bit like my shape-shifting as a junior reporter, except it had an immediate reward: a percentage of the sale.

But it wasn't just a cynical hustle. I had done my preparation, asking questions of my manager and the other salesmen and even of Mr. Hudson. I learned about the history of the brands we dealt in: how long they had been in business, what their reputation was, and, most importantly, what their lead times were. I learned the difference between Wilton carpeting and Axminster (the finest Wiltons were the most expensive items we sold).

And when I had slow, deliberative customers, I did not rush them. I asked them if they might enjoy a cup of coffee or tea: "Milk and sugar? Black? I'll just pop next door. You go ahead and make yourself comfortable. Try out the armchairs. Lie on the beds. Feel the silkiness of the Wiltons. My name is Patrick, and I am at your service."

Oh, I was good and I was making money. And this money was going into savings for my future ambitions, which, by the way, I never spoke of. I wanted upper management to think that they had a furniture salesman for life. Was that dishonest? I don't think so. My plan was to compete for a place into drama school within a year of starting work in the store. But my plan also depended on first *winning* a place at a drama school, and then figuring out if I could afford it, even with the money I was socking away. These were major challenges. If I failed at them, I needed to keep that job at Hudson's.

One benefit of working days at the furniture store was that I had my nights uncontroversially free for rehearsals. I was getting a reputation locally for being good at my "stupid amateur theatricals," and the roles I was being offered kept getting bigger and better. It wasn't all a ringing success, though; the Dewsbury Drama Club turned me down, which, honestly, I have never quite gotten over. In the actor's life, you shuck off the triumphs but hang on to the rejections, especially the early ones. I think that club's rejection was more disappointing to me than when, a few years later, Sir Laurence Olivier did not accept me into the National Theatre.

I was also enthusiastically continuing my visits to Ruth Wynn Owen and her haunted house. Sadly, Brian Blessed was no longer part of our group, as he had been called up to do his National Service in the army. But then, a stroke of luck: Brian was discharged from the military for having flat feet. He applied immediately to the Bristol Old Vic Theatre School and was accepted. Aarrghh. He was four years older than me, but I was jealous, and that fired my ambition even more. I'd decided that Bristol was where I wanted to go.

I discussed all this with Ruth, who concurred that Bristol was the place for me. I also laid out to her my financial limitations and how challenging it would be for me to afford drama school. One day, Ruth told me she had considered the matter and concluded that my best option was to apply for a West Riding County Council grant. It made sense. Gerald Tyler, who directed the yearly Mytholmroyd acting retreats I had so enjoyed, was an adviser to the West Riding County Council Drama Department. This was in the halcyon days when the British government, nationally and locally, saw value in arts education and allotted funds to further the dreams and skills of those interested in pursuing a life in the arts.

With Ruth's guidance, I filled out my applications for both an audition at Bristol and a grant from the West Riding council. I heard back quickly from the drama school. Yes, they would audition me, but it would be in a month or two, and I was to sit tight until they sent me a date. The council was less promising. I received a letter informing me that due to the high number of grant applications, it would be months before I might even be seen for an interview. In the meantime, I was to send them a résumé of my qualifications— of which, oh Lord, I had none. Left school at fifteen. Never sat an exam in my life. All I could do was mention my yearly Mytholmroyd courses and my local work in am-drams.

When the weekend arrived, in the spring of 1957, during which I was to audition at the drama school, I took a day off from the furniture shop and caught an overnight train from Huddersfield to Bristol. I got no more than a couple hours of sleep, which worried me. I ate an early breakfast at the station and walked to the Vic School. I was at first dismayed to discover that, physically, it was just two semidetached houses knocked together. I had expected something much grander.

I was instructed to take my seat and wait in the school secretary's office. The school was not in term, and the place seemed desolate. But a few minutes later, the door opened, and I was face-to-face with the director of the school, Duncan Ross—known to his friends as Bill, I later learned, though I never found out why. He was an unusual-looking man: lean and fit, his skin pale except for his pink cheeks, his hair short, curly, wiry, and orange. He held out his hand and shook mine, welcoming me to the school and leading me into a room. There was a huge bay window looking out onto the Clifton Downs, the open green space across the road. He motioned for me to stand in the center of the room. There was no furniture and I felt very exposed.

Mr. Ross asked me what I was going to perform for him. I mentioned the two pieces I had practiced with Ruth: a Shakespeare passage and a passage from Sartre's *No Exit*. He was silent for a moment, and I couldn't tell if he was impressed, disappointed, or intrigued. Then he said, "Start with the Shakespeare," and moved off to one side of the room, leaning against the window frame. It was a bright day, sunlight streaming in through the pane, and he was effectively erased from my vision. I almost felt as if I were alone, which might have been what he intended.

I heard Mr. Ross say, "Take your time. No need to hurry. When you're ready." By now, I was grateful for my lack of sleep because I think that my exhaustion served me well, tamping down my nerves. I took a couple of slow breaths and began. I felt good about my performance, but it was followed by another long silence.

Then, a voice through the sunlight: "All right, now the Sartre."

The *No Exit* piece was longer and more complicated than the Shakespeare one, but I negotiated my way through it quite well, actually enjoying myself in the process. Another pregnant pause.

Then, the voice again: "How old are you?"

I told Mr. Ross that I was sixteen. By this time, he had moved to where I could see him. He put his hands in his pockets—*Not a good sign*, I thought—and walked back to the window. His orange hair, backlit by the sun, seemed to be on fire. "What about National Service?" he said. "Are you going to do it, two or three years?"

I told him that I was too young by six months, and that I had heard the government was about to end the service requirement. "Yes, of course they are," Mr. Ross said. "I think it is a mistake." I certainly didn't, but I kept this sentiment to myself.

"You are very young," Mr. Ross remarked, "but you seem quite a lot older." Another agonizing pause. "All right, we will offer you a place, starting in September, and you will receive the offer in writing. Make sure we have your address. Thank you for coming."

Bloody 'ell, can this be 'appening? I thought. I took a steadying deep breath and said, "Thank you."

Mr. Ross escorted me back to the waiting area, where I picked up my bag, my heart pounding, and he saw me off, saying, "We'll see you in September."

When he left, I noticed that the secretary had a huge grin on her face. "I knew it, I knew it! Congratulations," she said.

I walked out, crossed the road, and found an empty bench on the Downs. I tried to slow my breathing, but it wasn't easy. I couldn't believe what had just happened. I had anticipated either a flat rejection or a "Thanks, we'll get back to you." I had not expected to be told at once that I was in. I wanted to tell somebody so badly, so urgently, but I was all alone in Bristol, where I knew no one . . . and, of course, this was decades before cell phones.

When I got home late that afternoon, I immediately spilled the news to my parents. Mam was amazed, bordering on bewildered, but clearly pleased for me. Dad appeared to take the news in stride, but he shook my hand, something he had never done before.

I needed a peer to share my stroke of good fortune, so I visited Barry, my newspaper pal. He provided the over-the-moon response I craved: "Bloody 'ellfire, Stewart, that's amazin'. Yer on yer way!"

In the next breath, Barry asked, "But how are you going to pay for it?" *Crash.* I had thought about that a lot on the train ride home. My savings were modest, and there was nobody in my family from whom I could borrow tuition money. I had put in the application to the council for a grant, but it seemed like a long shot, given my thin qualifications. But when I went to see Ruth that weekend for my usual class, she was much more confident. "Just wait until you are called," she said, uncorking a bottle of celebratory wine for a toast. Brian Blessed happened to be there, on break from the Vic School, which boosted my spirits.

That Monday, I decided to come clean with Mr. Hudson and tell him that I had been offered a place at Bristol. He seemed happy for me, his congratulations sincere. But he went straight to the money issue: "Patrick, how will you pay, though? That's not just two years of tuition. That's books, lodging, food, and a bit of pocket money." For a moment, I thought that Mr. Hudson was going to offer to lend me the money—he certainly had it—but it didn't happen.

So, I continued my work at Hudson's, saving as best as I could, hoping for good news from the council. My parents kindly told me that I no longer needed to give them a piece of my wages, as long as I diverted this chunk of income to my savings. I resisted, but they were insistent. For the first time in my life, I felt that Mam and Dad were united in their goodwill and pride, and I felt enormous gratitude toward them.

I also continued my am-drams, and word got out in the various drama societies that I had been accepted into Bristol. The support I received was wonderful. One of these groups had entered the production we were rehearsing into a one-act drama festival in Dewsbury. There were six societies in competition, including the Dewsbury Drama Club, which had ignominiously spurned me. When the festival week came, the names of the productions were put in a hat for a drawing that determined the order in which we would perform. We drew Friday, the penultimate evening. There would be a final show on the Saturday, followed by the jury's selection of winners for best production, best director, best actor, and best actress.

I was considered the favorite for best actor, and I confess that I believed such an honor to be only fair, an appropriate way for me to bid farewell to am-drams. The night after our performance, I caught the final production of the festival. The male lead was a very good-looking young man I knew slightly, and damned if he wasn't excellent.

Uh-oh, I thought, *this won't be the walkover I was anticipating.*

I should note that I never considered myself leading-man handsome, nor did anyone else. I did just fine with the girls, but in theater terms, my appeal lay in my acting ability, not in being a heartthrob. I'm not being falsely modest. I have a big nose and a heavy brow, and I wore unattractive spectacles in the classroom because without them, I was too nearsighted to make out the words on the blackboard. (I later switched to wearing contact lenses.) These issues were soon to be exacerbated by the premature loss of my hair. Not until I was well into my first run as Captain Jean-Luc Picard, during the early 1990s, did I have any sense of being dishy. And that was only because *TV Guide* published a cover story headlined "TV's Top Turn-ons," based on a readers' poll. I was deemed the top male "turn-on" in all of television. Absurd. All the more so given that my female counterpart (and costar on the magazine's cover) was Cindy Crawford.

So, this handsome chap in the other play was suddenly my rival for the best-actor honor. I admitted to our director that I felt threatened, but he insisted, "No, no, no, Pat, it's going to be you." There was a bar in the theater, and we had a nervous drink just before the awards commenced. The ceremony began auspiciously. Right off the bat, our show won best production. But then best director and best actress went elsewhere. And after that, so did best actor. I knew the reason at once: He was cute, and I wasn't.

In hindsight, I see that my non-cuteness was actually an advantage. Cuteness gives audiences, agents, and producers instant gratification and an anticipation of good things to come. But it doesn't always deliver on its promise. I have worked with many cute actors who haven't made it and many non-cute ones who have. Also, cuteness can fade with time, whereupon there has to be something to replace it. But often there isn't.

Confession time: That moment of not winning best actor has never faded. As I contemplate this memory, I still feel what I felt that Saturday night years ago in Dewsbury: failure. Like I said earlier, we actors perversely hang on to the lows that life has dealt us, brushing away the highs. To provide another example: I still remember, word for word, the one comment about me in a newspaper review of the first amateur production I ever appeared in, *The Happiest Days of Your Life*: ". . . and as Hopcroft Minor, Patrick Stewart was barely adequate."

Now, nobody wants to be rated merely adequate. But an especially deep pit of shame awaits the person who is *barely* adequate. What is wrong with me? Why do I cling to that quote? After sixty years of acting, I can acknowledge that, all things considered, I have done well.

Somehow, I survived the drama-festival slight and, at long last, received a notification from the West Riding County Council's grant department. I was to attend an interview with an examination panel in the town of Wakefield at four p.m. on an appointed day.

On the day in question, in the summer of 1957, I was allowed off work early to catch a bus from Dewsbury to the center of Wakefield,

where the imposing Victorian building that housed the council offices was located. I was instructed to sit and wait my turn—it would
be a while, as they were running late, having seen a lot of applicants
already, with the appointment before mine still in progress.

And so I sat—very nervously—in a handsome, wood-paneled
anteroom. This was it. The final hurdle. If I was turned down, it was
probably all over. If I got some kind of grant, *anything*, maybe my
dream of being a professional actor might work out.

I had no idea what would be expected from me in this interview. There had been no mention of an audition. Nevertheless, I
had prepared two speeches: the same Shakespeare piece I had done
in Bristol and a J. B. Priestley piece from his play *An Inspector Calls*.
I had dropped the *No Exit* speech from my repertoire on the suspicion that none of these councilors had ever heard of Sartre and
would have found me pretentious if I'd brought up his name. Priestley, on the other hand, was a proud son of Yorkshire, born just a few
miles away in Bradford. It was a calculated choice and I make no
apologies.

Suddenly, the double doors to the inquisition room opened and
a young woman in her late teens strode out. She closed the doors
behind her and let out a long sigh. Then she shot me a look, offering
a cheeky thumbs-up and an even cheekier wink. She will never know
what that did for me. I responded with a nod and my own long exhalation of breath, accompanied by what must have looked like an
idiotic grin. *Right! Let me get into that room*, I thought. But it wasn't
time yet—they kept me waiting, likely discussing my new friend,
the winking girl.

At last, the doors opened for me and a smiling man beckoned me
in. It was Gerald Tyler, my teacher in Mytholmroyd. My champion,
my ally! I contained my relief at seeing him, and he kept his cool, too,
wordlessly indicating that I should take a seat in the middle of a large
room before a row of dour-looking men, about eight of them, all
dressed in suits and ties.

I was politely (a Yorkshire version of polite, anyway) asked about
my background, my roots in Mirfield, how long I had lived there.

Why did I want to act? Why did I want to study in Bristol? Wasn't I a bit young?

This line of inquiry was easy to deal with, not remotely as challenging as I had anticipated. That is, until the grumpiest-looking councilor fixed me with a fierce look and said, "Suppose, Mr. Stewart, that we give you this grant. And suppose you make it through the two years in Bristol, don't get thrown out, and you graduate. What good are you going to be to West Yorkshire as an actor? How would you make us feel as if the expense had been worthwhile? What are we going to get out of it? Anything?"

I should not have been surprised by the man's theatrical belligerence, though I was. This was, after all, the rough-hewn West Riding, where the phrase "Wir thes muck, thes brass" ("Where there is dirt, there is money") was coined. Another inspirational quote, my favorite, goes, "Eyt all, sup all, pay nowt. Ear all, see all, se nowt, and if tha iver does owt for nowt, di it for thisen." In other words, "Eat everything, drink everything, pay nothing. And if you ever do anything for nothing, do it for yourself."

I cleared my throat and improvised a response. "Sir," I said, "you'll understand that an actor's job is very different from the usual work that most people do. You are a freelancer, going from place to place, and there is little chance of planning where it might lead. But I will tell you this: If there is a chance that I can make a career in the West Riding, I promise I will. This is the place that made me want to be an actor, and I shall forever owe it a debt beyond mere money."

I know what you're thinking: *What a load of bullshit, Patrick.* Well, in the moment, it was. But in my defense, my first professional job in the theater, a couple of years later, was as an assistant stage manager at Lincoln Theatre Royal, bordering on East Yorkshire, and my second job, as a company member, was at the Sheffield Playhouse, *in* Yorkshire. And roughly fifty years later, I was invited to be chancellor of Huddersfield University (again, in Yorkshire), a position I proudly accepted and held for twelve years. So there.

When my grilling was over, I caught the bus home to Mirfield, minus the delight and self-satisfaction I'd felt during my return ride from Bristol, but nevertheless with a feeling I had done the best I could. Then came another agonizing wait and a return to the routine at Hudson's, working six days a week. My emotions fluctuated wildly between hope and despair, confidence and depression. Even the memory of that bright-eyed winking girl failed to reassure me—she was so much more self-possessed than I had been.

Five weeks after the Wakefield Inquisition, I came home wearily from a long day of selling furniture and carpets to find my mother waiting for me in the hallway, holding a manila envelope in her hand. I saw at once that it had the return address of the West Riding County Council and that it was addressed to me.

I opened the envelope and read the letter within: "Dear Mr. Stewart, the Council are delighted to confirm that . . ."

In that moment, I did not read on but looked into my mam's eyes. "Well, love?" she asked expectantly.

I read on, aloud, and my mother and I discovered that I had been awarded something called a County Major Scholarship. We didn't know what that was. But the next day, I received another letter, this time from Gerald Tyler. He congratulated me and explained that only two County Majors were given each year, one apiece to a teenage girl and teenage boy. I was the first grant recipient in the council's history not to be a graduate of Cambridge or Oxford.

The scholarship would pay for everything: tuition, books, travel, accommodation, meals. My parents would not need to spend a penny, nor would I.

I was on my way. As an actor. An *actor*.

Chapter Five

L ife has a way of adding its own punctuation, dividing one chapter from another with an emphatic period. In the same stretch during which I was preparing to move on to Bristol, we said goodbye to 17 Camm Lane, the only home I had ever known.

I had been unaware of this, but for some time, my parents had been on a waiting list for a council house. In the UK, after World War II, the government invested in the working class by underwriting the construction of "council estates": affordable housing complexes that represented a step up from the primitive Victorian domiciles of old. In 1957, at long last, the names of Mr. and Mrs. Alfred Stewart were called, and our family moved from our old "one up, one down" to a semidetached council house on a small but brand-new estate of eight identical red-brick houses.

This new house brought about a complete transformation of how we lived. We had a small garden out front and another in the back, and, for the first time in my life, front *and* back doors. We also had a hallway, a kitchen, a sitting room, two proper bedrooms, and an indoor bathroom. All of these rooms were quite small, but to the three of us, it felt like the lap of luxury. We had left behind two rooms and an outhouse. Now we had six rooms and a view; out back, beyond the railway lines, we could see green fields that led up to the parish church and graveyard. We could also see Black Dick's Tower, a picturesque old stone structure I loved—a remnant of a house that was said to be haunted by Sir Richard Beaumont, a seventeenth-century baronet who had represented our area in the House of Commons.

The curving hillside street on which our house was built, Sykes Avenue, was also new. It looked out onto some detached houses, which, to us, represented a step up the social ladder as well. The one thing I missed about Camm Lane was the community feeling: the sense of friendship, caring, humor, and generosity it engendered. But I relished my newfound opportunities for privacy. Achieving the state of being alone no longer required taking a candle to a chilly outside toilet; there was always a room one could have to oneself. Paradise!

Another sea change: In the sitting room, my father installed a TV set. Nothing like today's giant flat-screen models—it was small, rented by the month, and only offered programming in black and white. But it brought the world into our house. This meant a lot to my father, who had traveled so much and lived abroad in his younger years, as well as during the Second World War. He badly missed those times, which I believe contributed to his frustration and occasional fury.

Dad also erected a small greenhouse just outside our kitchen window, which became something of a passion for him. He not only grew tomatoes, cucumbers, and green beans but also developed an interest in orchids, cultivating some handsome varieties. He even planted sunflowers, which struck me as profoundly atypical of the regimental sergeant major. I had never pegged Dad as a sunflower enthusiast. I took this as a good sign.

The weeks leading up to my departure for Bristol passed in a delirious blur. I gave my notice to Mr. Hudson. He and his staff were genuinely happy for me, which was heartening. I deliberately left a gap between the end of my employment and the start of drama school so that I could take some time off to collect myself and perhaps enjoy a little holiday somewhere. That didn't happen, though I continued to work with Ruth Wynn Owen as a way to gear up for the rigors of six days of class a week, twelve weeks per term.

I also had some shopping to do. The Bristol Old Vic Theatre School sent a list of the things I would need from day one. Among them: black dance tights, ballet shoes, and a "ballet support," what we would today call an athletic cup. I did some research and found a small store in Leeds where I could purchase such things. The prospect of requesting these things from a shopkeeper made me uncomfortable, so I took my newspaper pal Barry Parkin along with me for emotional support. I should have realized that Barry would do nothing but tease me throughout the entire excursion. But I cherished that time with him—he had by then joined the RAF, and I knew that our opportunities to spend time together were dwindling. As it turned out, we would meet for a few pub nights during Christmas and summertime breaks, and thereafter fall out of touch entirely.

I had been half-heartedly dating a local girl. Nothing serious, usually one night a week at the movies or at the Saturday dance at the town hall. But she cried when I told her my news. A week later, on our final date night, she told me that she didn't want to see me again, because what was the point? I couldn't disagree. In my head, I already had one foot out of Mirfield. Barry had advised me to leave without any lingering attachments, and I knew he was right. He also said, "Aaaand who knows who you are going to meet in Bristol?" Also a good point.

Life at our new home was a little strained. My mother was noticeably melancholy. Soon she would say goodbye to her youngest son, her baby. I continually reassured her that I would return at the end of every term, and that on the summer break I would get a job locally and move back into my bedroom. Rather recklessly, I even said that we would all go on holiday together again, a promise that I am sorry to say went unfulfilled.

I think she was also worried about being alone with Dad. For over twenty years, since Trevor was born, she always had at least one ally in the house, and often two. There had been a drastic reduction in the frequency of the rows with Dad, and as far as I knew, he was no longer violent toward her. But Trevor and I were uneasy about the notion of just the two of them in that council house, and the potential for trouble to arise. I took some reassurance from the fact that Dad was devoted to tending his orchids and sunflowers, and had even started making elderberry wine, which, unlike his ale, he drank at home with Mam in a civilized, married-man fashion.

As September 1957 approached, I found myself in a reflective state. A feeling had grown inside me that I was saying farewell to not only my family, but also my youth, my little town, and the way of life in which I had grown up. I took long walks around Mirfield, silently bidding adieu to the three schools I had attended, the fields I had played and dreamed in, the cinemas where I learned of worlds I did not know, and the river, canal, and railway lines I knew so well. For some reason, I was most sentimental of all about the rolling hills that surrounded my town. My contemplations of them prompted me to get on my bike and go farther afield.

It wasn't a fancy bike but the same sturdy Raleigh my father had bought for me when I was thirteen, the one I had used on my rounds as a newspaper reporter. With two of my childhood friends, David and Brian, I embarked on some all-day treks. We didn't merely cycle around our local streets but pedaled for long, punishing distances, heads down, breathing hard, as many as 115 miles on one Sunday that summer. Years later, I frequently received compliments about how shapely my legs looked in tights and in my slim Captain Picard uniform. My response has never changed: "Cycling, my friend, cycling."

On one occasion, David, Brian, and I ambitiously headed north toward the Yorkshire Dales, the upland area of hills and valleys in the

Pennines. I had only ever been on the fringes of the Dales in the past, but we rode twenty-odd miles to the towns of Otley and Grassington, and deeper into the valley of Wharfedale. Oh, those sheep-dotted green hillsides, those beautiful stone cottages, the magnificent silence! When the moment came to turn south and head back to the familiar childhood sight of sooty mills and factories, I felt a pang in my heart, a deep sadness.

On one of my last days before I left for Bristol, I rode back to the Dales alone, though I wasn't remotely lonely. Breathing in the cool air, I realized that I had never been anywhere more soothing, caressing, welcoming, or inspiring. I locked my bike to an iron gatepost and walked to the very summit of a peak called Ingleborough, from which I could see farther hills and dales, and, nestled within them, tiny, cozy villages. In that moment, I didn't want to leave Yorkshire, but I knew I had to. I was going to be an actor. And as beautiful as they were, the Dales offered no opportunities for that.

I have never forgotten that day, no matter where I have lived or worked. Many years later, in the *Star Trek: The Next Generation* era, I was driving my beloved British racing-green Jaguar XJS 12 through Los Angeles, headed downtown for some tiresome reason. "Driving" is a generous way to put it. It was four in the afternoon, rush hour was just underway, and we were all crawling, crawling along. I had the top down, which was crazy in those air-quality conditions. As I was enveloped by a massive low cloud of smog, I was struck by a thought: *I should buy a house in the Yorkshire Dales.*

With my brother Trevor's enthusiastic help, this dream became a reality. Six months later, my only home in England sat at the top of a hill, overlooking the Wharfedale valley, not far from the same hilltop where I had stood all those decades ago. The house was half a mile from its nearest neighbor. To its east, the deserted moorland stretched endlessly. I invited my friends and family to stay over, but more than one said that the house's isolation made them uncomfortable. My daughter, Sophie, refused to stay there alone, even for a single night. But I loved it and spent long periods in the house alone, never once feeling uneasy or unsafe. I sold the place some time ago, but for twenty-five years, it was my treasured retreat from Los Angeles, London, and New York.

But back in 1957, I wistfully said goodbye to my childhood stomping grounds. The day finally came when my suitcase was packed, my jacket was on, and there was a taxi waiting for me. I hugged and kissed Mam, and even hugged Dad. She was crying. He was stoic. Me? I could hardly breathe in my state of confusion. *I know I want this, but do I really? Do I? Too late to back out now. Goodbye, Camm Lane. Goodbye, Towngate. Goodbye, Sykes Avenue. Goodbye, Mirfield. Goodbye, West Yorkshire, and thank you for all you have given me.*

Bristol, a port city two hundred miles away from Mirfield, in South West England, impressed me from the off. I had barely taken it in the day I auditioned for Duncan Ross, but upon my return, I realized what a spectacular place it was. Just as San Francisco has the Golden Gate, Bristol has the mighty Clifton Suspension Bridge, high above the River Avon, which flows at the bottom of the steep, rocky Avon Gorge.

Bristol was, and remains, a major cultural hub, boasting the massive Bristol Hippodrome and the Theatre Royal, which houses the Bristol Old Vic Theatre Company, a revered, prestigious entity distinct from the Old Vic School. The Theatre Royal, built in the 1760s, is the oldest continuously operating theater in the English-speaking world, and it is ravishingly beautiful. Wrapping around the ground-level stalls is the area of seats known as the dress circle, its ornate filigrees matching the ceiling. Above the circle is another level of seating, the gallery, where behind the upholstered seats are several rows of wooden benches that date to the theater's opening in 1766. If you sit in the very last row of the benches, your head almost touches the ceiling. The closeness of the theater's seats to its stage heightens the intensity of the experience; to the audience and actors alike, the venue offers an uncommon intimacy for a 540-seater. The first play I saw at the Theatre Royal was *Waiting for Godot*—a show with which I would later become very familiar as an actor—and well before intermission, I had fallen in love with the space.

But I was not yet an actor in any professional sense when I first laid eyes upon that theater. I was new to Bristol and, for all the hearty congratulations I had received back home, insecure about my place at the drama school. I was reassured by the thought that Brian Blessed would be there, starting his second year, and that Roy Semley, another Yorkshire lad I knew from Ruth Wynn Owen's, was going to be starting in my year. The other students, however, would be strangers. I had managed to cast them all as well-to-do middle-class kids with private school educations, some of them even holding university degrees. They would all be from the South of England, and they would all talk like BBC newsreaders, and they would all have pockets bulging with cash that they could spend on whatever they wanted.

The school didn't have dormitories, but with the help of the school office, I had reserved a room in a private house where I would get a bed, breakfast, and dinner seven days a week for a very reasonable charge. When I got there, I was happy to see that the house, near the BBC's Bristol studios, was a well-cared-for home with comfortable furnishings. The live-in landlady was attractive and welcoming, with a middle-class accent. The one irritating hitch was that, when I was shown into my bedroom, I noticed that there were two single beds. I had not realized that I would have a roommate. I was somewhat reassured when I was told that it would be none other than Roy Semley. Roy arrived halfway through my dinner with the landlady and seemed to be as annoyed as I was by the living situation, though pleasant enough to me.

It was a fifteen-minute walk from my digs to the Vic School the next morning. I arrived early. I did not feel comfortable. Though I physically blended in, I felt the social handicap of my limited education. I had not excelled academically or traveled widely. I had no ready small talk and could make no smart allusions to current events and contemporary culture. As the room filled, I noticed that there were more young women than men, about twenty students total. I took a seat in the back, wanting to be as inconspicuous as possible.

At nine a.m., Duncan Ross walked in, accompanied by Rudi Shelley, the great movement maestro, and a middle-aged woman I didn't recognize. She was introduced to us as Daphne Heard, the senior acting tutor. Miss Heard, as we all deferentially called her, was a formidable presence. She did not lean back in her chair but sat bolt upright, holding her head high above her shoulders. We watched her open a purse and remove a pack of cigarettes and a lighter. Very dexterously, she took out a cigarette, placed it between her brightly lip-sticked lips, lit it, inhaled, and then breathed out a long, slender stream of smoke. She put the lighter and the pack of cigarettes back into the purse, from which she then produced a tiny ashtray, which she balanced in the palm of her left hand while her right held the lit cigarette, level with her chin. I stared at Miss Heard in fascination and admiration. It was as if she had already begun coaching us, and I was eager to learn this woman's secrets.

Mr. Ross laid out the coming academic year for us, particularly the events of the first term. We would be divided into two groups so that the classes were small. But every day would begin promptly at nine a.m. with the whole group doing a movement warm-up with Rudi Shelley. Monday through Friday, we would focus on the acting program, which included script study, character analysis, improvisation, solo speeches, and the contrasts and connections between medieval and Renaissance drama, as well as Restoration comedy, Victorian melodrama, European drama (e.g., Chekhov, Ibsen, Brecht, and Ionesco), and modern drama from Shaw to Shaffer to Pinter. We would also engage in a series of acting "games" that would test our capacities for invention, character absorption, and developing relationships between the characters we were playing.

Wow! Though I only half understood what Mr. Ross was talking about, I was excited. Ruth Wynn Owen aside, no one had ever discussed acting with me in terms like these, and certainly no director I had ever worked with in am-drams. In the five years that I'd done amateur productions, it was mostly a matter of memorizing lines, having fun, and thinking, *Let's pretend.*

Miss Heard told us that she would work with us on verse, starting with poetry and moving on to Shakespeare. She said that everything we learned about communicating the words of Shakespeare would assist us in communicating the words of every other playwright. She would also lead us in improvisation classes.

When Mr. Ross wrapped up the talk, Rudi instructed us to change into tights, T-shirts, and ballet pumps. He didn't mention the dreaded "supports" for us men, but I knew they would be required. Oh Lord. It wasn't that I was shy about wearing the cup; it was that in order to put it on, I would have to take off my underpants, and I had never before exposed my genitals to adults, not even to our doctor in Mirfield. Before we headed off to the changing rooms in the basement, Rudi recognized me. He came over to shake my hand and welcome me to the school. I couldn't help but notice that a few of my fellow students had observed this and glanced at each other. That gave me a little boost.

The large, low-ceilinged movement studio was also in the basement. As we all assembled, boys and girls in clingy, somewhat revealing movement clothes (by then I had applied my ballet support without incident), I was relieved to see that the other students were as self-conscious as I was: plenty of nervous laughter and shared looks of apprehension. I also noticed that one boy was not wearing a support, leaving nothing to the imagination, though he seemed not to care. I hoped that Rudi wouldn't comment on it, but he did—graciously, without identifying the person, simply making general points about comfort and safety.

The warm-up began simply enough, very similar to the exercises I knew from my gym classes at Mirfield Secondary Modern School: stretches, cardio fitness, and the like. Then Rudi put on music, which I recognized at once as "The Skaters' Waltz" by Émile

Waldteufel, a staple of the BBC Radio program *Children's Choice* and, to this very day, countless elementary school music classes. Rudi explained that there would be many mornings when we would do our warm-up without him. He was going to teach us a series of connected movements that we would perform for the entire length of "The Skaters' Waltz." It would be a kind of dance, Rudi said, but we were to do so alone, although connected to each other by performing the same precise choreography. We were to warm up this way every morning.

But that was not all. There would also be a vocal warm-up, as we were to sing words to the entire piece. I expected sheets of lyrics to be passed round. But no—every incoming class of students, Rudi said, were charged with writing their own lyrics. The second-year students would show us the ropes, visiting us the following day and singing us their version of the warm-up song. We would be given a week to ponder our version, and the following Monday morning Rudi, Mr. Ross, and Miss Heard expected to be entertained by the lyrical stylings of the incoming class of 1957.

I noticed at once that one of my fellow students was animated by this news: a puckishly handsome lad named Robin Phillips. He and I were the two youngest students in our year, and I found him charming and dazzlingly clever, the very traits I lacked. He had a cultured accent to go with his cultured air and appearance, though I later learned that his parents were a gardener and housekeeper for the film star Stewart Granger. When we got back to the changing room, Robin announced that he wanted to have a go at writing the lyrics. There were no objections.

The following morning, he came in with his words, co-written with a Canadian girl from our year, Patricia Armstrong. Together, they sang it for us at our morning break. Thereafter, our entire class sang their words every morning for our first year. This is all I remember:

Here at the school
We love each rule

We dig our movement
It's real cool.

Can't do it yet
But we won't fret
Keep smiling, darlings
You're not dead . . . yet.

Cole Porter it was not, but please remember that it was 1957 and we were young. We all loved what Robin had come up with, and he was immensely pleased with our positive reaction. I was particularly impressed; in my short life I had never met a contemporary as clever as Robin. He speedily became the star of our class and remained so until graduation. I am pleased to note that, later on in his career, he directed me in a production of *Two Gentlemen of Verona* at the RSC and became a renowned stage director in Canada.

The small size of our class ensured that we quickly got to know each other, and I learned how wrong my preconceptions were. Ours was a diverse group, representing a variety of classes and education levels. Margaret Barron came directly from high school and was even less worldly than me. Glenys Gardner was, like Roy Semley and me, from a humble Yorkshire background. Anita Hartwell Jones and Gillian Kitchen were sophisticated girls from London, but that didn't stop them from becoming my friends. Anita is the one member of our class with whom I remain in regular touch; I owe her a debt of gratitude for jogging some of these memories of the Vic School.

We also had three Canadians, one American, one Australian, and one New Zealander, a fetching young lady named Adrienne Finch. During our first term, I spent a lot of time with Adrienne and her flatmate, my friend Gillian Kitchen. I sensed in Adrienne a feeling of being unmoored—she was a long way from home, and everything around her was strange and unfamiliar, including me. Well, what better reason to get *more* familiar with her, then? By the end of the second term, Adrienne and I were an item.

And then there were the two guys in our class from Hungary. They were older than most of us, refugees of the Hungarian Revolution of 1956. That year, the Soviet Union, which controlled the country at the time, used force to put down an uprising by Hungarians against their repressive government, killing 2,500 people. This triggered a wave of emigration to, among others, England and the United States. One of our two Hungarian classmates, George Kishvalvi, was already an accomplished director who had run his own theater in Budapest. He was a delightful, gentle man with whom I became friends. The other, Sandor Eles, was an experienced actor, matinee-idol handsome but at times arrogant and condescending to the rest of us.

I must also note a man in our group who was nearly twice the age of everyone else, Leader Hawkins. He was in his late thirties and had lived an entire life before joining us, working for an oil company. In fact, he had hopped a cargo ship in the West Indies to travel all the way up to Liverpool, just so he could take a train down to Bristol and beg Duncan Ross to let him audition. Leader was admitted, I am pleased to say, and I was impressed by his ambition and dedication. He also became a dear friend to me and a successful, professional character actor.

I didn't end up staying long in my shared bedroom with Roy Semley, partly because neither of us liked the arrangement—and Roy would end up leaving the Vic School anyway—but mainly because a second-year student told me that there was a vacancy in his own digs. The housing was in a four-story terrace building behind the Victoria Rooms, a beautiful Greek-revival building on the campus of another school, Bristol University. Our house was known in our circle as the Lyons Den, as it was a family named Lyons that ran the place and looked after us all so well.

Living there had such a beneficial impact on me. As you by now are aware, I was always more comfortable in the presence of older people, and the second-year students, even with the minor age difference, had more experiences to share and advice to impart. There was also a young woman in our place, Deborah Hecht, who worked for the Old Vic's design department. She broadened my understanding of the nonacting people who help put on a show, whose jobs, as all theater folk know, are very much intertwined with those performing onstage.

Thanks in part to my mates at the Lyons Den, I became more confident and comfortable about participating in conversations, even though I often had no idea what I was talking about. When I had a speech or a scene to work on, there was always a flatmate who generously offered to read it with me, suggesting adjustments, provoking me into arguments, and pushing me to look for different options. This process became as important and enlightening as the education I was getting from my teachers.

I received an education of a different sort from my time with Adrienne. It all began innocently one Saturday evening at her flat. Gillian, her roommate, was away, and I came over to watch some TV. Adrienne and I shared a cheap bottle of Sauternes. That evening turned into a night, which turned into a morning.

I was no longer a virgin when I awoke that Sunday. I remember going out to get us both cappuccinos and finding that I couldn't walk properly. My legs wouldn't obey my brain, and I tottered unsteadily, expecting my knees at any moment to fold up and deposit me in the road: not the best look in a quiet, middle-class, residential section of a Bristol suburb on the Lord's Day. Finally, I reached the coffee shop, gripping the frame of the door to get myself successfully inside. I noticed there was a newspaper stand just inside the door, and I reached for a copy of *The Observer*. As I lifted it up, I went down, bringing the stand and the newspapers with me.

The shopkeeper ran over to help me and get his store in order. Once I was upright, the kind man asked me if I needed help.

"Help?" I replied. "Why would I need help? I am a *man*." Then I humbly ordered my coffees. But I never, ever went back to that shop again.

Adrienne and I, however, remained a couple through to our graduation and slightly beyond.

My education at the Vic School drilled me in technique: text, verse, speech, movement, improv. It was not unlike what I learned in the West Riding drama courses, only much more detailed and rigorous. I was no longer in am-dram territory, just winging it and having fun. I was learning how to construct a character, how to lift him off the page and let him breathe—and breathe in his own way, not Patrick Stewart's way.

I learned about objectives. If, while portraying a character, I became confused or uncertain, not sure where the guy was going, or even who he was, I simply asked myself, *What does he want?* It really is a simple technique. It doesn't always have to be right or true to the script; when you have the answer, or rather *an* answer, then it will be truthful at least.

We were taught to ask ourselves these questions in solitude, by the way. The rationale was that the only true way to work out the answers was to be solitary, unswayed by external influences. In school and in the early days of my professional career, I loved this process: sitting alone in my room with a script, a notebook, and a pen, nothing else needed.

What I am going to describe might seem obvious or rudimentary, but believe me, it is gold dust.

For starters, I read and reread the script many times, recording my discoveries in my notebook as I went. I still have a stack of notebooks with the BOVTS logo, filled with what might be called research. Each of these readings served a distinct purpose, which I kept foremost in my mind as I read.

Reading 1: What is the narrative, the story?
Reading 2: What is the play about?
Reading 3: What does my character say about himself?
Reading 4: What do other characters say about my character when he is present?
Reading 5: What do other characters say about my character when he is absent?
Reading 6: What is true in the play?
Reading 7: What is false in the play?
Reading 8: What does the character actually *do*?

Duncan Ross provided us with this approach. He told us that the day would come when we would no longer have to go through such an arduous process, that as our skills became sharper and more finely tuned, these questions would answer themselves instinctively. That is indeed what happened, and it was exhilarating when it did: Acting had entered my bloodstream. Still, to this day, I like to read a script multiple times, especially for a film or TV, making notes as I go of the feelings it generates.

Curiously, speaking of film and TV, we received no instruction in how to act for these media. It's a strange omission in retrospect, as plenty of great stage actors, including one of the Vic School's founders, Laurence Olivier, were consistently booking screen work. Acting for the camera involves a different set of techniques. The most impactful lesson I ever learned in this regard came nearly twenty years later from the great Rod Steiger, when he was the lead in a movie called *Hennessy*, which was filming in London. I had loved his work since *The Pawnbroker* and my formative moviegoing experience, *On the Waterfront*.

1975's *Hennessy* was my first film, and I was only to work on it for a day and a half. Upon hearing this, Rod invited me to have lunch with him in his trailer. I seized the opportunity and asked him what I needed to learn about film acting. He thought for a moment and then said, "You must understand, Patrick, the camera photographs *thoughts*." Simple but profound. No matter what kind of acting you're doing, you of course have to *think*. But the camera gets closer to you than any audience member ever will. What might be missed onstage, the camera will absolutely see.

My voice classes with the formidable Miss Daphne Heard continued in the spirit of those I had taken with Ruth Wynn Owen. My Yorkshire accent was mostly gone, but Miss Heard mentioned how much she liked it when my Northern vowels slipped through. She said they were "sexy"—so, of course, I strategically started using them more.

The one class I really struggled with was improv, which also fell under the purview of Miss Heard. I had zero experience in it. I knew only the discipline of reading words on the page and absorbing them, and I confess that, at first, I couldn't even see the point. Sure, I enjoyed watching my classmates improvise, especially the naturally funny ones like Robin Phillips, but others, me included, were hopeless.

After a while, I got so embarrassed by my lack of improv skills that I did something stupid: When I knew I had a solo improv or a two-hander coming up, I worked out in advance what I was going to do and where I would go with the improv narrative. A total negation of the whole exercise. Naturally, my teachers and classmates saw right through it, to the extent that sometimes I was booed.

After one such disastrous class, Miss Heard asked me to stay behind. When we were alone, she asked me what was wrong. I had grown to like and trust her, so I admitted that I was frightened of making a fool of myself.

"But, Patrick," she said, "you are so fearless in so much that you attempt in your other classes. Why should this be different?" I had no ready answer for her.

"Here is what I want you to do," she said. "The next improv class we do, prepare nothing. Just enjoy watching what the others do. And when you are called upon, make sure you absorb the circumstances of the improvisation. Take as much time as you need to prepare yourself, but not by planning ahead. Clear your mind, find the emotion that seems right to you, absorb it, and then *let it out*, in whatever form takes hold of you. And let go of your fear, because—and this is the most important thing—you can never be wrong. There *is* no wrong, except thinking ahead. It is not about being clever—it is about being truthful and vulnerable."

Vulnerable! Yes, of course, that was it! Therein lay my fear. I had come up in life believing that to be vulnerable was to invite the worst to happen. From five years old, my age when my father came home from the war, to be vulnerable was to put myself at risk. I'd never been to a therapist, of course, but it was curative to have this realization. How could Miss Heard have possibly known what was going on in my head? And believe me, she *knew*. As she reached the door, she turned around and said, "Never forget, Patrick, in this room you are always safe."

Again, how could she know? I had never breathed a word to anyone about my experience at twelve years old, stepping onto a stage for the first time and finding that I felt safer there than any other place I had ever been. That knowledge has stayed with me for my entire career, and it was Daphne Heard who made the connection. I never really got good at improv at the Vic School, but thereafter, I enjoyed those classes far more and understood their benefit.

If I am making it sound like the Vic School was uncommonly nurturing, it's because it was. Our teachers were always supportive and encouraging. I have heard some horrendous stories about abusive acting coaches and college professors who turn the studio into a boxing ring, throwing oaths and insults at students like punches. There is no room for humiliation in the theater—and no need for it—but my God, there are truly misguided teachers who delight in it.

But in certain respects, the Vic School did have its limitations. I sensed even then, having fallen in love with *On the Waterfront*, that the American acting scene was ahead of ours in the 1950s. We were all required to read Konstantin Stanislavski's book *An Actor Prepares*, the foundational text of Method acting, but Duncan Ross took Stanislavski's ideas only so far. "Living" or "becoming" the role was never part of our vocabulary or curriculum. Rather, our baseline was to convincingly "perform" the role, and I am sorry to say that that is where I got stuck for too long, right up through my early years in the Royal Shakespeare Company during the mid-1960s.

I was locked into a mindset that there was a "right" way of performing a role, and that until I found that way, I was getting it wrong. I felt almost as if a secret code had been given to all the really good actors, while stragglers like me resorted to trial and error. And even when I somehow cracked that code, I thought it was my duty to deliver the exact same performance, show after show. I don't mean to make that sound easy, because it certainly isn't. But I do mean that I was denying the audience a unique experience— what they were watching when they saw me perform was something that had already been seen many times before by many other audiences.

To be fair, that was the prevailing style of theater in the middle of the twentieth century. I saw and worked with actors who were dazzlingly brilliant in their unwavering consistency and their commitment to entertaining the audience. But an actor needs to grow, and sometimes I was slow to adapt to the times and the circumstances.

A good example comes—albeit years later, in 1987—from the first season of *Star Trek: The Next Generation*. My dear pals from that program love this story and particularly enjoy winding me up by reciting their own versions, which make me out to be an even bigger fool than I was. But this is my story, so here is my version.

My mentors Ruth Wynn Owen, Duncan Ross, Daphne Heard, and Rudi Shelley had instilled in me a commitment to discipline. In show business, it is essential. Whether on a film set, in a TV studio, or on a stage, conditions can be challenging. Sometimes, only discipline will see a company through the day. But demanding such discipline is a skill unto itself.

One day, about halfway through our first season, I called a meeting of all the principal *Next Generation* cast members. We were a new program, with no guarantee of renewal, and I had grown very concerned about said discipline on the set. To my eyes, there was too much fooling around, too much noise and laughter, and not enough focus and concentration as we prepared to roll cameras. I delivered a speech to this effect, in a tone that might be considered, I now reluctantly admit, rather pompous.

"There are people on this set who don't get early wraps and late calls and the occasional day off like us lot," I said. "We owe it to them to help make the days go as quickly as possible. Yet look at us: having our fun, indulging in unprofessional behavior. Disgraceful. Do better."

When I was done, there was silence. Until Denise Crosby, who played Lieutenant Tasha Yar, our chief of security, said, "Oh, come on, Patrick! We've got to have some fun sometimes."

Pounding the arm of my chair, I replied, "We are not here, Denise, to have *fun*." After a pregnant pause, the rest of the cast erupted in previously pent-up laughter. I think I even heard a smattering of sarcastic applause. I stalked off the set, furious, but primarily at myself: I knew that I had fucked up.

My castmates will *never* let me forget this anecdote, and they bring it up with exhausting frequency. What also always comes up is that, by the second season, I had become arguably and ironically the most unruly person on the set, insisting with conspiratorial glee that every one of us should be responsible for at least one big laugh every day.

But back to Bristol. In that first year at the Vic School, my greatest satisfaction came from the classes that explored and experimented with the physical aspects of acting. This might have been because as a schoolboy, my crowning successes were on the soccer pitch or the athletics track. My body was in good shape, and when Rudi Shelley made his crack that we walked like "pregnant fairies," I enjoyed it not just for the sassy wisecrack but because I eagerly anticipated learning how Rudi would change all that. Basically, I was a jock who liked being coached.

Rudi had us spending hours walking in big circles while he yelled instructions. Sometimes he pulled one of us out of the circle to use as a demonstration student. If it was me, for example, he would have the class watch as he corrected my gait, the way I held my head, shoulders, and hips, the angles at which I pointed my feet, and how my hands hung from my wrists and moved when I walked. His adjustments were so thorough that, through sheer correction, I gained an inch in height, going from five ten to five eleven. Like a miracle.

But Rudi wasn't just teaching us how to move elegantly, smoothly, confidently. In making us explore the impact that bad posture had on our bodies and our movements, he was helping us understand how to persuasively perform a character beset by age or illness. I was still a teenager. What would my body feel like in fifty years? How might I convey the physicality of an old man?

These lessons were of great value for me when, three years later, in my first season of working in repertory theater at Sheffield, I had to perform two different roles in back-to-back shows: the first one as a rich, suave twenty-two-year-old; the second as an eighty-five-year-old butler in an aristocratic household. In the second role, I was required to make an entrance toward the end of Act I in which I announced to a group of people and my employer, "Tea is in the tapestry room, Your Grace."

This role had been created in its original London production by Ernest Thesiger, a genuinely ancient actor born in 1879, with a career that dated back to the early silent-movie era. How would a man that old move? In considering this question, I decided to make my entrance long before my cue arrived. With my face fixed on the floor, I shuffled through the open door, taking steps of no more than two or three inches.

There was an entire scene going on downstage while I was doing this, and one of the actors in the scene noticed me and started giggling. Soon, two more onstage followed suit. This didn't go down well with some other members of the cast, who complained about me to the director, Geoffrey Ost. But Mr. Ost enjoyed what I was doing and told me to change nothing. So encouraged, I started to make my entrance even earlier, which only made the disruptive giggling get worse. Then the giggling began to affect me as well, until the evening arrived when I opened my mouth to say my line and all I could do was laugh. Even worse, the cast had become so used to my shenanigans that they started cracking up before I even entered. By then, I knew that I had taken things too far. For the last couple of shows, I shouted the line from offstage.

I am not proud of this incident, but I am grateful to Rudi Shelley for unlocking the possibilities of the body. The one thing that could not be denied is that my physicality in the role had pleased my director.

Decades later, once I had loosened up on *The Next Generation*, I related this tale to my castmates. Michael Dorn then dared me to re-create my elderly-butler shuffle for the cameras.

Somewhere in the Paramount vaults, there must be an outtake of me tottering onto the *Enterprise* bridge from the captain's ready room and saying, "Tea is in the tapestry room, Your Grace." Everyone on the bridge laughed, but our director had no idea what was going on and was none too pleased. Remember, we were not there to have *fun*.

Chapter Six

After my first term at the Vic School concluded, I returned to my family's council house in Mirfield for Christmas break. I also got a job for the holidays delivering mail in my corner of town. I loved it. Arriving at the post office before sunrise, sorting the letters, and having a coffee with the full-time crew gave me a wonderful sense of belonging.

But when one of the older men asked me what I was studying, and I told him that I was attending the Bristol Old Vic Theatre School, he just stared back, clearly bemused. It made no sense to him, unlike, say, engineering or textile design. I went to a couple of family parties where I was asked the same question, eliciting a similar blank response. I didn't entirely mind this, as a part of me enjoyed knowing that I might have been the first-ever product of Mirfield to study acting at a high level. But I could feel inside, with a touch of guilt, that my life was irrevocably changing. Mirfield had been my whole world, and now it had become almost meaningless. I pined for Bristol and all the friends I had made there and couldn't wait to get back.

My second term was a direct continuation of the curriculum. But our instructors ratcheted up the level of their demands and expectations. All of my first-term discomforts were gone, however. I knew now that I *belonged* at the Vic School. Despite my limited education, I no longer felt intimidated by my fellow students; I was their equal. I had long harbored a hunger to act, but now this hunger had purpose, focus, and a legitimate pathway forward.

One weekend, four of us drove up from Bristol to London to see some shows. At the London Old Vic Theatre, I caught a matinee of *Romeo and Juliet* that featured the dashing West End star John Neville and future film star Claire Bloom in the title roles. I have never particularly liked the play and, indeed, have never been in a production of it. I find it overlong and dull in places, especially during the second half. But watching this particular production was a revelation.

With my Vic School training, I viewed these top-of-the-line Shakespearean actors through a new lens, especially where John Neville was concerned. He was tall, slender, and shockingly handsome, and spoke the lines melodiously but also with powerful intent. I genuinely believed he was a dear friend of Paul Rogers's Mercutio, that they had a history long predating the action onstage. In the famous "Wherefore art thou Romeo" balcony scene, when he saw Claire Bloom's Juliet, there was a visible change in Neville's physicality, as if the sight of her beauty made him stronger, yet at the same time more vulnerable.

Then, when he whispered the line "But, soft! What light through yonder window breaks? It is the east, and Juliet is the sun," he was not the same man. Something had penetrated Neville so deeply that he was fixed in place, immobile, until Juliet concluded her speech by saying, "Romeo, doff thy name, and for that name, which is no part of thee, take all myself."

Neville swelled with purpose and fearlessness as he said, "I take thee at thy word. Call me but love, and I'll be new baptized. Henceforth I never will be Romeo." I was absolutely thrilled. A transition that profound had never been in my arsenal. It made me realize that I must have been plodding along when I should have been flying. That is why live theater can be so utterly captivating and consuming, both for the actors and the audience. I remembered that moment for years, and . . . see what I mean? I still vividly remember it now, more than sixty years later. I always hoped that one day I would meet John Neville and tell him what he had given me, but it was not to be.

With spring break approaching, I decided, despite the fact that my scholarship was very generous, that I needed to make some extra money. Why? Because I was rapidly losing my hair, and I wanted to be able to pay for treatment at a hair clinic in Bristol. I had grown up with thick, dark, wavy hair, but in my first year of drama school, when I was seventeen, it started to thin out at an accelerated rate. Every day as I walked from my digs to the school, I noticed this place that had in its windows before-and-after photos of balding men restored to their virile, pompadoured former selves. The more hair I lost, the more attention I paid to the clinic. Finally, one day, I screwed up the courage to walk in and have a chat with the people inside. They told me what the treatment would cost. That's when I realized I needed more cash in my pocket.

When I went back to Mirfield for spring break, I took similar initiative. Just up the road from my parents' house was the storefront of a small, private building contractor. I walked in, found the boss, and asked him if he had any unskilled work available just for three weeks. He told me that his chief bricklayer needed a laborer and that I could start right away. The job was right down the street. Perfect.

I ended up working harder than I ever had in my life. What I hadn't been told was that I was not going to be working for just any bricklayer. This man was a champion, a prizewinner. I kid you not. There are bricklayer competitions, and they are taken quite seriously in the building trade. My tasks were as follows: First I had to move the bricks from the pile where they had been delivered to an area close to where he was building a wall and stack a small pile for him. Then I had to mix the mortar. On a normal building site, this would have meant simply switching on a mechanical cement mixer. Not so for the champion! This guy insisted that his mortar had to be mixed by hand. Standing by the pile of bricks were bags and bags of sand and cement. I was given a shovel and a large, flat piece of plywood to use as a mixing surface. Another bricklayer gave me the champion's mortar "recipe" and let me know in no uncertain terms that I was to follow it to the letter, not varying it by so much as an extra drop of water. I was fine with that. It was like a chemistry class.

The champion was due to show up any moment, so I made a start, shoveling and mixing. Moments later, a short, stocky fellow arrived: the king of all bricklayers! He wordlessly gave me a nod, took off his coat, and reached for his trowel. He turned over my mixture once or twice and, to my relief, seemed satisfied. Then he began laying on the mortar. I had never seen hands move so fast. He was like a circus juggler, but instead of clubs, balls, and flaming torches, he had bricks, mortar, and a trowel. I marveled, mouth agape, at his skill and efficiency. Not a spot of mortar was wasted—it all went into the wall.

I quickly realized that I needed to get on with making another batch of mortar, as the first was disappearing by the moment. But I wasn't fast enough, and now the champion was waiting with a look of fury on his face. "Come on, yer lazy bugger!" he yelled. "I'm fooking waiting!"

Thank heavens there was a lunch break because otherwise I wouldn't have survived the exertions of that morning. We sat silently, side by side on a fallen tree, the master bricklayer and me, eating our sandwiches, until I dared to open my mouth and ask him about his trade. At first he just grunted monosyllabic answers. But little by little, he got caught up in what he was saying and in having an eager audience. And then I had the privilege of receiving a private lecture on working with bricks and mortar.

I am not being sarcastic. The champion's words were not wasted on young Patrick Stewart. About ten years later, when I was married to Sheila Falconer, my first wife, we bought our first house—a tiny fifteenth-century dwelling in Warwickshire that came with a quaint name: Wheatsheaf Cottage. And there, I put what I had learned from the champ into action. The period charms of the cottage's small sitting room were ruined by the modern, cheap-looking, gas-fueled heating unit that had been installed atop a concrete hearth in front of a brick wall. There was a big, ugly wooden frame around this unit, which at its top met with an ancient piece of thick timber about seven feet wide.

For weeks and weeks, I gazed at this old timber, and little by little, I became convinced that what I was looking at was the outline of a large inglenook fireplace, perhaps even as old as the building it was in. Late one night, after Sheila had gone to bed, I took out an old box of tools I had inherited from my father and removed from it a heavy-duty hammer and a large, blunt chisel. I went to work, hammering away until I was able to remove one brick, and then another, and another. Sheila, drowsy and understandably miffed, shouted down to me, wondering what the hell I was doing. I assured her that I would stop in a few minutes.

That night, I used a high-beam flashlight to look into the hole I had made in the brick wall. Behind it were large blocks of stone, similar to the ones the house was made of. That was all I needed to know. First thing the next day, I called to have the gas turned off and had someone come to disconnect the heating unit. In a couple of days, the hearth was mine to attack. It took a few days, but my demolition work revealed an old hearth, in good shape but damaged. I did some research and found a brick company in Gloucestershire capable of making bricks in period-appropriate Elizabethan style, narrower and longer than modern bricks.

Then I hand-mixed my own mortar and went to work. Laying those bricks was one of the most rewarding experiences of my life. My next-door neighbor was, I jest not, the village blacksmith. His forge stood across the road from us, and he made me a magnificent steel hood that drew flames and smoke upward. I had the chimney swept and then came the lighting ceremony. This was during my time with the Royal Shakespeare Company. I invited over some of my fellow actors, and we toasted the restored fireplace with sparkling wine as flaming logs lit up the hearth and brickwork, warming us. Thanks, champ.

Many years later, I chanced to drive by Wheatsheaf Cottage, now with different owners. Glancing through the window, I could see there was a fire burning in my restored inglenook. I took satisfaction in knowing I had built something that would last.

Did I mention that I had no hair atop my cranium as I worked on that fireplace? The clinic treatments in Bristol that I'd invested my hard-earned bricklayer money into achieved nothing. I must have had three or four sessions, which involved the placing of electrode patches on my scalp, some massaging by hand, and the application of various creams. But it was hopeless. By the age of nineteen, I was as bald on top as I am now.

This wasn't particularly worrisome where acting was concerned. I knew that I was no dreamboat, no John Neville. What I cared about, though, was dating. Attractive young women, I assumed, were *not* going to want to go out with a young bald guy—not like what's become socially acceptable, even desirable, in recent years. And while Adrienne was my steady companion when I was a bald-*ing* guy, I could feel it later on, after we broke up: that deflating sense on dates, when I was trying to connect with a woman, that she just couldn't see herself pairing up with a young fellow who had already lost most of his hair. A different era, to be sure.

Briefly, I attempted a comb-over, growing what remained of my hair longer and painstakingly spreading it around my scalp. But my Hungarian classmate and friend George Kishvalvi put the kibosh on that strategy. He was directing something I was in, and one day, he stopped rehearsals, walked up to me, looked me over, and said with indignance, "What are you doing?"

Then, with his hand, he mussed up my hair, undoing my careful arrangement. With vehemence, he proclaimed, "Be yourself, or you will never be an actor!"

George was already married, and when I next visited his house, he suddenly grabbed me from behind, restraining my arms. His wife came at me with scissors, pulling my hair up and chopping it very short. I yelled, "Stop, stop!" But George put his mouth to my ear and said, very softly, "*Now* you can be an actor."

I have not looked back since. *Köszönöm*, George.

As I reconciled myself to my fate—or is it pate?—I realized that I had been given a strategic advantage. Being bald, I was a wigmaker's ideal, a tabula rasa for all manner of hairstyle experiments. And I knew that I was not bound for instant stardom on the West End or Broadway; I would be working in British repertory theater, where budgets were limited. It became my custom to audition wearing a delicate little hairpiece—with fake hair, less is more—and then remove it for the director. "See what you've got?" I said. "You have a young actor in his early twenties. But you've got a character actor as well. Two actors for the price of one."

With summer approaching at the end of our third term, Adrienne and I began to talk about the plans we might make for a holiday together. I had already signed up for a month's work on a big building site back home so I could earn more pocket money and get really fit. Which I did. One of my tasks was to empty a truck loaded with concrete paving slabs, one at a time, by myself. Fortunately my mother bought me some heavy gardening gloves that saved my beautiful actor's hands from ruination.

My job commitments left me just three weeks for vacation. I invited Adrienne to come to Mirfield for a couple of nights to have some fun and see where I had grown up. It was a terrible mistake. She was a middle-class girl—her father ran his own business in New Zealand. Our council house and working-class community were not what she was expecting, and she did not enjoy herself.

This is not to knock Adrienne but me. I had failed to prepare her for Mirfield and my home life. At school, there was little discussion among the students of our pasts and backgrounds. We were all there because we loved acting and were good at it—otherwise we wouldn't have been among the select few chosen to be in our year—and we passed our free time talking passionately about our lives in the theater and our futures. And I was more reticent than most about where I came from; never would I have broadcast the fact that I'd shared a bed with my brother until I was fourteen. It wasn't shame, more like a self-protective reflex. To this day I have a natural connection with people who, like me, were hard up as kids; there's a certain understanding among us about what you do and don't talk about.

But at the Vic School, it would have been easy to assume I was middle-class. I had shed my Yorkshire accent and become increasingly at ease with myself, part of the mix. I should have told Adrienne in detail what she was getting into: the modest way of life, the moodiness of my father. On top of that, our council house, while palatial to me, had only two bedrooms. By this point, Adrienne and I were sexually active and used to spending the night together. But that wasn't going to happen under the roof of Alf and Gladys Stewart. So, she took my room and I slept on the sofa. I got Adrienne out of the house as much as I could, taking her to different pubs each evening and introducing her to some of my local pals, but she clearly wasn't having a good time.

To make up for this, I booked us, on very short notice, a holiday in Spain. While Adrienne had journeyed to England all the way from New Zealand, I had never before left the country. But I stepped out of my background, becoming the first Stewart ever to book a trip through a travel agency, a process I found intimidating and awkward. We had to take a train to London and then another to Folkestone, whereupon we caught a ferry to the French port of Dieppe and then took another train to Paris. In Paris, we hopped on a train to the seaside town of Tarragona, where we spent a week in a small hotel before returning to Bristol for our second year at school.

I did okay for a travel neophyte, though I did commit the rookie mistake in the Gare du Nord train station in Paris of engaging with one of those shady drivers who ask you if you need a cab. We got into the guy's car, and I immediately noticed that there was no meter. I knew at once that we were about to get ripped off, but we had already started moving. Fortunately, Adrienne and I had packed light, our bags in our laps, and we were able to escape from the swindler's vehicle at a red light. I was more embarrassed to be made a fool of in front of Adrienne than anything.

We passed some pleasant days on the beach and visited Barcelona, a city with which I immediately fell in love. The only real misfire was our decision to attend a bullfight in Barcelona's Plaza de Toros. Spain and bullfighting were synonymous, so why not?

We quickly learned. The proceedings began innocuously enough, with terrific music and the processional entrance of the matadors and their sidekicks and, finally, the arrival of the first bull. He was huge and cast a shadow over the slight figure of the matador. But then the matador's assistants, the banderilleros, ran at the bull and pierced his body with ornately decorated darts. This was the first queasy moment for Adrienne and me. Clearly the creature was in pain, with blood streaming down his neck and sides.

Then the climactic moment of the ritual arrived. The matador held a sword and the edge of a small scarlet cape in one hand. With a series of little hops, he got closer and closer to the bull, who had now lowered his head. But still the bull tossed his head when he could. There was then a moment when the bull and the man gazed at each other, both totally still. Then the man raised the sword and, taking a couple of quick steps, pushed it deep into the bull's back, almost to the sword's hilt. The crowd roared, while Adrienne and I sat silent. The matador stood to one side of the bull, whose head was now almost scraping the sandy ground, his nostrils bleeding.

Suddenly, his front legs buckled and he fell to his knees, blood pouring out of his mouth. He staggered a little before landing on his side and going still. The crowd went wild. Adrienne and I sat looking at each other in disbelief. I will never forget the shock and horror in her eyes. I momentarily stopped breathing. We left—the customary bill is six bullfights—and caught a train back to Tarragona.

Our second and final year in Bristol included some more explicitly preprofessional education, including one-off classes on basic makeup and wigs. I had a head start, pardon the pun, in the wig department, but as far as makeup went, I had a lot to learn. The most useful lesson was in how to apply a base. At the time, Leichner was the leading manufacturer of stage makeup. If you were a white actor who was not playing an older person or some kind of fantastical character, all you needed was one Leichner No. 9 stick and one No. 5 stick. The No. 9 was a reddish-brown color while the No. 5 was a creamy pink. You applied streaks of both all over your face—and in my case, all over my pate—and blended them together to a create a smooth tone.

This was the received makeup protocol because the heavy, primitive lighting of that era washed out most of the reddish brown, allegedly resulting in the appearance of natural, un-made-up skin. As lighting and makeup improved, the "5 and 9 look," as it was known in the business, went out of fashion, except among old-timers who persisted in wearing it out of force of habit.

I was far from an old-timer, but young habits indeed die hard. During an early technical rehearsal of my first play with the Royal Shakespeare Company, almost a decade after my time in Bristol, director Peter Hall yelled out from behind the production desk, "Patrick Stewart, what the hell have you got on your face?"

I probably blushed, though my makeup was so heavy it would have been hard to tell.

"Er . . . nothing, Peter," I called back. This prompted gales of laughter . . . and this rejoinder from Mr. Hall: "Then fuck off and wash that dreadful nothing before I see you again." Lesson learned. Goodbye, Leichner 5 and 9.

Recently I found, stuffed into a bottom drawer, my old makeup box from this era. My father had at one time kept his military service medals in it, but upon getting a fancier box, he gave me his old one. Inside it still were my original sticks of 5 and 9, lain unused for decades. There was also a purplish stick of something known in the theater as lake-liner, which you applied to the face to add furrows that made you look older. I was reminded of sharing a dressing room at the Sheffield Playhouse decades ago with an actor named Henry Beckett. He was in his eighties at the time, with a deeply lined face. This did not stop him from filling in his real lines with lake-liner. In the dressing room it looked ghastly, but from out front, it made him look convincingly ancient in a way that would not have projected otherwise.

We also had costume classes, as unlikely as that sounds, and they were more useful than you might suppose. We learned how one properly puts on and wears tights, doublets, and hose, and—of particular importance—what to do with your hands when you were not gesticulating or your costume had no pockets. The answer? Just let them hang by your sides, not as if you are standing to attention, but loosely. This applies equally when your costume does indeed have pockets. When I see an actor frequently placing his hands in his pockets onstage, I pick up on his insecurity—such a stance gives off an artificial appearance of relaxation, which is not good unless you're actually trying to convey artificiality.

If you'll allow me, this also applies to political theater. In 2000, I supported Al Gore in his campaign for US president. I was working at the Paramount Pictures facilities at the time, and one day the studio head, Sherry Lansing, asked me if I would introduce Vice President Gore before a speech he was to give on the lot. She had intel that he was a *Star Trek* fan. I was delighted. I met Mr. Gore backstage, and he won me over with his sense of humor and relaxed manner.

I did my introduction and he walked onstage to enthusiastic applause. But he no longer appeared relaxed: he'd put one hand in a pocket in that artificially nonchalant way. I moved off to the side of the stage and listened to him give a powerful and inspiring speech. But every few sentences, he would switch out one hand in a pocket for the other hand in a pocket, and I felt it was undermining his speech, because in real life, nobody does that.

When his event was over, I decided to gamble on giving the vice president my tried-and-true, theater-tested advice on hands in pockets. He listened carefully and thanked me. However, I was disappointed to see, as I followed his campaign on TV, that he continued to do his alternating-hands-in-pockets maneuver.

I am not suggesting that this is why he lost the election to George W. Bush; Lord knows that there were plenty of other factors. But a few years later, at another event in New York, I attended an environmental charity event at the American Museum of Natural History at which he was to speak. I didn't even know Al Gore had arrived until I felt a hand on my shoulder. I turned around, and there was the former vice president. With a big grin on his face, he said, "Patrick, if I had listened to you, everything might have been different."

The shows we performed in our second year of drama school were more varied in idiom. We did an evening of three short plays by the absurdist Romanian-French playwright Eugène Ionesco, *The Lesson*, *The Chairs*, and *The Bald Soprano*. I was in the last of these three, playing the husband, as you can imagine.

I had never heard of absurdist theater before then, but I enjoyed the ride. Performing Ionesco was fun, fascinating, and, at times, scary. He is regarded as one of the most important dramatists of the twentieth century, though his status seems to have dimmed since the 1970s, and I have never performed his work professionally. He did play a role in loosening up the British stage, though, paving the way for the early plays of Harold Pinter, Samuel Beckett, and Jean Genet, all of whose work I have appeared in over the years. There is a British playwright named N. F. Simpson who too often gets left off this distinguished list. In repertory, I did his plays *One Way Pendulum* and *A Resounding Tinkle* (you read that right) and found them delightful.

A big play that we did in our final year was *Under Milk Wood*, by the Welsh genius Dylan Thomas. He originally wrote it for the radio, and thirteen-year-old Patrick Stewart was listening when it was broadcast on the BBC for the first time on January 25, 1954, curled up in the old armchair that occupied a corner of our one downstairs room, my ear as close to our old radio as my mother would allow.

I had no idea who Dylan Thomas was, but I was transfixed. A resonant voice spoke the words, "To begin at the beginning. It is a spring, moonless night in the small town, starless and bible-black . . ." I recognized the voice instantly as that of Richard Burton, Thomas's fellow Welshman.

Thomas originally set up the play to have two narrators, called First Voice and Second Voice. But for the production we did in Bristol, Duncan Ross, who was directing, combined the two voices and cast me as the one Narrator. We had only three weeks to rehearse, but Mr. Ross gave me a heads-up about my casting, giving me an extra couple of weeks to learn my lines.

This was my first large, leading role in a bona fide pro-level production, and I was both excited and apprehensive. Mr. Ross explained to me that I controlled the evening, setting its tone and tempo, and that the Narrator differed from a conventional leading role in that he served as an onstage storyteller, directly addressing the audience.

Our rehearsals were full of fun and laughter. (Ahem.) For the first time, I had a sensation that I have since come to love: of leading a company of actors who also happen to be friends. Everyone respected the enormity of what I was taking on and was supportive. My self-confidence grew with each rehearsal.

Then came the first performance with a live audience. There would only be three. By design, I kept myself apart from the other actors in order to be focused and ready.

The lights went to blackout and I stepped onto the stage, quietly heading for my lightly glowing mark in the very center. I hit it and a narrow spotlight came on, illuminating only my head. I took a breath to speak the first line. This was the moment. But my mouth wouldn't open—it simply refused to. A moment of panic began to swell in my chest. But some greater force overpowered it, parted my lips, and I got out the first two words: "To begin..."

After a tiny pause, I spoke the remainder of the phrase: "...at the beginning." My heart rate slowed, and then I found myself speaking calmly, gently, as if there were only one person in the audience. As it happened, the face I keyed in on, in the center of the first row, was that of Daphne Heard, my teacher. She looked right back at me and... smiled. That was all I needed, and I was away. In what seemed like a matter of minutes, I was speaking the play's final words, "The suddenly wind-shaken wood springs awake for the second dark time this one spring day."

Here is the oddest thing: As we gathered for the curtain call, all I could think was, *I want to do it all again, NOW!* And I would have, had the audience not subsequently filed out. I've had that feeling several times since, and there is nothing like it.

As my time as an acting student was drawing to a close, I was told by the school secretary one morning that Mr. Ross wanted to see me later that day. There was no further explanation. As the hours passed, I became increasingly nervous about this meeting. I had never been summoned to his office before, and usually, when a student received such an invitation, it meant bad news. Oh Lord, was I in trouble?

Finally, at about six o'clock, I found myself sitting on the opposite side of Mr. Ross's desk. For perhaps twenty minutes, he spoke calmly and encouragingly about my two years of work in his school. He was complimentary about what I did in *Under Milk Wood*. He noted certain challenges and difficulties I had been through, but it was all constructive. And then there came a moment when he paused for a few seconds and rubbed his hands rather violently through his thinning ginger hair—a gesture that I knew heralded something complicated or awkward was about to come up.

"Patrick," he said, "you will never achieve success . . ."

Oh God, no.

". . . by insuring against failure."

Well, it began badly but ended okay. The final four words redeemed the first six.

But if I'm being honest, it took many years for the complex wisdom behind those ten words to take root. Mr. Ross was not only saying that I should not be concerned about failure, which was something I was overly concerned with for far too long a time, but also that I should replace this concern with courage, with boldness, with ambition, with fearlessness. He recognized my talent but sensed in me a tentativeness that was holding me back.

I believe now that Mr. Ross's advice to me that day was the best I have ever received. It took me until early middle age to find the determination for fully immersing myself in the counsel I had been given. I'm not saying that I wasted the intervening years, because they were full of creative adventure. But I know that I missed out on a lot of joy and creative opportunity by thinking too much about failure.

Now, however, Mr. Ross's wisdom has been fully absorbed into my work and my life. I will reveal a secret I have withheld until now. Every time I am about to make a first entrance in a play, or the camera is about to roll on an important scene, I say to myself, out loud but very softly, "I don't give a *damn.*"

Of course I *do* give a damn. But uttering that statement aloud releases me, and I can walk onstage or cross in front of the camera with confidence, naked and unafraid. Thank you, Duncan Ross. When I give a talk to a group of acting students, I am invariably asked if there is just one piece of advice I can impart. I always say "Yes," and offer an abbreviated version of Mr. Ross's advice to me: "Be fearless."

At the Vic School, the two-year program culminated in what were called the final shows. They were a big deal because the Bristol Old

Vic Company, the professional entity, loaned us their gorgeous Theatre Royal in King Street for the three days we performed these shows. What's more, the school sent out invitations to important agents, managers, theater directors, and producers. Also, once the shows were cast, each student could, if he or she felt comfortable with it, send his or her own invitations to directors and agents. Even though we were a hundred miles from London, our school had developed an excellent reputation for producing talent.

My buddy Brian Blessed, for example, was already on his way. Right out of school, a year earlier, he'd landed a position as an actor and assistant stage manager at the Nottingham Playhouse, which at the time was possibly the leading repertory theatre in the UK. I visited him there his first year and he gave me a very colorful, if not lurid, account of his time as a grown-up, red-blooded acting professional in rep theater. I was envious, believing that I would never reach such heights. In a short time, Brian was a TV star, one of the leads in a new police procedural series, *Z-Cars*, that ran for over sixteen years. He and his character, Police Constable William "Fancy" Smith, became household names in Britain.

The plays chosen for the final shows were *The Critic*, an eighteenth-century satire by Richard Brinsley Sheridan, and *The Shewing-Up of Blanco Posnet*, a George Bernard Shaw play I had somehow never heard of, let alone seen. Mr. Ross was to direct *The Critic*, and Robin Phillips, our class's star, was cast as the lead character, Mr. Puff. Among us students, the prevailing belief was that the powers that be wanted a role in which Robin could shine for the show business professionals.

But none of us could understand why we were doing *Blanco Posnet*. It's lesser Shaw, not particularly amusing or interesting, and while my Canadian classmate Alan Gibson had been cast as Posnet, a town drunk accused of stealing a horse (the play was set in the American West), I was to be his eighty-year-old father. I knew from the outset that I wouldn't, couldn't, pull off this role. Couldn't convincingly do an American accent, couldn't convincingly play an old American duffer. And I didn't. I was dreadful and everyone knew it.

My accent, my look, my strained attempts to be "old" . . . everything about my performance was ghastly. The director, William Moore, was one of our acting teachers, and while he saw me struggle, he couldn't find a way to help me at all. In retrospect, I think that *he* would have been good in the part.

The Critic, by contrast, went over triumphantly, and Robin dazzled in the lead: so confident, so in control, so watchable. I had a tiny role in the show as a Tower of London beefeater and shared a dressing room with Robin in the Theatre Royal, an honor of sorts. When the professional company was in residence, in fact, the dressing room's occupant was Peter O'Toole. He did not share it with anyone.

Robin was a gracious, popular, effervescent young man. In fact, he was the first person I ever recognized as gay. No doubt there were plenty of gay people even in my hometown of Mirfield, but they wouldn't have made themselves known as such in the 1940s and '50s. Robin was uninhibitedly himself, perhaps a healthy byproduct of growing up around show business people.

But it was painful to share a dressing room with him for one reason: Following every performance, almost immediately after the curtain had fallen, there was eager knocking on our door. The first night, I made the stupid mistake of opening it, therefore being confronted by a queue of smiling faces from the professional theater world, eager to meet Robin and confused when they saw me standing before them. I was embarrassed and mortified. Per the Vic School's protocols, I had written around sixty invitation letters to the directors of various repertory companies, from the most important—Manchester, Birmingham, Liverpool, Glasgow—to the most lowly and obscure. All I got back were a few form letters saying thanks but no thanks. Nobody wanted me. A few weeks later, a few invitations from some of the lesser reps trickled in, and I auditioned for them, but still, nobody hired me.

After the second and third performances of *The Critic*, I let Robin open the door while I hid behind it, against the wall. Robin's guests rarely stayed long, but they stuck around long enough for me to hear the torrents of praise and congratulations directed at him.

Robin was sensitive to my plight and tried to draw me into the conversations, but when we were alone for a moment, I begged him not to. "It's okay, Robin," I said. "Just let me keep out of the way."

By the end of the third and final night of shows, I was seriously in bad shape. All the goodwill and positive vibes of my drama-school experience seemed a mirage. I had fucked up and probably wasted two years of my life. I can't remember where Adrienne was during all this, but I imagine she kept a healthy distance. My work had deteriorated with each performance, and I could see the disappointment register in the faces of Mr. Ross and my other teachers.

That night, there was a party in the Theatre Royal lobby, celebrating not just the end of our modest run but the end of our student days. The following morning, we would all go our separate ways. That is, if you had a way to go. Robin had already accepted an invitation to join the Bristol Old Vic Company—the prestigious theater in which we stood was going to be his new home.

The lobby was cheerfully rowdy, rocking with the sound of laughter and clinking glasses. I couldn't take it. I filled a glass with wine to the brim and walked back into the theater itself, which, to my relief, was empty. I sat in the middle of the stalls, gazing at the empty stage and the beautiful auditorium. I came to realize that in my head, I was saying goodbye to it, forevermore. But not just to the space—I was saying goodbye to *all* of it: my career, my dreams, my life in the British theater, even though it had yet to start. I knew it was not going to happen. I would have to go home to Yorkshire, tail between my legs, and explain to my family and friends what had happened. How could I survive that?

This was the closest I ever came to considering the idea of ending it all. I let the thought cross my mind: *The cold, black waters of Bristol harbor are a two-minute walk away.*

But I stayed, sitting where I was. Why? Not because I had a thunderbolt visitation of self-confidence, but because drowning myself would have really spoiled the good fun everyone else was having out in the lobby. All those terrific people I had just spent the best years of my life with? I couldn't do that to them.

My operatic moment of despair was unexpectedly interrupted by the sensation of a hand on my shoulder. It was Bill Moore, my director and teacher. He was asking if I was okay. All I could do was shake my head. Bill immediately climbed over a row of seats and took the one beside me.

If you're expecting a tender moment of comforting, consoling words, turn the page, because that ain't going to happen.

Bill said to me, "Patrick, may I speak frankly?"

Not a good start. Nothing good has ever come of this phrasing. If anyone ever asks you this question, tell them to bugger off.

But I said what I was required to say: "Yes."

"Patrick, you are going to be a good actor, a character actor," he said. "And you will work, but it could take another twenty years before you come into your own."

See what I mean? You should have turned the page.

Twenty years! *Twenty bloody years?* That was longer than I had lived! I have no idea how I responded, but I remember what I thought: *Fuck you, Bill, you're talking fucking shit. You wait. I'm going to be a fucking actor, NOW.*

I downed the glass of wine, went back to the party, and found Adrienne. We embraced and bid each other an affectionate farewell, unsure if we would ever meet again. I graciously said goodbye to my friends, for whom I was genuinely happy. And then I returned to my digs, packed my bags, and the next day caught the train back to Mirfield.

My first morning home again, I caught the bus to Dewsbury and signed on at the Labour Exchange as unemployed, thereby deserving of said benefits. In plain English, I went on the dole. I think my father was ashamed for me, but my grant was all used up and I wanted to give Mam something for feeding me, and I also needed to have pocket change for bus fares and the occasional pint.

The Stewart family, for all its problems and hardships, never lacked for work ethic. Nobody in my family had "signed on" for years, and in our particular working-class community, doing so was usually seen as idleness, of being "work-shy." I truly felt bad that I was letting my family down, though my mother, unlike my father, was sweet and caring, assuring me I would find a job soon. I knew she wasn't thinking of an acting job.

It was a low moment for me, but I kept telling myself that something would turn up.

And then . . . something did. In my third week back home, I received a telegram. It was from the artistic director of the Theatre Royal in Lincoln, a city in the East Midlands. His note explained that there was a place for me in their next season if I was still interested, but they needed a response ASAP. There was a telephone number, but we still had no telephone. So I made sure I had lots of small change in my pocket and walked to the telephone box by the Dusty Miller pub, a quarter of a mile away.

I was put through to a Mr. K. V. Moore, the artistic director in question, and he told me, yes, there was an opening, but it was for an assistant stage manager and actor: most likely a combination of menial duties and tiny parts. It was not quite what I had hoped for, but it was a job in the theater, and I immediately accepted. My weekly wage? A penurious sum of six pounds, ten shillings. Fine.

They wanted me to start the following Monday, which told me that I received the offer only because someone else had pulled out. But so what? If I wasn't their first choice, I was wanted now. I asked about lodging, and Mr. Moore connected me to his assistant, who gave me a couple of phone numbers to call. I still had some coins in my pocket, so I decided not to waste any time. I called one of the numbers, spoke to the landlady who answered, and was told she had an availability. Room and board, which included breakfast and dinner, was three pounds, ten shillings a week. I thought this was a great deal and told her I would see her that Sunday.

I had entered that telephone box outside the Dusty Miller an unemployed guy with no resources and no future. I left it as an assistant stage manager and *actor* in repertory theater, with a weekly wage and somewhere to eat and lay my head. I went from despair to walking with my head up, and I couldn't wait to share my news with Mam and Dad.

They were pleased for me and appreciated my excitement, but I could see that my mother was a little sad. I think she had enjoyed my being back at home and hoped that my stay might last a while. In fact, though none of us knew it then, those three weeks were the longest time I would ever spend with them again.

Chapter Seven

My comrade in arms for my final big night out in Mirfield was Barry Parkin, my newspaper pal. We went to the pub, drank far too much, and, when the pub closed, caught the bus to Ravensthorpe, where Barry lived with his parents on a council estate. His folks were out, and Barry knew where his father had stashed a bottle of scotch. We put some Lonnie Donegan on the turntable and started sipping.

Lonnie Donegan was the big star of skiffle, the UK precursor to rock, a sort of homemade folk-jazz played on banjos, acoustic guitar, washboard, and tea-chest bass. As unlikely as it sounds, Lonnie was a huge star in the 1950s, inspiring the future members of the Beatles, the Who, and Led Zeppelin to take up music. A few years ago, I was at an event with my wife, Sunny, and I got to talking with a nice middle-aged guy who told me how sincerely he wished that his father had still been alive to witness our meeting. His dad, he said, had been a popular musician and a huge fan of *Star Trek: The Next Generation*. I asked for his father's name and he said, "Lonnie Donegan." I was gobsmacked and thrilled . . . and, for a moment, fourteen again.

Lonnie's music, however, was not to blame for the state I found myself in late that night at Barry's. Having polished off the booze with my good friend, I realized the time and knew my mam would be worried about me. The buses had stopped running for the night, so I walked home. It was only a mile and a half, but the journey was twice delayed by projectile vomiting and once by a mortifying tumble to the pavement.

Well, I was officially a man of the arts now, and I could live it up if I wanted to.

The city of Lincoln was nigh on impossible to get to from where I lived, but I somehow reached my destination via multiple connections on the appointed Sunday, arriving at last by train. Lincoln is a dramatic place to approach because the surrounding landscape is as flat as a pancake. From miles away, you can see the old town center because it is built on the only hill of significance in the county of Lincolnshire. Atop that hill stands the building for which the city is celebrated: Lincoln Cathedral. There is no other structure like it in England. Some of it dates back to the eleventh century, and behind its massive, ornate facade rise three very tall towers topped with pointy Gothic spires. While in Lincoln, I visited the cathedral at least once a week and always found a new nook to explore, such is the building's size and architectural ambition. The cathedral was conveniently a short walk from my digs, which were also walking distance from the theater. Would that every job was like that.

The theater's season was already underway when I arrived, and I started rehearsing my first professional production the next morning: *Treasure Island*, based on the beloved novel by Robert Louis Stevenson. I was cast as Morgan, one of the pirates. The role was small, but I had responsibilities elsewhere, given that half the reason I'd been hired was to serve as the company's assistant stage manager.

That title sounds reasonably respectable, but in truth, I was on the lowest rung of the ladder, a gofer at everyone's beck and call. The one thing I loved about the job was that I was given the key to the stage door and was the first person through it every morning.

Upon entering, I was to fill a big urn with cold water and light the gas beneath it to get the water boiling for coffee. My next job was to sweep the stage with a wide broom. I shall not name names, but I have since been on TV and film sets where a young actor has complained of having to share a limo to the studio with another actor, or thrown a fit because the walk from the trailer to the set is too long. I want to tell such actors to get a grip, because they are so oblivious to their privilege. I am glad that my TV and film career didn't take off until I was in my forties, because by then I had known pretty much each level of working-actor life that there was. I wish that every actor was compelled to start out by sweeping the stage and making coffee.

Sometimes, in my assistant stage manager capacity, I was "on the book" for rehearsals and performances: following the script, prompting actors as needed, and, during tech rehearsals, cueing lights, sound, and entrances. During live performances, I found myself running upstairs to call actors for their entrances because we didn't yet have such modern technologies as walkie-talkies and backstage loudspeakers. My favorite activity, though, was shopping for props. I confess that this was the case because the other assistant stage manager was a dynamic and pretty young woman just out of drama school— yes, another crush. We were never anything more than good friends, but she had a naughtiness to her that gave me a charge. Often when we were on prop hunts together, she talked me into taking a break and calling into a little tea shop for a snack, something I wouldn't have dared do alone.

At the end of each performance, I waited for the last actor and the staff to leave the theater before switching off the lights and locking up for the night. Actually, I left on one light in accordance with an old theater tradition, whereby a single bare bulb is left on, hanging over the center of the stage.

With the theater otherwise deserted, I stood beneath this light every night, taking a moment to breathe in the auditorium and the vibrations of the audience that had just left it. I looked at the set, only recently populated by our company of actors. I was part of all this now. Indeed, I had responsibilities to fulfill, even if they were as a lowly assistant stage manager. *This*, I thought, *is now my home.*

Our theater in Lincoln—named, like Bristol's, the Theatre Royal— was devoted to weekly repertory, meaning that our company mounted a brand-new production *every seven days*. It's astonishing to contemplate that (A) we pulled this off and (B) there was an audience for such a high volume of material. But this was the heyday of the repertory movement, begun early in the twentieth century by a Manchester company whose leaders were keen to bring theater to the masses. Much as the working-class people of Mirfield enthusiastically supported am-drams, so did the whole of England support a constellation of repertory theaters in cities small, medium, and large, all with a resident acting company.

The repertory movement was also a system for nurturing and promoting talent, akin to English football, with its multiple levels below the Premier League, and American baseball, which has three tiers of minor leagues below the majors. Weekly rep was like Single-A baseball: lower in price, talent, and quality of the product but an enjoyable night out nonetheless. The next level up was biweekly rep. At the very top of the heap were the Royal Shakespeare Company in Stratford and the National Theatre in London.

Much of this was made possible by large grants from the government. I was fortunate to grow up in a time when there was a compact between the government and the people dictating that the arts were a necessity of life, not a frivolity. At every level of the rep movement, there were large, enthusiastic audiences, which is why I am irked when the theater is dismissed as an elitist art form and a waste of public money. These hateful attitudes were not widely held until the late-1970s ascent of Margaret Thatcher, who I feel did so much damage to the fabric of society. I fear we shall never again see such an era of public investment in the arts and emerging artists.

As crazy as the weekly-rep schedule was, though, it produced some remarkably entertaining shows. Usually, we were allotted four and a half days for regular rehearsal and one day for tech rehearsal. These were followed by opening night, and the next day by a matinee and an evening show.

Sunday was our one day off, which the actors used to learn their lines for the next play. If you were a lead, you had basically one day to absorb your lines and get off-book. Formidable! But I was too young and excited to actually be working with a professional rep company to consider the insanity of this schedule.

Our artistic director, K. V. Moore, had an eccentric approach to casting the lead roles. After the latest slate of plays was announced, he met with a small group of the company's veteran actors for a few rounds of poker. Whichever actor won three hands first was given the privilege of casting themselves in a plum role. The precise details of the system remained unknown to me, but at least I understood why, at times, some actors were badly miscast. In my youthful naivete, I believed this practice to be normal in the theater, so I resolved to learn poker in the hopes that I, too, might one day secure a good role. But never in all my years of British repertory theater did I ever again encounter another version of Mr. Moore's dubious casting system.

My personal indoctrination into the seat-of-the-pants world of weekly rep came in a play called *Saturday Night at the Crown*, which, as its title implies, was set in a pub. In keeping with my low place in the company hierarchy, I was given the role of "Pub Customer," sitting at a table, mostly mute, for the better part of Acts II and III. The female lead, however, had a ton of lines to commit to memory. In one performance, in the middle of the second act, she began to flail, losing her way in a speech. An assistant stage manager whispered a prompt, but as is often the case in these situations, the actress was in too much of a panic to hear it.

This was where I nobly stepped in. I knew the cue and fed it to her, reciting one of her lines as one of my own. With a look of relief and gratitude, the actress picked up where I left off and continued happily on her way. I was immensely pleased with myself, even more so when a couple of other actors onstage acknowledged my save with nods and smiles.

But! There followed a second catastrophe. The actress was still in the midst of her big speech when, we all noticed, she slowed down her delivery and finally came to a dead stop. At that moment, I realized what I had done. I'd fed her a cue from Act *III*, not Act II, and the speech I'd merrily sent her off on was the one that winds up the play. And here was where the resourcefulness of trained actors came to the fore. We collectively realized what was going on and, via improvisation, wound the play back about thirty pages, resetting it so that the third act flowed sensibly from the second.

The audience was none the wiser, but the director certainly was. He gave me a right bollocking after the show. In a different performance of the same play, I had another such disaster in my capacity as assistant stage manager. Scurrying up two flights of stairs, I let an actor know that he had missed his entrance. He immediately dashed for the stage and threw himself through the scenery door, where he was greeted with silence and quizzical stares by the rest of the cast. He came back offstage and whispered to me sharply, "It's not me that's off. It's *you*."

I was stunned that I wasn't fired after that incident. But I came to realize that such cock-ups are reasonably common in weekly rep, and that the Lincoln company enjoyed the memory of such stories, especially where I was concerned, and especially when my career began to take off. Theater people love disaster stories—after the fact.

My time in Lincoln turned out to be short-lived. Two months in, out of the blue, I received a call from Sheffield Rep, a company for which I had auditioned near the end of drama school, only to hear nothing back, just like the others.

Geoffrey Ost, Sheffield's artistic director, offered me a position as a full-time actor, working for the princely sum of eight pounds, ten shillings a week. So, while I was very grateful to Mr. Moore for starting me off, I gave notice and moved on to Sheffield, commencing rehearsals on a new play less than twenty-four hours after my departure from Lincoln. What's more, Sheffield was a fortnightly rep, which meant we had two whole weeks to rehearse a show, so I was movin' on up.

Shortly before I bade Lincoln goodbye, I heard from Adrienne, my Vic School girlfriend. She told me that she'd just been hired to be part of a rep company—mine, in Lincoln! We only overlapped for a few days, and while our reunion was pleasant, it was also a bit awkward. We had drifted apart.

But fate sometimes has a nice way of tidying up loose ends. Adrienne's first play at Lincoln Rep was directed by K. V. Moore's deputy, John Brittany, a smart and talented young man. John and Adrienne hit it off right away. A couple of months later, when I was settled in Sheffield, I received a letter from Adrienne telling me that she and John were engaged. I am pleased to say that they were wed in 1960 and remained happily married until John's death decades later. Adrienne, I am sad to have recently learned, passed away in July 2020. I shall never forget her.

Working in Sheffield brought me back to Yorkshire, albeit on the southern fringe. Sheffield was and still is a proudly working-class, industrial city, the UK's main steel town, with two major football teams and a populace not to be messed with. It is the home of both Cockers, Joe and Jarvis, the latter of whom, as the leader of the rock band Pulp, wrote the populist anthem "Common People" (which, incidentally, was incongruously covered by my predecessor as captain of the *Enterprise*, William Shatner).

One more piece of irresistible Sheffield lore: I was having a drink one night with a stagehand much older than me, who asked if I had ever heard of the gangs of female steelworkers. Allegedly, on Friday nights after the pubs closed, they walked down the center of the city's streets, singing at high volume and yelling belligerently at any man who gave them the stink eye. The stagehand told me that these women were known for administering severe beatings to guys they didn't like the look of; even the police stayed clear of them.

None of this had any bearing on the delicate tastes and temperament of our artistic director. Geoffrey Ost was in his sixties, complete with a posh accent and a long track record at the Playhouse, the theater that was the home to Sheffield's repertory company. I always felt self-conscious in his presence given my humble background, and these feelings only intensified when a fellow actor told me that Geoffrey took care to have at least one actor from the British upper class in the company. Why? Because he enjoyed hosting these actors' families when they came to Sheffield.

Geoffrey was also an extremely proper man who could barely abide sex, romance, loudness, swear words, and violence—a really odd trait for a director. When a steamy scene was being played, I noticed, he actually left the auditorium until it was over, like a child covering his eyes and plugging his ears.

On the other hand, he was always ready to give a note if you improperly pronounced a word, violated a social protocol, or, in my case, let your Yorkshire accent creep in when you were playing an affluent young man with a double-barreled name who was dating a debutante.

One Monday afternoon, when we were doing a full dress rehearsal before that evening's opening-night performance, everything that could go wrong did. Entrances were missed, lines were forgotten, someone put on someone else's costume, someone threw up in the wings, someone fled the stage in tears, and, near the end, a large piece of scenery fell forward onto the stage, barely missing one of the actors and revealing much of the backstage area. We even botched the curtain call in our discombobulated state.

We were prepared for the worst from our director. But Geoffrey simply made his way down to the foot of the stage and said, "Marvelous, well done, all of you! So good, so good, I'm delighted." And then: "Oh, just one thing. Patrick—your umbrella is folded the wrong way."

Sheffield was, artistically speaking, a very traditional theater, with little risk-taking. One night after a show, a group of us repaired to a bar, where we were joined by a member of the theater's board. Somebody mentioned the previous year's production of Ibsen's *The Wild Duck*, which had evidently done poorly at the box office. Another actor in our group said that he wasn't a fan of Ibsen, but he loved Chekhov and wanted to do *The Seagull*. The board member banged his glass down on the bar and said, "No! No bloody way! We're 'avin' no more o' them bloody bird plays!"

Nevertheless, we did good work. We had an experienced company, except for me, and Geoffrey was skillful at blocking out the physical aspects of a production, the movement and placement of actors—he was adept at painting a "stage picture." In essence, he was more of an organizer than a director, and there was nothing wrong with that.

During my time in Sheffield, I learned primarily from my peers. The actor who impressed me most was Keith Barron. He stood out for a variety of reasons. Like me, Keith was from the West Riding of Yorkshire. Unlike me, he never even made it as far as drama school. After he finished high school, he somehow persuaded Geoffrey to let him audition. Geoffrey was impressed, but Keith had to accept a deal in which he worked as an intern and paid the theater for that privilege rather than the other way around.

By the time I arrived, though, Keith was a full company member, usually the juvenile lead in the plays we did, and newly married to a wonderful young stage designer named Mary Pickard (an auspicious surname, that). He and Mary quickly became my good friends, inviting me over every Sunday for lunch in their spacious ground-floor flat. Keith went on to have a brilliant TV career in Britain, starring in Dennis Potter's Nigel Barton teleplays and the police drama *The Odd Man*, and working continuously right up through the end of his life, appearing in such programs as *Midsomer Murders* and *Foyle's War*. He was the first real "name actor" with whom I had the honor of working.

Another company member from that era who comes to mind is Amanda Grinling, a fine actress of aristocratic background—maybe she was one of Geoffrey's social ringers—who starred in the title role of our production of *The Reluctant Debutante*, the play in which I played the posh fellow with a double-barreled name. What I most cherish about Amanda is that she taught me her secret to curing hiccups. Since it remains a secret, I cannot get too much into the details of how it works, but it involves gazing intensely into the eyes of the hiccuper, with utmost seriousness—if anyone giggles or smirks, the spell is broken. My children believed in my powers so completely that even when they got older and had moved out of the house, they phoned me to cure their hiccups, which I did, even without eye contact, every single time.

Indeed, not long ago, while I was giving my wife, Sunny, and her parents a tour of Stratford-upon-Avon, we encountered a salesperson in a chemists' shop who apologized to us for the dreadful attack of hiccups she was suffering. I looked her firmly in the eye and said, "They've gone." And her attack had truly ended. When the young woman realized this, she began to cry. It was a moving experience all around. Now, my father-in-law is a retired emergency room physician, an educated, science-based man. When we left the shop, he grabbed my elbow and said, "How the hell did you do that?" I told him exactly what I am telling you now: I cannot disclose my methods. But thank you for all time, Amanda Grinling.

I spent eighteen months with Sheffield Rep, and I consider that time as crucial a chapter in my education for becoming an actor as drama school was. I spent a lot of time in the wings studying my fellow company members as they performed, learning both how to act and how *not* to act. I took in the craft and dedication of those actors who committed themselves fully to their performances. I saw the sorry end result when an actor had failed to prepare adequately and simply phoned it in. I studied how some actors delivered powerful performances boiling over with energy while others shone with equal impact by making the most of stillness.

Above all, I opened myself up to the idea that there is no single "right way" of delivering a performance, and that I must always be prepared to sublimate my ego to the demands of the work itself. This applies to every job I take, right up to the present. For example, during the pandemic lockdown, I filmed a silly but very fun commercial for Uber Eats with *Star Wars* actor Mark Hamill. We shot different lengths and versions of the script, but even the longest was only forty-five seconds. Our director, a young man named Guy Shelmerdine, kept saying, "It's too long, can you speed it up?" Despite my reservations, I did, getting to a point where I thought we were just gabbling incomprehensibly. But when we watched the playback, it was perfect. The requirements of the project demanded a new kind of performance from me, and now I am keen to experiment further with rapid-delivery dialogue.

During my second year in Sheffield, I was elected to be our company's representative in the British Actors' Equity Association. I'd become a provisional member of the union in Lincoln and a full-time member after logging forty weeks of service as a professional actor. Having come from a strong union family, I was proud that my fellow actors had entrusted me with this responsibility, even if the reality was that the rest of them didn't want the job and were only too happy to pass it on to the kid.

The union still very much exists, though it is no longer the powerhouse it once was. Margaret Thatcher, during her time as prime minister, saw to it that the rules were changed, making union membership no longer compulsory for professionals—another reason why I so intensely disliked her and her government. When I am part of a company, I always try to persuade nonmembers to join, as does my dear friend Sir Ian McKellen. Our experiences in Actors' Equity have taught us that life is better with union protection.

As I was learning the ropes of life as a professional actor, I was also learning how to be an adult—sort of. For the first time in my life, I rented not a room but a proper flat, in a section of Sheffield known as Nether Edge. The building was perfectly fine, a red-brick semi-detached; the flat, less so. It was accessed through a back door and was basically a basement room, with its kitchen, bedroom, and sitting room all occupying the same four-walled space. The sole window faced the back garden, allowing barely any sunlight in, so I had the lights on all the time. Still, just up the road was a bus stop from which I could catch a ride into the city center and then take a short walk to the theater. I was thrilled by my independence.

Upon moving in, I realized that I needed to stock up on pantry staples, so I visited a small market and a greengrocer's. Bear in mind that I had never before cared for myself and prepared my own meals. So, while I was fine buying things that came in jars, packets, boxes, and tins, when it came to loose products, such as fresh produce, I was at a bit of a loss. I mean, in my Camm Lane days, I had run errands for my mother, but she had always written out a list of what and how much she needed.

But for the life of me, I could not remember what the appropriate quantities were for a family, much less a single person, and at that time, a phone call home represented an extraordinary expense—and my parents still did not have a telephone anyway. So I was on my own. Four oranges, two onions, a dozen carrots—that all seemed to make sense. But what about potatoes? I vaguely recalled the word "stone" (the equivalent of fourteen pounds) somehow being part of the ordering process. But was it two stone? Five? Half a stone? I had no idea.

To be on the safe side, I ordered eight stone. The greengrocer looked at me with a curious frown, but then he shrugged and went to the back room. He returned, sometime later, with an assistant, both of them carrying a number of bags. When I saw this, I looked questioningly at the grocer and said, "Eight stone?"

"Oh, yes," he said.

I knew in that moment that I had messed up. But I was too young and too fearful of creating a scene to say, "I'm so sorry, sir, I am new at this and have come to recognize that I have grossly overordered in the potato department." That would have been a rational and reasonable way to rectify the situation. But, too scared to call further attention to myself, I simply went along with it and brought home my eight stone of potatoes, well over a hundred pounds. It took me four trips on foot.

Now came another problem. Where, in my small flat, would I store all these potatoes? The only place I could find was a cupboard under the kitchen sink. I opened it and became aware of an unpleasant, mildewy smell. Examining the space, I noticed damp permeating everywhere, loosening the nasty old wallpaper and staining the wooden baseboards—not just in the cupboard but throughout the flat, with water splotches even on the ceiling. However, the flat came equipped with a decent gas-powered fireplace. As it was late autumn, I decided to make the most of it. The gas fire kept me warm and, I hoped, would dry out the damp.

But it did not—the place never lost its faint but insistent smell of rot. Fortunately, I was on a month-to-month lease, and with Christmas approaching, I found something more like my digs in previous stops: an attic room with a private bathroom in a lovely detached house owned by a well-off couple. The day I left my damp, nasty flat was cold and gloomy, with pouring rain. I couldn't wait to be out of there and was pleased to find myself loading my suitcase and other belongings into a taxi. I was about to leave the key in the flat's door for the last time when I decided that, for peace of mind, I should do an idiot check and make sure I was leaving nothing behind. It would only take a few moments—it was only a room, after all.

I opened nearly every door and cupboard, and, as I suspected, I had cleaned them all out. But then my eyes fell on the cupboard under the sink. In my mind, I was certain there was nothing to be found within, but thought I should look anyway. I unhooked the latch. At this, the cupboard's two doors violently burst open, and my head and shoulders were suddenly devoured by green snakes. I screamed and fell on my back, my arms flailing like a victim of an alien attack in a sci-fi movie.

Yes, the eight stone of potatoes had taken their revenge. I had forgotten about them, and the dark, damp, warm cupboard had provided an ideal environment for them to sprout and grow slimy green tentacles. Mortified, I sent the taxi away and spent the next half hour cleaning up the spud carnage. What's especially surprising about this story to me is that it is not unique. I have discovered over the years that many friends have similar tales of youthful potato-storage misadventure.

My new accommodations, however, were more civilized in every way. My landlords, a couple named Arthur and Sarah, invited me to join them on my free evenings in their sitting room, which usually had a blazing fireplace going and something playing on the TV, which was large and luxurious by 1959 standards. When the program we were watching was over, Arthur turned the TV off and said, "So, what did we think?" He didn't want just a response of "good" or "bad" but thoughtful assessments, judgments, and analysis. This was new and good for me, in that it made me think seriously about entertainment and critically about the news—expanded my horizons, if you will. A little guiltily, I envied the middle-class kids for whom such a home environment was the norm.

At the start of my second season in Sheffield, I noticed a new addition to the stage management team, a beautiful, dark-haired young woman named Jill Pomerance. She had just graduated from Bristol University. We must have been studying there in Bristol at the same time when I was at drama school, though we had never met. I was instantly captivated. Jill had a brilliant mind and a great sense of fun, and she was a local girl, born and raised in Sheffield.

We began seeing each other casually, but agreed it would be best to keep our workplace romance undercover. One Sunday evening, she invited me to her home, as her parents were going to be out late. The house was absolutely gorgeous, and we spent the evening in the library, watching TV and drinking a few glasses of wine. We cuddled a little while doing this, but that was as far as it went. I could not have been more content, and wished only that I had more time with Jill before I scuttled home to my digs. Maybe it was this wishful thinking that caused us to lose track of time, for suddenly, we heard the front door open.

To say that Jill's parents were surprised to see me is an understatement. They clearly disapproved of my presence, even though Jill and I were over twenty by then, not teens in heat. In a decidedly unfriendly way, her father sized me up with judgmental eyes and said, "I'll show you out." Then I was "escorted" to the front door, Mr. Pomerance's hand firm on my shoulder. I wasn't *literally* thrown out, but came close, as I was physically nudged over the threshold, and as the door slammed shut, it nearly hit my back.

For twenty minutes I walked through the darkened streets of Jill's fancy neighborhood and could think only about what might have come after I left. It couldn't have been pleasant for Jill. When we met the next morning, she told me she was sorry about what had happened, but we wouldn't be able to meet like that again. I had been banned from the house, even though we had done nothing wrong. Jill's parents had big ambitions for their daughter, and I was clearly not among them.

I experienced a few other episodes of this nature early in my adulthood. About two years later, when I was with the Manchester Library Theatre Company, I got my first lead in a Shakespeare play, as the title character in *Henry V*. A talented young actress named Karin Fernald played Princess Katherine, whom King Henry was to marry. As I would discover over the years, it's a perilous business to keep telling someone you love them as required by the script, because if you say it often enough, you start to believe it in real life. Although Karin only did this one play before leaving Manchester, she and I began a long-distance relationship. I simply adored her.

However, Karin's father, John Fernald, was an important man in the British theater, the director of the Royal Academy of Dramatic Art in London. Like Jill's parents, Mr. Fernald and his wife, the actress Jenny Laird, had grand plans for their daughter, which again were unlikely to have included that no-name regional-rep actor Patrick Stewart. I met Karin's parents a couple of times, and while they were civil, I sensed a distinct chill. At some point, Karin landed a leading role in a West End production and our relationship fizzled out, though I did not want that.

These experiences hurt. How could they not? I confess to sometimes playing out a little fantasy in my head. What if *Star Trek*–style time travel was a reality, and I was able to come face-to-face with these disapproving parents as my future self, Sir Patrick Stewart OBE, associate artist of the Royal Shakespeare Company, with the West End, Broadway, multiple TV series, multiple films, and two beloved cultural franchises on my résumé? Would it make any difference?

Probably not. These parents didn't want me associated with their daughters because I had a working-class background in which borderline poverty had occasionally played a role, and no proper education to speak of.

If I am honest, I paid a price for these rejections. I felt unfairly treated, and a part of me believed in my heart that these people were right—I wasn't good enough. Those feelings dragged me down for years.

I am sure that some friends who knew me as a young adult would say, *That's nonsense, Patrick. You were always brimming with self-confidence—it oozed from your every pore.* Well, it might have appeared so, but it was just that: an appearance, not the truth. Even today, I find myself in situations where these feelings resurface and I want to hide. Not because I feel "less than" as an actor—I am over that—but because I am struggling just to be an acceptable Pat Stewart.

One day during a rehearsal in Sheffield, word came to me that I had received a telegram, which was being held for me at the box office. It was from the London Old Vic Company, requesting that I call the telephone number listed if I was still interested in joining the Old Vic World Tour.

Hang on, I thought, *the Old Vic what?*

I had never heard of an Old Vic World Tour. Nor had I applied or auditioned for such a thing. I didn't have an agent or manager— all I had was a job I liked with Sheffield Rep. I have never solved the mystery of how this opportunity came my way, though I do wonder if this telegram was the brainchild of some disapproving father, using his influence to get me away from his daughter: *What if we shipped the Stewart kid off to Melbourne and points beyond? That's the ticket!*

I consulted Keith Barron and other members of the company, and the unanimous conclusion was that there was no harm in at least calling the number and finding out what this telegram was all about.

So I did, and was put through to Douglas Morris, the general manager for the tour. If I was interested in joining it, he would send me details of the offer, with three scripts and the roles I would be playing. But he needed a yes or no this very moment, right now, before the end of our phone call. Mr. Morris's tone as he related all this was impersonal, bordering on unfriendly.

It was an unfair position to put me in. But: An offer from the *London Old Vic*? A *world tour*? I was twenty years old. How could I turn that down? I accepted the offer on the spot and crossed my fingers that the Playhouse would let me out of my contract. When that day's rehearsals ended, I broke the news to Geoffrey Ost, who looked astonished and didn't seem to entirely believe me. But then he said that if it was a genuine offer, I should accept it and he would let me go, with regret.

Two days later, a package arrived for me. Within it were three scripts, a letter, and a contract—Mr. Morris was as good as his word, and it all appeared legitimate. The letter said that rehearsals would begin in London in four weeks and that the company would fly to

Australia two months after that. In all, the tour was scheduled to last eighteen months. The Australia–New Zealand leg would include stops in Melbourne, Sydney, Brisbane, Adelaide, Perth, Auckland, and Wellington. We would spend six months down under, followed by an eight-city tour of Central and South America, details to follow.

I looked at the three scripts. *Twelfth Night*, by William Shakespeare. Well, I was familiar with that one. But *The Lady of the Camellias*, based on the 1848 novel by Alexandre Dumas, and *Duel of Angels*, an English-language adaptation of Jean Giraudoux's *Pour Lucrèce*? Never bloody 'eard of 'em.

Then I looked at the roles I was assigned. In *Twelfth Night*, all I saw was "Second Officer." For the other two, it said, "to play as cast," meaning in whatever assorted nonspeaking roles they needed a body for. Ouch. This was sounding decidedly *not* good.

But then I looked at the pay: a stratospheric thirty-five pounds a week, way beyond what anyone in my family had ever earned. And the star of all three plays and headliner of the tour would be . . . Vivien Leigh. Yes, Miss Scarlett O'Hara herself, one of the greatest film stars my country had ever produced—and, until the year before the tour, Lady Olivier, the female half of Britain's powerhouse acting couple.

Well, *now* things were getting interesting. And the letter noted that I would be required to pack evening dress—a tuxedo and a black bow tie—because there would be numerous formal events to attend throughout the tour.

Despite the unpromising casting news, I went to bed that night giddy over the possibilities such a tour would present. After that night's show, my pals in the company took me to the Playhouse's bar and bought me several rounds in tribute. Even Jill, my forbidden amour, was there. She raised a glass, happy for me but with tears in her eyes. The next night, Keith and Mary threw me a farewell party at their flat. The following morning, I was on a train back to Mirfield to pack for eighteen months away.

I had already written to my parents about the exciting new development in my life, and they had told all of their neighbors—and, of course, my paternal grandmother, Mary Stewart. This, by the way, was the moment when she summoned me to her home near Blackpool to tell me about my vanished grandfather's acting career. However, I should let you know of one more story that Mary told me on the same day that Mam and I went to visit her. When the Stewarts were still living in Tyneside, they had a spare room that they sometimes rented out by the week, usually to entertainers passing through town while performing at the local variety theater. Among their regulars was a young married couple. One year, they turned up with a new baby in tow and asked my grandmother if she could look after him in the evenings while they performed. My grandma said that this baby was an uncommonly jolly infant who she delighted in looking after.

His name? Stanley Jefferson. Later, when he was grown and performing himself in the United States, he changed his surname to Laurel. Yes, my grandmother was (briefly) the one and only Stan Laurel's babysitter.

The other unusual experience of my brief home visit to Mirfield was the press coverage I received: my first, apart from a few small mentions in reviews. In the way that news travels in small towns, word of my pending travels abroad reached the ears of my old employer, Mr. Wilson at the *Dewsbury and District Reporter*. One of my former newsroom colleagues was assigned to interview me for an article.

The headline that ran with the piece was something along the lines of LOCAL BOY TO TOUR WORLD WITH VIVIEN LEIGH, which was putting things generously where I was concerned. But admittedly, I didn't mind the attention.

Chapter Eight

We rehearsed for the world tour in the Finsbury Park Empire, a cavernous, two-thousand-seat theater dating back to 1910 and the heyday of vaudeville and music hall. Now it was weathered and gloomy, a few years away from its demolition. Still, I was excited to be in a proper London theater for the first time as a working actor.

I couldn't afford to stay in a hotel, so I found lodgings nearby in a tatty-looking four-story boardinghouse that was even shabbier inside. A gruff elderly woman led me upstairs to my room, which had two double beds in it—one currently occupied by a young man who was fast asleep. When he awoke, he pleasantly introduced himself in a thick Irish accent. Shortly thereafter, he led me to the large dining table downstairs and introduced me to the other residents. They were all, like my roommate, young and Irish. At once, they began peppering me with questions: Where was I from? Who was I working for?

None of them had ever heard of the Old Vic Company. One of them asked, "Are they building contractors?"

The penny dropped. These young men were all laborers who had come from Ireland to make money on building sites. The Republic was going through a dire time economically, with few jobs for lads like them. I was the odd man out: an Englishman of the arts. I felt sheepish revealing to them that I was, in fact, an actor, in London to rehearse for a world tour.

But far from ridiculing me, they were impressed, quizzing me about the tour and the plays involved. They also loved that my first name was Patrick. When I explained to them that Stewart originated as an Irish name before it was taken up by the Scots, well, that was it—I was in, one of them. Their routine on a Sunday evening was to follow dinner with a visit to their favorite local pub, a crowded, noisy place whose clientele, like our boardinghouse's, was mostly Irish. I was proudly introduced by my new friends to the pub's patrons as Patrick the Actor. When I saw how many men were now in our group, I began to fret—not because I was intimidated, but because I didn't have enough cash to buy everyone a round. I confessed this to my housemates, who erupted in laughter.

"Drinks are on us, Patrick!" said one. I was their honored guest.

I fell asleep that night pondering the prejudices with which I had been raised. If I had been walking down a street at night and seen these lads gathered in a pack, I would have turned around or crossed to the other side. They were *Irish*. I had led a rather sheltered life in Mirfield, where stereotypes died hard. I had always been told not to trust Irish people. They were no good. They were violent. They were cheaters. They just wanted your money. All it took was one night in London for me to shake off these horrible misconceptions once and for all.

I did not receive as warm a welcome on the first day of rehearsals in the Finsbury Park Empire Theatre. The Old Vic's director, Michael Benthall, introduced us to our play's director, Robert Helpmann, a small, slender Australian who had first made his name as a ballet dancer. Helpmann was a big deal in the theater world, having conquered not only dance but drama as well, building a formidable career as an actor and director. You might remember him from your childhood as the grotesque, long-nosed Child Catcher in the movie *Chitty Chitty Bang Bang*. I was fascinated by the man. When he moved, he appeared to do so in exquisitely choreographed dance steps, and when he stood still, it always seemed as if he was striking a pose.

But I took issue with the manner in which Helpmann handled our first day. He singled out some members of our company by name, but many (like me) not at all. And when the time came for Benthall and Helpmann to leave the stage, they offered gracious goodbyes and handshakes only to the actors who had been named. I found that odd and, more than that, insulting. We didn't work that way in regional theater, and I expected the standards of conduct in London to be higher, not lower.

Thank goodness for Vivien Leigh. After she was introduced, she made a point of speaking with everyone in the cast, asking us our names with sensitivity and genuine interest. I had something of an out-of-body experience meeting her, as I had never before met anyone so famous, nor, for that matter, so talented. She was forty-seven years old and had weathered a very public divorce and bouts of tuberculosis and mental illness, specifically what we would today call bipolar disorder. But there were no indications of this in person. Vivien was bright, friendly, hardworking, and as beautiful as she appeared in the movies, with that mane of cascading dark hair. Whatever reservations I had about this tour and my place in it, I was thrilled to be in her presence with the knowledge that, very soon, I would be sharing a stage with her. Vivien's boyfriend, a handsome actor named John Merivale, was also part of the touring ensemble, and he, too, was outgoing and friendly.

We wasted no time, getting right into rehearsal for *Duel of Angels*, a play that Vivien, it turned out, had already starred in, to much acclaim. Now I was beginning to understand our peculiar triple bill a little better. Vivien had a massive workload to take on, and her familiarity with this play made for one less mountain to climb.

I also met Douglas Morris, the company manager and the man who had brusquely demanded a "yes or no" answer from me on the telephone. He was even worse in person: an officious, sneering, nasty man whose smile was more like a grimace. He was always dressed in a suit and tie, as if to constantly remind us that he was the production manager, a figure of senior rank. In front of the other actors, he presented me with an envelope and said, "Stewart, here are the details of your casting," enunciating that last word with sarcastic emphasis. I couldn't help but notice a smirk on his face, and knew then and there that he had it in for me.

In a matter of days I had befriended some of my fellow actors of low billing, in particular the witty, sardonic Bruce Montague. Bruce had worked with Douglas Morris before and confirmed my suspicions that he reveled in tormenting young actors. In fact, Bruce said, the people at the London Old Vic had a delicious nickname for this cruel man: Mugless Doris.

As soon as I got out of the theater on that first day, I opened the envelope that Mugless had handed me. Inside was a sheet of paper listing the specifics of all the roles I was to play. For *Duel of Angels*, it said "Townsperson" and "Man Sitting at Café Table." Neither of these characters spoke. In *Lady of the Camellias*, I was to play the Duc du Giret. That sounded promising, but when I got home and reviewed the script, I leaned that *le duc* appeared in only one scene, right at the beginning of the play, and had no lines. After that, I had two more appearances in the show: as "Party Guest" and "Servant." Two plays, no words.

Then there was *Twelfth Night*, in which back in Sheffield I had already played Antonio, a respectably sized role. But with the Old Vic Company, I was only to play . . . "Second Officer." He appeared only in Act III, Scene 4, and had a grand total of three lines: "Antonio, I arrest thee at the suit of Count Orsino"; "Come, sir, away"; and "Come, sir, I pray thee go." Wow, what a rich array of Shakespearean dialogue. Three plays and a total of nineteen words. Oh, and in *Twelfth Night*, it appeared I had another nonspeaking role, as "Sailor."

The kicker was that I was also to understudy one role in *Twelfth Night*, an arrangement that no one had discussed with me in advance. And it wasn't for a major role, but for a priest who appears in the fifth act. He had one speech of around eight lines.

I was devastated. This was less onstage work than I had been given as a first-year student. Not what I was expecting to play after eighteen months in rep.

I felt humiliated. What would I tell my friends and family? They would be shocked. My first impulse was to call Mugless Doris, whose smirk had by now explained itself, and tell him that I was out of the tour.

Back at the boardinghouse, I joined my new Irish friends at the dinner table. One of them picked up on my foul mood and asked me what was wrong. At first I hesitated, but then I realized how much hope they had invested in me, and I decided to spill it all out.

"That's fecked" was the first response I got.

Someone else said, "Don't call 'em, just don't show up. Feck 'em."

But my roommate spoke sense. "Look," he said, "you've met some new people you like and you're going to be working with a famous director and a star actress. But most important, you're going to be making decent money and someone is paying for you to travel the world. You're only twenty. Something like this may never come up again. Think of all the experiences you'll miss, the places you might have gotten to see."

Another fellow at the table added, "And think of the food you'll eat and the fecks you might get."

While that final prediction failed to come to fruition, my friends were right. I would be crazy to pass up this world tour, and I also realized that Mugless could easily make my name shit around the West End. The decision was made—I would grit my teeth and stay.

A fringe benefit of my lack of stage time was that I was hardly needed during rehearsals and got to explore London.

I loved walking down the Mall, which I had seen so many times in the newsreels that preceded movies in the cinema, especially when there was an important overseas visitor in town and both sides of the Mall were lined with alternating Union Jacks and the national flag of the visiting VIP. Like any tourist, I checked out Trafalgar Square, Piccadilly Circus, Shaftesbury Avenue, Regent Street, Park Lane, St. Paul's Cathedral, Tower Bridge, and the Houses of Parliament. Mostly, though, I relished getting lost in London's narrow, winding, tucked-away streets.

I also explored rowdy, hopping Soho, the nexus of London's music and youth scenes, though I was intimidated by it. The bars pulsed with dangerous energy, and outside of them and their neighboring bordellos stood sexily dressed prostitutes, some of whom called out, "Y'want some fun, love?" I never visited any pub more than once because there were so many and I wanted to drink a pint in all of them. I got a kick out of chatting with the barmen. Some of them were lively, laughing jokesters. Others, especially the older ones, were quiet, but I drew them out about the war years— nearly all of them had served—and found them happy to share their fascinating stories. Every barman asked me where I was from. When I said Yorkshire, they invariably shook their heads and said, "Nah, never been up there." They couldn't have been more dismissive of my home turf, but I didn't care.

The only calls I got for the first few days were for costume fittings, visa processing at the embassy, photo calls, passport examinations, and a meeting with a wigmaker (Helpmann wanted the Duc du Giret to be very old, so I was to wear a white wig). I also bought an evening dress suit from a secondhand clothing store in Charing Cross Road. It was double-breasted and in a very heavy, uncomfortable material, and I looked, frankly, stupid in it, but it was the only one I could afford. Miss Leigh announced to us one day that *Gone with the Wind* was going to be rereleased theatrically, and she requested the pleasure of our entire company at the premiere, which would be my first. And so, also for the first time, I had to wear that tux in public.

I had by this time bid farewell to my friends and moved out of the boardinghouse, to slightly nicer digs that were walking distance from the London Coliseum in St. Martin's Lane. This meant that I would not need to get out of a taxi and walk the red carpet—I knew that I looked idiotic in my tuxedo and wanted to keep a low profile. Inside, there was a champagne reception before the film in the upstairs bar, and my castmates had a field day making fun of me and my shit suit. Evidently, Miss Leigh caught sight of this scene and took pity on me. For all of a sudden, her boyfriend, John Merivale, was at my side, whispering into my ear that he was going to be sitting on one side of Vivien at the screening and that she had requested that I sit on her other side. I was already besotted with her, and this act of kindness only intensified my feelings.

The capper was that, once I was seated beside her, I addressed her as "Miss Leigh" and she took my hand in hers.

"Patrick," she said, "you are to call me Vivien."

My erstwhile Irish roommate was right: The memorable experiences were already piling up. One more happened that evening. The film had been running for about an hour when Vivien—I still couldn't quite believe I got to call her that—turned to me and again took my hand. I could see that she was crying.

"I am so sorry, Patrick, but I am going to have to leave," she said. "So many of these dear people I worked with are now dead, and it is making me so sad. I hope you enjoy the rest of it." And off she went into the night.

Rehearsing my tiny role in *Lady of the Camellias* wasn't entirely a downer. I should explain that in the play, Vivien portrayed a woman named Marguerite Gautier, who was herself based on a notorious real-life nineteenth-century prostitute named Marie Duplessis, who died at the age of twenty-three. A bit of a stretch for our middle-aged leading lady, but Vivien had the grace to pull it off.

The first scene of the play is set in the Paris Opera, specifically in a wide corridor that serves all of the opera's luxury boxes. The evening's performance is about to reach its intermission, and soon the stage is filled with the lavishly dressed occupants of these boxes, who gossip about Marguerite, who is seated in the center one. For this scene, Vivien wore a long, beautiful white gown, with a white feathered cloak over her bare shoulders.

When the intermission of the show within the show ends, the audience members return to their boxes as the music starts up again. The Duc du Giret, Marguerite's lover, is escorted onstage by a lackey, who opens the door of Marguerite's box. The Duc bends to kiss Marguerite's hand before the door closes again.

This was all the audience in the real theater got to see of me. Mind you, even if they had heard of me, I would have been unrecognizable wearing a white wig and a false white beard, and I walked with a cane and an old man's stooped posture.

The fun part was something the audience never saw. The moment the door to the luxury box closed, Vivien and I were no longer visible to the audience, but we couldn't leave the stage until the long scene finished playing out. So Vivien, in dress rehearsals and throughout the tour that followed, took to throwing off her feathered cloak, turning to me with a smile, and whispering, "So, Patrick, tell me what kind of day you've had. What have you been up to?" We'd softly chat until we were cleared for exit. So, three times a week, there was a little moment when I had the great Vivien Leigh all to myself.

These moments mitigated the shabby treatment I received elsewhere. When the time came for us to have our photos taken for our work visas, the Old Vic hired a photographer who set up shop in a small room close to the Empire Theatre's stage door. The photo sessions were being run by Mugless. I dutifully arrived early and patiently waited my turn—but my name was never called. When other actors came in, they were immediately escorted into the makeshift studio, even as I was conspicuously sitting there. When I finally protested, in as lighthearted and self-effacing a way as I could manage,

Mugless said, "Patrick, we are doing this in the order of billing. As you are at the bottom, you must wait." He didn't confide this to me quietly, either; he said this in front of my actor pals and the stage management team, to maximize my embarrassment.

Why he chose me as his punching bag, I still do not know. As noted by Bruce Montague, I suppose it might have been some sort of hazing ritual in the world of the West End, Britain's highest stratum of professional theater. Or maybe Mugless was simply an arsehole. Nowadays, someone in the position I was in might have legal recourse against such blatant workplace bullying. But back then, I just had to grin and bear it.

As for Mr. Helpmann, he wasn't exactly mean, and he was a more than capable director, but he definitely fancied himself a very important man who couldn't be bothered to engage with the little people. In the first week of rehearsals, he never looked my way, much less spoke to me. The first piece of direction I ever got from him came when he simply took me by the elbow—unlike Geoffrey Ost, he directed on the stage rather than from the seats—and moved me to where he wanted me to stand, as if I were a piece of scenery rather than a human being.

By the end of the second week, those of us in small roles came to understand that Helpmann had no idea who we were and no interest in learning. If he wanted to make an adjustment in the staging, he would yell, "You, over there! No, not you, you fool, *you*, the other one!" Or, if he wanted to be a little more specific: "You in the green shirt, horrible color, you're standing too close to Miss Leigh. Move! And you in the red tie—go stand with green shirt."

I would not today tolerate a director handling his company with such condescension and coldness. But I was young, and the tour offered a wealth of experiences to offset the indignities. There was, for starters, the trip from London to Melbourne—and young Pat Stewart's very first airplane ride. And what a ride it was: a thirty-hour journey with stops in Frankfurt, Athens, Cairo, Karachi, Calcutta, Bangkok, Singapore, and, in Australia's Northern Territory, Darwin. Some of these were fueling stops, while others were to pick up and drop off passengers. We were flying the local, essentially. I was beyond thrilled.

Bruce Montague and I made a vow to drink a glass of beer at every stop—and we did. I also bought a postcard in every airport, wrote a short message on it, and mailed it to my parents. Not long ago, searching for something else in an old chest of drawers, I came across a box with an elastic band around it. Inside, I was moved to discover, were these very postcards. On the first, sent from Frankfurt, I had written, "So far, so good," as if I'd been competing in a marathon.

We had been instructed by Mugless to dress well for the journey, because we were representing not only the Old Vic but Britain itself (Vivien and Helpmann traveled separately from us, presumably in first class or on a chartered plane with a less punishing itinerary). There were no Jetway bridges then, so to board the plane, we all walked across the tarmac as a group to the plane's stairs. There were press photographers to record our departure from Heathrow, and all of our actresses looked amazing, wearing hats and gloves, even though we were flying coach.

As I recall, we opened the tour with a week of *Lady of the Camellias*, followed by a week of *Duel of Angels*, and then a week of *Twelfth Night*. So I had to wait two weeks for my first spoken line as a member of the touring company of the London Old Vic.

All three plays went over well, but the Shakespeare was my favorite. To watch, mind you—I utterly hated playing the Second Officer. As his title suggests, he was subordinate to a First Officer, who was played by Leslie Moxon, though I bore no ill will toward him. I was always so relieved when our scene was over, although the play was not done with us—the two officers reappear at the start of the final scene, the longest in the play. Leslie and I stood way downstage left for about twenty minutes. I kept myself awake by observing the performances and how they varied night to night. If one actor was on fire, his energy became infectious and elevated everyone else's level of performance. Occasionally there were flubbed lines—the longer the tour went on, the more likely it was that a misspoken word would lead to a fit of giggles. In my experience, super-serious actors are the ones most susceptible to giggling. John Merivale was especially guilty in this regard.

One night, we had just started the first scene, which was actually *Twelfth Night*'s second—Helpmann had flipped their order. As Viola—another role for which she was a little older—Vivien, standing among several sailors after a shipwreck, said, "What country, friends, is this?"

At this, the theater went dark—a temporary power outage. I was playing one of the sailors, carrying a prop lamp that happened to have a battery-operated light in it, though I was never called upon to use it. I switched the light on and quickly scuttled forward, holding it up near Vivien's face. Vivien offered me a nervous smile, and we went on and played the scene as directed, with another actor guiding her off the dark stage. By the next scene, the stage lights were back on.

At intermission, an assistant stage manager told me that Miss Leigh wanted to see me right away. Her maid was waiting by the door of Vivien's dressing room. She opened it and called inside, "Patrick's here." I entered and found Vivien sitting at her dressing table. Looking at my anxious face reflected in the mirror, she held out her hand.

"You brilliant man," she said. "You saved the scene. We couldn't have gone on and it would have been calamitous."

Summoning all the nonchalance I could fake, I said, "Well, there was nothing else to be done."

"Nonsense," she said. "What you did was beautiful. Thank you." Our hands were now joined. I bowed forward over them, let go, and left the room, glowing with pride.

I know that I have already confessed to several crushes, but can you blame me for developing one on Vivien Leigh, too, especially given how kind she was to me?

One more story along these lines, though I fear it might make me sound like an obsessed fan. Vivien's maid was a nice woman who happened to be married to the actress's chauffeur. I liked them both and got to know them reasonably well. At every theater we played, Vivien's dressing room was on stage level. Whenever she made an entrance in *Lady of the Camellias*, the maid preceded her with one of those old-fashioned perfume spray bottles, the kind mounted with a tube and a puffer bulb. The maid sprayed the air that Vivien was about to walk through before quickly retreating to the wings. Some of our company thought Vivien demanded this because the stagehands were smelly. Not so—she was playing the great courtesan Marguerite Gautier, and the perfumed mist was part of the character.

I even knew which perfume it was, as I had seen it on Vivien's dressing table: Joy, by Jean Patou. In the course of my backstage movements, I sometimes took a small detour and walked through that part of the wings, just so I could breathe in Vivien's scent.

Our time in Melbourne happened to coincide with a momentous event, my twenty-first birthday. It fell, conveniently, on a Sunday when we had the night off, so I knew that I could freely invite everyone to join me in celebration at the large flat I shared with Bruce Montague and three young actresses from our company. Unsurprisingly, neither Helpmann nor Mugless showed up, but Vivien and John did, as did everyone else in the company. She presented me with a handwritten card and a gold linen handkerchief. The hankie was, wouldn't you expect, perfumed with Joy. I still have it.

The London Old Vic was a very gay company. Benthall, its artistic director, was gay, as was Helpmann. Together, they successfully created what we would today call a safe space, in which the company's gay men could be open about their sexuality.

In Sydney, where we spent something like six weeks, I shared a spectacular flat near Bondi Beach with three gay actors: Roderick

Horn, Nicholas Wright, and Frank Middlemass. I felt honored to be included in their gang, for, as cliché as it sounds, they were wittier and more cultured than any man with whom I was used to hanging around.

I have since come to have many dear friends who are gay, and I have played a gay man in Paul Rudnick's comedy film *Jeffrey*. But because of my upbringing, the gay sensibility was entirely new to me back then, and living with those three guys was as wonderful an education as any I ever received. I felt at home among them. Frank, who played Sir Toby Belch in *Twelfth Night* and later flourished as a character actor, was a fantastic cook who prepared lavish dinners on our off-nights. Nick, a physically beautiful specimen of a man, became a successful Tony-nominated playwright. And Rod, a native New Zealander and an excellent guitarist, became a close friend; we roomed together for a time in Manchester, where he educated me in classical music. Sadly, Rod tested positive for HIV in the 1980s and returned to his home country to live out his final days.

Unconsciously, I assumed my flatmates' behavior, adopting a gay affect in their company. Today this would be called appropriation or, perhaps, fakery. Certainly problematic. But as I think about myself back then, I was an uneducated kid finding my way, trying to fit in. It was part and parcel of my aptitude for acting—I was good at learning *how to be*, just as I learned how to be someone who was comfortable calling Vivien Leigh simply "Vivien," despite my reservations. But my friendship with my flatmates was no performance. I loved them dearly.

Nearly every day, I went to Bondi Beach to swim and bodysurf. I had never before seen a beach so beautiful. I loved the fine sand, the waves, the water temperature, and the guy whose job it was to spray suntan lotion all over you. I am not kidding. This man had a big plastic tub of lotion attached to a spray hose that, in a couple of minutes, evenly coated your body. You could go back to him for top-ups, as needed.

So, during my weeks in Sydney, I developed the best suntan I've ever had, dark and even. Mugless Doris was furious with me, as it is an article of faith in the theater to stay out of the sun unless a tan is specifically called for. I ended up having to use a greenish kind of makeup to hide my bronzed features and make the Duc du Giret look as pale and deathly as he was meant to be. But it was well worth it to look great and stick it to Mugless.

So little was demanded of me as an actor that I had the time to be a tourist. With Bruce Montague and another company member, David Dodimead, I visited the Great Barrier Reef. On an island called Quoin, up the coast from Brisbane, I saw kangaroos in their natural habitat. We spent Christmas—summertime in Australia—in the charming city of Adelaide, where Vivien generously hired a riverboat for an all-day cast outing.

Vivien, though, was the only one of us who faced genuine pressure, not only as the lead in all three plays but as our touring company's chief ambassador. I had heard through the grapevine that she was going through a rough time physically, struggling to sleep and feeling run-down. She did a good job of disguising it, but one night in Adelaide, after a two-show day, we were all invited to a grand estate with a huge house in the heart of it. Our hostess had invited the most important families of Adelaide to attend, and black tie was compulsory. Vivien arrived in her limo while the rest of us were shuttled via bus.

After a round of formal introductions were made, Vivien turned to our hostess and said, politely, "Lead us into dinner."

"Ah, no," the hostess said. "Before dinner, we have a reception in the ballroom. There will be speeches, of course, but it shouldn't take too long." There was an uncomfortable silence.

"You clearly don't understand," Vivien said. "We have been working all day and it is now after eleven o'clock. We must have dinner. Either we eat immediately or we will leave."

From the expression on our hostess's face, it was clear that she was unaccustomed to being spoken to in such a way. Her mouth tightened, she took a deep breath, and then she called out a name. A man appeared at her side: her butler. "Serve our guests dinner now and inform our other guests in the ballroom that they can eat when they choose," she instructed him. Our hostess, to her credit, then led us into a vast dining room ringed with tables loaded with delicious food. "Help yourselves," she said, and walked back into the hallway.

Vivien gave us a huge smile and said, "You heard her. Help yourselves!"

But as the weeks went on, Vivien's struggles with exhaustion became more apparent. Her boyfriend, John, got the idea that it might help if every night, after the show, three or four of us in the company could join her at their apartment to drink some wine and play party games with Vivien until she got sleepy and could be tucked into bed. Tough assignment, right? John warned us that Vivien was unpredictable, and that there was no way of knowing how late she would want to stay up. But we bravely soldiered on in our noble mission to help a famous movie star get to sleep by partying with her.

I was part of the first group of actors, four of us in total, who were chosen to go to their apartment. John and Vivien had laid out an impressive spread of snacks, spirits, and expensive wines. Vivien suggested that we play charades: three teams of two people. We rolled dice to determine the pairings, and wouldn't you know it, I found myself partnered with our star. The groups split up so as to secretly come up with titles of movies, plays, books, and TV shows.

Vivien, laughing gleefully, pulled me into the master bedroom, where we sat on her bed, side by side, trying to come up with great titles. I was useless in this regard—all I could think was, *I am sitting alone in Vivien Leigh's bedroom . . . with Vivien Leigh.*

During the actual game, Vivien was given a title for me to

guess. I worked out quickly from her mimed cues that it was the title of a song and that it was four words long. But I struggled to come up with what these words represented. Suddenly, Vivien signaled that she was going to act out the entirety of the title at once. Fine.

Vivien began as if she was walking through a field with tall grass, or hay, or something like that. I was already confused. And then her face brightened, and as she walked, she started performing a gesture that I could only identify as male masturbation.

What on earth was she doing? The only word I could think of was "wanking." But there was no way that "wanking" could be part of a song title—or, as far as my innocent mind was concerned, part of Vivien Leigh's vocabulary. I had no idea what to say or do.

John Merivale saved me. "Give in, Patrick," he said. "Let her just tell you what it is." Vivien agreed to do so, but not, she said, before giving me one last chance to guess.

Her masturbatory miming got even bigger. So did my bewilderment.

Finally, she yelled at me, "'Coming Through the Rye'!"—the traditional Scottish minstrel's song based on a poem by Robert Burns.

Vivien's exclamation received a burst of laughter. As for me, I received a sympathetic hug from her. The games went on for several more rounds. Finally, around four a.m., our hostess announced, "Breakfast time!" She went into the kitchen and cooked us plates full of bacon and scrambled eggs, which we wolfed down. Then Vivien finally said good night, and our little group went back to our own flats.

The following day, John told me that Vivien had gone to sleep immediately after our departure, resting soundly until noon. He also said how grateful he was. In my mind, I could only think, *For Miss Leigh, anything.*

My spirits were further uplifted when we got to Auckland, where we proles of the touring Old Vic company enjoyed the satisfaction of seeing the imperious Mr. Robert Helpmann socially embarrassed. Just before a matinee performance in that city, we were notified that there was a VIP in the audience, Queen Salote of Tonga. She would be coming backstage afterward.

Queen Salote was a charismatic woman who stood over six feet tall. I was excited to meet her. I had seen her in the Pathé newsreels of Queen Elizabeth's coronation, smiling and waving to the crowd from an open carriage on a rainy day. Well, let's face it, I was unlikely to actually meet her, given Robert Helpmann and Mugless Doris's hierarchical protocols. We were to line up in two rows, we were told. The front row would include Miss Leigh and Mr. Helpmann, followed down the line by the leading members of the company. The rest of us would just line up behind them.

After the final curtain, we took our positions and Her Tongan Majesty was escorted onto the stage by Helpmann. He introduced the queen to Vivien, with whom she had a very animated conversation, and then moved down the line, with Mr. Helpmann making the introductions. When they reached the end of the line, he gestured for Queen Salote to walk back to where Vivien was waiting— but Her Majesty stood her ground and, looking at the rest of us, said, in a loud, clear voice, "Oh, *no*. I want to meet *everyone*."

Helpmann was standing right in front of me, and I saw confusion and panic flush his face. *He didn't know who the rest of us were.* I believe that Her Majesty had picked up on his snobbish attitude and wanted to put him on the spot. The first actor, an Aussie named David Nettheim, saved our director from embarrassment by extending his hand to the queen and saying, "David Nettheim, Your Majesty." We all followed suit. Queen Salote smiled and briefly conversed with all of us before making her way back to Vivien. This was one of the happiest moments of the whole tour for me, because the queen lived up to and beyond expectations, and I could see that Vivien, though she was close to Helpmann, delighted in this moment of comeuppance.

As the first leg of our tour was winding down in New Zealand, there was lots of speculation about our next stops: India and Japan? South America? It was a fog of rumor, and someone even intimated that the remainder of the tour was going to be canceled.

Finally came definitive news. A week after our last show in Wellington, New Zealand, we would open in Mexico City. We would spend a week there, followed by a week apiece in the following cities: Caracas, Venezuela; Lima, Peru; Santiago, Chile; Buenos Aires, Argentina; Montevideo, Uruguay; and São Paulo and Rio de Janeiro in Brazil.

I was over the moon. Remember that while I was not well-educated, I was well-read. I would be visiting the homes of Aztec and Incan civilizations. Me, a kid who, a year earlier, had only just spent his first significant time in London. We were also to be given five days off to get from Wellington to Mexico City. My castmates Nick, Frank, and Bruce and I decided to investigate flight routes and were thrilled to discover that, for the same price as whatever the "official" Old Vic itinerary was, we could make expenses-paid stops in Honolulu and San Francisco, covering only the costs of our lodging before we got to Mexico.

So it came to be that my first time on American soil was in the newest of the United States, Hawaii. The boys and I were unprepared for how busy Honolulu was, choked with traffic and tourists, but we found a decent hotel on Waikiki Beach, drank way too many piña coladas, and I learned that I was no good at surfing. I rented a huge board and was violently thrown off of it by the very first wave I tried to catch. I went under, and the board whacked me hard on the head. For a moment, I genuinely thought I was going to drown, but mercifully, my feet touched the sea's sandy bottom and I was able to walk toward the beach, pretending that nothing had happened.

We flew on to San Francisco, where we spent only one night, but it was enough time for me to fall in love with the city's steep hills, architecture, and suspension bridges. It would be another seven years, by which time I was a member of the Royal Shakespeare Company, before I got to revisit and truly explore that beautiful place.

One unfortunate aspect of our tour of Mexico and South America was that we no longer performed *Twelfth Night*, the one play in which I had lines. What really irked me was the reason the play was out of the lineup. Helpmann held the incredibly patronizing belief that South American audiences would not sit still for an entire Shakespeare play, and therefore devised an evening of "Great Scenes from Shakespeare," in which he and Vivien performed a series of famous vignettes, with the rest of us filling in with any supporting dialogue that was needed.

We were appalled by Helpmann's supposition, and indeed, everywhere we went, we learned that famous European theater and opera companies had toured these same cities and put on the same "challenging" bills of fare that they performed at home, to sold-out audiences and enthusiastic response.

Our opening night, at the Palacio de Bellas Artes in Mexico City, did not go well, with the audience restless precisely because the program was so choppy. The first scene of the evening was Helpmann himself performing the opening soliloquy of *Richard III*. What Helpmann should have said was, "Now is the winter of our discontent / Made glorious summer by this son of York." What he actually said was, "Now is the summer of our discontent / Made glorious . . . *winter* by this son of York."

I sincerely hoped that Helpmann heard our tittering in the wings. Unfortunately, Vivien also had an uncomfortable start. The second extract was from *A Midsummer Night's Dream*, the first time that Titania encounters Oberon. Helpmann entered from the downstage wings. Vivien entered by running up four steps positioned upstage, in the center. But in so doing, she caught her foot in the hem of her ankle-length white dress and crashed to the floor. Oh, dear. At least Helpmann lived up to his surname and lent aid.

Because we moved on to the next stop on the itinerary every Sunday, I didn't get to do much exploring. We were all exhausted, especially Vivien, and everywhere we went, we were compelled to attend an opening-night reception, usually formal. But through sheer determination, I managed to get myself not once but twice to the ancient city of Teotihuacán, thirty miles northeast of Mexico City. The first time, I went with a tour group. The second time, I went alone because I wanted to lose myself in the monumental scale of the place. Its Avenue of the Dead stretches over a mile in length and is lined by gorgeous temples and monuments, the most impressive being the huge Pyramid of the Sun. Since then, I have visited and been awed by many later Aztec and Mayan temples and ruins, but none have impressed me more than those in Teotihuacán.

Of the other cities we went to, I think we were all the fondest of Buenos Aires. Our audiences were lively and appreciative, and the city stayed up late, offering us plenty in the way of post-performance nightlife. One day, the entire company was driven by bus out to a large estancia in the country for a cookout: grilled meats from the very acreage where we sat. No steak I have eaten in my life has since matched what we were served that day.

As if that hadn't been enough adventure, on the way back, our bus driver pulled over into a lay-by and spent several minutes talking to someone on a radio telephone. When he was done, he informed us that while we had been gone from the city, a military coup had taken place, and that we should not be surprised if we saw tanks in the streets. Other than that, he assured us, everything was normal.

Someone in our company asked him if that night's performance would be canceled. *Typical actor*, I thought, *always angling for a night off.* But our driver said that, to the contrary, people would be fighting to get tickets and enjoy a good night out. It was always that way after a coup, he said, as if describing the most everyday circumstances in the world.

At the tour's end in 1962, there were hugs, tears, exchanges of tele-phone numbers, and promises to keep in touch. But with the excep-tion of Rod Horne, my future housemate in Manchester, and Frank Middlemass, who became a lifelong friend, I never saw any of my fel-low company members again. Worst of all, Vivien died five years later from complications of tuberculosis. I had by then been married for two years to my first wife, Sheila. When I received the news, I must have looked crestfallen. Sheila asked me what Vivien had meant to me, and for the first time, I related to her all the stories I have just told you, which, to that point, I had not shared with anyone.

Our trip home to London was the antithesis of our initial hop-scotch to Melbourne—we caught a direct flight from Rio to Heath-row. I was determined not to suffer a post-tour letdown, so, before it was over, I had sent a letter to Geoffrey Ost about picking up where I'd left off in Sheffield. As it turned out, he was in the throes of put-ting together his 1962–63 season and offered me a supporting role in its first production, in some obscure play I had not heard of. I read the script and wasn't impressed, but I accepted the offer anyway.

I had also written to Manchester Library Theatre, Liverpool Rep, and the Bristol Old Vic, companies all reputationally superior to Sheffield. My thinking was that I had just finished eighteen months working with Vivien Leigh and the London Old Vic Company, so I was therefore ready to work at a higher level.

I was pleased to receive a response from the artistic director of the Manchester company, David Scase. He told me that he was coming to London and would be happy to meet with me.

I had heard through the theater-gossip grapevine that Scase was brilliant but also extremely budget-conscious. So I found my hairpiece and went to the meeting wearing it. I liked David at once and let him know that if he had a place for me in his new season, I wanted it. Then I took off my hairpiece and did my two-actors-for-the-price-of-one routine. His eyes lit up, and he told me he would be in touch. I felt a swell of optimism, along with a bit of gratitude for my premature baldness.

The following day, I received a telegram from David asking me to call him. He came straight to the point. He had an entire season laid out for me, which included Duke Orsino in *Twelfth Night* (*Hmm, not too shabby*) and King Henry in *Henry V* (*Yes, yes, FUCK, yes!*).

My salary would be no better than what it had been in Sheffield (*Hmm, not great*), but I decided not to let this get me down. I had saved some money from the Old Vic tour and I was about to play two Shakespearean leading roles, one of them an all-time great. Either way, I remained a working actor.

Chapter Nine

I had never dared articulate the thought aloud before, but my ultimate ambition as an actor was to be part of the Royal Shakespeare Company. Honestly, I had barely allowed myself to consider the notion privately—it seemed too extreme a goal for a mere Mirfield boy. But as I was gaining confidence in myself, it started to seem an attainable goal, if not an immediate one. My plan was that I would spend a few years in regional theater for the experience and a good résumé, and then make my pitch to the RSC. I wasn't counting on this happening anytime soon because I was only twenty-two and unlikely to be cast in the big, juicy roles that reflected my age: the juvenile romantic lead, say, or Hamlet. As my drama teacher Bill Moore had not-so-helpfully pointed out, I was a character actor destined to wait a while until I came into my own.

But my mentors Ruth Wynn Owen and Cecil Dormand had put the Bard in my head and my belly, and I was happy to let him gestate there for a few years before offering myself to the greatest Shakespearean company in the world.

In the meantime, the Manchester Library Theatre was an excellent place to be. It represented another step up the ladder, providing its company with an astonishing *three* weeks of rehearsal before the first performance.

The only difficulty was that I had committed to the one play in Sheffield, a forgettable work with the unfortunate title *Love in the Time of Bloomers*, and Geoffrey Ost had subsequently invited me back for the whole season. I sheepishly told Geoffrey that I was moving on to Manchester, only thirty-five miles away. Geoffrey was a very polite man, but I could see his frustration with me. He had, after all, given me a huge break just two years earlier. But a friend assured me such was the nature of show business.

Janet Manners, the actress playing opposite me in *Love in the Time of Bloomers*, was a young South African fresh out of drama school in London. A year or so later, she reverted to her real name, Janet Suzman. A wise choice, for under that name she rocketed to stardom on the British stage and, by the 1970s, in film and British TV; in '71 she received an Academy Award nomination for playing Tsarina Alexandra in the film *Nicholas and Alexandra*.

Janet confided to me that we two were in the same boat: David Scase had also invited *her* to join the Manchester rep for the coming season. There were some people in Sheffield who felt that Janet and I were selfish and had let Geoffrey down. But we were both young and ambitious, and grasping every opportunity to advance was essential in the very competitive world of professional theater. Janet and I were also in the midst of a five-minute romance, another good reason for us to go to Manchester together.

It was a sign of my growing confidence that during my second week in Manchester, I did something uncharacteristically forward. A popular English radio comedian, Frankie Howerd, was spending a week in the city for a mini-residency on his tour of UK theaters, and he was staying, to my surprise, in the same actors' lodgings as me. I looked forward to meeting Frankie, as I'd grown up listening to him. But our paths never crossed—from what I gathered, he never left his room until late in the day, when I was still in rehearsals, to be at the theater where he was performing.

But I was determined to meet Frankie, so I devised a plan with the landlady: When she took up his breakfast one morning, she would purposely "forget" something. I was given the job of carrying a missing teacup upstairs to Frankie's bedroom, and thusly, I would meet the great funnyman. When I knocked on the door, I heard the unmistakable voice of Frankie Howerd saying, in his characteristically campy way, "Come in, dear."

When I appeared, he shrieked, "Oooh-hooo! Who are you?! Go away, dear!" This was classic Frankie Howerd, and I burst out laughing. Then he pulled the bedcovers over his head and, from underneath them, started whispering, "Who is he, who is he, dear?"

What I hadn't realized was that Frankie was gay, and his manager, Dennis, who was sitting up in bed beside Frankie, was also his lover. Dennis looked at me sharply and said, "You'd better give me that cup and bugger off, or there will be trouble." Frankie added, "Yes, dear, yes, trouble. Go away."

Not quite the dream meeting I had imagined, but it was sort of perfect—very much in keeping with his style of comedy. A couple of years later, Frankie was starring in the musical *A Funny Thing Happened On the Way to the Forum* in the West End. I snagged a ticket and afterward went backstage. I knocked on his dressing room door and was invited in. I was just about to say my name when he good-naturedly cut me off and exclaimed, "I know who you are, dear! You invaded my bedroom in Manchester!" All was forgiven.

Life was good at the Manchester Library Theatre. We had a fantastic company, and David Scase, our director, was an exuberant, fun-loving man, the temperamental opposite of Geoffrey Ost. You'd find him bouncing on and off the stage, doubled over with laughter in the stalls, yelling at us from the back row like a drunken punter, or tenderly whispering something in an actor's ear to give them confidence. He loved his job and he loved actors.

Our first play of the season, *The Buried Man*, conveyed an advantage upon me: It was set among working-class Yorkshire folk.

I reveled in reverting to my childhood accent, but Janet struggled to develop one of her own, so I was engaged as her unpaid Yorkshire-dialect coach. She tried so hard, but I am afraid her accent came and went. She struggled with the line "I just saw him go past the window." As you may recall from earlier, in the West Riding we never said "the window" but "t'winder." Poor Janet tied herself in knots trying to get it right.

But she was much more in her element in *Twelfth Night,* in which she played Viola opposite my Orsino. Janet was clearly on a fast track, scoring leading roles right out of school. What's more, she told me one night, her agent had informed her that Peter Hall, a legend of the British theater and the esteemed artistic director of the Royal Shakespeare Company (and the husband of the stunning Leslie Caron), would be coming to see the production because he was interested in plucking Janet from our company to be in the next RSC season.

Inwardly, I was quite envious. It was all happening for her already. But I also saw this as a window of opportunity. Having Peter Hall see me as Orsino was not a bad way to kick off my long-game seduction of the RSC. And having him see me in a production was a hundred times better than stumbling into Stratford for a ten-minute audition.

I couldn't resist fantasizing about a shortcut, though. On the night that Hall was in attendance, Janet told me that she was meeting up with him afterward at the nearby Café Royal for a drink and a chat. I considered positioning myself at the other end of the bar while they met, and then, after getting up to leave, casually stopping by and saying, *Good night, Janet. Oh, Mr. Hall, what a delight! Hello! Thank you for seeing the show tonight. I hope you had a good time.* Then I would grab Peter Hall by the lapels and push my face close to his, muttering, *You loved me, didn't you? I was the best, wasn't I? Well, play your cards right and you can have me. It will be an unforgettable experience for you. Even better than being married to Leslie Caron. Here's my number. Think about it.*

Of course, when the show was over, I just caught a bus home.

I think I made the right choice. I pictured the Manchester papers blaring the headline DRUNK ACTOR ARRESTED FOR THREATENING RSC DIRECTOR and thought, *Nah, not worth it.*

A few days later, I met Janet at the stage door, and the grin on her face said it all. She had been invited to join the RSC immediately, as soon as *Twelfth Night* was over. Her first role was to be Joan of Arc in the Wars of the Roses tetralogy, which the RSC had already announced as the kickoff of their new season.

No life-changing phone call came for me right then, but an intriguing new angle did present itself. Another fellow company member in Manchester, Charles Thomas, who was playing Sir Toby Belch in *Twelfth Night*, told me excitedly that Maurice Daniels, the head of casting at the RSC, had written him. Peter Hall would be returning to Manchester to see Charlie in *Henry V*, which was to open in late January, after our Christmas show.

Talk about the agony and the ecstasy. Charlie had only recently graduated from college. Like me in my Lincoln days, he was only a part-time actor who also performed duties as an assistant stage manager—yet *he* was the one getting this big chance!

On the other hand, though, I would be on display in the title role. Mr. Hall could hardly overlook me. Suddenly, my slow and steady plan of working my way through regional theater had gone out the window. I wanted the RSC, and I wanted it *now*.

As we performed our family-friendly Christmas show, *The Princess and the Swineherd*, I spent my spare time closely studying *Henry V*. The role came quite naturally to me, and not because I harbored secret dreams of invading France. I simply loved the character and had been immersed in Henry's great speeches since my Sunday afternoons with Ruth Wynn Owen. Only now, I was not a fifteen-year-old but a man, with completely different frames of reference. I had a better understanding of authority—what it felt like and how it worked as a tool for achieving one's desires.

I was also learning to *listen*, something I was never explicitly taught about in drama school. As an audience member, I was always intrigued by the actor whose job it was in the scene to pay attention as someone else had a long speech. The best listened with a presence and power that is its own advanced form of acting. I was determined to learn this skill. Henry's first scene includes a lot of listening, and his second adds a layer of suppressed fury toward the English traitors. I loved most his great night scenes before the Battle of Agincourt: his simplicity, patience, and resolve. Was I ever going to nail this role! The RSC was no longer a dream deferred; it lay within immediate reach . . .

. . . or so I thought. I got so lost in the excitement of playing Henry that I dissociated myself from how the audience reacted to my portrayal. The only thing I noticed was that after every matinee, at the curtain call, Martin Jarvis, who played the cowardly wretch Pistol, got louder cheers than I did. Peter Hall and Maurice Daniels did indeed come see the play, and they did indeed offer Charlie Thomas a season at Stratford. But I heard nothing from them.

I allowed myself to be devastated, but only for about five minutes. I'd simply gotten ahead of myself and needed to look on the bright side. I had a terrific job in Manchester, and at least the RSC's powers that be knew of me and my work.

There had been a rumor going around the Manchester Library Theatre that David Scase, our beloved boss, was moving on to a new job. Given my RSC frustration, I desperately wanted this not to be true. When David called me in for a meeting, my anxiety grew, but he assuaged it all at once. He confirmed that he was leaving Manchester, but he wanted me to join him at his next stop: the Liverpool Playhouse, an equally fine rep theater. Even better, he wanted me to *lead* the company. Liverpool was the same distance from Manchester as Manchester was from Sheffield. All I needed in a year's time was to get a job in Hull, and I would have been the rep-theater king of England's industrial North.

During the Manchester winter, I had purchased my first car, a

1939 Ford Prefect. At the outbreak of World War II, its original owner had garaged it and basically never used it again. But let's face it, it was a 1930s Ford with an antique-looking upright body, tall grille, and round, bug-eye headlights, and it looked ancient in 1962, the year of *Dr. No*, the first James Bond movie. Still, it was a car and it was all mine. The drive from Manchester to Liverpool was the longest I had undertaken in my young life. Though Los Angeles traffic has over time done its best to dim my ardor for driving, I still love being behind the wheel.

But after a year of tolerating the sit-up-and-beg style of driving that the Prefect demanded, I sold it and bought a marginally more modern 1949 MG YT. I adored this car and drove it for three years until it conked out on me on the A4 road in the South of England. My next car was an even flashier MG, a TF 1250 convertible, which I gave up only in 1967, when my first child, Daniel, was born. It had to go, for the TF 1250 allowed no space for a pram, a cot, or any other baby stuff. Dan still claims that I resent him for this reason.

I was only to spend a single season in Liverpool. The first show we did was *The Rough and the Ready Lot*, a gritty play about mercenary soldiers by a young playwright named Alun Owen, whose star was ascendant because he had just written the screenplay for the Beatles' first movie, *A Hard Day's Night*.

Liverpool, you are no doubt aware, is where the Beatles come from, and while I naturally knew who they were, I was more of a classical-music guy, and not completely up on their history. In the course of commuting to work by ferry from my flat on the other side of the Mersey, I discovered a backstreet shortcut from the ferry dock to the playhouse. About halfway up this backstreet was a door with a sign above it that read THE CAVERN. There were often young people milling about and taking photographs of this door, which seemed to lead to some kind of subterranean space. On my life, I tell you, I had no idea what the Cavern was or why these kids were hanging about, even though it was 1964, the peak year of international Beatlemania.

On the other side of the street from the Cavern was the loading dock of a Boots Chemists shop. The reason I remember this is because, if you walked past this spot at lunchtime, you were likely to see a group of young female Boots employees on break, smoking and looking tough. As young men like myself walked past, these women showered them with taunts, hoots, and catcalls. Never before or since have I encountered a scene like this. The tables were turned and it was delicious.

The third play we did that season in Liverpool was Noël Coward's *Hay Fever*, a world away from Alun Owen. In keeping with my character-actor reputation, I played the family patriarch, David Bliss, a role usually assigned to a middle-aged actor. One incident, though, sticks in my memory and really had nothing to do with the play.

Jennifer Stirling was the actress playing my character's wife, Judith Bliss. Jennifer had placed herself on a very stringent weight-loss program that required her to drink one large diet shake and consume nothing else the rest of the day. I was concerned for her well-being and expressed that I wasn't sure if such an approach was safe, especially since we were putting in twelve-hour days. But she assured me that there was nothing to be worried about.

One evening, we were about five minutes into the play when I heard a shout from the direction of the stage. I was in the greenroom at the time, chatting with a stage manager, because my first entrance didn't come until well into the first act. But I knew that Jennifer had just made her entrance for a scene with the actors who played our son and daughter.

I heard the shout again: someone calling "Father!" in character. I hurried through the pass door into the wings, where I saw the actor playing the son calling out, "Father, Mother needs you!"

The actors playing our children were huddled over a sofa, behind which I saw a pair of high heels jutting out, still on Jennifer's feet. She lay there on the floor, seemingly unconscious. Our "children" saw me and gestured for me to come onstage. The stage manager encouraged me to go on, too, but I protested, whispering, "No! Bring the curtain down."

By this point, a few other actors had gathered in the wings. The one who was due to make the next entrance went on and began an improvisation with the children, soon to be joined by another actor. This improv became an attempt by the four of them to lift Jennifer onto the sofa. By this time the audience was abuzz with confusion. Was it a bit? An emergency?

I heard some people laugh. I also heard a man actually shout, "Is there a doctor in the house?" However you looked at it, though, this situation was no joke, and the stage manager was paralyzed with indecision. So I dashed over to the safety-curtain lever and activated it. The curtain came down, thank goodness, and yes, a doctor rushed to the stage. He brought Jennifer back around and helped her to her dressing room. Within ten minutes, she had recovered to the point that she was confident that she could go on with the play.

When the show resumed and Jennifer made her entrance, the audience gave her a standing ovation.

I, on the other hand, was the evening's bad guy. Not to the audience, but with the cast. I had refused to go onstage and help. I don't think the actors playing my son and daughter ever forgave me.

Here, however, as best I can reconstruct it, is my line of thinking from that night. I did not want the audience's belief in what we were performing to be betrayed—even in a lighthearted show like *Hay Fever*. If we had brought down the curtain right away, the world of the play would have been preserved. As it was, we had shared with the audience that something was very wrong and tried to make this crisis part of the show. The world of the play was not merely interrupted— it was destroyed. I was thrilled and relieved that Jennifer pulled through and finished the performance like the trouper she was. But our make-believe had been exposed, and I hated that. I couldn't help it.

But that was as dramatic as my time in Liverpool got. *Hay Fever* was very well received, and I took pleasure in helping David Scase launch his tenure as artistic director in that city. But for the following season, I moved onward—and southward—to the Bristol Old Vic. This was the company I had only dreamed of joining when I attended its neighboring drama school, but now, at the wise old age of twenty-four, I was a seasoned pro. I was pleased to be cast as Fagin, Charles Dickens's grubby king of the pickpockets, in a stage adaptation of *Oliver Twist*.

I had read the novel years earlier and pictured myself in the role, so I knew exactly how I wanted to look. I worked with the wardrobe and makeup people to achieve this vision: grimy skin, matted hair, dirty beard, crazy eyebrows, and blacked-out teeth. I walked with stooped shoulders and a sort of sideways shuffle. All of this was accompanied by a whiny, rather caricatured East London Jewish accent that I loved at the time, but now realize was probably offensive to many members of the audience. I was happy with my performance then, but regret it now. Sometimes the sentiment *It was a different time* isn't enough of a justification.

In the middle of the play's run, I developed a really bad case of influenza, perhaps my karmic punishment: coughing, sweating, trembling, a high temperature. We did not have understudies, so I had to go on. Our third day of performances was a Saturday, which meant a matinee and an evening show. Halfway through the latter, I keeled over and sprawled on the floor. I remember someone in the cast trying to help me up and my shaking them off, choosing instead to play the scene while lying on the ground. I was in a state of delirium, and I believe that at one point, I ran all of my speeches together, not pausing for other characters to speak, so desperate was I to get offstage. I'd be morbidly curious to see a video of my portrayal of a very ill Fagin, though I'm rather certain no such thing exists.

Later that season, I played Shylock in *The Merchant of Venice*. As familiar as I was with the play, it having been my baptism into

Shakespeare thanks to Mr. Dormand, I was way too young for the role—as I had been for Fagin—and it showed, with me trying to compensate for this age disparity with more broad, showy attempts to appear grotesque. Fortunately, this was not my last Shylock. I have since played him four more times, with increasing returns, the last time in a modern-dress production set in contemporary Venice.

Possibly the most consequential development of this season in Bristol was my introduction to a fine, raffish-looking actor by the name of Gawn Grainger. I have already mentioned the downside of an actor's life, in which budding friendships often fizzle out when the shared job comes to an end. But with Gawn, that never happened. On the contrary, we have remained the best of friends, and my love for him—and for his fabulous wife, Zoë Wanamaker—has grown with every decade.

I like to say that Gawn allowed me to finally experience my teenage years—in my mid-twenties. As much as I have recounted my nights out at pubs and early attempts at romance, the truth is that I was working so hard as an actual teen, both to save money and to become a professional actor, that I had never truly enjoyed the wild freedom that most people associate with those years.

Gawn, the rascal, changed all that. He started up a Wednesday night poker game with me and two other buddies. He took me to the betting shop around the corner from the theater and taught me how to play the ponies. Then there was drink and dating, often combined. Given my father's history with alcohol and my one misbegotten night getting plastered on my friend Barry's dad's scotch, drink was never high on my list of desires beyond the occasional pint. But Gawn liked cocktails and taught me how to drink like a civilized gentleman. His influence continues in this regard to the present day: My wife, Sunny, and I enjoy a cocktail almost every night. She makes a killer Aviation, a gin cocktail that is as beautiful as it is refreshing, thanks to its inclusion of crème de violette liqueur.

Only once did Gawn's influence turn malign—and really, I am equally responsible for what happened. The final production of that Bristol Old Vic season was George Bernard Shaw's *Saint Joan*. We had a terrific cast, with the excellent Barbara Leigh-Hunt in the lead and parts for Gawn and my world-tour pal Frank Middlemass. I played the Earl of Warwick and loved every performance—but one.

Gawn and I had an afternoon off and decided to have lunch at the Coronation Tap, a pub in the Bristol suburb of Clifton. The Tap is famous for its cider, especially its scrumpy, a particularly strong and cloudy version. The scrumpy served at the Coronation Tap was so strong, in fact, that if the barman didn't know you, he would only serve you half a pint at a time. He was quite the character. When closing time came, he would put on a pith helmet—the type that the British Army wore in India—that had, written across its front, the phrase I'VE MY PITH HAT ON, SO PITH OFF!

Gawn and I washed down our lunch with two pints of cider each. This did not concern us, as it was only 1:30 p.m. and we didn't have to be onstage until 7:30 that evening. My little basement flat was just around the corner, so when I got home, I lay down for a restorative nap.

By the time I woke up, it was 6:30. Not good. And when I got out of bed, I stumbled. Oh Lord, I knew it at once—I was still pithed.

Nevertheless, I was sure that the brisk half-hour walk to the theater would freshen me up. I got in and applied my makeup without incident, but when I tried to get into costume, I struggled to get my tights on, and when I finally did, I realized I'd put them on back to front. Yep, still significantly pithed.

I was in the third scene of the play, a very long scene in which my character enters into a complicated negotiation with the intellectual Bishop of Beauvais, who was played by actor Terry Hardiman. Just before the scene started, I managed to grab Terry's arm and tell him what had happened that afternoon, and that I needed his help.

Terry's face broke into a huge smile. He was clearly looking forward to this.

The scene was about twenty minutes long, and I assure you, it was the longest, scariest twenty minutes I have ever spent onstage. Not only was I having difficulty getting the words out coherently, I was also having difficulty remembering them. As I had anticipated, Terry was having a ball. A smile—more accurately, a smirk—never left his face. Afterward, I couldn't remember much of my performance, though my fellow members of the company were still quoting my deranged, nonsensical lines for weeks.

But there was an upside to this debacle. A life lesson—I never again drank before a show.

But, I hear you ask, what about Gawn? Did he get away with it? Lucky bugger, he did. His character was a drunken squire named Robert de Baudricourt. That night's performance might have been the best work he has ever done. Right, Gawn?

In the same season, we did a musical called *Lock Up Your Daughters*, in which I played a corrupt judge named Mr. Squeezum and experienced West End performer Joan Heal, eighteen years my senior, played my wife, Mrs. Squeezum. It was the first full musical I ever did and remains, to my sadness, my last. I have to admit that, musically, Joan carried me through the show.

Our choreographer was the talented Sheila Falconer. As I was to learn, she had already enjoyed a decorated and demanding career, first as a classical-ballet dancer, then as a dancer in West End shows, and later as an assistant to the renowned English choreographer Gillian Lynne. One of Sheila's colleagues told me that whenever a Broadway musical was transferring to London, the production always tried to hire her as the lead dancer because she had an innate grasp of American-style movement. I think that *Lock Up Your Daughters* was something of a challenge for her, if only because she was tasked with turning Gawn and yours truly into actual dancers.

She mustn't have been too annoyed by me, though, because by the end of the run, Sheila and I had become romantically involved. She had a great sense of humor and an innate understanding of how important acting was to me, for she, too, was deeply committed to her work in dance. We had such mutual respect for each other, and romance had finally worked out for me, as soon we were engaged to be married.

As 1965 went on, Gawn and I were both welcomed back to Bristol for a second season, but with a condition attached. In the season's second half, the company was going to be divided, with one contingent staying in Bristol and the other doing a tour of the United States. Included in this tour was a new production of *Hamlet*, directed by Sir Tyrone Guthrie, with Gawn Grainger as the Prince of Denmark. I, meanwhile, was part of the group asked to remain in Bristol.

I was so happy for Gawn, and I wanted to be part of the tour. I begged Val May, our artistic director, to cast me in *Hamlet*, but he rather bluntly told me that there were no roles for which I was suited. I have long held the belief that Val deliberately separated me and Gawn. And perhaps, if this is true, he was right to do so. The two of us on a tour of the United States could have gone very wrong, especially after hours.

During the season, I spent a couple of weeks in London. One night, I went to see the Royal Shakespeare Company's latest production of *Hamlet*, directed by Peter Hall and starring David Warner. The critics had gone nuts with rapture over the production, but I was nevertheless unprepared for the impact it had on me.

At the show's very start, the stage lights and house lights went out together—even the exit signs, a fire-safety offense—which plunged the audience into total darkness and silence. I think we all jumped—all 1,200 of us in the sold-out theater—when out of the shadows came a voice, that of the actor playing Barnardo, shouting the play's first line, "Who's there?"

As for David Warner, he quite simply made theater history. To those of us who witnessed his extraordinary performance—a burgundy scarf wrapped around his neck, his blond hair in a Beatle fringe—it was as if Hamlet's words were being spoken for the very first time. He and Peter Hall had created a youth-tinged version of *The Tragedy of Hamlet, the Prince of Denmark*, that chimed with the times.

David was only twenty-four, the same age as me, but this production elevated him immediately to the rank of star, not only to theater types but to the same teens who were screaming over the Beatles and the Rolling Stones. That I would later become David's friend and colleague was something I could not have imagined at the time, much less that, almost thirty years later, he and I would lock horns in one of the all-time-greatest episodes of *Star Trek: The Next Generation*, the two-parter "Chain of Command."

That production of *Hamlet* intensified my desire to be part of the Royal Shakespeare Company. By this point I had signed up with my first agent, and I decided that I would no longer demurely wait for someone to notice me—I would seek out an audition.

I had already been cast in a slate of shows at the Bristol Old Vic for the autumn of 1965: in Chekhov's *The Cherry Orchard*, in *The Merchant of Venice* (as Shylock), and in that year's Christmas production, *The Happiest Days of Your Life*—the same farce in which I had made my amateur drama debut in 1953. This time, I was playing a bossy, arrogant parent rather than a schoolboy. My agent came through in securing me an audition at the RSC, but because I was working so steadily in Bristol, I would have to audition on a Sunday—and get to and from Stratford-upon-Avon in twenty-four hours. Done.

I took a huge gamble at this point, telling my agent that after the Christmas show, I wouldn't be returning to Bristol. It just wouldn't be as much fun without Gawn. This was a potentially reckless move on my part, because if the RSC didn't take me, I would be out of work for the first time in my career.

My audition, with the RSC's casting director, Maurice Daniels, was set for six p.m. on a late-November Sunday—an odd but manageable hour, as my friend Charlie Thomas had a spare room in his flat in Stratford. I would audition, spend the night with Charlie and his wife, and scoot back to Bristol at dawn.

The RSC asked me to prepare two contrasting pieces. I thought it best to stick with characters I had already performed, so I decided on one monologue by Shylock and another by Henry V.

Charlie's flat was on the other side of Clopton Bridge from the RSC campus, and it was a fifteen-minute walk to the stage door of the Royal Shakespeare Theatre. It was a cold, rainy evening, and I crossed that famous bridge with my shoulders hunched and my head down, running through the two speeches in my head. The famous theater loomed on the other side of the Bancroft Gardens. As I got nearer, my nerves began to kick in. *Am I good enough? Am I inventive enough? Can I bring anything new that they haven't seen before?*

I rang the bell and was buzzed in. I shall never forget giving my name to the man stationed at the entrance, who told me to go through the door, turn left, and go through another door that led to the wings and the stage. He said that Mr. Hall was waiting for me.

Mr. Hall? As in Peter Hall? The legend? I had been under the impression that I was meeting with Maurice Daniels.

Technically, this turned out to be true. When I finally walked through the wings and out onto the empty stage of the Royal Shakespeare Theatre, I saw, halfway back in the stalls, three men. One of them, a gray-haired guy, ambled down the aisle and introduced himself as Maurice Daniels. "And those two," he said, "are Peter Hall and John Barton"—the artistic director and his associate director. My brain produced one thought: *Oh my God, this is it.*

Mr. Hall waved and said, "Hello, Patrick. Welcome." Mr. Barton said, "Thank you for coming on such a terrible night. Let's start. What are you going to do for us?"

The theater was otherwise deserted, with only the deep red of the stalls' seats providing any warmth or color. I had never felt so alone and exposed. *What* am *I going to do for them?*

I opened my mouth to answer, but sensing that I was just going to croak, I paused, swallowed, and then said, "Thank you." Then I told them the two pieces I would be performing.

Right at that moment, it dawned on me that just a year earlier, Messrs. Hall and Barton had directed their own production of *Henry V*, starring the British actor I looked up to probably more than any other, Ian Holm.

Was I out of my mind? Too late. Into the deep end . . .

What's he that wishes so?
My cousin Westmoreland? No, my fair cousin:
If we are mark'd to die, we are enow
To do our country loss; and if to live . . .

And finally, forty-six lines and seemingly twelve hours later . . .

. . . That fought with us upon Saint Crispin's day.

There was a brief silence. Then John Barton came down to the front of the stage and said, "Good, good. Just now, you were speaking to a small group of nobles. What if you were speaking to just one? Just to Westmoreland. Give it a try. But take your time, no hurry."

What an unusual and interesting idea! I did indeed take my time, absorbing the new situation. Barton walked back up the aisle, and when he turned around, I began the speech again.

I got about a dozen lines into it when Peter Hall said, "Good. Now what if you were saying the same speech to the *whole English army*? Start again."

Ah, I get it, I thought. *It's not just about how well I can act. It's about how well I can take direction and make adjustments.* I took a moment, gathered myself, and then addressed my speech to ten thousand soldiers. It was so much fun that I wanted the game to go on. This time, they let me go the whole way through the speech, and when I finished, all three men gave me a little round of applause.

"All right," one of them said, "let's see your Shylock."

I took a small walk around the stage to get Henry out of my head. As I was doing so, I realized for the first time that Shylock, just like Henry, is actually speaking to only one man, though several others are present and listening. I made an instant pre-speech adjustment.

> *Signior Antonio, many a time and oft*
> *In the Rialto you have rated me*
> *About my moneys and my usances . . .*

Again, the three men let me get all the way through to the end of the monologue. Then they walked down to the edge of the stage to offer warm handshakes. Peter Hall said, "Thank you, good. We'll be in touch."

Arrrggh. No offer on the spot.

Feeling just a stir of disappointment, I left the stage, thinking, *Did I just blow it? Will I never again have this opportunity? Will I never grace this stage in an actual production?*

Walking back across the damp, cold Bancroft Gardens, I replayed what had just happened over and over in my head, reading the tea leaves, trying to figure out how it had gone. It was fruitless, for in truth, I had no idea.

When I got back to Charlie's flat, I told him all about my experience, word for word. He said he was sure I was to receive the thumbs-up, and that I would be hearing from Maurice Daniels's office the next day.

I did not. But I did the day after that. The dream came true— Mr. Daniels, via my agent, made me an offer to be part of the Royal Shakespeare Company's next season, encompassing both parts of *Henry IV* and *Henry V*, for thirty-five pounds a week, to play "as cast."

Those last two words left me slightly uneasy, as they conjured up unwelcome memories of Douglas Morris and his sadistic pigeonholing of me in meaningless parts on the Old Vic World Tour.

But my agent assured me that no such indignity would be visited upon me this time. And he was right. In *Henry IV, Part 1*, I was to play Sir Walter Blunt, and in *Henry IV, Part 2*, Lord Thomas Mowbray. These were small but worthwhile roles. And best of all, there was more. Peter Hall was bringing his London production of *Hamlet* back to Stratford, with David Warner reprising his starring role as the prince, and I was to play the First Player, an actor who brings his troupe to Elsinore Castle, and the Player King, who performs the lead role in *Hamlet*'s play-within-the-play. In *Henry V*, I was to play Louis, Dauphin of France.

Yes! These were *roles*. Not the biggest ones, but they were full-blooded characters of ambition and presence. My head was spinning—everything I'd worked for was finally being realized.

The first person I broke the news to was Gawn, who let out a whoop of happiness. That night, after performing in the show that was on in Bristol—Brendan Behan's *The Hostage*—we raised two tumblers of scotch on the rocks in a toast to each other's success. We had both gotten what we wanted, including being in *Hamlet*. True, we were doing the show on different continents in different productions with different responsibilities. But whereas Gawn would be touring the United States, I was going to be in the *Royal Shakespeare Company in Stratford-upon-Avon*.

The run-up to Christmas and our Bristol production of *The Happiest Days of Your Life* seemed to drag on forever. I enjoyed doing the play, lightweight as it was. But my life was changing—Sheila, the RSC—and I wanted to get on with it.

Fortunately, we had a wonderful cast, and in it was a talented and pretty young actress with red hair named Jane Asher. Everyone knew that Jane was dating Paul McCartney, but we were all very circum-spect around her and careful never to mention his name. Still, this was 1965, the year of *Rubber Soul* and the sold-out show at Shea Stadium in New York City. It was hard not to be starstruck by proxy.

One night after a performance, we were all sitting in the Old Duke pub when someone suggested a party game: We would go around the table, and each of us would answer the question, "If you were given a million pounds, what would be the first thing you bought with it?"

When it was my turn, I didn't hesitate. "An Aston Martin DB4," I said. "It's a fabulous car."

Jump forward to the following Saturday. Word got around during the matinee that Paul McCartney was in Bristol and he was coming to the evening show! We were all beside ourselves with ex-citement, though we did our best to conceal it from Jane.

After the performance, I was alone in my dressing room, chang-ing into my street clothes, when there was a knock on the door. Still in my underwear, I called out, "Come in."

The door opened and there, in the flesh, was Paul McCartney. "Hello, Patrick," he said. "Jane tells me you like Aston Martins. Here, drive this." He tossed a bunch of keys my way.

Then he went off to get Jane. I was stunned—I pulled on my trousers and pinched myself to make sure this was real life.

The three of us made our exit out through the stage door, with Paul signing autographs as we went. His silver Aston Martin, a DB5, was parked at the end of the alley. We got in: me in the front, Paul and Jane cuddled together adorably in the back.

"I'll tell you what, I have never been to Bath," said Paul. "Why not drive us there?"

Gearhead that I am, I was as excited to be behind the wheel of an Aston as I was to chauffeur Paul and Jane. Traffic was light, and I was able to operate the car with ease. Several times, Paul encouraged me to put the pedal to the metal. "Yes, go on, overtake!" he said. "Faster, faster. You can make this! Go!"

I appreciated his encouragement, but the thought did cross my mind: *If I kill Paul McCartney, it will be the only thing I will be remembered for.*

But we got back to the theater safely. I dropped myself off where my old MG was parked, and Paul and Jane moved up to the Aston's front seat. They had both been lovely, and Paul had been so generous.

Decades later, I met Paul again at some random event. He had been uninterruptedly one of the most famous people in the world every day since we had first met. I had achieved my own level of fame only relatively recently, courtesy of *Star Trek* and Jean-Luc Picard. In the intervening years, I had been through dozens of acting jobs, my fortunes ebbing and flowing. I expected that Paul might, at least, find my face familiar. Maybe.

But what he said when we met for the second time was, "Hey, Patrick, do you remember when we met in Bristol and I let you drive my DB5?"

I was bowled over, for all that had happened in his life, he'd matched the middle-aged man before him with the young man he had met in Bristol.

But that's Sir Paul for you. Not too long ago, I was having dinner at the Tower Bar at the Sunset Tower hotel in West Hollywood— a very glamorous spot where celebrity-spotting is normal—when the room stirred with excitement. Why? Because who else had walked in but Sir Paul. He greeted me warmly, as is his wont. A few minutes later, there was a second stir. Why? Because who else was joining Sir Paul but the recently knighted Sir Richard Starkey, a.k.a. Ringo Starr.

My dining party had a head start on theirs, and we finished our meal before they did. As I got up to leave, Paul came over to hug me goodbye. He said in my ear, "Do you know Ringo?"

Everybody knows Ringo, but I had never met the man. So, Paul motioned Ringo to join us, and suddenly we were in a huddle, three modestly born men from the North of England in a fancy Los Angeles restaurant.

"Hang on a minute," Paul remarked. "*Sir* Ringo. *Sir* Patrick. *Sir* Paul. Hey—we've got the Knights of the bloody Round Table!"

But this was all still to come for me. Back at the end of 1965, by the time Jane and Paul had sped away, it was after midnight, but I wasn't sleepy. Rather, I was in a daze of *Did that just happen? Will anyone believe me?*

The Old Duke was closed, so I couldn't share my story with anyone. I did need a drink, though. When I got back to my basement flat, I was glad to find a few drops left in my one bottle of scotch.

Sitting with a glass of whisky in my hand, I decided, *Yes, that joyride in Paul McCartney's Aston Martin really did happen. It happened because I am joining the RSC and getting married to Sheila. Good things are happening.* A guardian angel had patted me on the shoulder.

Chapter Ten

O ne thing I had not anticipated in my dream of working for the Royal Shakespeare Company was the complexity of domicile. Often our rehearsals were held in London, but our performances took place in Stratford-upon-Avon, seventy-five miles away. Sometimes it was the other way around: rehearse in Stratford, then perform in London, where the Aldwych Theatre served as our second home.

Sheila and I decided that it made more sense to get married in London, during rehearsals, as once we were in Warwickshire County, where Stratford is situated, life would be more complicated—she had her own show to rehearse in London.

We sublet a flat from a friend in Notting Hill Gate for four weeks. When the two of us had a day off, we drove up to Stratford to look at the housing that the RSC made available to company members. A lot of the options were rentals just across the street from the theater, but I didn't want that. If we were going to live in Warwickshire, I wanted to be based in the countryside, not in town, which most of the year is besieged by tourists. Luckily, the RSC had a lead on a small detached bungalow in the little hamlet of Wixford, about eight miles from Stratford. It backed onto a huge cornfield, with not another house in sight, though there was an old country pub a five-minute walk away. Perfect. Sheila and I were just beginning our lives together, and already we had city and country homes.

My first day of work as a member of the Royal Shakespeare Company took place in London, in a building at 41 Earlham Street in Covent Garden. Today this space is known as the Donmar Warehouse and puts on first-run plays and musicals. Back then it was known simply as the Warehouse. Covent Garden, which is now filled with high-end shops, was still dominated by an old-fashioned urban market where vendors sold all manner of fruits and vegetables from little stalls.

I was nervous as I climbed up the Warehouse's long flight of stairs for the first time. The Royal Shakespeare Company was what I had wanted for so long, but to be in the inner sanctum, working with actors and directors I had upheld as gods, was another thing entirely. What were their methods, their secrets? Would I be able to keep up?

We were there to rehearse *Henry IV, Parts 1 and 2.* Right away I recognized Ian Holm, the actor I regarded as the best of the best, and two more RSC greats: Paul Rogers, then nearly sixty, and Tony Church, a founding member of the RSC, whom I had seen as Polonius in David Warner's *Hamlet* and was now playing King Henry. Whew! Not in Kansas anymore.

Then came the entrance of the RSC's top brass: Peter Hall; John Barton; the Welsh director Clifford Williams; the general manager, David Brierley; and John Bury, the company's towering, bearded head of design. There must have been at least fifty of us in that room.

At ten a.m., the stage manager called the meeting to order. Peter Hall introduced himself with disarming modesty and explained that we were on a tight schedule. Given the vastness of the work we were to perform, he, Barton, and Williams would all be directing, and there would be several rehearsals going on at the same time, often in the evening. "Stand by to rehearse *Henry IV, Part 1*, Act I, Scene 1, starting in ten minutes."

And just like that, we were off! All of the actors in that first scene were asked to pull their chairs together into a circle. That included me, for I had been cast as Sir Walter Blunt, a faithful lieutenant to the king.

Clifford was responsible for directing this scene. I thought we were going to do a simple read-through of it, which would be light work for me—Sir Walter has no lines—but Clifford didn't open his script. He just turned to his left and asked Tony Church to talk about the scene. Tony did just that, explaining, at some length, his thoughts on King Henry and how he would be exploring the king's intentions. When Tony was done, Clifford nodded to the actor on Tony's left, Michael Jayston, who was playing Westmoreland, and he talked about the scene in similar fashion.

King Henry and Westmoreland are the only characters with lines in Act I, Scene 1, but there were four more of us in the scene who had no dialogue. When Michael was done speaking, Clifford gestured for the actor to my right, who, like me, had no lines, to pick up the conversation. To my horror, I realized that I would be called upon next. But I had nothing to say. Because I had no lines, I had not given the scene much thought.

When my turn came, I muttered something along the lines of "What they said, yeah," along with the dull observation that Sir Walter would support whatever the king chose to do. Pathetic. Twenty minutes into my first RSC rehearsal and I had been found out as a pretender. Off to a smashing start.

After all the scene's participants had spoken, Clifford informed us that John Barton—the lord of text at the RSC—had reassigned some of King Henry's lines in the scene to Sir Walter. Meaning that I indeed had lines in Act I, Scene 1, and that I should have already familiarized myself with the material, the way a real actor would.

In Shakespeare's text, King Henry gestures to Sir Walter and notes that his friend has brought "smooth and welcome news," which the king himself delivers. John Barton's clever idea was for me to deliver Sir Walter's news in my own voice, to enliven the scene. These were now lines that I was to speak:

> *The Earl of Douglas is discomfited:*
> *Ten thousand bold Scots, two and twenty knights,*
> *Balk'd in their own blood did mine eyes see.*
> *On Holmedon's plains. Of prisoners, Hotspur took*
> *Mordake the Earl of Fife, and eldest son*
> *To beaten Douglas; and the Earl of Athol,*
> *Of Murray, Angus, and Menteith.*

The good news was that my speaking role had almost doubled in size. The bad news was that I had inadequately prepared for my very first day of my dream job. Sitting on the train that night, returning to Notting Hill Gate, I swore to myself that I would never, ever allow myself to make such a terrible error again.

That scene was all I had to do that first day, but I'd asked the stage manager if I could stay and watch the remainder of the rehearsal. With a look of surprise, he said, "Of course." The next scene featured Prince Hal, Falstaff, and Ned Poins, which meant a chance to watch Ian Holm, Paul Rogers, and Daniel Moynihan in action.

You cannot overestimate the benefits of watching fine artists like these at work. And I mean watching *everything*: how they interact in and out of character, as actors and as people; how they pursue truth and embrace spontaneity; how they enjoy themselves. When things are going well, the room is redolent with a shared pleasure like no other high. That, I am certain, is one of the main reasons we actors commit ourselves to such a strange, capricious profession.

Ian Holm was so "there" from the very first day: still, watchful, responsive, delicate. I had nine months ahead of me in which to observe him almost daily, and perhaps put into practice some of what I was learning from him. I didn't want to bother Ian or ingratiate myself to him, to become his pal, his chum, his mate. But I did hope that I might somehow make him aware that we were sharing the stage. And that did happen in a performance, once.

There is a great scene in *Henry IV, Part 1* between Prince Hal and his father, who savagely criticizes his son for being a wastrel. The scene ends with the prince passionately convincing his father that he will make him proud. The king, in response, says:

A hundred thousand rebels die in this:
Thou shalt have charge and sovereign trust herein.

Enter Sir Walter Blunt.

I had to come through a heavy door of metal and timber. It was an ordeal to open and move, but I had grown used to it. One night, to add some extra pizzazz, I decided to slam the door behind me and then swiftly move toward the king, kneeling before him. I did the door part, but I never got to kneel because my cloak had gotten caught in the door, pulling me back. I tried to free the cloak, but it wouldn't budge. Some people in the audience had begun to laugh, so I decided to deliver my seven-line speech to the king while standing upright, and then hightail it off to the wings.

Ian was standing downstage of me, and when I turned to say one of my lines to him, he had a huge smile on his face. As we made eye contact, he slyly raised an eyebrow at me. For a moment I couldn't go on. But then he resumed looking serious, and I pulled it together to finish my speech. Tony, as the king, said his lines, and then the three of us moved to exit. Ian beat me to the door and opened it, releasing my cloak. Tony walked off first. Ian indicated with his arm that I was to exit next: inappropriate protocol in the royal court, but I did what I was being told to do. When we were in the wings, he put his arm around me, gave me a squeeze, smiled, and disappeared into the darkness.

That was the only moment of true connection I had with my role model in the nine months we worked together, but it was enough. I had been acknowledged by him, and in the very kindest way. Ian was, in every sense, a prince.

Right in the middle of those first few whirlwind weeks in 1966 with the Royal Shakespeare Company in London, Sheila and I got married in the Kensington and Chelsea Register Office. Our witnesses, and the only people who attended the ceremony, were my actor pal Donald Gee and his wife, Shirley. She was heavily pregnant at the time, and when the ceremony began, the registrar called Shirley and me forward, clearly assuming that she was my fiancée and that this was a shotgun wedding.

Donald was the first to grasp the mistake and call a halt to the proceedings, lest his wife become a polygamist. Well, at least my marriage to Sheila had started off with a laugh. We had no reception afterward, just a quick lunch, because Sheila and I both had to return to work in the afternoon. We reunited at the end of the day in a lovely room at the recently built Hilton Hotel at the bottom of Park Lane, overlooking Hyde Park. There, we quickly got changed and hailed a taxi to the Aldwych Theatre; weeks earlier, unsure of our wedding date, I had bought tickets for this very night to see Harold Pinter's *The Homecoming*, a brutal play of sexual politics and marital tension, because Ian Holm and Paul Rogers were in it.

It was a totally inappropriate play to see on one's wedding night, but there was no way I was going to miss it. While getting into the taxi, I was so overwhelmed by anticipation and confused by how to tip a hotel doorman—not in my repertoire back then—that I walked headfirst into the roof of the cab. I sustained a cut on my scalp, and Sheila spent the drive to the Aldwych cleaning me up with tissues. When we arrived at the Aldwych, I had a huge bump and a splitting headache. I saw a cracking show, though, in every sense.

The first public preview of *Henry IV, Part 1* in Stratford was a matinee—my debut as a member of the Royal Shakespeare Company. As I stood in the wings waiting to make my entrance as Sir Walter Blunt, I was overwhelmed by a combination of excitement and disbelief. Not because of the role, which was less challenging than many I had played elsewhere, but because *this was the RSC*. I felt like Neil Armstrong on his moon walk, planting my feet in a place I could only have dreamed of visiting as a boy.

As soon as the two *Henry IV* plays opened in Stratford, we began rehearsals for the next show, *Henry V*. I loved playing the Dauphin. What an appalling character—he is arrogant, obnoxious, boastful, and a misogynist who declares, "I had rather have my horse to my mistress." And after the Battle of Agincourt, he turns whiny and suicidal.

Unfortunately, the Dauphin fades out of the play fairly early, but Peter Hall had the great idea of bringing him back into the French court when King Henry comes to woo the Princess of France, Katherine. I had no lines at all, but I got to act nonverbally, sulking and at times being on the verge of tears. Ian, as King Henry, played some of his lines off me, which justified my being there. I also got to wear a very pretty costume, a rarity in my career.

One newcomer in our cast was a young fellow with piercing blue eyes named Malcolm McDowell. He had not been in the business long, and none of the roles assigned to him had any dialogue; he was, in effect, a walk-on. I remember seeing him in the wings quick-changing from an English tabard to a French one. Malcolm did, however, have responsibilities as understudy, if in very small roles. One of the characters was a messenger who enters as Henry is finishing the famous St. Crispin's Day speech ("We few, we happy few, we band of brothers").

There came a day when Malcolm was pressed into duty. The entire company was called in early one Saturday morning because a supporting actor in a significant role was unwell and could not perform. This triggered a cast shuffle, as we had a next-man-up system of promoting people in smaller speaking roles to the more medium ones, and the walk-ons to the smaller speaking roles. Therefore, our directors thought it prudent to run a rehearsal of this shifted lineup, which ended up taking so long that there was no time left to go over Malcolm as the messenger; the audience members were already waiting to take their seats. The stage manager told Malcolm he would be fine because Malcolm was used to being onstage as a background cast member when the messenger said his three lines, which were as follows:

My sovereign lord, bestow yourself with speed.
The French are bravely in their battles set,
And will with all expedience charge on us.

Malcolm concurred with the stage manager, and we all scooted off to get ready. Throughout the performance, backstage, I kept noticing Malcolm standing off in a dark corner, muttering these lines to himself. Finally, Ian started the St. Crispin's Day speech and Malcolm positioned himself in the wings, waiting for his cue and still muttering his lines.

At last, the cue came. Malcolm ran on, knelt before Ian, looked up at him, looked away, looked at Ian again, and these were the words that came out of his mouth:

Come on, come on! They're coming!

And then, after a pause:

I'm sorry.

Malcolm has given me his blessing to share this story, as it serves as an inspirational message to young actors who have endured onstage brain-lock and forgotten their lines: Two years later, Lindsay Anderson cast Malcolm as the lead in his film *If . . .* , and two years after that, Malcolm was the lead in Stanley Kubrick's *A Clockwork Orange.* He and I were reunited in 1994, when he played the villainous Soran in my first *Star Trek* feature film, *Generations*, and we had a roaring great time together.

We only had two weeks to prepare *Hamlet*, which wasn't as crazy as it sounds because it was a revival of the previous year's firecracker production at the Aldwych and all of the principal roles were to be played by the same actors, with the exception of Ophelia, who had originally been played by Glenda Jackson, then by Janet Suzman, and now in our version by Estelle Kohler.

I, too, was a newcomer, if a less consequential one. Still, my presence in *Hamlet* as the First Player and the Player King—respectively, the prince's actor friend and the character the actor friend plays in the show he stages for Hamlet—warranted a one-on-one session with Peter Hall.

I barely got an hour, but what an hour. First Peter had me perform the whole of the First Player's big speech ("Anon he finds him / Striking too short at Greeks . . ."), and then he gave me a couple of notes and said, "Do it again." This time I had barely gotten out the first line of verse before he stopped me to give another note. He told me to have my script in hand, even though I knew the speech by heart, so that I could write down his observations. I started again, and he gave me another note, and another, and another. By the time we were done, I had no space left on the page.

When at last I got to the end of the speech, he said, "You don't have to remember all of my notes, but you can work on them on your own. Okay, one last time." I delivered the speech once more and then our hour was up. When I got home that night, I looked at my script and realized that there was not a single line of verse that I had *not* underlined. How was I going to remember all of his suggestions?

I was determined, though—I worked and worked at it. Then came the day when the full cast did its first run-through of *Hamlet*.

When my first scene was over, Peter caught my eye and flashed two thumbs-up. I was glowing inside for the rest of the day.

This was my first *Hamlet*—I would return to it thirty-two years later in a modern-dress production, playing King Claudius, with David Tennant in the lead. Tennant was a joy to work with—so free, so gifted at connecting to each and every actor with intensity and generosity.

At the time of the David Warner *Hamlet*, though, the RSC was a sports-crazy bunch, with our own summer cricket team and winter soccer team. I was among the regular players for both. The summer of '66 was a glorious one for England, in that our country hosted the World Cup tournament and the home team made it all the way to the final.

That match, against West Germany, took place during one of our Saturday matinees. It was the game of a lifetime and remains the most-watched television event in British history. We were no different from everyone else in England—but we had a show to do. So under the stage, some crafty members of the crew mounted a small TV set. When we actors weren't onstage doing a scene, we were crouching down below, watching the match and, despite ourselves, cheering and yelling.

At the intermission, the house manager came backstage to let us know that there were many audience complaints about intrusive barking and yelping noises. He lectured us about keeping it down, though I must note that among the most vociferous offenders was Hamlet himself, David Warner.

We had other ways of following the match when we couldn't sneak under the stage. One actor, wearing a long wig for his part, was able to conceal an earpiece in it that was wired to a radio hidden in his costume. Right when we were about to do the play-within-the-play scene—my big moment—this actor muttered to me, "West Germany have scored." For heaven's sake, how was I supposed to launch into the First Player's speech with *that* news in my head? Fortunately, England won, 4–2. Happy days.

One luxury of not having a big role was that on a normal performance night, I was allowed to leave the theater early, as my character disappeared in the third of *Hamlet*'s five acts. But on the night of our first public preview, I was required to stay until the final bows.

Given the production's success in London the previous year, David Warner, who was still only twenty-four, had been transformed into a national heartthrob. It wasn't uncommon, after any given performance, to find a smattering of fans assembled at the stage door. But on this night, the first of previews, there was a throng.

When I pulled the door open to leave, I was met by a surge of humanity. Many of these fans had autograph books, programs, and pens in their hands. Most of them were female and young. A pretty blond girl in a miniskirt thrust her program in my face. But as I reached for it and her pen, she pulled it back.

Very demandingly, she inquired of me, "Are you anybody?"

What a curious question. I had never before been asked it. But given the circumstances, I knew exactly what she meant. Smiling, I shook my head. The crowd immediately parted and let me through.

Was I disappointed? Yes. A little hurt? Yes. But as I drove home that night, still smiling, I realized something: That girl had given me a gift. She had pressed the ambition button. I was reminded of feelings that I had suppressed during rehearsals, caught up as I was in heeding Peter Hall's notes and marveling at the actors around me. I *was* ambitious! I *did* belong with the RSC! And then it dawned on me how I should have replied to her question: *Not yet. But watch this space.*

As I have mentioned, the back of the rustic bungalow I shared with Sheila abutted a cornfield, and the area abounded with wildlife. On one side of the house was a small orchard planted with apple, plum, and damson trees. I had never had my own fruit trees before, and in the early autumn, I took bags of our trees' yield into the greenroom of the theatre, where they were quickly devoured. I also planted sunflowers and was amazed when they not only thrived but grew taller than me.

It sounds idyllic, but in truth, Sheila and I did not get to spend much time together. She was on tour as a choreographer and dancer, and was also filming a part in the movie *Half a Sixpence*, a vehicle for the 1950s teen singing idol Tommy Steele. Film was still beyond my comprehension as a career goal, and I was impressed that she had landed this job.

Since I had no one waiting for me at home, I followed the lead of other RSC actors in heading off after an evening performance to a Stratford institution, a pub and hotel known to us as the Dirty Duck, though it was actually called the Black Swan. Soon enough, I was sufficiently in the know that when closing time came and the pub's doors were locked, it became an after-hours club of sorts for RSC members who were formally approved to patronize it.

I seriously do mean "formally approved." It took me a while to be treated as someone who could be trusted with the Duck's secret. Fortunately, I found two ready sponsors in Norman Rodway and Godfrey Quigley, both Irish actors. They vouched for me and I was in as one of the club. But it wasn't just for drinking—we played darts, cards, and billiards. Occasionally, on account of the drink, there might be a flurry of angry words and a thrown fist or two. We were, after all, intensively engaged in the great works of William Shakespeare, which could rile up one's emotions.

As the RSC's 1965–66 season was nearing its end, my anxiety intensified. I had loved my ten months with the company, but there was no guarantee that I would be asked back.

The reality was that I had achieved my dream job on the cusp of turning twenty-six. I had never been so happy, so stimulated, or so surrounded by fine and dear people. I desperately wanted to remain, but this choice was out of my hands.

I was informed by my colleagues that it was Peter Hall's custom to invite each actor in the company to a private meeting in his office at season's end for a sort of performance review. I had also heard that a couple of actors had already been told there would be nothing further for them when the season ended, and that it was time to move on. I had no plan B. If it was the move-on list for me, I wasn't sure what was next. I wasn't hungry to be in films or TV, and there was no other company comparable in quality to the Royal Shakespeare Company. A quiet despair set in.

Finally, the day came: my momentous appointment with Peter Hall. I waited outside his office in a state of acute tension as another actor endured his appointment. It seemed to be going well: I heard laughter and cheerful voices. When the door opened, this person, who was someone I liked, was in the process of shaking Peter's hand. As he passed, he gave me a huge smile and a thumbs-up.

I was up next. Peter invited me in and sat down behind his desk, where I faced him. In my mind, I was twelve again and Mr. Bassett, the man who whipped my hands to a pulp, had returned.

Peter motioned me to sit down, though I was reluctant to—if he was letting me go, I would just have to get up again and drag out the misery.

The first thing Peter said was, "Well, this won't take long."

Oh God, it is Mr. Bassett all over again.

Peter continued: "Patrick, we have something we call the Associate Actors Group at the RSC. The main feature of it is that its members commit to a three-year contract. Most actors agree, but some prefer to have more flexibility and independence, which I understand. But I hope that you will accept this offer. I want to keep you in the RSC."

I wanted to jump up and down, scream like a banshee, and pull Peter over the desk so I could kiss him sloppily on the mouth. But this wasn't drama school, damn it; this was the Royal Shakespeare Company! So I gave my best Ian Holm–style performance. With calm and steely resolve, I said quietly and respectfully, "Thank you, Peter, I would love to accept your offer. It is what I wanted."

We shook hands. Peter explained that the next season's programming was still up in the air, but he and the associate directors were planning an exciting season of productions. I was to be in that office many more times in the years ahead, but this particular moment in it has never left me.

Outside, close to the entrance of the RSC Library, there was an old-fashioned red telephone box. I marched straight to it, calling Sheila with the news. I put in my coins and she answered.

"It's me," I said.

"How did it go?" she asked, tentatively.

I opened my mouth but couldn't speak. I just began to sob.

"Oh, love, I'm *so sorry*," she said.

"No, no—it's good!" I said. "I've got a contract for three years!"

That phone box is somehow still there, and I never pass it without giving it a grateful nod. I want it to stay there for all time.

Chapter Eleven

I was to spend fourteen years as a full-time member of the Royal Shakespeare Company, with my three-year contract renewed four times. The RSC offered me as stable a life as any professional actor could wish for, akin to being a tenured professor at a top-notch university. This allowed Sheila and me, as busy as we both were, to settle eventually into a comfortable domesticity. When it became evident that my time with the company was going to be lengthy, we gave up the rented bungalow and bought a modest but cozy four-hundred-year-old cottage—the one whose ancient inglenook fireplace I excavated—in a village called Barford, a twenty-minute drive from the Royal Shakespeare Theatre. Our first child, Daniel, was born in 1967, followed five years later by our daughter, Sophie.

My time with the RSC was everything I had hoped it would be and more. There was one quality to the experience that I hadn't anticipated: The people who filled that historic auditorium in Stratford were excited just to be there. Many of them had traveled great distances, halfway around the world, to be with us. Patrons had saved money for the express purpose of seeing William Shakespeare's work performed in his hometown by the foremost Shakespearean actors in his home country.

As a company, we held a serious responsibility and we knew it. We sensed the expectation and anticipation before the curtain went up and heard the excited rounds of applause that greeted the first dimming of the house lights. A play at the Royal Shakespeare Theatre was not just another show; it was an event. We became experts at knowing where in the house a tour group of non-English-speaking theatergoers was sitting, usually because the section was conspicuously silent. We wanted these audience members to have as good a time as everyone else, so we worked hard to please them. If it was a comedy, for example, we amplified the physical hijinks to get them to laugh. Our efforts did not go unappreciated. Often, the most enthusiastic applause during our final bows came from the people in those seats.

Still, in my early days at the RSC, the blessing of my wonderful job and my equally wonderful job security took some getting used to. After my first season wrapped, we moved back to London for the break, leasing a flat in Bayswater near Hyde Park. Sheila and I filled it with secondhand furniture, and I rented us a TV set, my first. Given the outsize role that television was to play in my future, it's funny to think that I never had one until I was twenty-six years old.

As an associate artist under contract to the RSC, I was getting paid even though I wasn't working—a situation so alien to me that it felt wrong. I was restless. I wanted to be working. As luck would have it, I encountered the director John Barton while attending a play at the Aldwych, and I admitted to him that I was at loose ends. John asked me if I was based in London, and, if so, would I like to do some verse work with him at his flat two or three times a week.

With one of the greatest directors in Britain? I jumped at the chance, and for two months, we worked on sonnets, speeches, verse, and prose. Though John was academic in his approach, he welcomed the injection of emotion and physicality into delivering verse if it suited an actor's objectives. Whereas Peter Hall took a more traditionalist approach, preferring that you hit your line endings as Shakespeare intended, John regarded line endings more fluidly, as a means of launching you into your next thought. I still keep this in mind whenever I study a script. It was such a privilege to have those one-on-one sessions in John's tiny Marylebone office, a script in my lap.

When we reconvened for the next RSC season, I learned that I was to play Grumio, the dimwitted comic sidekick to Petruchio, in *The Taming of the Shrew*, directed by Trevor Nunn, and the banished Duke Senior in *As You Like It*, directed by David Jones. I had not worked with David, but I already had the year before with Trevor. He was the wunderkind of the RSC, an associate director even though he was only six months older than me. We were to become dear friends, but our relationship got off to a rocky start. The previous season, he had recruited me for one of the RSC's non-Shakespeare plays, *The Revenger's Tragedy*, a play ascribed then to Cyril Tourneur and now to Thomas Middleton, both of them the Bard's contemporaries.

Trevor told me that the play was centered around two brothers, Vendici and Hippolito, who seek revenge against a duke who disgraced their family and shamed their sister. The great Ian Richardson was to play Vindici, and Trevor wanted me for Hippolito. *What? When do we begin?*

But I didn't know the play, and when I got the script, I realized that something wasn't right. The first scene is indeed a dialogue between Vendici and Hippolito, but Vendici has long speeches and basically all Hippolito gets to say is stuff like "Yea, brother, 'tis so," and "Verily, brother, thou speakest right." Yes, I was in most of Ian's scenes—and it was thrilling to be onstage with him—but I had virtually nothing to say. I thought Trevor had misled me. I could have stayed angry at him, but I liked him too much. At the previous year's Christmas party, he had gotten up onstage with a guitar and sung Lonnie Donegan songs. How could I not want to work with this guy?

As the new season began, I realized there had been heavy turnover in the RSC. Most of the actors from the previous season were gone, and we were a very different ensemble. There were two young actors I knew nothing of until I met them. One was Roger Rees, and the other, Ben Kingsley. In *The Taming of the Shrew*, they were both cast as huntsmen, essentially background characters.

But it took only a couple of seasons for Ben and Roger to become stars of the company. Both were lovely guys, both took their turn playing Hamlet, and both went on to bigger things: Ben in *Gandhi* and Roger in the mammoth eight-hour RSC production of *Nicholas Nickleby* that traveled from London to Broadway (he also had a nice recurring part as millionaire antagonist Robin Colcord on the TV series *Cheers*). Whereas Roger was a quiet, private man, Ben was the exact opposite, and he and I became good friends.

Another actor new to the RSC that season was Roy Kinnear. His was a face well-known to British TV and film audiences as a regular on the parodic sketch program *That Was the Week That Was*, and as one of the exasperated foils of the Beatles in the movie *Help!* One of Roy's first roles with us was as Touchstone in *As You Like It*. Shakespeare himself described Touchstone as a clown, and Roy fit the bill: He was short and portly, and audiences laughed at the mere sight of him. But Touchstone is also brilliant with language, and Roy made the most of that. He became notorious in the RSC for ad-libbing, which irked some purists but not me.

Here's how I look at it. Hamlet, in his speech to the First Player, says, "And let those that play your clowns say no more than is set down for them; for there be of them that will themselves laugh, to set on some quantity of barren spectators to laugh too." In other words, Shakespeare himself had worked with comic actors like Roy, and the writer in him was annoyed with these actors for doing precisely what Roy was doing, deviating from the text, saying "more than is set down for them." But Roy was so good that I think Shakespeare would have approved.

I'll give an example. Touchstone delivers a delightful speech in which he offers a taxonomy of lies, declaring that there are seven different kinds, to which he assigns silly names, e.g., the Retort Courteous, the Reply Churlish, and the Countercheck Quarrelsome. After this speech, the character Jaques asks him, "Can you nominate in order now the degrees of the lie?" Touchstone then says, "O sir, we quarrel in print by the book, as you have books for good manners," and then obliges Jaques's request. But Roy, instead of following up immediately with the "quarrel in print" line, would first roll his eyes and say, "I thought you were going to ask me that."

I was in this scene, and for over a year, at every performance we did, in England and later on when we toured the US, I laughed, the rest of the actors onstage laughed, and Lord, did the audience ever laugh. Later on, when Roy had commitments elsewhere, I agreed to take over as Touchstone, a decision I still regret—how on earth could I follow someone that comedically brilliant?

At the end of the season, the RSC offered me my first proper introduction to America. In downtown Los Angeles, construction had just been completed on the Music Center, a huge performing arts complex that included the Dorothy Chandler Pavilion, the Mark Taper Forum, and the Ahmanson Theatre. It was a risky move for the city's tastemakers to build such a place, because downtown LA was a dead zone at the time, and it wasn't clear if Southern California was ready to support a Lincoln Center–like cultural mecca.

One component of the Music Center's strategy was for the Taper Forum to have a Royal Shakespeare Company–like resident company with which we would have a cultural exchange program, with us sending our UK productions to them and vice versa. That plan never fully materialized, but we did bring *As You Like It* and *The Taming of the Shrew* to the Ahmanson, the larger of the Music Center's two theaters.

We left London on a cold, damp January day in 1968, all of us quite pleased to spend six weeks in sunny California. These feelings only intensified when we saw our new digs: a huge Beaux Arts–style apartment complex called the Bryson Apartment Hotel, on Wilshire

Boulevard near MacArthur Park. The building is still there, and I later learned that it was owned by the actor Fred MacMurray of *Double Indemnity* and *My Three Sons* fame.

My apartment in the Bryson had only one bedroom, but the ceilings were high and the windows vast, with views down Wilshire and beyond into the Baldwin Hills in the southern distance. I didn't realize it at the time, but somewhere in this haze stood the old Metro-Goldwyn-Mayer Studios in Culver City, today the property of Sony Pictures. MGM made many of the films I cherished as a boy. Had I been aware of my proximity to those studio gates, through which the film stars of my youth had driven in and out, I'd have gone all limp.

The company was given a full day to rest and acclimate, but I couldn't sleep, and anyway, I was too eager to get out and explore. I walked aimlessly, and just when hunger was getting the best of me, I came across a hamburger stand on the corner of Beverly and Rampart Boulevards. There was a big sign on its roof that said TOMMY'S and quite a long line to get in, always a good sign. I noticed a couple of California Highway Patrol cars parked outside. When a third arrived, I observed that the cops, when they got out of their cars, didn't take their places at the end of the queue but went straight to the front and ordered. Already, a bit of local culture!

What I had stumbled upon was the first location of the venerated local hamburger chain nowadays known as Original Tommy's. As I waited in the queue, I asked the man standing in front of me what I should order. He looked at me in disbelief, but I think my English accent convinced him of my innocence.

"There's only one thing you want to order," he said. "Tommy's-to-go, with everything."

Of course he was quite right. The burger was huge and oozed with chili, melted cheese, sliced pickles, onions, and tomato. The counterman wrapped it firmly, and I walked briskly back to the Bryson because I had picked up a six-pack of beer and stowed it in the fridge. Such was the scale of the burger that I had to drink three beers, one after the other, to properly accompany each bite.

I became evangelical to my pals in the RSC about Tommy's, and within a couple of days, everyone in the company knew about my find. It became our habit to hit Tommy's after every show. The novelty of a parade of Shakespearean actors at the burger stand was not lost on the locals, and even the cops began to recognize us.

As fate would have it, this was just the first episode in the annals of Pat Stew's public adventures in culinary Americana. About ten years ago, at which time I was engaged to Sunny and we had just purchased a place together in Park Slope, Brooklyn, our day began uneventfully. We had slept in and missed breakfast, partly on account of being a little hungover, and we were hungry. Sunny led me to a local place, Smiling Pizza on 7th Avenue. I was surprised that she wanted to order a whole pizza. "No," she said, "we're each getting a New York slice."

I had never heard of a New York slice. When it arrived, I struggled to stop all the fillings from sliding off the slice onto the ground. "You have to *fold* it!" Sunny yelled at me. "That's why it's called a New York slice." I was so excited by this historic development in my food education that I had Sunny take a picture of me proudly holding my folded slice. We posted it on Twitter with a caption reading "My first ever pizza 'slice'" and gave the matter no further thought. Until . . .

In the next twenty-four hours, me and my slice became an international media sensation. Part of this stemmed from a misunderstanding: People believed that a well-traveled man then in his seventies had never before eaten pizza, which, indeed, would have been bizarre. All I meant was that I had never ordered by the slice before and eaten it on the go, folded. Still, this did not stem the planet's insatiable curiosity about my personal pizza history. I was contacted by multiple media outlets for interviews—including the BBC, from whom I had not heard in years. But now they wanted to talk to me. About a slice of pizza.

The RSC's productions at the Ahmanson, my first before an American audience, were a triumph. I discovered to my delight that when Americans see shows at a theater, they are out for a good time and don't hold back. In fact, I sometimes find that after playing a show in the US and then taking it to the UK, the experience is a bit of a letdown, because in London, it can feel as if the audience is holding back—afraid, perhaps, of offering a "wrong" reaction.

While the RSC was performing in LA, we received stunning news: Peter Hall was resigning as our artistic director in order to move on to the same position at the National Theatre, where Sir Laurence Olivier had announced his retirement. Peter's replacement would be Trevor Nunn. Those of us in LA were surprised but delighted—as inexperienced as Trevor was, we believed in his talent, and he was a known quantity, and a friend, to all of us.

This was, in fact, the beginning of a long and fruitful working relationship between Trevor and me. As for Peter Hall, alas, I was to work with him only once more, eighteen years later. That I have done just one play at the National, Peter Shaffer's *Yonadab*, in 1986, is one of my few professional frustrations.

While we were in LA, we also learned that the opening production of the RSC's 1968 season would be *King Lear*, directed by Trevor, with Eric Porter as Lear. Later in the season, Trevor was to direct *Much Ado About Nothing*, with Janet Suzman, Helen Mirren, Bernard Lloyd, and Alan Howard headlining. Directing plays as disparate as *Lear* and *Much Ado* in one's debut season struck me as a bold choice; years separated their writing, and their texts showed it. *Much Ado*, from 1598, is broad in its comedy, characterizations, and narrative, whereas *Lear*, from 1606, is mature, bitter, nuanced, and complex.

I was to be the Duke of Cornwall in *Lear* and Borachio, a comic bad guy, in *Much Ado*. Cornwall dies before the play is half over, but he is a delectably monstrous character—he is the man who scoops out the eyes of the Earl of Gloucester. I chose to play Cornwall as a bullying, angry, impulsive man who was also watchful and opportunistic because he has long periods of silence. In the blinding scene, as staged by Trevor, I stamped on Gloucester's face, jerking out of his head a prop eyeball. Then, as Cornwall gouged out the other eye, I got to speak one the ugliest lines in all of Shakespeare: "Out, vile jelly. Where is thy lustre now?"

Cornwall dies offstage shortly after this scene from his own wounds. For a while, this was the moment when intermission fell, meaning that my night was over and I could saunter over to the Dirty Duck for a drink before going home; take it from a pro, nothing clears the mind after an eye-gouging like a scotch and soda on the rocks. But Trevor was compelled to experiment with moving around the placement of the intermission, because many audience members weren't making their way to the bar after the "vile jelly" scene but for the toilets, in order to retch.

Much Ado About Nothing was a considerably lighter affair, both the play itself and our experience of performing it. Ben Kingsley was cast as Conrade, the sidekick of my character, Borachio, and oh, did we have fun. Too much, evidently; toward the end of its run, someone in the cast made a formal complaint to Trevor Nunn that Ben and I were adding excessive shtick to our scenes and even improvising lines, thereby holding up the production. The complaints were fairly accurate—I played Borachio with a Cockney accent, which alone spelled trouble—and Ben and I were admonished to clean up our act. Privately, though, Trevor told us that he had really liked what we had been inventing and felt its absence.

One cast member who made no secret of his annoyance with me was Bernard Lloyd, the actor who played Claudio, one of the romantic leads, in *Much Ado*. He was six years older than me and strikingly handsome, with a thick head of hair that made me deeply envious. Bernie took his work incredibly seriously, to the point of sometimes ruffling the feathers of his peers—me included. One day in rehearsals, unhappy with my broad portrayal of Borachio, he turned to our director and said, as if I weren't there, "Trevor, is he going to do it like that? Because if he is, we are wasting our time."

With indignation, I responded, "Bernie, who is this 'he'? I have a name."

"Yes, you're right, I'm sorry," he said. Then, with crack timing, he added, "Nevertheless, I want to know." The room broke out in laughter, defusing the tension between him and me forevermore.

My relationship with Bernie deepened into a true friendship in early '69, when some of us in the RSC returned to Los Angeles to perform *Much Ado* and another show from that season, Christopher Marlowe's *Doctor Faustus*, which I wasn't in. Since I had one play off, I urged Sheila to join me in my palatial flat in the Bryson with baby Daniel in tow; I knew I would have plenty of time to proudly show them the city I had gotten to know. In the bargain, they, too, fell prey to the charms of the actually quite nice Bernie Lloyd.

Later on, in the 1970s and '80s, Bernie and I would tour the United States together, sometimes as part of a traveling educational program that we put together with our actor friend Tony Church and an American academic, Homer D. Swander. Our group usually numbered five actors in total, with at least one woman in the mini-company. We traveled from one college campus to the next, spending a week at each, lecturing and performing—mostly to theater and English-lit majors, though we also visited some psychology and mathematics classes, whose pupils were often even more enthusiastic. On two nights of these weeks, we presented a staged performance of a Shakespeare play, operating on a shoestring, with just the five of us playing all the roles. It was a lovely way to spread the gospel of Shakespeare, and each one of us was paid $1,000 a week during these tours.

Bernie Lloyd did several of these tours, and I came on as many as I could. As the decades passed, he became like family to me, close to my son, Daniel, as he pursued his own acting career, and, in his later years, to my wife, Sunny. On our last visit with Bernie in 2018, this formerly rugged man was, to our sadness, bedridden and in considerable pain. Sunny offered to give him a massage, which he rather shyly agreed to. For half an hour, she gently administered to him. He sweetly thanked her for alleviating his pain and then began to fall asleep. We tucked him in, and before he drifted off, he smiled at us and we both kissed him, telling him we would see him again soon. When we got into our car, Sunny and I sobbed helplessly. He passed away three weeks later.

In my office in our house in Los Angeles, there is, to the left of my desk, a framed black-and-white photograph of Bernie and me in our glory, in costume as Camillo and Leontes in *The Winter's Tale*. Bernie has his hand on my arm and is looking at me with true tenderness. He remains forever at my side.

In 1970, back home in the UK, we members at the RSC were excited to hear that the other great Peter of British theater—director Peter Brook—was returning to Stratford to oversee *A Midsummer Night's Dream*. Brook was the heavyweight's heavyweight. In 1964, at the RSC, he had directed the first English-language production of *The Persecution and Assassination of Jean-Paul Marat as Performed by the Inmates of the Asylum of Charenton Under the Direction of the Marquis de Sade*, better known to audiences and theater historians as *Marat/Sade*.

That legendary production transferred a year later to Broadway, with Ian Richardson and Glenda Jackson in the leads. *Marat/Sade* won the Tony Award for Best Play, and Peter Brook the Tony for Best Director. I had worked with Peter only once at the RSC, in a staged reading at the Aldwych of a piece called *The Investigation*. Our large cast was seated in rows of chairs, and we took turns stepping up to a pair of lecterns to read. The script, by Peter Weiss, the author of *Marat/Sade*, was based on the Frankfurt Auschwitz trials of the early 1960s, in which twenty-two defendants faced criminal charges for their roles in the Holocaust. I have, over the years, met several people who have told me that they were present at that Sunday night reading, and that it was among the most powerful nights of theater in their entire lives.

So it goes without saying that I was eager to work again with Peter Brook, this brilliant man who could simply give an audience an experience so profound. I thought that *A Midsummer Night's Dream* was a curiously light choice for a man known for doing serious work, but that was no deterrent. As it turns out, *he* was the deterrent. I met with Peter and we talked, but he didn't cast me. I was utterly dejected and took it personally—I wasn't good enough for Peter Brook. Such is an actor's life, even a successful one. These feelings don't go away.

I ended up being cast in another of Shakespeare's comedies, *The Two Gentlemen of Verona*, but it seemed like a consolation prize. I had seen the play once and had not been impressed—it is one of Shakespeare's earliest, perhaps even his first, and his skills as a dramatist were not yet fully developed. But my spirits lifted when I learned that its director was to be none other than that blue-eyed boy of my class at the Bristol Old Vic Theatre School, Robin Phillips. And the cast was not too shabby: Helen Mirren, Ian Richardson, Estelle Kohler. It brought me comfort to consider that perhaps they, too, had been rejected by Mr. Brook.

I was cast as Launce—yes, another comedy servant, this time serving Proteus, the male romantic lead, who was played by Ian. Not so promising. But then I realized that I had forgotten something important about Launce: He has a companion, a dog named Crab. I loved dogs, but I had never before acted onstage with one. Suddenly, Verona was looking a lot more palatable than Athens.

I decided that casting my canine costar was going to be exclusively my business—an instinct that only seemed more justified when, in my first conversation with Robin Phillips about Crab, he showed me a photo of the dog he wanted to use: a large, handsome, long-haired collie. No, no, no, no, no, no, no. That was totally wrong for Launce's dog: too elegant, too middle-class, too pretty.

I did some research and learned of a kennel for stray dogs in Alcester, about ten miles from Stratford. I made an appointment and drove over to meet the owner. As we sat in his office and I told him what I needed, he cut me off. "You're in the wrong place," he said. "We don't have trained performing dogs here. Just ordinary rescues."

"Exactly!" I replied.

I didn't want a gorgeous, flashy, stage-ready dog, but one that in real life you wouldn't look at twice. Though it would be nice, I said, if he had a personality.

The kennel owner, though skeptical, took me on a tour of his grounds. The dogs I encountered were sweet and adorable, but none of them felt to me like Launce's friend.

"Let me put this another way," I told the kennel owner. "I'm looking for a dog that gives an impression of being independent, perhaps a loner."

At this, the man's face lit up. "Well, why didn't you say so?" he said. "Follow me."

In his own back garden, lying idly in the grass, was a medium-sized black dog with a graying muzzle. He just gave me a bored look and then went back to the bone he was chewing on. I got a tingle. This creature might be Crab—unremarkable, nondescript, just like me. His name was Blackie, which was also somehow perfect.

I told Blackie's keeper that I would need the dog to live with me from the time rehearsals began until the end of the run, a span of about five months. I also explained that I had to clear Blackie with the director and get the theater's permission to admit an old rescue dog into the company. I had brought my camera with me, so I took photos of Blackie, a process he completely ignored. No fussing, no tail-wagging . . . he was just *there*, present in the moment, a real Method dog. Rod Steiger would have loved him.

After getting the green light from Robin and the Royal Shakespeare Theatre, Blackie came to live with us in Barford a few days before we began rehearsals. He was the picture of good behavior, gentle and house-trained, and he dutifully walked into the garden when he needed to pee or poop. He loved to lounge and nap in front of our big inglenook fireplace.

On our first day of rehearsals, I left Blackie in the stage manager's office and went into the conference hall to join the entire company.

Robin welcomed us all and spoke of his plans for the production. I had arranged with Robin that when his talk was over, he would turn the floor over to me, whereupon I would introduce our production's Crab.

First came a speech. I explained that this dog's name was Crab and that he should be called nothing else (at home, Sheila and I did the same; Blackie had already become accustomed to being addressed in character). I also told my fellow actors that Crab was Launce's dog and therefore mine. Other than an occasional ear-scratch, the cast was not to interact with him—an edict with which Helen and Estelle were to struggle, not that I could blame them.

I further insisted that everyone should behave as if Crab weren't there at all. Ian Richardson, to his credit, bought into this entirely; his character didn't like Crab, and Ian pointedly scowled at the dog whenever he came near. Several times in rehearsal, and later in performance, I heard Blackie/Crab very quietly growl at Ian. The audience heard this, too, and loved it.

Finally on that first day of rehearsal, with my speech complete, I brought our newest cast member into the room. Naturally there was an instant chorus of "Awww," but I shushed everybody and sat him down alongside my chair. Blackie/Crab was a little inquisitive, looking around a bit—it was a very large room filled with lots of new faces. But before long, he grew bored, stretched out, and fell asleep. We did our first read-through and were shown set designs, including a small plunge pool downstage right, a novel touch. The costume designer asked me if I had considered dressing Crab up, and I responded, perhaps a little too hotly, "Certainly not!" In fact, I even took off his collar for every performance. He was meant to be an old street dog, with no identification.

I took Blackie/Crab for a walk around the backstage area, but I could tell that he didn't like the dark. Nevertheless, he never wore a leash at any time when he was in the theater. I wanted him to be untethered and do whatever he liked. At first he was uncomfortable when we stepped onto the stage proper, and the auditorium itself, being so vast and dark, palpably unsettled him. But he quickly got used to his surroundings. Still, I could not avoid worrying about how he might react when there were 1,200 people in the audience looking at him. I just hoped that during tech rehearsals, he would get used to strange people and noises out there.

Rehearsals went well. Blackie/Crab and I made our first entrance together, just the two of us, in Act II, Scene 3, which begins with a thirty-five-line speech from Launce, mostly complaining: "I think Crab, my dog, be the sourest-natured dog that lives: my mother weeping, my father wailing, my sister crying, our maid howling, our cat wringing her hands, and all our house in a great perplexity, yet did not this cruel-hearted cur shed one tear . . ."

As we rehearsed this scene over and over, the dog became used to the repetition. His habit was to settle down near me, put his head on his paws, and close his eyes, only occasionally having a look around, which was perfect. Then, one day during a run-through, in the middle of my speech, he looked up at me and yawned in prolonged, exaggerated fashion. The rehearsal room erupted in laughter, with Helen Mirren shouting out, "He's got your number, Pat!"

Blackie/Crab was a natural. I learned never to worry about him onstage, even when there was a full house, because he was so consistent in his performances. Well, not *entirely*. One evening, he had settled himself down near the edge of the plunge pool. Halfway through my speech, I sensed the audience's attention swinging fully away from me and toward Crab. I gave him a furtive glance and saw that he was staring fixedly at the water. In the moment, I realized that he was transfixed by the complex reflection of the stage lights on the pool's surface. He held himself utterly still, his gaze focused. It was, perhaps, the most potent acting lesson I had ever been given—the powers of concentration are critical for a stage actor, though they must be used selectively. I have locked my eyes in such fashion a few times in my stage career, and every time, I have said to myself, *Thank you, Crab.*

On the advice of the kennel owner, I always carried a few incentivizing doggy treats in my pocket. Crab knew they were there, though he never made a fuss about them. But every time we made an exit, I made sure to give him such an incentive. One night, and in one performance only, he got up and wandered off into the wings during my speech. I had prepared for this. I simply looked off into the wings and put my hand in the pocket where the treats were. Professional that he was, Crab ran right back onstage. I rewarded him with a treat on the spot and the audience rewarded him with a round of applause.

And now for my canine costar's finest hour. We were in our usual setup: Launce giving his speech, Crab sitting listlessly at his side, head nestled on forepaws. But suddenly, my costar pushed himself up into sitting position. Then he proceeded to lift one leg in the air. I noticed, in the same moment as the audience, that he had a large, pink erection between his legs.

Of course, instant uproar. For a moment or two, the loud laughter and applause distracted Crab. But only for that long. Soon enough, his attention returned to the task at hand. He bent his head, stuck out his tongue, and gave his penis a long, slow lick.

The roar returned, only this time it was much louder, and some audience members were now on their feet, applauding and cheering. The play had come to a complete standstill. I couldn't speak and there was no action I could take. I could only look at him and smile.

Luckily, Crab soon lowered his leg and his penis disappeared. To the audience, this moment must have seemed rehearsed, and I did not want to let on to them that the Method dog had audaciously engaged in improv.

Still, it took several moments before the laughter subsided enough for me to go on. Finally, I said my next line, which just happened to be "I am the dog."

This triggered another uproar. I contemplated cutting the rest of the speech, but I couldn't think of an elegant way to do that, so I went on: "No, the dog is himself, and I am the dog— Oh, the dog is me, and I am myself; ay, so, so." At every punctuation mark came a new explosion of laughter.

Me at sixteen months old—
around 1941. PHOTO COURTESY
OF THE AUTHOR

An aerial view of Mirfield, which includes Camm Lane, my brother's house, my school, and
t'bottom field. PHOTO COURTESY OF THE AUTHOR, SOURCE UNKNOWN

Theatre Royal, Bristol,
when I was a student.
ARCHITECTURAL PRESS
ARCHIVE / RIBA
COLLECTIONS

ABOVE: Trevor and me at Blackpool Pier, 1948. PHOTO COURTESY OF THE AUTHOR

LEFT: 1947—Trevor and me with Rover, and my mam in our doorway. The adjoining house is where Lizzie Dixon lived. PHOTO COURTESY OF THE AUTHOR

Circa 1946, Trevor and me in the bed that we shared for five years. PHOTO COURTESY OF THE AUTHOR

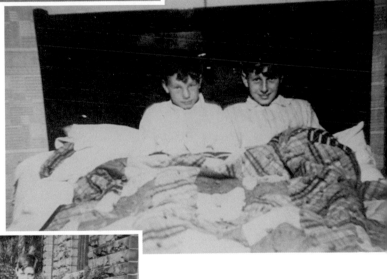

Me with a friend and Rover, outside my Auntie Annie's house. PHOTO COURTESY OF THE AUTHOR

Me at age nine with Mam and friends, Blackpool Promenade. PHOTO COURTESY OF THE AUTHOR

My form, Crowlees Boys' School, with me seated on the headmaster Mr. Haigh's right, 1951. PHOTO COURTESY OF THE AUTHOR, SOURCE UNKNOWN

Me and Denis Marshal as Mirfield parish church choirboys. PHOTO COURTESY OF THE AUTHOR

1951, Easter Parade. PHOTO COURTESY OF THE AUTHOR

Crowlees Boys' School, with me seated second from left and Fred Fisher in the black sweater, back row. PHOTO COURTESY OF THE AUTHOR, SOURCE UNKNOWN

Me with Mam and Dad, en route to Stratford-upon-Avon. PHOTO COURTESY OF THE AUTHOR

West Riding County Council drama course, 1953. Me (front left) as a harlequin. Norman Lambert is standing third from the left, and Brian Blessed is standing fourth from right; second from right is Trevor Parks. PHOTO COURTESY OF THE AUTHOR, SOURCE UNKNOWN

Trevor and Pat's wedding, 1956. My brother Geoffrey and me on the right
(please note the length of my new suit sleeves). PHOTO COURTESY OF THE
AUTHOR, SOURCE UNKNOWN

Hudson's Furniture, 1957.
You wanna buy a bar?
PHOTO COURTESY OF
THE AUTHOR

Opening season as the First Player in *Hamlet* at the Royal Shakespeare Theatre, April 28, 1966.
David Warner is down right. PHOTO BY TOM HOLTE THEATRE PHOTOGRAPHIC COLLECTION
© SHAKESPEARE BIRTHPLACE TRUST

Me playing Duc du Giret. PHOTO COURTESY OF THE AUTHOR; DILIGENT EFFORTS HAVE BEEN MADE TO LOCATE THE ORIGINAL SOURCE, WHICH REMAINS UNKNOWN

Royal Shakespeare Company—*King John*, June 1970. PHOTO BY JOHN COCKS STUDIO

Launce and Crab in *The Two Gentlemen of Verona*, 1970.

Me as Snout in Peter Brook's *A Midsummer Night's Dream*—Royal Shakespeare Company, New York, 1971. David Waller (left), Glyn Lewis (right).

Richard Johnson, me, and Janet Suzman rehearsing with Trevor Nunn.
PHOTO BY REG WILSON

The Winter's Tale, with me as King Leontes and Bernie Lloyd as Camillo.
PHOTO BY REG WILSON

LEFT: Oberon: *A Midsummer Night's Dream*, May 3, 1977. PHOTO BY JOE COCKS STUDIO COLLECTION © SHAKESPEARE BIRTHPLACE TRUST

ABOVE: *Antony and Cleopatra*, with Alan Howard as Antony and me as Enobarbus, 1978. PHOTO BY REG WILSON

RIGHT: Royal Shakespeare Company's *Titus Andronicus* with Leonie Mellinger, September 1981. PHOTO BY JOE COCKS STUDIO COLLECTION © SHAKESPEARE BIRTHPLACE TRUST

Dune—my first day. With Max von Sydow, Kyle MacLachlan, and Jürgen Prochnow, 1983.

Me as King Claudius in the 2009 film
Hamlet. ©

Even a Borg has to check the script. COURTESY OF © PARAMOUNT

A happy day on the *Enterprise*. Clockwise from left: LeVar Burton, Jonathan Frakes, Michael Dorn, Brent Spiner, Marina Sirtis, Patrick Stewart, and Gates McFadden. COURTESY OF © PARAMOUNT

ABOVE: My most favorite production photo. George in *Who's Afraid of Virginia Woolf?*, 2001. PHOTO BY © CAROL ROSEGG FOR THE GUTHRIE THEATER

RIGHT: Me as Antony in *Antony and Cleopatra*, 2006. PHOTO BY PASCAL MOLLIERE © RSC

With my children Daniel and Sophie in the Yorkshire Dales, 1985. PHOTO COURTESY OF THE AUTHOR

My favorite rehearsal photo. Director Greg Doran (back to us), to his left me, then Oliver Ford Davies, David Tennant (Hamlet), Penny Downie, Peter De Jersey, and Mariah Gale, 2008.
ELLIE KURTTZ © RSC

RIGHT: Not a party, but a rehearsal room. Return to Stratford for *Antony and Cleopatra*, 2006. ELLIE KURTTZ © RSC

Royal Shakespeare Company—as Claudius in *Hamlet,* with Penny Downie as Gertrude, August 2008. ELLIE KURTTZ © RSC

Royal Shakespeare Company—Shylock, *The Merchant of Venice*, May 2011. ELLIE KURTTZ © RSC

My treasured Jaguar XJS 12. I still have it. PHOTO COURTESY OF THE AUTHOR

The ball pit wedding photo that went viral, 2013. PHOTO COURTESY OF THE AUTHOR

LEFT: X-Men! Long-lost brothers: me and Sir Ian McKellen. PHOTO COURTESY OF THE AUTHOR

ABOVE: The famous "first slice" pizza photo, 2013. PHOTO COURTESY OF THE AUTHOR

Public push-ups while being immortalized in front of TCL Chinese Theatre, Los Angeles, 2020. PHOTO COURTESY OF THE AUTHOR

Sunny and me in Florence, December 2019. Could life be any better?
PHOTO COURTESY OF THE AUTHOR

RIGHT: Me and Ian promoting *Waiting for Godot* in New York's Coney Island, 2013. PHOTO COURTESY OF THE AUTHOR

LEFT: My infamous Halloween costume seen 'round the world, 2013. PHOTO COURTESY OF THE AUTHOR

Shakespearean actors often lament that we can do nothing new; everything that can be done has been done over the last four-hundred-odd years. But I think this qualifies as an incident where that philosophy didn't apply. And it was also the second time I ever gave Crab a treat onstage. That evening at the Dirty Duck, I didn't have to buy one drink.

I loved that dog. He always joined me for curtain call, as ever without a leash. After our final such call, as Crab reverted to being Blackie once more, the company gathered around him, gave him pets and hugs, and bade him goodbye. The next day, I drove Blackie back to his home in Alcester. Sheila, Daniel, and I missed him very much. I shall never forget him, and it pleases me that Blackie will live on forever in the annals of the Royal Shakespeare Company.

Chapter Twelve

For all that life had offered me to this point, I had somehow still never made it to New York, let alone acted on one of its world-famous stages. Fortunately, that was about to change, and the person who set my path to Broadway in motion was, of all people, Peter Brook, the director who had spurned me in the Royal Shakespeare Company.

I was reluctant to say so aloud, but when I saw his version of *A Midsummer Night's Dream*, I was astonished by it. Our production of *The Two Gentlemen of Verona* was well received, but (Blackie's revolutionary performance notwithstanding) it was completely overshadowed by Peter's show. For starters, his production of *Dream* was ultramodern and strikingly minimalist in its design. The set was a stark white box, the floor covering included, with no furniture at all except for that in Titania's bower, a nest of red fluff that could be lowered and raised from above, and at one point with Titania and Bottom on board.

The roles of Theseus and Oberon were doubled, with Alan Howard playing both, and the same went for Titania and Hippolyta, played by Sara Kestelman. The female lovers wore flowing white gowns and the male lovers white pants paired with brightly colored shirts. Did I mention the trapezes? Yes, from time to time, Peter had some of the actors harnessed and hanging from the rafters, performing acrobatics and swinging back and forth, and even forward over the audience. It was almost psychedelically whimsical yet also quite physical, demanding an uncommon athleticism of the cast.

I can't remember a hotter ticket at the RSC than Brook's *Dream* in the autumn of 1970. When word got out of what he was up to, every performance sold out. So it wasn't a surprise when it was announced that the show was going to Broadway after its Stratford season was over. Soon thereafter, I heard rumors that some cast changes were in the offing, that Norman Rodway had not enjoyed playing Tom Snout the Tinker and was likely to leave. But I did not expect to receive a call to meet with Peter Brook about replacing him in the New York production, which was to open in January 1971.

Snout is one of the smallest speaking roles in the play. He is one of the show's six "mechanicals," the generally rather dim and incompetent amateur Athenian actors who perform in *Dream*'s play-within-the-play, *Pyramus and Thisbe*.

I can't say that there was anything about the part that turned me on. I was also offered the position of understudy to Alan Howard for the Theseus and Oberon parts. Alan was a sturdy pro who was unlikely to miss a performance, especially in a limited run, so that wasn't a huge lure. But let's face it: The prospect of working with Peter Brook and going to Broadway in such an extraordinary, high-profile production was all the motive I needed. So, of course I gave Peter a firm yes on Tom Snout.

Sheila was more than supportive of my choice—she was excited because, while she would just be along for the trip rather than working in New York, she was thrilled to be able to attend multiple Broadway shows and see what was going on in American dance. Daniel was not yet in school, so we brought him along and set up house temporarily in a nice apartment building on West 72nd Street near Central Park.

We were to spend eight weeks on Broadway at the Billy Rose Theatre, now known as the Nederlander, followed by three weeks at the Brooklyn Academy of Music. This order seemed the wrong way around, but Peter was keen for our Broadway production to be followed by a gritty immersion in the "real world" of downtown Brooklyn.

The rehearsal time was tight; basically, I was stepping straight into Norman's shoes. But Peter let me know that I could experiment with Snout as I pleased. That was all the encouragement I needed. I decided to play him with a heavy Yorkshire accent, hoping an American audience would somehow grasp the humor in it.

There was one line where that strategy worked perfectly. The mechanicals are discussing how they will stage their play. In this play, the title characters, forbidden lovers, are meant to speak through a "crannied hole" in the wall that separates their two houses. But how to execute the logistics of presenting such a wall onstage? This quandary is raised, which was my cue. I chose to remain silent for a long moment before offering my wisdom: "You can niver bring in a wall." Even in Brooklyn, *especially* there, it got a big laugh.

The mechanicals resolve the issue by having Snout himself play the wall. He enters and says:

> In this same interlude it doth befall
> That I, one Snout by name, present a wall.
> And such a wall, as I would have you think,
> That had in it a crannied hole or chink,
> Through which the lovers, Pyramus and Thisbe,
> Did whisper often very secretly . . .

The traditional approach in any given performance of *A Midsummer Night's Dream* is for Snout to hold up a finger of each hand to create the "crannied hole" through which the lovers speak. But I had what I thought was a better idea, based on how Snout seems to be saying that he is using props: "This loan, this roughcast and this stone, doth show I am that same wall; the truth is so."

I had found some old bricks at the back of the theater, where construction had been going on. What if I held a brick in each hand, placed one atop the other, and then theatrically cracked them open to create the "crannied hole," with Snout clearly believing that his idea is a stroke of genius?

The next rehearsal was a stagger-through of the play, so nobody knew what I was about to do. Bricks at the ready, I did my thing. It worked—even Peter laughed, which was rare.

Two days later, with the clock ticking toward opening night, we did a full run-through. When I came to Snout's speech, I did the bricks business again. At once Peter called out "Stop!" and said, "Patrick, why are you doing that?"

"Well, because I thought you had liked it," I said.

"That was two days ago," he shot back. "Do something different." This, in front of a full rehearsal room.

I don't mean to make Peter sound like a rude, insensitive bugger, though I was wounded in the moment. He didn't want me to commit to that bit just yet. Peter encouraged exploration that never ceased. So, I heeded his request and put the bricks down.

When we were in previews, just days away from our January 21 opening, I happened to be walking from the subway to the theater one afternoon when, crossing Times Square, I ran right into Peter. He asked me how I was doing in the show. I said, "Fine . . . just a couple of things." He stopped dead in the middle of the street, took my arm, faced me, and said, "Tell me." As I started to speak, I realized that the traffic was moving again, with cars swishing past us and angry cabbies honking. I spluttered out whatever concerns I had while piloting Peter and myself to the safety of the sidewalk. At the theater, we parted, with Peter heading for the front of the house and me for the stage door. Right before I entered, I heard Peter call out my name. "Patrick! Do you remember the business you did with the bricks? Put it back. I like it!"

So back in went my brick shtick. It was a reliable audience-pleaser in what Clive Barnes, the *New York Times*'s veteran theater critic, called in his review of our opening-night performance, "Without any equivocation whatsoever, the greatest production of Shakespeare I have ever seen in my life." The tickets flew out the door, and there were lines at the box office after every performance of audience members eager to return.

One slightly odd development was that two young women conspired to sit in the same front-row seats at almost every show. It was flattering to a degree, but these ladies became a problem, because after a time they laughed at our jokes before the punch lines arrived, spoiling the fun for everyone else. We asked the front-of-house manager to have a gentle word with them. He did, and they obliged his request to pipe down, but we noticed them tying themselves in knots to contain themselves.

Such was our show's popularity that even we, its participants, started gawking. At the beginning and the end of the play, those of us who were not onstage or involved in the action were able to sit or stand on the balcony running along the top of the set. We covertly spied on the audience to see which celebrities were present. When we spotted one, we passed along our intel through whispers: "Third row, five seats from the left aisle—Robert Redford"; "Second row, on the left aisle, Lauren Bacall." At the end of each show, we made a point of leaving our dressing-room doors open so that in the event one of these stars decided to pay a visit, we would get to catch a glimpse of them passing by.

One night, I heard voices outside my dressing room and quickly scuttled to the doorway to see who was there. Standing before me were Paul Newman and Joanne Woodward. Mr. Newman explained they were looking for Alan Howard's dressing room, but had gotten lost. Of course they were looking for Alan—he was the star of the show—but I was privileged to be the actor who gave them proper directions. Once I'd done so, Paul and Joanne both shook my hand and said, "Congratulations." *Now that*, I thought, *was cool*.

This might be the time to mention that during our wildly popular Broadway run, Snout the Tinker acquired his very own fan club.

I learned this from a young woman who was hanging out by the stage door one night. She told me that "You can niver bring in a wall" had become a catchphrase among in-the-know New Yorkers for describing something that was hard to do. Needless to say, I was both taken aback and absolutely delighted.

As scheduled, the show eventually moved to the Brooklyn Academy of Music. Here the auditorium was vast and the lighting different, making our star-spotting pastime significantly more challenging. Nevertheless, the audience reaction was, if anything, even more ecstatic, with curtain calls that went on and on. That alone was a thrill, but what made our experience so especially enjoyable was that our cast was populated entirely by great people: Alan and Sara, along with Ben Kingsley, Frankie de la Tour, Barry Stanton, Terry Taplin, Philip Locke, John Kane, and David Waller. An unforgettable era in my life.

So began a love affair with New York City that continues to this day. On our first day of rehearsal at the Billy Rose Theatre at the top of 1971, I arrived early and noticed a deli on the corner of 7th Avenue and 41st Street. I walked in to find it extremely busy, which I didn't mind, because it gave me time to consider the extensive sandwich menu on the wall behind the counter, which contained some words I didn't understand.

The place had a raucous atmosphere, with the men behind the counter—and they were all men—shouting out orders to the guys farther down who were actually making the sandwiches. Suddenly, I heard a voice cry "Next!" and I realized that a server was looking me in the eye, impatiently waiting for me to speak. I somewhat hesitatingly said, in the manner of an overwhelmed Englishman: "Oh! Er . . . yes, good morning. I'd like, um, yes, a . . . a corned beef sandwich on rye bread, please, thank you. And, erm, could you put some . . . erm, salad on it, and, erm, I'd like to take it with me. If that's all right."

The counterman looked at me as if in total incomprehension. Then, quite deadpan, he yelled at the workers in the back, "Two corny cows coming through the rye drag it in the jungle to go." Ah, New York!

Chapter Thirteen

As the cliché goes, there are no small roles, only small actors. A part of me bristled at being cast as Launce in *The Two Gentlemen of Verona* and Snout in *A Midsummer Night's Dream*, but my resourcefulness, along with the sheer joy I took in working with my peers, made these experiences worthwhile. But that doesn't mean I was willing to settle for being a reliable supporting player in the Royal Shakespeare Company for the rest of my life.

While I diligently prepared to go on in the event of Alan Howard's absence during *Dream's* run in New York, I never anticipated actually doing so, for Alan was tough and lived to act. I admired him deeply. He was always on top of what he was doing—understanding the role, embracing it, investigating it. But he also had a bit of a temper. I saw him lose it once or twice. If he was absorbed in the work and believed someone else onstage was not as committed, he could turn rather nasty. Back when Ben Kingsley and I were with him in *Much Ado*, having loads of spontaneous fun as a comic team, he was one of those who protested that Ben and I should stick to what we had rehearsed. Nevertheless, I highly respected Alan.

As I had anticipated, he never missed a performance during the Broadway/BAM run. But when we brought the white-box production back to London for a stretch in the Aldwych, I learned that Alan suffered from diabetes, symptoms of which could flare up at any time. One night he gave a performance in which he seemed uncharacteristically tentative. The next evening I was in the dressing room that I shared with Ben and Barry Stanton when our stage manager knocked on the door and announced that Alan had not yet signed in. It was ten minutes after the "half," meaning twenty minutes to curtain, but I had little doubt that Alan would arrive, late for some reason and grumpy about it. But then the "quarter" came and there was still no Alan, and by the time the "five" was called, the stage manager told me to start changing into Alan's costume.

He wore an ankle-length purple garment and white slippers—that was all. I went to Alan's dressing room and quickly began to get ready, but I felt that I should wait before putting on his gown, a garment that for nearly a year had only been associated—rapturously, I might add—with him. Being in his dressing room made me uncomfortable, but I took deep breaths and warmed up my voice, practicing his opening lines: "Now, fair Hippolyta, our nuptial hour draws on apace."

Suddenly, the door burst open and the stage manager said, his voice trembling, "Patrick, Alan isn't here. You're on." So on went the gown, with no time for makeup.

At the top of the show, as conceived by Peter, the entire company burst through the two doors on either side of the stage, with Oberon the first through the one at stage right. As I waited to enter, I stood surrounded by the company, hands touching my shoulders, squeezing my arms, Sara Kestelman kissing my cheek: all very reassuring. Then the audience quieted because the house manager had walked onstage. We heard him say, "Due to a sudden indisposition of Alan Howard, in tonight's performance the part of Oberon will be played by Patrick Stewart."

I knew exactly what was going to happen next. There was a groan from the audience and then a burst of aggravated chatter. Alan was very popular—who was this charlatan daring to take his place?

The house lights went down. I pushed the door open and strode on. The audience applauded as it always did. It took a moment or two for the entire cast to get to their positions. Then I said the first line, and away we went.

We got to the intermission and all was well. I drank a cup of coffee (probably not a good idea) and did some breathing exercises in my dressing room while my castmates kept putting their heads around the door to assure me I was doing a good job. Then the stage manager appeared and said, "Patrick, I have had a talk with the tech people, and we all feel your flying in the second half should be cut. It is way too dangerous."

But buoyed by how smoothly the first half had gone, I said, "No, no, I have done it right once and I can do it again. I'll be fine."

The stage manager shook his head and said, "No, it's too risky." I persuaded him that I would be fine—and the daft bugger agreed and let me do the full menu of acrobatics! I felt some moments of abject fear during that second act, but miraculously did not injure myself or sully the show. Before I knew it, I was standing in the wings with my peers, all of us waiting to go on and play the final scene.

Ben Kingsley gave me a hug and asked me how I was feeling. "Great," I said, "but I have so many little interjections in the play scene, and I'm not sure where they all come."

"Hang on just a minute," Ben said, and he hurried away. He returned a moment later with a book under his arm, just as I was making my entrance. In the final scene, we all sat on the floor and while Philostrate, the master of the revels, gave his long speech, Ben came beside me and slipped a script behind my thigh, where it couldn't be seen by the audience. What a thing for a fellow actor to do! Thank you, Sir Ben, for making my debut as Oberon finish up so well.

The next morning, I got a call from Alan, who thanked me and apologized, explaining that he had taken some medication that knocked him out, making him unaware of the time until it was too late. "Anyway, I'll be okay for tonight," he told me.

"Great, Alan, that's good," I said. But what I was actually thinking was, *Have yourself another long nap if you like, Alan. I want to do that AGAIN.*

I did get another opportunity to sub for Alan as Oberon eighteen months later, when yet another version of Peter Brook's *Dream* played in Liverpool and both Alan and his understudy were indisposed. I was busy doing the RSC's 1972 "Roman season" in Stratford—with roles in *Julius Caesar, Antony and Cleopatra,* and *Coriolanus*—but jumped at the chance.

Unfortunately, the Liverpool company was by and large completely new, and the dedication of the New York and Aldwych gang just wasn't there. Because the principal and the understudy were absent, the cast expected the show to be canceled. But that was not how the RSC worked. It was a Shakespeare labor force in those days, so I was duly plucked out of Rome (Stratford-upon-Avon) and dropped into Athens (Liverpool). Some of the cast were so irritated by this that, as a protest, they did not attend the afternoon rehearsal of my scenes. In fact, I met a couple of castmates for the first time that night onstage, in front of the audience. I wound up doing four consecutive performances in Liverpool as Oberon. Meanwhile, my own understudy in Stratford was pleased to go on in my stead.

I did at last get to play Oberon from the inception of a Royal Shakespeare Company production in 1977, when John Barton and Gillian Lynne, my wife Sheila's mentor, together directed their own version of *A Midsummer Night's Dream,* with Marjorie Bland opposite me as Titania.

For this production, I was given gloriously long tresses of the kind Daniel Day-Lewis later had in *The Last of the Mohicans,* only his hair was real. My costume (such as it was) consisted of a very abbreviated loincloth. A photograph of me in this production has circulated widely on the internet, which I will magnanimously accept as a compliment, though my *Star Trek* colleague Jonathan Frakes never misses an opportunity to mock me for my turn as the "famous nude Oberon."

Nudity figured into my 1972 Roman season, too. In *Coriolanus*, I was cast as Tullus Aufidius, the titular general's nemesis-turned-ally-turned-killer. The battle scenes found me and my army of Volscians wearing very brief skirts of a length you might associate with NFL cheerleaders. There is also a scene in which Coriolanus shows up unexpectedly at Aufidius's home. Reviewing the script, I picked up on an erotic charge to their interactions. I asked our costume designer if I could wear nothing but jewelry and a skirt—ankle-length but diaphanous, of the lightest silk. This outfit produced the desired result: Circling my frenemy Coriolanus, played by Ian Hogg, I was no longer a warrior but a feminine, graceful, and, quite possibly, horny Aufidius. Finding this double life in the role became the most interesting part of playing the character, and I am grateful to Trevor Nunn for letting me go there.

I was a committed young actor and in good shape as well, so I never balked when a director chose to explore nudity or near nudity with me. In a 1968 production of *Troilus and Cressida*, those of us who played Trojans wore skimpy outfits very much like the Volscians' battle gear. And when we were first working out my interpretation of Launce in *The Two Gentlemen of Verona*, Robin Phillips proposed that I try performing a scene—one in which Crab and I were alone onstage—while completely naked.

I admit that I was startled by this idea. But in rehearsals, I went for it. Robin cleared the auditorium of everyone but stage management. Off came my black T-shirt and black jeans and, finally, my underpants. Whoo, drafty in this theater, isn't it?

Being naked onstage was not as unnerving as I had expected it to be. Indeed, there was an element of liberty in how I felt and how I delivered my lines. Crab, also naked, though it was nothing new for him, did the scene with me, and we walked off with confidence. But when Robin called me back onstage, using my real name, my feelings changed.

As Launce, in the world of the play, I had felt safe. But now Patrick was onstage, and Patrick felt way too self-conscious to be stark naked in front of an audience. I could no longer give myself over to the work in these circumstances.

I told Robin this. He said he understood and that I looked great, but that we would not further pursue this idea. I got dressed and said farewell to full-frontal nudity.

During the Roman season of 1972, I was cast as Cassius in *Julius Caesar*, the one who enlists Brutus in his conspiracy to kill Caesar. Mark Dignam was a wonderful Caesar, but the performance that thrilled audiences was that of the intense, long-faced John Wood as Brutus.

I had seen John's work before and admired it very much, but I firmly believed that we had been cast the wrong way round. Cassius is volatile bordering on scary, yet painstakingly articulate—John exactly. Brutus is more cautious, thoughtful, and self-aware—a better fit for me. In rehearsals, I just didn't feel comfortable. John was playing Brutus as if the character had a Cassius-like personality. I felt I had nowhere to go. I spoke privately to Trevor, but he assured me that there was nothing wrong and he loved what we were doing.

But by previews, I felt even worse. Someone had warned me about John before we began rehearsals, saying, "Watch him or you're in trouble." I took this to mean watch *out* for him—John was also known as a slippery character—but this caution was meant literally. John liked everyone onstage to literally watch him act. Sure enough, after a few performances, he complained to Trevor that when he was speaking, the rest of us were not paying his Brutus enough attention. If we weren't all fixated on Brutus, what he was saying didn't count, or so John thought.

I might have received this critique more sympathetically were it not for one thing: John was notorious for not giving other actors so much as a glance when *they* were onstage with him.

This was true even in my big head-to-head scenes with him. I would start talking, and John would look down at his feet, or out to

the audience, or up at the ceiling. Hardly ever at me. The most infuri-
ating thing he did came when I finished a speech. Often, he would
remain perfectly still, and I could swear he tuned out of the play
entirely. Then, as if startled, he would look at me, shake his head,
and finally speak his lines and kick the play back into gear.

In other instances, he glanced at me as I was arriving at my final
line, smiled, and did his dismissive head-shake. Most humiliating of
all, he sometimes started his speeches before I had finished mine, as
if to say, *Yes, yes, yes, we've heard all this before. BORING! Now let's
hear the real actor speak.*

These incidents occurred with increasing frequency until one
night, I lost it. It started during the scene in Brutus's tent, where he
and Cassius have a terrible quarrel and then try to make up. It was art
imitating life imitating art—me trying to make nice with this man
who was continuously ill-tempered and ill-mannered toward me:

CASSIUS
Hath Cassius lived
To be but mirth and laughter to his Brutus,
When grief, and blood ill-temper'd, vexeth him?

BRUTUS
When I spoke that, I was ill-temper'd too.

CASSIUS
Do you confess so much? Give me your hand.

BRUTUS
And my heart too.

John could not have said that last line more insincerely and indif-
ferently. Yet onward we went.

CASSIUS
O Brutus!

BRUTUS
What's the matter?

CASSIUS
Have not you love enough to bear with me,
When that rash humour which my mother gave me
Makes me forgetful?

BRUTUS
Yes, Cassius; and, from henceforth,
When you are over-earnest with your Brutus,
He'll think your mother chides, and leave you so.

John's delivery dripped with sarcasm, which, to me, undercut the
scene. I continued, with my Cassius offering loving, tender conces-
sions to his friend, in diametric opposition to how I was feeling.

CASSIUS
O my dear brother!
This was an ill beginning of the night:
Never come such division 'tween our souls!
Let it not, Brutus.

BRUTUS
Every thing is well.

CASSIUS
Good night, my lord.

BRUTUS
Good night, good brother.

I could barely get out those last lines, I was so angry at John. I had
tears in my eyes during the curtain call and stalked back to my dressing room as soon as I could. I was in no mood to speak to anyone.

But there was a knock on my door. "Come in," I said irritably.

In walked John, who closed the door behind him. He asked me what was wrong. Oh, was I ready to show him! In a fit of pique, I grabbed him by the throat with both hands and began slamming his head against the door, snarling, "You selfish fucker!" I felt positively murderous, and I'm glad that John spoke up before I smacked him around any further. But precisely what he said, I couldn't quite make out over my blind rage.

It took me a moment to compute what he had said to me: "I have cancer."

I let go of him at once.

"Wait . . . *What?*" I said.

"Cancer," John repeated. "And it's bad."

I felt absolutely horrible; the anger drained from me at once. I put my arms around John, held him tight, and profusely apologized. He thanked me and soon left.

I had a dreadful, sleepless night, full of utter sadness for John and relentless remorse over my behavior. Where had this burst of violence come from? I raised but quickly dismissed the notion that it was my father coming out in me: My dad's violence always came on when he was drunk, but I had not been drinking. Was it envy deep down of John's unmistakable brilliance? Was it because John got leading-man parts and I didn't? Was it an immature inability to accept that he had his methods and that I should have been more tolerant of them?

In any event, I vowed never again to let violence take hold of me—a vow I have upheld.

The next morning, as I approached the stage door, I saw John walking toward me. When we drew close, I put a hand on his shoulder, repeated my apology, and asked him if he was all right, in light of his health issues.

"All right?" he said with condescension. "I'm fine. There's nothing wrong with me."

He turned away and went into the theater. Was he serious?! The lying, manipulative bastard!

Furious once again, I made an appointment to see Trevor later that day. When we met, I told him what had gone down between John and me and that I wanted out of *Julius Caesar*. But almost like John in the play, Trevor shook his head and interrupted me.

"I know this isn't easy for you, Pat," he said, "but what you and John are doing up there is brilliant. The dynamic between you is fantastic. That scene *works*."

And in hindsight, I guess it really did. We persevered through the Stratford season and a later run in London, where John's performance won raves and mine got notices that were . . . okay. It was our audiences who told me all I needed to know. Nevertheless, our scenes as Brutus and Cassius often received a round of applause at their conclusion—a rare thing in British theater, especially in a tragedy.

In the years to come, John and I did two more plays together, as well as a movie, Trevor Nunn's 1986 film *Lady Jane*, starring a twenty-year-old Helena Bonham Carter. John died in 2011 at the age of eighty-one . . . not of early-onset cancer, and not, thankfully, at my hands, either.

Was I destined to remain forever a supporting player at the Royal Shakespeare Company, never the actor who snags the title role?

I did finally get cast as King John in Shakespeare's play of that name, but with a couple of asterisks. One, that *King John* is not one of the Bard's more beloved or produced works. And two, ours was a sort of fringe production, squeezed into the RSC calendar and produced on a shoestring budget. We were only given the main stage for midweek matinees, so our performances were few and the audiences were modest in size, consisting mostly of school groups.

But these indignities were mitigated by the opportunity to work with the director: a tenacious young woman with the unlikely name Buzz Goodbody. I was in awe of her. She'd gotten her foot in the door as John Barton's assistant, and when her brilliance became too obvious for John and Trevor to ignore, she was given *King John* to direct.

Mary Ann was her given name, but as a child, her energetic curiosity won her the nickname Buzz. She and I became fast friends, and it was my privilege to lead the company of the first RSC production overseen by a female director. Buzz was an ardent feminist and radical Marxist who was keen to tear down the absurd perception that Shakespeare and the theater in general were elitist indulgences. In her view, *King John* was a parable about the futility of war as it had been waged for centuries by headstrong, misguided men. Buzz also worked with Trevor as a sort of assistant director on *Coriolanus*, with the Volscian scenes as part of her remit, so we got to work together closely on that project as well.

A visionary as well as a director, Buzz convinced Trevor Nunn to create a new space at the RSC for a small experimental theater. She wanted to call it "the Other Place." The productions would be spartan compared to the lavish main-stage affairs, but the trade-off was that the tickets would be way more affordable. The Other Place found its home in a repurposed storage hut made of corrugated tin. On warm days, it was hotter than Hades inside, but it was her vision made manifest: Shakespeare and experimental plays at a discount price, with tickets costing a measly seventy pence, or less than a US dollar.

One night, Buzz took me out for a drink and told me she'd been given a new assignment to create a London version of the Other Place. The RSC was leasing a dance studio on Euston Road, and she had found a marvelous play with which she wanted to open this new space, which was to be called simply the Place. The play, *Occupations*, by Trevor Griffiths, was about the relationship between Sardinian Communist activist Antonio Gramsci and Bulgarian Communist activist Christo Kabak. Buzz asked Ben Kingsley to play Gramsci, the softer character, and me to play Kabak, the more militant one, with Estelle Kohler playing Kabak's mistress, a Russian aristocrat who lies dying in bed throughout the play. I know this all sounds like

self-serious agitprop theater, but Buzz made it exciting and fun—
her enthusiasm was infectious, and she knew what she was doing.

Working with Buzz and Ben was so freeing and loose, and there
was a part of me that never wanted rehearsals to end because the exploration was so joyful. *Occupations* was but a blip on the radar of
British theater, but those who saw the play enjoyed it.

In 1975, Buzz gave Ben his first big starring role, in her modern-
dress version of *Hamlet* at the Other Place in Stratford. Alas, she
would not live to see her and Ben's great reviews.

When I got the news, I was back in LA, this time on a US tour of
the RSC's production of *Hedda Gabler*, with Glenda Jackson. Sheila
and little Daniel had joined me, and we were splashing around in our
hotel's pool when the front desk notified me that I had an urgent
phone call. It was from Trevor Nunn, who was also in LA. He told
me to meet him at the theater, and when I got there, he was standing
in the frame of the stage door, clearly distressed. He immediately
wrapped me tight in his arms and tears poured out of his eyes.

"Buzz is dead," he said. "She died in the night."

She had overdosed on sleeping pills. Gone at only twenty-eight
years old. Neither Trevor, Ben, nor I had any idea that anything was
wrong in her world. I was devastated. Buzz was destined to be as big
a star as Peter Brook or Peter Hall, and I had anticipated working
with her for decades to come. She remains a strong presence within
me. "Buzz" is a much-used word these days, and whenever I hear it, I
see her face.

In 1976, the Royal Shakespeare Company chose to end its season
with something different: Eugene O'Neill's *The Iceman Cometh*. The
play is set in a New York flophouse and bar, situated in my mind on
the Lower East Side of Manhattan at its pre-gentrification dirtiest, a
world away from Shakespeare's royal courts and Roman battlefields.
There is a large cast of nineteen characters: twelve dead-end drunks,

three prostitutes, two barkeeps, and two cops. I got to play Larry Slade, an anarchist described by one of his fellow alcoholics as "the old foolosopher."

The Iceman Cometh is a challenge no matter how you look at it, in that it's emotionally harrowing and runs for over four hours. But going in, it was entirely worth it to me, for the lead role of Hickey, the charismatic traveling salesman to whom all the others look up, was to be played by Ian Holm, the actor I revered more than any other.

Only three of us in the cast—Norman Rodway, Patrick Godfrey, and me—never left the stage for the play's entire length. This meant that we three were the only ones to witness the additional drama that unfurled during the tech rehearsals and previews.

At the start of rehearsals in London, Ian proved to be as awesome in reality as he'd been in my memory. He was already "off-book" (no need for a script) for most of the first act, and within days, he was the first of the company to know his role entirely, which was nothing short of astonishing. As the days passed, he lost himself further and further into Hickey; another actor told me that Ian walked to and from Covent Garden every day from his flat in Fulham, which took over an hour each way, and recited his lines as he traveled.

By the time we reached the day of the play's first complete run-through, all four-hours-plus of it, the difference between Ian and the rest of us that Friday was more evident than ever. He was acting in a separate solar system from the one we inhabited. His performance that afternoon was as extraordinary as anything I had ever witnessed by an actor. We all went home that weekend brimming with excitement over what was to come.

Except it didn't. That rehearsal turned out to be his peak. What followed the next week was his unraveling. With each passing day, Ian faltered, becoming increasingly insecure about blocking, timing, and even the lines he had so impressively committed to memory ahead of the rest of us. He required prompt after prompt to find his way through the material, and the distress this caused him was changing his features, dimming his bright eyes. He was also becoming less socially interactive with us, solitary and noncommunicative.

Our director, the gifted Howard Davies, confided in me that he'd had a private talk with Ian, but little had come of it. Howard simply didn't know what to do. The dreaded word "breakdown" entered our conversation, though we wished with all our hearts that it hadn't.

Ian seemed to recover a bit during tech rehearsals. The broken, fragmented nature of those days, with frequent stops by Howard to discuss lighting and sound cues with the crew, created moments that allowed Ian to collect himself. But when we arrived at the first dress rehearsal, Ian's performance was the worst yet. Over and over, he asked for prompts, and an actor who had gone out front to watch part of the performance said that sometimes, Ian was so quiet that he couldn't be heard from the seats.

There was then talk of pushing back opening night and giving Ian a few days off. But ultimately, Howard decided to carry on with the first preview in the hope that the presence of a full house would focus Ian.

The house was indeed packed and we got off to a terrific start. But Hickey, Ian's character, doesn't enter until about fifty minutes into the first act. When the moment arrived, the entire cast except for Ian filled the play's bar, all looking upstage. The swing doors pushed open and there he stood, on the little platform in front of the door. He received an entrance round of applause from the audience, just what he needed. As the adulation enveloped him, Ian took a couple of deep breaths and his whole body seemed to have a light emanating from it.

But when the time came for Ian to speak, he simply didn't. He took a few steps and paused at center stage, only a few feet from where I was perched at the bar. Awkward silence. Norman Rodway, bless his heart, was playing Harry, the head bartender, and he was ready for this scenario. He began to ad-lib dialogue, shaking Hickey's hand and giving him a hug. A few other actors clapped, which was appropriate to the world of the play, as everyone in the bar looked up to Hickey and had eagerly anticipated his arrival.

Finally, Ian began to speak his lines. But just as abruptly, he stopped. He took another deep breath and exhaled. Then I heard him say, very, very softly, "It's no good, it's no good."

Somehow, with everyone else contributing a great deal of improvisation, we straggled through the last page of the act. The curtain came down. Ian hadn't moved from the spot where he'd stood for the applause.

Norman Rodway took Ian by the arm and led him to his dressing room, which was adjacent to mine. I heard the director David Jones, who was in charge of the RSC's London shows that season, go into Ian's room and offer gentle encouragement. "Everything is going to be all right," he told Ian.

What I didn't know at the time was that the production was already prepared for this eventuality. Ian's understudy, Alan Tilvern, who played another of the bar's regulars, the disgraced ex-cop Pat McGloin, had been alerted some days earlier that if Ian broke down onstage, there would be a break, whereupon David Jones would go out front to notify the audience that the play would continue without Ian. And this was exactly what happened.

Alan did an amazing job given the circumstances, and another actor, Raymond Marlowe, effortlessly stepped in as McGloin. I have never known a time when an audience didn't rise to the cause of an actor going on at short notice, and Alan received a great ovation at the end, as well as the thanks and praise of the cast. But it was all so desperately sad. Later that night, when I was having a drink—or two—with David Jones, he told me that when he went into Ian's dressing room, he found our star, my idol, lying on the floor, curled up in a fetal ball.

Ian did not go back onstage for years. Fortunately, he found an outlet for his talents in film, whose stop-start pace better suited him psychologically. In fact, he received the greatest acclaim of his career to date in Ridley Scott's landmark 1979 film *Alien*, in which he portrayed Ash, the spaceship *Nostromo*'s science officer. Ian then moved from strength to strength in the movies, appearing in the Oscar-winning *Chariots of Fire* (a Best Supporting Actor–nominated role), *Brazil*, *The Fifth Element*, *A Life Less Ordinary*, and, finally, winning international adoration as Bilbo Baggins in Peter Jackson's *The Lord of the Rings* and *The Hobbit* films.

And he finally conquered the demons that kept him from the stage, playing King Lear in 1998 at the National Theatre in a sort of late-stage victory lap. He won the Laurence Olivier Award for this iconic role and was knighted that same year.

Postscript: In 2003, I played Halvard Solness in a West End production of Henrik Ibsen's *The Master Builder*. For the final rehearsal-room run-through, director Anthony Page invited some guests to watch us. I noticed among them a small elderly man with a white beard. When the run-through ended, all of us, guests included, repaired to the theater's canteen for a cup of tea. The old man ambled over to me.

"This is brilliant," he said, "and you are so powerful and complex, and . . ."

And that was all I heard of what he said. Because at that point, I realized who he was: Sir Ian Holm.

Chapter Fourteen

For all the ups and downs I'd experienced and witnessed in the theater, the stage was really the only place I ever wanted to be. I had no designs on film or TV stardom and never demanded of my agent that he hustle me off to auditions and screen tests.

Yet in the mid-1970s, through no action of my own, some screen work started coming my way. In '75, Rodney Bennett, a well-known British TV director, told me that he admired my work with the Royal Shakespeare Company and offered me the male romantic lead in a TV miniseries called *North and South,* based on a Victorian novel by Elizabeth Gaskell that explored class and regional tensions in England. It just so happened that I had read another of Gaskell's novels the previous year and liked it a lot, so I was glad to jump in. I was a known Yorkshireman in British acting circles, so naturally my character was a Northerner, the owner of a mill.

More significant was my first movie. It was a thriller I have noted earlier called *Hennessy,* starring Rod Steiger, the very actor whose film *On the Waterfront,* in which he costarred with Marlon Brando and Eva Marie Saint, had transfixed me and awakened me to the infinite possibilities of acting when I was a boy in Mirfield.

Rod, in the title role, was playing an Irishman whose wife had been killed by a British soldier, turning him into a militant bent on blowing up the Houses of Parliament. My part was not big, offering only one and a half days of work, and the script was not particularly good. But every moment I had in the film, in which I played an IRA man trying to prevent Hennessy from going rogue and ruining the organization's more carefully laid plans, was with the great man himself. And the script called for me to shoot a scene with Rod in the back of a car, just as Rod had done with Brando. I mean, what choice did I have?

The first of my days began with us rehearsing logistics—setting up the shot of me bundling Rod into the car, all rather complicated. But a half hour before our lunch break, we had the scene shot, including all of Rod's coverage, the footage taken from various angles to ensure the director had choices later in the editing room. But I still had my own coverage to shoot. The assistant director said, "Okay, Rod, that's you done. Why don't you go to lunch now and we will pick up with you after?"

There was a moment of silence followed by Rod saying, very quietly, "What about Patrick?"

The assistant director said, "Oh, we'll have someone read in for you."

From my left, where Rod was sitting, I suddenly felt a wave of . . . I don't know, *something* building up.

Rod said, still very softly, "What the fuck do you think I am? You fucking asshole. You think I'm gonna walk out on him and go to lunch?" Suddenly, his voice was no longer soft. "You fucker, you piece of shit! We'll shoot Patrick's coverage *right now*."

I said, "It's okay, Mr. Steiger, that's fine. I—I don't—"

"No!" he shouted, cutting me off. "It's not fucking fine, not on my fucking movie! And my name is *Rod*, not Mr. Steiger! Set it up!"

And so we shot my coverage, with Rod off camera but looking me right in the eye. It felt good, working this way. Not to mention to have the star, someone who I greatly admired, advocating for me.

We wrapped and Rod asked me what I was doing for lunch. I told him I didn't know, since this was my first movie.

"Really?" he said. "Then you're having lunch with me. You get it over there in that tent, and then come to my trailer."

I was overwhelmed. *Hennessy* wasn't much of a picture, but it gave me the gift of a dream one-on-one lunch meeting with one of my all-time inspirations. Rod asked me where I was from, what I had done before, what I wanted to do. I asked him a couple of things about Sidney Lumet's 1964 film *The Pawnbroker*, which got Rod an Oscar nomination for his role as a concentration camp survivor, and he was clearly pleased that I knew the movie and happy to discuss it; he considered his performance in it his career best. The whole experience was delightful.

When I came in the next morning for my second and last day of shooting, I was disappointed that he hadn't been called. But I was content with my time on the film, and I learned an important rule about film acting, beyond the wisdom he offered over lunch that "the camera photographs thoughts": If you have off-camera lines, be there for them. It's the right call. You would be surprised at how often I have worked with actors who don't bother.

About fifteen years later, I was busy filming *Star Trek: The Next Generation*, no longer the obscure actor from *Hennessy*. I walked into a Beverly Hills restaurant and spotted Rod at a corner table with three other people. Suddenly, I was a starstruck novice again; I hesitated to approach him, lest he think me a bothersome fan. But then he noticed me, stood up, and called out, "Patrick!"

I contemplated, as a joke, using on him his old line to the AD: *What the fuck do you think I am?* But I didn't; instead, he embraced me and we chatted for a few minutes. He hadn't forgotten me at all, and congratulated me on my success as Captain Jean-Luc Picard. A class act, from the moment I first saw him on-screen all those years ago in Mirfield.

In 1976, I received my best TV offer to date: to be part of BBC Television's serialization of the epic Robert Graves novel *I, Claudius*. I needed no persuading—as a teen, I had devoured the book and its sequel, *Claudius the God*. To play any role was going to be a thrill, but somewhat to my surprise, I was cast as Lucius Aelius Sejanus, one of the series' very, very bad guys.

Long before the Harry Potter and *X-Men* franchises became bonanzas for stage-trained British actors, there was *I, Claudius*. It was one of the first prestige serialized dramas to earn a huge international viewership, and its cast was chock-full of UK luminaries: Derek Jacobi as Claudius, George Baker as Tiberius Caesar, Siân Phillips as Livia, John Hurt as Caligula, Margaret Tyzack as Antonia, Patricia Quinn as Livilla, and, most excitingly for me, my teenage pal from the West Riding, Brian Blessed as Caesar Augustus. Brian and I were in only a couple of scenes together, but as the years pass, the occasion is increasingly momentous to me. Believe it or not, *I, Claudius* was the only time that he and I ever worked together professionally.

My character, Sejanus, had at one time been just a Praetorian soldier. But through ambition and some canny sucking up to Tiberius, he has become the leader of the Imperial Guard. And after seducing Livilla, Claudius's sister, he believes himself set up to ascend to the Roman throne. Is he ever a scheming, pompous bastard! My favorite scene is the one I play with Patricia Quinn, in which I tell her that I am not going to marry her, as our characters have planned, but will instead wed her very young daughter. Sejanus assures Livilla that it's just a workaround that will allow him into her family, and that the daughter means nothing to him. But Livilla isn't having it. "And you'll service us both, then, like a stallion?!" she screams at him.

I have only felt genuine fear in the presence of another actor twice, and both times, my opposite in the scene was a woman. When Patricia set upon me physically, shouting, "You bastard!" I was certain that she was going to end my life. The other time I was as terrified was when Kate Fleetwood, as Lady Macbeth, came after me in a production of *Macbeth* directed by her husband, Rupert Goold.

I was in just four of the thirteen episodes of *I, Claudius*—

Sejanus meets a very nasty end on the Senate steps—but they gave me as much pleasure to perform as almost anything I've ever done. There is still a faction of people out there who know me primarily for this series. Not too long ago, I walked into a restaurant in Chicago and a woman shouted out, "Oh my God—it's Sejanus!" An astonishing moment, all these years later.

My next noteworthy screen appearance was in David Lynch's 1984 adaptation of Frank Herbert's classic science fiction novel *Dune*. But the road to *Dune* passes through Trevor Nunn's 1982 production of *King Henry IV*, so let's start there.

In '82, the Barbican Centre, a long-in-the-planning performing arts complex located in London, was finally completed. It occupied an area that had been almost totally leveled during the German Blitz of World War II and was part of a grand plan by the movers and shakers in London's financial center to build a new neighborhood from the ground up, with luxury apartment buildings, parks, artificial lakes, and waterfalls in addition to the arts center. The Barbican was a controversial project because it suffered from delays and cost overruns, and its architecture was brutalist in style.

But the Royal Shakespeare Company had committed to making the Barbican's main theater its London base. Trevor chose to christen the theater with a marathon one-two punch of *Henry IV, Parts 1 and 2*: a seven-hour production with a dinner break between the two parts. You may recall that I was in these plays in my very first RSC season, in the small roles of Sir Walter Blunt in *Part 1* and Mowbray in *Part 2*. This time, hurrah, I was to play King Henry himself. And so it was that I enjoyed the distinction of being the first actor to speak in the first full-fledged performance on the Barbican's new stage: "So shaken as we are, so wan with care . . ." King Henry's opening lines could not have been more appropriate, given the years of stress that had accompanied the construction of the space where we now worked.

I was fond of the new auditorium, though many people found the place drab. My main quibble was that essentially everything was underground. My dressing room had just one window, which looked out onto the underground car lot's access ramp. The stage was three floors below ground level, and the rehearsal room one floor further. One could report for work, go down the elevator at ten a.m., and not see the sky again until eleven p.m., when the streets were desolate; the neighborhood was not exactly a charming place to go for walks.

But it was my joy and privilege to appear in a production that, auspiciously, was opening with all eyes upon it, for its arrival heralded an even bigger one, that of London's most ambitious postwar cultural center. Such was the sense of celebration that the audience applauded before we even began, as the house lights dimmed. And it was a fine production. I took particular pleasure in Henry's famous sleep soliloquy, a rallying cry for insomniacs for centuries: "O sleep, O gentle sleep, Nature's soft nurse, how have I frightened thee . . ."

One shrewd choice that Trevor made was to have me play King Henry not as a whiny monarch bemoaning how hard his job is, but as a workaholic fighter whose reserves of energy have been stretched to the hilt. I played the role actively rather than passively, and my soliloquy's famous final line—"Uneasy lies the head that wears a crown"—was delivered not with self-pity but amused irony. I have of late been curious about our new king's thoughts in this regard. I've met the man several times and liked him, and I wish him and the queen consort well.

Henry IV played to sold-out audiences and good reviews, but it did not exactly catapult my career to new heights. The following year, I found myself accepting a supporting role in a Japanese film, the star of which was a pop idol who had never acted before. It was a paycheck, nothing more, but on the plus side, I didn't have to work much and the film took me to several pleasant European locations where, in the movie, the singer's character was performing.

I was gazing out of my window in a hotel overlooking Germany's lovely Mosel valley, making the most of a late call time on my first day of shooting, when the phone in my room rang. It was my agent on the line from London, asking me if I remembered a script he had sent me some months earlier: an adaptation of the Frank Herbert novel *Dune*. I assured him that I did. Prior to reading the script, I knew little of science fiction, but I found myself captivated by the material. There was no specific role on offer to me at that point, but I told my agent that I wanted very much to be in the film if they would have me.

Weeks had already passed and there had been no follow-up from my agent. I assumed the film team had passed on me, a major disappointment because I had discovered that *Dune*'s director was to be David Lynch. He was an upstart whose first two movies, the bizarre, unsettling *Eraserhead* and the beautiful *The Elephant Man*, were brilliant—emotionally dark but not without humor, and visually brave. Lynch struck me as my kind of director. But as I had already learned from my years in the acting business, you had to let go of dashed hopes and move on. The day my agent called, I was going to put in my hours on the pop idol's film and then enjoy a ramble through Germany's wine country.

But my agent, it turns out, had a reason for bringing up *Dune*. "You have been offered the role of Gurney Halleck, and they want you to fly to Mexico City on Saturday," he said.

"What? How can I do that?" I said. "I'm shooting in Germany!"

"Don't worry about that," he replied. "We've worked it all out. *Dune* will shoot around your European schedule, though it does mean you will be commuting for three or four weeks between Europe and Mexico."

"And everyone is happy about that?" I asked.

"Totally," my agent assured me. "David Lynch really wants you."

Well, how flattering was that? And what a turn of events. One day you're in a schlocky production of a film you don't much care about, the next you're in a big-budget American picture directed by a visionary and starring such amazing performers as Francesca Annis, Max von Sydow, Jürgen Prochnow, Kyle MacLachlan, Dean Stockwell, Siân Phillips, José Ferrer, Brad Dourif, Freddie Jones, Kenneth McMillan, and Virginia Madsen.

The travel was going to be an ordeal, from Frankfurt to London, and then London to Miami, and then Miami to Mexico City. But I still loved flying in those days, so a full day spent on airplanes was no deterrent.

I called Sheila immediately to give her the news. She was thrilled, and also, sensibly, said that she would meet me at Heathrow with a case packed with clean clothing suitable for Mexico. I asked her if she could also procure for me a copy of Frank Herbert's book, since it would inevitably offer so much more characterization of Gurney Halleck, a warrior and troubadour, than the script did.

On the appointed day, Sheila met me at Heathrow with my suitcase, a very thick paperback copy of *Dune*, and a bag of home-baked goodies. It was a big goodbye—I had learned from my agent that *Dune* was going to be a long shoot. "Keep the next six months clear," he'd said. We would be shooting at the Churubusco Studios in Mexico City, and I was to be put up in a luxury hotel.

Sheila and I ate breakfast in the terminal and agreed that as soon as the kids were let out of school for the summer, they and she would join me in Mexico for some family fun. We'd spent so much time apart because of our work schedules, so six or seven weeks together in a faraway place would be enjoyable for all of us—in some respects, Daniel and his little sister, Sophie, had been growing up with not much of a father around.

My flight was called, and after a loving farewell, I hustled to the gate, joining a long queue waiting to board my Pan Am flight. When I reached the door, I handed my ticket to the flight attendant, who looked at it with confusion.

"You're at the wrong door, Mr. Stewart," she said. "You are in first class."

What? I couldn't contain my astonishment. The big time! It had taken me forty-three years, but finally, the trainspotting boy from Mirfield was getting to fly first class!

I reveled in every second of the experience. At the first-class door, there was no line, only a charming flight attendant who warmly welcomed me *by name* before I showed her my ticket. Another equally charming flight attendant escorted me onto the plane, guiding me to the left and into the temple of privilege. There was only one seat in the first-class cabin not taken. Fortunately, it proved to be mine. The attendant took my bag from me, placed it in the overhead compartment, helped me off with my coat, and more or less tucked me into my seat, which offered acres of legroom, a pillow, and a blanket. I could not believe this was happening to me.

Beside me sat a beautiful young woman. She explained to me that everyone else in the first-class cabin was one of her relatives. They were an Indian family traveling the world together—they'd just spent three days in London and were now moving the party to Miami, with more stops to come in the next month. As we talked, a glass of champagne had found its way to my tray, along with a small plate of treats. This was a way of living of which I had known nothing until my seat neighbor explained it to me. *I could get used to this*, I thought.

We carried on conversing, this young woman and me—it turned out that she revered the theater and had seen *As You Like It* in Stratford. At one point a man came over, introduced himself to me as her father, and sternly asked if his daughter was bothering me by talking too much. I assured him that she was delightful and I was having a grand flight. He leaned over and in a soft voice gave me his name. "If she becomes a nuisance, just call out for me," he said. "I have some seats back in coach and can send her there." No bother at all, I replied, amused at such luxury as actually having empty seats on reserve.

The surrealism of it all continued when, without my asking, I was presented with a bowl of caviar with all the trappings: blini, crème fraîche, toast points. This was overwhelming, for I had never before seen caviar, let alone eaten it, and I didn't know the protocol. Fortunately, my companion did, and I studied her every move to make sure I did it right.

I had ordered roast beef as my main course. I expected it to arrive on a plate already carved. But no, a flight attendant pushed a trolley before me bearing a magnificent joint of beef, glistening and aromatic. I was consulted as to which part of the joint I would like. Getting the hang of things, I chose my section and asked for some English mustard on the side. To my surprise, I was told that they didn't have English mustard. *What? This is an outrage!* In the space of a couple of hours, I had gone from a Northern rube to an entitled toff. Well, actually, I of course let it go and had a great dinner.

When the pilot announced that we were thirty minutes from landing in Miami, my new friend stood and pulled me up with her. She announced to her family that I was an actor with the Royal Shakespeare Company. I received a spirited round of applause from them, just for being on a plane. I received warm farewells from everyone in their lovely group when we disembarked at the end of what remains, even now, the best flight of my life.

The turnaround to Mexico City was fast, and when I arrived, there was little time for messing about. I was met at the door of the plane by someone from the production team, who whisked me through customs and immigration and out to a waiting car. When I got to my hotel in the Zona Rosa neighborhood, it was late, but there were wardrobe and makeup people waiting for me, as well as an assistant bearing a new script and news that I would be picked up at eleven a.m. the next morning to meet with David Lynch.

Terribly jet-lagged, I slept horribly. But I was bang on time for my meeting with David. He was staying in a nearby hotel, and I had been given his room number and told that I should go straight up to it, with no need to call at the front desk.

The door was ajar. I knocked and heard a man's voice call out, "Come in." There sat David, with his soft, blank face and thick head of hair. He was engrossed in something he was reading but looked up when I entered.

Silence.

"It's Patrick . . . Patrick Stewart," I volunteered.

He still didn't speak—or move, for that matter. He just stared at me. Finally, after what seemed a lifetime, he slowly stood up and shook my hand. The shake was not enthusiastic, and my discomfort increased. We both sat down and the strange silence continued. I felt it was up to me to try to normalize this weird situation, so I told him it was great to meet him, I was a big fan, and I was flattered by the invitation to join the cast.

David just nodded his head and then let it fall down onto his chest. Something was clearly amiss, and I wondered if there had been some kind of terrible mistake. Thank goodness for Max von Sydow, who suddenly entered the room, greeted David, and then turned to me and said, "Patrick! Welcome to *Dune* and Mexico. We are so happy you are doing this, Kyle in particular. He'll be up here soon—I just passed him in the lobby."

These were all the things that I had hoped and expected David to say, but so be it. When Kyle MacLachlan and Jürgen Prochnow appeared, the atmosphere changed completely for the better. Kyle, a Shakespeare buff who was aware of my standing in the RSC, offered me a hug, and from Jürgen, a hearty handshake. I was expected after all. What a relief.

Their arrival also activated David. He moved some chairs into a circle so we could all discuss the next day's work. There were a few things I didn't understand, so I asked David some questions. But every time I did, he directed his answers not at me but to the whole group. *What on earth is going on here?* I thought. Kyle's outgoing friendliness kept me from losing my mind and succumbing to self-doubt. He invited me to supper with some of the other cast members that evening and made me feel welcome. But David's behavior was still bothersome.

I was also dismayed at the condition of the Churubusco Studios, which were old and threadbare. We didn't have trailers but interior rooms, with ratty-looking furniture and temperamental air conditioning. But the most crucial feature was the costume rail, which had hanging from it the one-piece rubber suits that we all had to wear nearly every day.

These costumes were a nightmare to get into, requiring two wardrobe assistants and a lot of time. We were told that we were not allowed to remove the suits until the day's work wrapped, as they would prove impossible to get back on once we began sweating. It was a small mercy that we were allowed to wear T-shirts to alleviate our epic perspiration. Although I will admit that when these suits were zipped up—a challenging task in and of itself—they did look pretty cool and futuristically intimidating.

I was still green as a film actor, unused to endless waiting while the director set up his shots. Kyle, Max, Jürgen, and I sat there sweltering in our rubber suits inside a small, helicopter-like contraption called an ornithopter. I admired David, though, for the care he took in his setups and his multiple takes. The company of those three actors went a long way toward making the day tolerable, but when "That's a wrap" was called, all I could think of was pouring a large scotch and soda, slipping into a hot bath, and then going straight to bed.

David Lynch, I should make clear, was devoted to his cast. He never gave the impression that he was concerned only with visuals and special effects. He checked in with us constantly and was at times even complimentary . . . though never to me, personally.

Something was most definitely up. Every day, I reported for duty expecting a thaw or at least a normalization of our director-actor relationship. I was convinced that David simply hadn't gotten to know me well, and that as soon as he did, we would relate in a looser, dare I say human, manner. Yet it never happened. Yes, he sometimes did address me directly, telling me to stand here or move there, but that was the extent of it. In the months we worked together, he never once gave me a personal or acting note, a true piece of direction. At times I felt like a part of the set and nothing more. And I had no idea why.

Had it not been for my warm and friendly relationships with my fellow cast members, I don't think I could have survived the experience. I already knew Siân Phillips and Freddie Jones from working with them in British TV, and Kyle, Max, and Jürgen were ready friends who propped up my spirits. I should also mention another actor I had never before met until *Dune*. Four years earlier, I'd seen Alan Parker's *Midnight Express*, a terrifying but brilliant film. Its memory stayed with me, particularly the scenes featuring a huge man-mountain of rage named Hamidou, a Turkish prison guard capable of impulsive acts of brutal violence.

One late, hazy afternoon at Churubusco, I had just found myself a quiet corner in which to curl up with a novel when I heard someone say, "Patrick? Patrick Stewart?" Through the shadows emerged a tall, bulky figure who I immediately identified as—*No, it can't be!*—Hamidou himself. Instantly, I flipped from reality to my recollections of that film—I was not in Churubusco Studios but a cell in Istanbul, about to be beaten to a pulp. I stood up in shock, genuinely frightened, and raised my hands to defend myself. But from the huge man extended an equally huge hand that gently enveloped both of mine. Then I heard a charming, amiable voice say, "Patrick, hi, I'm Paul Smith. It's an honor. I saw you onstage in London and you were amazing. I can't believe that we get to work together."

Such is the power of performance—of total conviction, skill, and art. Paul Smith, an Israeli-American actor, turned out to be one of the most mild-mannered, kindest men I have ever met. But even so, as I write this, I can't help but feel a little frisson of terror at being alone in a room with him.

A couple of weeks into the shoot, I arrived on set to great excitement. Word was going around that someone called "Sting" would be joining the *Dune* cast. Please bear in mind that I am primarily a fan of classical music and not the most pop-culture-fluent guy around.

This Sting chap arrived the following day. I was at once struck by his gorgeous looks and his modest manner.

A day or two later, we were appearing in the same scene. As is inevitable on a film set, we found ourselves waiting to work, sitting side by side while David Lynch and his crew set up a shot. I thought I would indulge the man in some conversation.

"So," I said, "I understand that you are a musician?"

"Yeah, that's right," he said.

"What instrument do you play?"

I detected a slight smile. "Bass," he said.

"You know," I said, really holding forth now, "I have often wondered what makes a musician choose to haul around such a huge instrument as that. It must be impossible."

"No, I don't play a double bass," he replied. "I play the bass guitar. An electric one."

I was beginning to feel some unease with this Sting fellow, as if I'd put a foot wrong. "Do you . . . play in a group?" I asked.

"Yes, with the Police," he said.

I broke into a broad grin. "You play in a police band?" I said. "Wow! How marvelous!"

I have never fully recovered from the sheer embarrassment I suffered when word got out on the set about my exchange with one of the world's biggest rock stars. A few years afterward, I saw Sting in concert at the Royal Festival Hall in London and was utterly exhilarated by his music. He has since forgiven me for that first conversation we had.

The other huge benefit of shooting *Dune* besides meeting wonderful people was that I got to explore more of Mexico than I did during the

Old Vic World Tour with Vivien Leigh, when I fell in love with the pre-Columbian ruins I had seen. This time, I explored Mexico City further: the National Museum of Anthropology, with its astonishing collection of Aztec, Mayan, and Olmec artifacts, and the narrow city streets with their endless varieties of markets, architecture, and food. I stood mesmerized for about an hour watching an elderly woman effortlessly make tamales with grace and speed.

I averaged just one or two days of work a week, so I went farther afield. On the recommendation of Max von Sydow, I enjoyed a quick getaway to a beach town called Zihuatanejo (which some of you film lovers might recognize as a pivotal location in *The Shawshank Redemption*), where I stayed in a hotel that had a small collection of waterfront villas, one of which I had all to myself. When Sheila and the children arrived, I rented a delightful house in Polanco, an affluent area of Mexico City. There came a time during the shoot when I was informed that I would not have a work call for ten days, so we went traveling as a family for the very first time.

We flew down to Mérida near the northern tip of the Yucatán Peninsula, where I had booked us in what I had heard was a lovely place with a lot of character. And it was—just not in ways we had expected. Sheila and I had just finished checking in when, looking around the spacious lobby area, we noted lots of pretty, scantily clad young women. An absurd thought popped into my head. "Sheila," I said. "Look around. Are we . . . in a brothel?"

She didn't hesitate for a second. "Clearly," she said.

Before I could suggest that we consider other options, my wife, ever the pragmatist, said, "Look, it's already getting late, and who knows how hard it will be to find a room elsewhere. Let's ask to be shown one of the rooms and then we will make a decision."

So that was the plan. We discovered that the room was vast and nicely appointed with antique furniture. The bed linens were clean, with no sign of anything that would make us run from the building screaming and in need of decontamination. Granted, all four of us ended up sleeping in the same bed, but we enjoyed a peaceful night followed by a first-class breakfast the next morning. At the very least, it was the most family-friendly brothel one could hope to find near the Gulf Coast.

I had rented a car, so we proceeded to drive across the Yucatán to Cancún, which struck me as nothing more than a tropical, upmarket Blackpool, but the children loved it. After three days there, we spent a night in Oaxaca City, my favorite city in all of Mexico, which I adored for its food, its people, and its artisans devoted to weaving, carving, and painting.

All of this sightseeing and family time mitigated the uneasiness of my current work situation. I had begun to notice that when David Lynch addressed us collectively as a cast, he had no trouble making direct eye contact with the other actors, such as Kyle and Max. But when his head swiveled my way, his eyes still passed over me, as if I were invisible. It was hurtful and discouraging.

Watching *Dune* even all these years later is not a comfortable experience for me. I can sense my lack of connection to the work, and have to say I am not proud of my performance. However, at least I finally got to the bottom of what the hell was going on with David Lynch, thanks to Raffaella De Laurentiis, the film's producer.

Raffaella is the daughter of the legendary Italian movie producer Dino De Laurentiis and a formidable cinematic force in her own right. One day during the shoot, she asked me if I was free to have dinner with her that evening. I was surprised and delighted, as I had grown to like Raffaella.

As soon as we'd both had a glass of wine, she began to talk about David. She was aware, she said, that he was being distant and strange with me, and equally aware that I was upset by David's behavior.

"There is a reason he's like that with you," she told me.

"I'm dying to hear it," I said.

Remember when I said that the road to *Dune* goes through *King Henry IV*? Raffaella explained that, a year earlier, she and David had gone to the Barbican to meet with a young actor in our cast whom they were considering for the part that ultimately went to Kyle MacLachlan. While Raffaella and David were waiting in the Barbican's backstage greenroom, David was struck by another cast member who had wandered in: a middle-aged man with long, dark hair, going gray, that hung limp around his gaunt, pale face. David told Raffaella to find out the actor's name because he loved the way the guy looked.

Fast-forward to a year later, by which time *Dune* was already in production. David and Raffaella had a serious problem: The actor they had hired to play Gurney Halleck dropped out of the film abruptly for personal reasons and needed to be replaced. In the middle of a meeting with the casting department, David asked Raffaella if she remembered the name of the ragged actor they had seen backstage in London. She had made a note of it: Patrick Stewart.

"See if he is available," David had said. "He would be a perfect Gurney." At once, the casting director phoned my agent, who told her what I was up to. This was what had led to me being whisked away from Germany with all due haste, the costs be damned.

As Raffaella related this story to me in the restaurant, it all began to make sense. David Lynch thought he was getting the dramatically wasted-looking King Henry IV he had seen at the Barbican, the man whom I had become through acting, disciplined eating, and excellent hair and makeup people. But into his hotel room had walked this hairless, suntanned, healthy-looking fellow.

Oh Lord, it was all so embarrassing to ponder now: David's silence and confusion when I introduced myself as Patrick Stewart; his immediate realization that he had no choice but to have me play Gurney, as my deal was done, the contract was signed, and he was pressed for time anyway. I also understood, just a little, why he sometimes seemingly couldn't bear the sight of me. I actually felt a little bit sorry for him. Still, I wished he would have said something to clear the air and not make me feel so uncomfortable.

Even as all the pieces of Raffaella's story came together, I was stunned. I sat there at the table, completely at a loss. "Erm, does David know that you're telling me all this?" I finally asked.

"No," she said, "and I don't want him to know. He has enough to worry about. I just wanted to make sure that *you* know. And for what it's worth, Pat, I think you're doing an excellent job."

Gradually, over time, David became more comfortable around me, more accepting of the fact that the bald, tan man was in his cast and not the one he remembered from the Barbican, even though wardrobe and makeup would have solved that issue in a jiffy. Near the end, after we principal actors had wrapped our roles in the movie, Raffaella threw us a farewell dinner at a nice restaurant in Mexico City. To my utter astonishment, David stopped for a moment to sit beside me, and for the very first time, we socialized. My hunch is that the cat was out of the bag—he had learned that I knew the story of my (mis)casting, and now that we were about to part, he wanted to make up for the discomfort he had caused me.

I have not seen David Lynch since *Dune*, but I have enjoyed all of his films since, particularly *Mulholland Drive*, and like everyone else, I was in awe of his groundbreaking TV series *Twin Peaks*. We connected once more after Mexico. In the 1990s, I got into Transcendental Meditation, of which David is one of the world's foremost advocates. He somehow learned of my embrace of TM and asked for my support in his campaign to introduce it to students in school. I was happy to help. I think it's a great idea.

Soon after *Dune*, I was cast in a film by another cult director: Tobe Hooper, the horror-meister behind *The Texas Chain Saw Massacre*. The movie was called *Lifeforce*. Let's just say that it was significantly less prestigious an endeavor than Mr. Lynch's: something to do with space vampires who inhabit human bodies, if I recall correctly. But it was another foray into science fiction, a genre that, auspiciously, seemed to have room for me.

My main memory of *Lifeforce* is a scene in which my character, a doctor, was supposed to kiss a beautiful woman lying naked on an operating table. The stunning young French actress Mathilda May played the "space girl" with whom I was to lock lips, after which she would take the form of Carlsen, the movie's male lead, played by Steve Railsback. We were ready to shoot the scene, with me hovering over the unclothed Mathilda, when Tobe abruptly decided that the space girl should turn into Carlsen the moment *before* I kissed her.

Steve is a nice-looking fellow, but this was a major comedown. The one consolation was that Mathilda sweetly told me that she, too, was disappointed that we would not get to have our intimate moment. Anyway, thanks to Tobe Hooper, it is a matter of public record that the recipient of my first on-screen kiss was Steve Railsback.

Chapter Fifteen

My parents did not live long enough to see me become a globally known actor, but they were able to enjoy my success on the British stage. As dyed-in-the-wool Northerners, they never traveled as far south as London to see me perform with the Royal Shakespeare Company, and only once went as far as Stratford. But if I was doing a show in Sheffield, Manchester, or Liverpool, they were there like a shot.

This made me happy. As harrowing a youth as my father had imposed on me, I was so pleased to make him proud of my chosen profession; he was the only father I had, after all. As for my mother, she had given me nothing but unconditional love and support, and I was beyond moved by her devoted efforts to see me perform, often with her sister, Annie, in tow.

Mam didn't quite get some of the fringier stuff in which I appeared, but it gladdened me that she took pleasure in seeing her son make good on his dreams of an acting career. I was also delighted when she told me that her neighbors reported to her with excitement that they had seen "our Pat" on TV (Dad received similar reports from his mates in the pub, which I'm certain gave him a thrill).

In 1977, Mam unexpectedly passed away. My brother Trevor called me to deliver the bad news, and I sped north to Mirfield for the funeral. I've never bought into my older brother Geoffrey's macabre theory that Dad finally went off and murdered Mam by smothering her with a pillow. The truth is that she had lived a hard seventy-six years, marked by poverty, spousal abuse, and exposure to chemicals in the mill, and there was only so much her heart could take before it gave out.

The day before Mam's funeral, I went alone to the undertaker's to say goodbye to her. Suddenly, I was back in my newspaper-reporter days, squeamishly sharing the room with a dead body. But this was different, at once harder and easier. The undertaker said, "Take all the time you need," and closed the door behind him to give me privacy.

Still shocked at the news Trevor had delivered, and still wary of getting close, I moved slowly toward the open casket in the center of the room.

But just before my eyes fixed on her face, I heard her say, "Oh, hello, Patrick, love." I know I heard it. I did not imagine it.

I stood over her for a while, tears in my eyes. I remembered the grieving relatives I had met while gathering information for obituaries, and how they always said of their departed loved one, "Doesn't he [or she] look grand?" Now that was me. And in all sincerity, she *did* look grand.

I kissed her on her cheek, told her I loved her, and bid Mam farewell.

Three years later I found myself in the same room, moving slowly toward Dad's coffin. He was about the same age that Mam had been when she'd passed, but once again, it was an unexpected death, and yet again I heard the news via an urgent call from Trevor. In his final three years, Dad lived alone in their council house. He had evidently collapsed and fallen down a flight of stairs. He was not discovered until the following day.

As I now inched toward his coffin, I prepared myself for Dad, like Mam, to speak to me. But no such supernatural greeting was forthcoming.

Nonetheless, I felt a charge in the room, as if he might, at any moment, sit up and hit me. I wasn't filled with sadness, as I had been

when saying goodbye to Mam. My primary feelings toward him—
still—were of anger and fear. I did not offer him a final kiss, but I did
say goodbye.

I have often wished that my parents could have stuck around
long enough to see me achieve bigger things, whether in *Star Trek*,
the *X-Men* movies, or onstage in *Macbeth* and *Waiting for Godot*. I
am certain that my mother would have adored my one-man adaptation of Charles Dickens's *A Christmas Carol*. And I most definitely
would have brought them to my knighting at Buckingham Palace.
They were fundamentally proud to be English, and my investiture as
Sir Patrick Stewart would have given them profound joy.

I do not, however, think that I would have gone the route of
springing for a new house for them. Not because I wouldn't have
offered, but because they wouldn't have wanted it. Their council
house on the new estate was so far removed from 17 Camm Lane
that they believed they were already living in luxury. Besides that,
my mam's whole universe was in Mirfield. There was nowhere else
she ever wanted to be.

In the early 1980s, I was free to do films like *Dune* because, as the '70s
were winding down, I notified the Royal Shakespeare Company that
I no longer wished to be a full-time member of their company. This
exit was neither dramatic nor final—I continued to do plays with
them, only with reduced frequency, one or two shows per season. I
had lived the bucolic Stratford dream; now I was getting fairly consistent work in film and television, so the timing seemed right. Sheila
and I sold our house in Warwickshire and opted for a London base
and a life of greater flexibility.

But I am associated with the RSC to this very day. And in 1981, I
was invited to play Leontes in Shakespeare's *The Winter's Tale*. It is
one of his later works and is often considered problematic and ton-
ally inconsistent. Leontes, the main character, is a Sicilian king who

succumbs to paranoia and destroys his family and friendships, yet somehow enjoys a redemptive final act.

Given my performance history with the RSC, I was not about to turn down a leading role. But I had never read the play, and when I finally did, I had to agree with those who find it a bit puzzling—the script gave me no idea how to play the part.

One day in Stratford, I walked into the Theatre's greenroom and happened upon Dame Peggy Ashcroft, one of Britain's greatest stage actors, sipping a cup of tea and quite alone. She was in her seventies by this point and a legendary figure. Acting against my cautious nature, I said, "Dame Peggy, have you got a minute?"

"Yes, of course," she said with a whimsical smile, motioning me to the chair beside her.

I explained that I had been offered the role of Leontes, my first leading role in a main-stage RSC production, but I didn't have a notion of who he was or how to play him.

Dame Peggy's response was immediate. "Don't do it," she said, grabbing my arm. "You'll hate it. Nobody likes him. *You* won't like him. He is loathsome."

I was taken aback by her vehemence, but I was not about to distrust someone as knowledgeable of Shakespeare in performance as she.

Then she redirected our conversation. "I know you're a Yorkshireman," she said, which prompted me to think, *Dame Peggy actually knows who I am?* "So I imagine that you must play cricket," she continued. "You are a batsman, I bet." And the remainder of our talk was about cricket, not Leontes. I later learned that Dame Peggy played for the RSC team when she was in Stratford. Cricket was her offstage passion, which only shows that you rarely know who actors really are.

Meanwhile, despite it being the opportunity of a leading role, I turned Leontes down.

Two days later, I received a call from *The Winter's Tale* director, Ronald Eyre. He was no slouch himself, a veteran whom a friend of

mine had described as "the most intelligent man in British theater."
So I agreed to his request that we meet.

I told Ron right away what I didn't like about the character and
how I couldn't figure out how to play him. He sat silent for a while,
then said, "Patrick, you won't have to act him. I have seen a lot of
your work. I know that Leontes is inside you already. All you have to
do is let him out."

Perhaps I should have been insulted that he believed such a de-
plorable character resided somewhere within me. But I was intrigued,
and I agreed to read the play once more. I shut myself in my dressing
room and hung a DO NOT DISTURB sign on the doorknob. As I read, I
focused on Leontes's demons: his rages, his insecurity, his disturbed
language, his tendency to see everyone around him as contemptible
and deceiving, even his own child.

In so doing, I found my mind trailing back to my childhood—
hearing my father's threats, replaying his violence against my mother,
wishing that he would somehow just die.

It was then that I began to understand Leontes. As Ron had assured me, he *was* inside me. To be clear, he was *not* my father; that
would be too facile. Rather, he was a refraction of all the complicated
feelings I had about my father as I was growing up, the volatile mix of
love, hate, pride, resentment, fear, and confusion. What I needed to
do in order to play Leontes, I decided, was tap my sense memory of
those times.

I did an about-face and accepted the role, putting myself on the
threshold of many weeks of misery and fascination. I had never before gone into a rehearsal room with my head and body totally invested in these kinds of feelings. Bernie Lloyd, my dear friend, who
was aptly playing Leontes's close companion Camillo, took me aside
one morning and asked if I was okay. He said he hadn't ever seen
me behaving as I was, seemingly depressed and full of energy at the
same time.

I confessed to Bernie how I was approaching the role, and although there was some doubt in his eyes, he pledged to support me,

whatever I should need. I am again, as I write this, looking at the photo of the two of us that I keep in my office. I see his trust in me from then and also his genuine concern. I miss him so much.

The production opened in the main auditorium at Stratford in the summer of 1981. I would like to tell you that I received raves for my deeply personal approach, but the reviews were mixed. Still, Ron Eyre's simple observation that the character already resided within me resonated in profound ways. I feel that he unlocked the gate to the final phase of development I needed to go through to become a complete actor, operating on a level approaching the Ian Holms and David Warners of the world. It was unexpectedly liberating.

In my tours of US college campuses with our small educational Shakespeare troupe, I had become close friends with David Rodes, a professor at UCLA's Department of English. David, bless his heart, actually flew over to England to see my performance as Leontes. His ironic take was that the newspaper reviews and audience response would have been much more positive had viewers not felt that what they were watching was too private and personal to be on a public stage. I told David that, on the contrary, he had given me a great compliment.

Armed with this new insight, I found myself, in the mid-1980s, doing what I believed to be my best stage work yet. In 1985, I was, in a rarity for me, cast in a play at the RSC's rival, the National Theatre. It was a new work called *Yonadab*, by Peter Shaffer, the masterful playwright of *Equus* and *Amadeus*. Peter Hall was directing.

Yonadab, sometimes spelled Jonadab, is a real figure in the Old Testament, a nephew of King David and a devious pot-stirrer in the king's court. In Shaffer's play, he manipulates David's son Amnon to rape his own half sister, Tamar, and when Tamar flees to another brother, Absalom, he counsels Absalom to seduce his already traumatized sister. Yonadab seems to believe that these incestuous pairings will lead to the creation of a new ruling superclass in the promised land. Or maybe he's just a crazy pervert.

If this doesn't sound like the makings of the feel-good hit of 1985, it's because it wasn't. *Yonadab* got mostly bad reviews, which did not sit well with the man in the title role, Alan Bates. Alan was a beloved British institution, a face of 1960s theater who originated roles in the works of John Osborne, Simon Gray, and Harold Pinter and later moved on to film stardom, notoriously wrestling naked with Oliver Reed in Ken Russell's *Women in Love*. He did not have time for what he perceived as middling nonsense.

I was playing King David, and I could sense even in rehearsals that we had a real turkey on our hands. But not because of the problematic material or Alan specifically. It was more the mismatch of the two—Alan realized he didn't like playing Yonadab and therefore never fully committed to the character.

On the Sunday of the week that we were to begin our tech and dress rehearsals, Sheila caught me pacing our sitting room, brooding about the unease I felt. She picked up immediately on my anxiety and asked me what was wrong.

When I was done spilling my guts, she suggested that I call Peter Hall to tell him my concerns. This was deeply out of the ordinary in the theater, for a cast member to request a conversation with the director about the state of the show, particularly this late in the preparation process. I had never in my career taken such a drastic step, but I felt that Sheila was right.

Peter answered the phone right away. I took a big breath and tentatively went into explaining my anxieties, gaining momentum as I realized that he was letting me go on without interruption. When I had finished, Peter quietly said, "What do you think we should do?"

I took another big breath. Then I suggested that we delay the play's opening and return to the rehearsal room for a week: another drastic, highly unusual step.

Peter was silent for a moment before he spoke up. "I think you're right," he said. He explained that he needed to make a few calls, but would soon get back to me.

It was evening before I heard from him again: "Sorry, it's simply impossible." We were bound by contractual terms and the theater's schedule. He thanked me for my candor, however, and that was that.

When critical pans came in, the cast was demoralized and the mood backstage was grim. Alan openly told anyone who would listen that the production needed to shut down—that, or simply let him walk from the show. Peter tried to reassure him that things could be worked out, but to no avail.

Another Sunday morning came around and my phone rang. It was Peter again, this time calling from Heathrow, asking me if I would take over the role of Yonadab. There was no one more qualified than me, he said. It would only entail twelve performances, after which the production would close. Peter assured me that I would get three full days of rehearsal. I told him I needed to think about it, but he said there was no time for pondering—he had to know before he boarded a plane bound for New York.

Now, for all the terrible reviews the play had received, I was morbidly fascinated by the character that Shaffer had created. And Yonadab never leaves the stage. And it was a proper lead role at the National Theatre. How could I refuse? I said yes.

This made me rather unpopular with the cast, whose members were hoping in vain that the remaining performances would somehow be canceled. But they warmed up a bit during the emergency rehearsals we held to get me up to speed—I'd found something in the role that Alan unfortunately hadn't, that Yonadab was fearful and desperate rather than masterfully manipulative. This discovery changed the tenor of the show, elevating the material. Peters Shaffer and Hall were tremendously supportive and grateful.

We did those twelve shows, sometimes to as few as twelve people. But ticket sales picked up a little when word got around that we had figured out a better approach to the play. Though *Yonadab* limped to the end of its run at the National, Peter Shaffer got in touch with me afterward. He explained that his friends in the Shubert Organization, which owns many Broadway theaters, were keen to give the play another try in New York, and he was game—on the condition that I continue to play the eponymous role. Peter was going to do some revisions to the material with me in mind, and he would consult with me in the course of doing so. It might take a couple of years, but he was confident that we were Broadway-bound.

I was immensely flattered to hear all this, naturally, despite the play's uphill battle. *Yonadab!* That's what I envisioned myself doing in 1987.

In 1986, in another indication that my leading-man career was finally going places, I received a call from David Thacker, the artistic director of the Young Vic Theatre on the South Bank. The Young Vic is, you will not be surprised to hear, an offshoot of the Old Vic, presenting plays and musicals that skew in a more experimental or youth-orientated direction. David wasted no time on the phone. He explained that he was about to begin rehearsals of Edward Albee's *Who's Afraid of Virginia Woolf?*, whose feuding lead couple, George and Martha, were memorably played by Richard Burton and Elizabeth Taylor in the movie version.

David told me that he was in a bind: the actor who had signed up to play George had abruptly dropped out. This made me, in no uncertain terms, David's second choice. But hey, I was wanted, and I was wanted *now*. I asked David if I could take a day to read the script before deciding, and he granted me this request.

Virginia Woolf is a long play. After reading the first act in the garden-facing sitting room of our London home, I got up to make myself a cup of tea. I remember Sheila was in the kitchen and asked me what I thought of the script so far. I said I didn't want to talk about it until I had finished the whole thing, and I returned with my tea to the sitting room. I'm glad I withheld judgment. I'd started out liking the play just fine. But the farther I got in, the stronger my feelings became. By Act III, they became so intense that I had to pause more than once to do some deep breathing.

Finally, I reached the point where George and Martha's guests, a young couple, say good night to their hosts and leave. George and Martha are alone for the first time in nearly three hours, and the impact of the evening, particularly on Martha, has left them subdued and exhausted. For the first time, George is quiet and gentle with his wife, while she is distressed and wrung out. Halfway down the last page of the script, I began to weep, and when I was done, I found myself sobbing uncontrollably. The fact that Albee's play had touched on some profound truths about my own marriage moved me—and also, it must be said, scared me. I pulled myself together before I arrived back in the kitchen, but Sheila saw my tired, tear-streaked face.

"You really liked it, didn't you?" she said. I admitted that I did, and that it would be my next project, starting in four days. I didn't speak of what had triggered my emotional outburst, however.

My opposite, playing Martha, was Billie Whitelaw, a legendary actress in London, highly respected for her work in Samuel Beckett's plays. Matthew Marsh and Saskia Reeves played the younger couple, Nick and Honey. My chemistry with Matthew and Saskia was fabulous, but my most important relationship in the show, onstage and off, was with Billie. Sadly, it wasn't an easy one. In the rehearsal room, she was distant, seeming to know exactly what she wanted to do and doing it, but what Billie did was often not in sync with the rest of us. When we played scenes together, I felt that nothing I did was being absorbed by her, while I was trying as much as possible to absorb Billie's performance into my own.

From the audience's point of view, my concerns were irrelevant. They and the critics loved her Martha and our production in general. Toward the end of our run, a producer introduced himself to us and announced his intention to bring the show to the West End.

I was thrilled—until I learned that Billie did not want to be part of it. This was a serious blow, because she was the star actor in the production, the box office draw. I felt even worse when I met with director David Thacker, who informed me that the main reason Billie had opted out was that she did not want to work with me. David told me, to my shock, that Billie found me an "intimidating" presence. I'd had no idea of this and wished only that Billie had approached me herself. I had known and suffered from feelings of intimidation myself on the stage and truly hated it.

I chose to try and learn from this experience—to evaluate my behavior retrospectively and see if I could polish whatever rough edges might have telegraphed the wrong message. But I was also deeply disappointed. I had envisioned us playing on the West End for a good run, six months or even longer. And then, by the time that was over, Peter Shaffer and the Shuberts would be ready to fly me to New York to get to work on the new and improved *Yonadab*. The grand plans I'd envisioned were falling apart.

In the meantime, though, my schedule was wide open. I was forty-six years old. I had recently done what I had considered my best work, but I was at a loose end.

I commiserated on the phone with UCLA professor David Rodes, who had become a confidant as much as a friend. Whether out of sympathy or genuine interest, he made me a kind offer, inviting me for a short visit to Los Angeles, during which I would stay at his place and do some workshops and Shakespeare master classes. It would be a perfect antidote to the *Virginia Woolf* disappointment and a sunny respite from gray England as well. Sheila thought the same, and although I would miss my family, I was soon off.

A few days into my mini-stint in LA as a visiting Shakespeare professor, David asked me if I could help him out. He was scheduled to give an evening lecture in Royce Hall on the UCLA campus—not to students, but to anyone in the general public who wished to attend. He wanted to liven up the proceedings by having a couple of actors read some play extracts to illustrate his points. He'd already roped in an actress friend to play the female parts. Would I play the male parts? My "pay" would be a hundred-dollar fee plus dinner afterward at the newly opened Westwood location of TGI Fridays. For David, I was happy to participate, and we all—performers, lecturer, and attendees—enjoyed a delightful evening from start to finish.

I did not, however, think of this night as remotely consequential vis-à-vis my future.

Early the following morning, David's home phone rang. He found me in the guest room and said, handing over the receiver, "It's for you. Says he's your LA agent."

At the time, I was represented in America by the agency ICM. The way it worked for English actors of my caliber back then was that we didn't really have our own personal talent agents based in Los Angeles. But in the unlikely event that someone in Hollywood expressed interest in our services, we were nominally represented by someone there who would handle our Stateside affairs. The man on the phone waiting to speak with me, Steve Dontanville, was this agent where I was concerned. I had never spoken with him, let alone met him in person.

Steve got right to the point when I took the phone from David and said, "Hello?"

"What were you doing at UCLA last night," he asked, "and why would Gene Roddenberry want to meet with you this morning?"

Chapter Sixteen

J ean Roddanburry? That's how I envisioned the name when I heard it. And I didn't have an answer for Steve Dontanville as to why Jean Roddanburry wanted to meet with me, for a simple reason: I didn't know who the hell Jean Roddanburry was.

It will not surprise you to learn that the guy who thought that Sting played a double bass in a policeman's band knew next to nothing of *Star Trek*. When Steve brought up that title and explained that the creator of this legendary late-1960s science-fiction program was developing a new version of the show, for which I was evidently being considered for a part, I realized that it sounded vaguely familiar. I recalled—to myself, not to Steve—that on Saturdays in my kids' younger years, when I came home for tea between performances of a matinee and an evening show, I'd find Dan and Sophie sitting in front of the television watching a program with guys in colored long-sleeved shirts. It was called *Star Walk* or *Star Track*, something like that, and though I never sat down and watched it with them, I was aware that the kids were rapt and did not want to be pestered by Dad until the episode had ended.

Steve sighed over the phone when I explained my relative ignorance of what he was talking about and, as if speaking to a small child, connected the dots for me. Paramount Pictures, the famous

Hollywood studio, was creating an all-new version of *Star Trek* to be called *Star Trek: The Next Generation*, its action taking place nearly a hundred years after the adventures of William Shatner's Captain Kirk and Leonard Nimoy's Spock, with a whole new cast of characters. A producer of the new series, Robert Justman, had been at Royce Hall the previous evening and enjoyed my performance organized by David Rodes. He suggested to Gene Roddenberry—for that was the *Star Trek* creator's actual name—that they meet with me. I was to report to Gene's home at eleven a.m. that very morning, which gave me just enough time to collect my bearings, brush my teeth, and go.

I drove my rental car to a house somewhere in the Hollywood Hills. It was a single-story, 1950s-era house, very ordinary-looking, even in need of some TLC. When I knocked on the door, it was opened by a smiling, silver-haired man who introduced himself as Robert Justman. As I stood on the welcome mat, he told me how much he had liked the Royce Hall event and the many parts I played in it. Then he led me into the house.

I noticed that throughout the structure—in the hallway, the living room, and every other space I glimpsed—the floors were covered in thick shag-pile carpet in a nauseating shade of green. Waiting for me in the living room were two other men. One of them, tall and burly, struggled to get out of his armchair to shake my hand. He introduced himself to me as Gene Roddenberry.

It was all very awkward. A few pleasantries were exchanged among us, but I was not invited to sit down. Indeed, it was a matter of mere minutes before Roddenberry called the conversation to a halt, turning to me abruptly and saying, "Thanks for coming."

Clearly, the meeting was over. Robert Justman escorted me to the door and again warmly shook my hand. He was lovely, but the whole experience had felt very uncomfortable and I was relieved to get out.

Months later, after I had gotten to know him better, Robert apologized to me for the way the meeting had been handled. Upon my departure, he said, Gene railed at him for recommending me. A couple of months after that, by which time the producer Rick Berman had joined the nascent *Star Trek: TNG* team, my name came up again in a casting conversation. Rick, like Robert, expressed enthusiasm about me, which evidently triggered an even more vehement response from Gene: "Patrick Stewart's name should never, ever be mentioned in my presence again!"

I knew none of this at the time, though, and after my strange, brief meeting returned to David Rodes's house and told him that it had all been a big zero. I did a couple more workshops with him at UCLA and then drove up to Santa Barbara to do a few more. Then I went back to London, the Roddenberry meeting barely a memory, apart from the hideous carpet. My mission at the time was to line up a replacement for Billie Whitelaw so that our production of *Who's Afraid of Virginia Woolf?* might at last reach the West End.

But I had no luck in that regard, and very little work even in England, to be honest. In midlife, at a crossroads, a realization came to me. Perhaps this was all that was meant for me as an actor? No real breakout role in the cards for Pat Stew? For whatever reason, I decided that maybe I could turn myself into a British squash champion. I had always enjoyed the game but never pursued it seriously. This time, I went for it, training vigorously, playing every day. But maybe what I was really doing, repeatedly hammering a rubber ball against a wall, was getting out my frustration about where I was at as an actor.

And I had to be honest with myself: Steve Dontanville's call had awakened a new desire in me. What about Hollywood? Why not pursue TV and film work in America? Other British actors had made the move and it had paid off. Should I give it a try? Or had I already blown my only chance?

As I sat mired in this mix of ambition and existential funk, I received a phone call from, of all people, Steve Dontanville. His news was astonishing: The *Star Trek: TNG* producers wanted me to return to

LA, this time to audition for a specific role—yet unspecified, but substantial.

I was on a plane as soon as I could be, and at the Paramount gates not long thereafter, excited as hell. After being whisked through the gates, I was shown to a room where before me sat a table lined with producers and casting people. The sides, as we call the script pages for auditions, were vague—I think I might have read for Q, the role that eventually and deservedly went to the masterful John de Lancie. The audition seemed to go well and everyone was cordial, with the exception of Gene, who did not address me at all. And that was that—LAX to Heathrow, back home to Sheila, the kids, and further unemployment.

I was not even over my jet lag when Steve called again—I was wanted in LA early the following Monday, at nine a.m., this time to read for Paramount's TV executives. And there was more. This was an audition for the lead role, the USS *Enterprise*'s new captain. There were two finalists for the part, one of whom was me. This was it: the big one.

I had four days to get myself together for this callback. David Rodes invited me to stay with him again. I arrived on a Saturday. Paramount had already messengered the new sides to David's house in Brentwood. I saw that the character I was reading for was addressed as "Captain," but I had yet to be introduced to the name Jean-Luc Picard.

I also learned that some hairy drama had ensued while I was in transit. Right as I was boarding my plane at Heathrow, my London agent called Sheila at home and notified her that the Paramount people had been in touch, asking if I owned a hairpiece, and if I did, could I bring it to the audition? Sheila diligently retrieved my "audition wig" from its space in my closet and boxed it up, whereupon a British Airways representative collected it and placed it on a later flight to Los Angeles.

I do not know if my hairpiece flew first class. But by Sunday, it had arrived, and I drove back to LAX to retrieve it. It was packed in my briefcase when I drove to the Paramount Studios lot on Monday morning.

One more novel twist to the whole experience: On that same Sunday, I was contacted at David's home by Corey Allen, who explained that he was the director of the new *Star Trek* show's pilot episode. He admitted that he was operating outside the chain of command, and that his call was unauthorized by the higher-ups in the production, but he wanted to know if I was interested in meeting up with him ahead of the audition, at eight a.m. the following day, so that the two of us could read the script together. I told him that it sounded like a splendid idea. Also, his name rang a bell, but I just couldn't place where I knew it from.

That Monday in April did not begin auspiciously. I drove up to the famous main gates of Paramount Studios, announced my name with authority and flair at the security kiosk, and waited to be waved through. But as I idled in my rental car, I watched two security guards confer in puzzled tones until one of them returned and explained that I was not authorized to park on the lot—I would have to turn around and find a space somewhere on a side street. I protested that I had a very important meeting scheduled and was unfamiliar with the streets of Los Angeles. But the guards were unsympathetic.

As all this was happening, a queue of cars had developed behind me, full of impatient employees, which only added to my stress. But I was saved by the driver in the car immediately behind mine, an attractive young blond woman. She came storming up to the kiosk and said, "Don't you know who this is? This is Patrick Stewart and he has a very important meeting with some studio executives and you can't make him late!" The security men immediately obliged her and let me pass. And she returned to her car so quickly that I could neither thank this Good Samaritan nor find out who she was.

Once I was on the lot, I felt a lot better. Here I was, a boy from Mirfield who'd grown up on Hollywood movies, making his way through the famed streets of Paramount Pictures, passing soundstages and production offices! It's an especially romantic-looking studio and the only one that has continuously operated in the actual neighborhood of Hollywood since its inception.

I found my way to Corey Allen's "office," which was actually one of those temporary cabin-like trailers you sometimes see on studio lots. He had a pot of coffee waiting, and we got right into the reading. Corey was a gentlemanly fellow in his fifties and an excellent dialogue coach. He gave me numerous helpful notes, particularly the advice that I should dial down the size of my voice, making it more conversational. Having mostly done theater and epic-style movies, I was used to speaking in stentorian tones, so this was something that I really needed to understand. Corey also reiterated that nobody knew that he and I were meeting, and that I should keep it to myself. Clearly, I was the candidate he was rooting for. The clandestine nature of our get-together made me a little uncomfortable, but I was so unaccustomed to the ways of Hollywood that I didn't make too much of it.

After forty-five minutes of dialogue work, we headed out to the *Star Trek* production offices. Corey advised me that if we ran into anyone else on the way in, we should simply say that we met in the street. He led me to a side office, where a hairdresser was waiting for me, ready to get my hairpiece in place for the audition. And who was that hairdresser? None other than the young woman who had taken a stand for me with the security guys at the gate. Her name was Joy Zapata, and it was the start of a lovely friendship between us. Joy had recognized me from the headshots she'd been sent in preparation for my arrival—it was she who was charged with fitting my hairpiece for the audition, and she had been diligent in her research. Joy went ahead with the job of getting my wig in place that morning. Then it was off to a room next door where the Paramount suits were waiting.

There were three executives and a couple of people from casting, one of whom said she would be reading with me. At this, Corey, who'd been silent until that point, piped up and said, "Would you mind if I read with Patrick? I think that, being an actor myself, it would be helpful." Ah, Corey had been an actor, that was it! Later on, I worked out why his name seemed familiar: I had seen him as Buzz

Gunderson, the thug who challenges James Dean to a car race and plunges to his death in *Rebel Without a Cause*. Now he was an in-demand, Emmy-winning TV director.

No one objected to Corey's suggestion, and he nodded at me. "Ready, Patrick?" And away we went. There were two scenes. After we read the first, Corey said I'd done well, but he gave me a couple of notes and we read it again. After that, one of the execs said, "I don't think we need to hear anything more. Thank you, Patrick. Someone will be in touch."

We didn't even get to the second scene. Was that a good thing or bad? I had no idea. Such is the fate of an actor—we know nothing until we know something.

I retreated to the little next-door room, where Joy Zapata was waiting with a big smile on her beautiful face. In a breathy whisper, she said, "That was great. Let's get that thing off your head." We did, and I indeed began to breathe a little more easily. But there was a sudden knock on the door, and in walked the three executives. *Shit, here comes the bad news.* But all they did was thank me once more, wish me a good day, and take off. When the door closed, Joy began jumping up and down gleefully. "You know why they did that?" she said. "They wanted to see what you looked like without the hair-piece. And I think they liked what they saw!"

I knew that the other candidate for the role was coming in to audi-tion, and I certainly didn't want to run into whoever he was. (I have seen the names of several actors floated in *Star Trek* histories, but I have never definitively learned the identity of this person.) I hurriedly stuffed my wig into my briefcase, gave Joy a hug, and made my way outside. My intention was to head straight for my car and drive some-place to enjoy a late breakfast. But the thought occurred to me that I might never again have an opportunity to be on the Paramount Stu-dios lot, so I decided to give myself a little tour. I walked past all the soundstages, wishing I knew which of my favorite movies had been shot there. I made my way with wonder through the backlots where entire urban neighborhoods had been erected. I came across the "tank" where they shot water scenes, behind which stood a huge green screen that allowed a director to add a background from any location in postproduction.

Then I realized that I was starving, having still not eaten anything that day. Wistfully leaving the studio lot and driving around, I found a nice coffee shop on Melrose Avenue, near which stood a big newsstand that sold Sunday UK newspapers. Perfect! I bought several, settled into a booth looking out onto Melrose, and ate a huge American breakfast as I read my papers and watched the world of Los Angeles go by, possibly for the last time.

In the meantime, absolutely nobody knew where I was, nor could they reach me. It's all so unimaginable now, so tethered are we to our phones, but in the late 1980s one could simply vanish from the radar at will. Which was exactly what I wanted to do, if only for a short while. If I had been a shrewd, tuned-in Hollywood actor, I would have immediately gone into a vigil by a landline telephone, waiting for Steve Dontanville to call with either good or bad news. But in the moment, I just wanted to decompress—which I did, for two and a half blissful hours.

I will now present to you my head-spinning reconstruction of what happened while I was enjoying my breakfast.

Soon after my audition, around 9:30 a.m., Steve got a call from Paramount, telling him that they wanted to offer me the role of Captain Jean-Luc Picard in *Star Trek: The Next Generation*. Steve already knew I was staying with David Rodes and immediately called his number. David wasn't there, but his then-partner, Jim, told Steve that David was teaching a class at UCLA. Jim suggested that if the matter was urgent, Steve should call the English Department at the college, which could connect him.

Steve did just that and explained that he needed to contact Patrick Stewart, houseguest of Professor David Rodes, as soon as possible. The English Department had already had happy dealings with me, so they were only too pleased to help. Someone brought a note to David in his classroom. As soon as he read it, he gave his students instructions to read without him and then made his way to his office. Fortunately, he remembered me telling him that I was having lunch that day with Professor Homer Swander, the American academic with whom we'd originally devised the traveling Shakespeare educational program. Homer, universally known as "Murph," for some reason, was based at the University of California, Santa Barbara, but David knew him well enough to know which hotel Murph stayed at whenever he was overnighting it in LA.

The plan was for me to pick up Murph at his hotel, and then we would go to lunch. I knocked on the door of his room, and just as Murph opened it, his room phone rang. He answered it, then said, with some puzzlement, "It's actually for you. It's David."

David Rodes, breathless with excitement, told me that my agent Steve was urgently trying to reach me, but he didn't know why. So I excused myself to Murph and called Steve right then and there. Steve, with full-throated Hollywood-agent fury, bellowed, "Where the fuck have you been?!"

Then, in slightly more measured tones, he continued: "I've been looking for you for hours! Paramount is offering you the role of the captain. We have to meet tomorrow to discuss this and get back to them. We'll have an early lunch." He named a restaurant opposite his office in the old ICM building on Beverly Boulevard. "Twelve noon," he said. "See you there. Don't be late. Oh—and congratulations, by the way." Like I said, head-spinning.

At David's house that night, my host cooked us a special dinner and we drank a lot of wine. I was a little hungover the next morning, but by the time I was to meet with Steve Dontanville—for the very first time in person—my head was clear. I liked him right away. He was, to my surprise, a smallish man dressed not in a power suit but casual clothes. He was way more easygoing in person than on the phone, but he naturally exuded don't-mess-with-me authority.

Steve walked me through the offer, which was printed out on many sheets of paper. A lot of it was incomprehensible to me, but when we got to the paragraphs about "compensation," Steve simplified it. The one thing that was clear to me right away was that this was money of a magnitude I had never before known or even imagined. I subsequently learned that it was a modest deal for an actor playing a lead role in an American TV series, but what did I know then? When Steve mentioned the per-episode figure of the first season, I had to ask him to repeat it. Then I wrote it down on a scrap of paper. *Nope*, I thought, *I've never seen numbers like that in the vicinity of my name.*

The real shocker, however, came when Steve explained that with each successive season, I would benefit from an increase in salary. I asked what he meant by "each successive season," and he replied, somewhat irritably, "Well, you will be contracted for six."

Six seasons? Six years of my life? What? I might have actually said those words aloud. Steve was nonchalant about it all. "That's standard," he said.

"But I can't do that, Steve," I said. "I've . . . I've got other things to do. There's, you know, this Peter Shaffer play called *Yonadab*, and, erm, you know . . ."

He looked at me as if I had gone insane.

"There has been nothing more important or financially beneficial than this in your entire career to date," he finally said. "And who knows, maybe it'll have a future. But. It is my opinion that you'll be lucky to make it through the first season. I don't think anyone can replicate the success of the original *Star Trek*. You'll be lucky to make it to Thanksgiving, to be honest."

I was unprepared for how frequently I would hear those same words at nearly every meeting I took in the months to follow. I had a few actor friends who knew the business well and had done stints in LA, and when I consulted them, they all echoed what Steve said. I distinctly remember one of them noting, "Look—just sign the contract, do the work, make some money for the first time in your life, get a suntan, maybe meet a girl or two, and then go home."

There was, however, a single dissenting voice. Ian McKellen was not yet a close friend, but we had gotten to know each other casually in the Royal Shakespeare Company, where our tenures overlapped yet we somehow were never cast in the same show. I admired Ian's work very much, but, as I had been with other actors whose skills I considered superior to mine, I was rather shy of him. But Ian happened to be in LA as all of this *Star Trek* drama was unfolding, so I had him over for lunch.

When I told him I was going to sign the contract, he almost bodily prevented me from doing so.

"No!" he said. "No, you must not do that. You *must* not. You have too much important theater work to do. You can't throw that away to do TV. You can't. No!"

There are few people, particularly with regard to acting, whose counsel I trust more than Ian's. But this time I had to tell him that I felt theater would return to my life whenever I was ready for it, whereas an offer of the lead role in an American TV series might never come again. Ian shook his head sadly, as if I were enlisting in the army, but, nevertheless, wished me good luck and gave me a big hug.

In the years since, we have become dear pals and *X-Men* colleagues, and Ian has acknowledged that he was wrong and I was right. More than once, in fact—primarily because I like making him say those words.

Ian's sentiments had an impact on me, though. I swore to myself that I would commit to this show with everything I had, no matter how pessimistic my colleagues and seemingly most of the industry were about its prospects. I was not going to treat *Star Trek: The Next Generation* cynically, as a paid holiday for a slumming British actor. It would become my obsession, and I would devote myself to it to the exclusion of everything else. I took this vow more seriously than was healthy for me, I realize now, but I was in my mid-forties, not a kid anymore, and I was running out of big chances. I am now almost twice as old as I was then, but sometimes I still feel the same way.

Believe it or not, I was so addled by the developments of that fateful Monday that I completely forgot to call Sheila to give her an update, and by the time I remembered, kicking myself, it was too late in the day, given the time difference between Los Angeles and London.

Subconsciously, I think now, I dragged my feet in calling Sheila because I knew that it was going to be a difficult conversation. When I flew over to the States for that final audition, I knew that she was not enthusiastic about the prospect of my getting the role. We both knew that the job would require me to spend much of my time in California, and there was already some tension between us regarding my ambitions to follow screen work wherever it took me. My rationale was that a move to California would have a positive, restorative effect on our marriage—it would be a fresh start—but Sheila was no fan of Los Angeles and had a thriving career of her own in England.

The call, when I placed it on Tuesday, didn't go badly: Sheila congratulated me and expressed happiness that I had won the role. But then came the logistical questions. "When do you start?" she asked. "Where will you live? Do you have a sense of how much of the year you'll be away from home?"

I'd jumped in feetfirst, not wanting the opportunity to pass, and I admitted that I had given no thought to any of these things. But now here they were, and here was Jean-Luc Picard, right in my face. *Patrick*, I thought, *your life is about to undergo some serious changes.*

Chapter Seventeen

I flew back to London a few days after signing my contract, having been told that shooting would begin on May 29, 1987. I had only a few weeks to get my English life in order before committing to my California life. I took a quick trip north to Yorkshire to let my brother Trevor and his family in on the big news—I wanted them to know why I wouldn't be seeing them for a while.

Back home, my kids were amused that I, of all people, was to be the new captain of the *Enterprise*. They were the *Trek* fans, not me. But they were generous in giving me a crash course on the Original Series, as it's now known, and the meaning it held in the wider world of popular culture. *Star Trek* had run for only three seasons on NBC in the late '60s. In syndication during the 1970s, repeats of the show acquired cult status in America that rapidly developed into a massive international following. By the 1980s, with Paramount's backing, Gene Roddenberry had revived the *Star Trek* franchise as a hugely successful series of films starring the original cast. We were the next phase of Gene's globe-conquering plan.

I should add that my children, Dan and Sophie, also took the opportunity to rib me about my *Trek* cluelessness. They would trade lines of dialogue between William Shatner's Kirk and Leonard Nimoy's Spock in front of me, knowing that I wouldn't catch the references, and reveled in my befuddlement. But they, of course, were thrilled. They couldn't believe that their boring old dad who spoke blank verse onstage would be doing something that they could connect with. Sheila put on a brave face, hoping she and I would figure out a way forward with us living several time zones apart. As for the kids, they were simply excited to go to Los Angeles for their school holidays.

To that point, there had been four *Star Trek* feature films made that starred the cast of the Original Series: *Star Trek: The Motion Picture, Star Trek II: The Wrath of Khan, Star Trek III: The Search for Spock,* and *Star Trek IV: The Voyage Home.* I watched them in order in preparation for my new job. The films struck me as a better reference point than the TV episodes from the '60s, because they were more up-to-date in terms of sensibilities and production values, and because I knew that actors are likely to deliver sharper performances in movies than they do on series television, which can become a monotonous grind.

With this prep under my belt, I returned to LA in mid-May, grateful for David Rodes's suggestion that I spend my first month on the job with him and Jim at their place in Brentwood. I was so wracked with insecurity that it meant a lot to come home to a "family supper" rather than wallow in profound loneliness and takeout food in a huge metropolis within a country not my own.

Later on that first season, I moved to an English acquaintance's Bel Air home that came complete with sweeping views and a swimming pool, which I used every day to stay Picard-fit. As luxurious as that place was, I am glad I spent my earliest weeks on *Star Trek: The Next Generation* as a coddled houseguest. Every evening at David and Jim's, my hosts had dinner waiting when I came home from work, providing me necessary companionship, good food, and comfort. Often they invited other guests, who were always very interesting people. In return, I brought home tales from the set, of which there were plenty.

What a crew we were, the new officers of the *Enterprise*! We had only two "name" actors, and they were the kids among us:

thirty-year-old LeVar Burton, who at nineteen had become a house-hold name as Kunta Kinte in the epic miniseries *Roots* and then com-pounded his fame in the '80s by hosting the highly influential PBS children's show *Reading Rainbow*; and fifteen-year-old Wil Wheaton, who had impressed the world a year earlier with his tenderness and poise in Rob Reiner's hit film *Stand by Me*. LeVar was playing Geordi La Forge, the blind helmsman who wears a special visor that allows him to see. Wil was Wesley Crusher, the precocious son of the ship's chief medical officer, Dr. Beverly Crusher.

The rest of us were chancers and hustlers from a variety of backgrounds, still angling for our big break. Gates McFadden, who had classical training in dance and a whole separate career as a chore-ographer, played Dr. Crusher. Jonathan Frakes, who had bounced from one TV drama to another, played William Riker, a.k.a. Number One, Picard's first officer. Brent Spiner, with a background in New York theater and sitcoms, played the android Lieutenant Com-mander Data. Michael Dorn, towering and equipped with a basso profundo voice, had played in rock bands, acted in the cop drama *CHiPs*, and was now our Klingon tactical officer, Worf. Denise Crosby, a granddaughter of the legendary singer Bing Crosby, had first broken through in soap operas and was our security chief, Tasha Yar. And Marina Sirtis, English of Greek parents, conservatory-trained, and a recent transplant to LA like me, played Deanna Troi, the ship's telepathic and empathic counselor and seer.

In the early days especially, I clung to Marina like a life raft be-cause I so desperately needed someone with whom I shared some cultural points of reference. She is from North London rather than the North of England, but we had in common our working-class and drama-school backgrounds and our passion for soccer. Marina was and is a passionate supporter of Tottenham Hotspur, a football club currently of an entirely different rank than my club, Huddersfield Town. But Huddersfield has a hundred-year history as distinguished as any club in the English Football League, and it brought me so much relief that there was someone on the bridge of the *Enterprise* who had even *heard* of Huddersfield Town.

As a group, we immediately bonded over the sorry state of our trailers. Don't get me wrong—we were all beyond thrilled to have our jobs and pitched no diva fits. But when you're working in series television, your trailer is your home for twelve or more hours a day, five days a week: your refuge for script study, your napping place, the space you need to clear your head. And ours? Well, I'd had better accommodations in regional theater. Each of us was afforded a small, boxlike cabin with a ledge running down one side, upon which lay a thin mattress of the type you might find in a prison cell, plus a small table and a hard, uncomfortable chair. And no toilet or sink. We had to share the facilities with everyone else on the lot. None of us expected luxury from Paramount, but a little convenience and comfort would have been nice.

Early on, the *TNG* cast was written up in the arts-calendar section of the *Los Angeles Times*, and I was referred to as an "unknown British Shakespearean actor." It was like going back to 1966 and the frenzied autograph seekers who were disappointed that I wasn't David Warner: "Are you anybody?" But I was mature enough to take this description in stride, and my peers were quick to play it for laughs. The day after that article appeared, I arrived at my trailer to find taped to its door a notice reading BEWARE: UNKNOWN BRITISH SHAKESPEAREAN ACTOR.

This, I quickly learned, was the work of Brent Spiner, an indication of his burgeoning status as the cutup of our group. Incidentally, this sign came up for auction a few years ago, and I had to inform the auction house in question that they had a fake on their hands. I have the certified Spiner original, which is a cherished part of my personal archive.

Little by little, this motley group of strangers of wildly disparate résumés began to coalesce into an ensemble, and I didn't feel so alone. At some point during the shooting of the pilot episode, I was taken aside for some media interviews. As I sat on a soundstage speaking to a journalist, I was unaware that LeVar was nearby, listening to the whole thing. When it was over, he appeared in front of me and said, simply, "Cucumber soup."

"I'm sorry?" I said.

"Cucumber soup. You are as cool as cucumber fucking soup."

I still consider this one of the most flattering compliments I've ever received, because LeVar is the coolest person *I* have ever met.

He, Jonathan, and Brent kept me sane that first season, each of them extending a hand of friendship and doing all they could to get me to lighten up. Because Lord knows, I needed to lighten up.

As I promised myself, I took the role of captain extremely seriously. Not just as the commanding officer within the world of the show, but at our workplace, with our cast. I believed that *TNG*'s success or failure was largely contingent on creating a wonderful ensemble, and not just of actors but also producers, directors, designers, and crew. And the truth is, I was terrified that I wasn't up to the job.

When we started work on the show, I must confess I found myself a little uneasy with Wil Wheaton's Wesley Crusher, and with Wil himself. I felt that the teen-on-the-*Enterprise* concept was a little gimmicky, but I was also put off by Wil's adolescent self-assurance. To me, he initially came off as cocky. But as I examined my feelings, I realized that they were not really about Wil or some notion that he should know his place as a juvenile actor—they reflected my own vulnerability. In those first weeks, I wished I had Wil's confidence.

My life that first season was one of monastic discipline and very little fun. I must have been the dreariest person to be around because I did little but *The Next Generation* prep, such was my terror that I would arrive on the set inadequately prepared. From Monday through Friday, we worked long days at Paramount. On Saturday, I would have a little lie-in and then wash and fold my laundry, which I still do. It's an obsession of mine. This stunned Jonathan Frakes, who couldn't fathom why the lead actor in a TV series did not send out his laundry or hire a housekeeper to do it for him; Jonathan still jokes with me that I have a "poverty mentality." Old habits die hard, I suppose.

On Saturday evenings, I often went to the Music Center downtown to listen to the Los Angeles Philharmonic. I was glad to see the arts complex flourishing two decades after I'd played a small role in launching it, via the productions that the Royal Shakespeare Company brought to the Ahmanson Theatre.

I also sometimes went on Fridays—if it looked like my day might wrap early, I scanned the LA Phil schedule I kept in my trailer. If there was a concert that night that I thought I would enjoy, I tore off my captain's uniform, changed into my civvies, and drove downtown to the Dorothy Chandler Pavilion with all due haste. I had a connection in management, and they always graciously found me a single seat and a pass to the patrons' bar. Since I had no work the following morning, I was free to enjoy a late solo dinner in the center's main restaurant. Not that I would have minded a little company—I did invite my coworkers to join me, but Gates was the only one of our cast who occasionally accepted my invitations.

All of Sunday, I devoted myself to script study of the episode we were shooting on Monday and Tuesday of that coming week, and, if time allowed, of the workdays to follow. I'd get annoyed if I was told, "Sorry, Patrick, we haven't gotten the scripts quite finished yet."

And what of Jean-Luc Picard himself? I had to crack his code. I knew he was a French-born, English-speaking graduate of Starfleet Academy. His preferred beverage was "tea, Earl Grey, hot" (clearly not a Yorkshireman). But how was I to find him within me, the way I had with Leontes and King Henry IV?

As has so often been the case in my life, William Shakespeare came to my rescue. I quickly came to understand that *Star Trek* is not naturalistic television, especially where its captains are concerned. There is a formality to the way they speak and comport themselves that reminded me of numerous Shakespearean situations I'd been in onstage. I should play Jean-Luc, I realized, as if he were a character in *Henry IV*, which is about brave men.

I also received some rare advice from Gene Roddenberry when he took me to dinner one night at a fancy restaurant near Paramount.

Gene never warmed to me. He sometimes visited the set and watched the proceedings from an inordinately high director's chair. As I sat in my captain's chair on the bridge, I sometimes caught him looking at me with a frown. But he eventually resigned himself to my presence and decided that the civil thing to do was to invite me out for a meal a couple of times. These were awkward affairs. At the second gathering, a lunch at his club, he spoke only of golf, a sport of which I do not partake. At the first get-together, he spoke mostly of his early days in television, pre–*Star Trek*, before I steered him to the subject of Jean-Luc.

"Did you ever read the Horatio Hornblower books?" he said.

"I did, yes—when I was a teenager," I replied. The publication of the Hornblower books, written by English novelist C. S. Forester, coincided with my childhood in the 1940s and '50s, and they were right up my alley—Horatio is a fictional officer in the nineteenth-century British Royal Navy who, thanks to his intelligence and daring, rises from a scrappy, unpromising background to the position of admiral.

"Read 'em all again," Gene said. "That's who Jean-Luc Picard is."

I found this somewhat frustrating, as if Gene were brushing me off, assigning me a stack of reading instead of offering his own thoughts on Jean-Luc. I felt as if I was being dismissed, and rather disrespectfully. That furthered my feelings of aloneness, for I had grown accustomed in British theater to a collaborative process of open, friendly discussion with the writers and directors of the plays I acted in.

But my solitariness had an upside, in that it pushed me into one aspect of Jean-Luc that I hadn't before considered: He is, by nature, a loner. In a sense, his job as captain, especially in the *TNG* days, required this to be true. I might have leaned too hard into Picard's go-it-alone attitude in the early episodes, though. I have certainly made him a more open and accessible man over time, especially in the recent *Picard* series.

One additional and potent influence in shaping Jean-Luc was my father, Regimental Sergeant Major Alfred Stewart—from him I drew Picard's stern, intimidating tendencies. But I like to think that my mother is in the captain, too, in his moments of warmth and sensitivity. They both live on through the character.

And in one very specific aspect, I owe a debt of gratitude to William Shatner. There came the time when I had to record the famous "Space, the final frontier" speech that opens each episode of *The Next Generation*, as it did the Original Series. The only difference between the 1966 and 1987 versions, much remarked upon at the time of *TNG*'s debut, is that whereas Kirk concludes his voice-over with "To boldly go where no man has gone before," Picard says, "To boldly go where no *one* has gone before," reflecting more enlightened times. I carefully listened to Bill's voice-over in preparation to do mine, and realized that there was nothing I could do to improve upon it. He'd done it perfectly, the tone and cadences spot-on. So I basically did his version syllable for syllable—the only time I intentionally copied Bill's performance as the captain.

Our pilot, "Encounter at Farpoint," was a double-length episode. In it, Picard meets his on-and-off nemesis Q, played devilishly by the aforementioned and dimple-chinned John de Lancie. Taunting Picard, Q appears in a variety of historical human getups to demonstrate the savagery and intellectual inferiority of *Homo sapiens*. Q, who is part of some kind of advanced, near-omniscient species, literally and metaphorically puts Picard on trial, demanding that the captain demonstrate that humanity is not inherently savage. With the aid of the *Enterprise* crew, Picard does just that, using peaceful tactics rather than violence to advance his aims, and freeing from captivity a huge, jellyfish-like alien creature so that it may rejoin its mate. The episode even included a cameo appearance from veteran actor DeForest Kelley, Dr. Leonard McCoy from the Original Series, now a 137-year-old admiral passing the torch to our new cast.

It was a well-written episode that did a good job of setting up all the main characters. I couldn't wait to get to work, but to my disappointment, my name was not on the call sheet for the first day of shooting. The producers elected to begin with a location day in Griffith Park, filming the scene in which Riker and Data meet for the first time in a patch of woods—which is actually inside the *Enterprise*'s holodeck, as the starship's holographic environmental simulation room is known.

I went anyway. If Captain Jean-Luc Picard was the lead character in *Star Trek: The Next Generation*, then I wanted to be fully part of the show from day one. So off I drove to Griffith Park.

It turned out to be a blessing, my not being on the call sheet, because there was no pressure on me the first day, and I got to observe Jonathan and Brent, whose chemistry was so instantly evident. This buttressed my hopes. If these two guys, who had never before worked together, could pull off a scene with such ease and comfort, then maybe I stood a chance.

My first day of work in front of the camera came twenty-four hours later. It was a scene in which I am walking purposefully through a corridor of the *Enterprise* and I pass a turbolift, whose door opens. Out steps Commander Riker, who speaks to me. I look at him but do not reply, walking on.

When we completed the first take, Jonathan shouted out, "Wow! So that must be what they call British face-acting!"

The whole set laughed. Now, I know of actors who would have been outraged by such insouciance from a lower-ranking officer, or at least an actor playing one. But I joined in the laughter, and it was genuine, because Jonathan's ribbing made me feel included. I was so scared and outside of my comfort zone, and I desperately needed the comic relief.

But I could be a severe bastard as well. My castmates doubled over in laughter when they flubbed multiple takes, and in rehearsals they sometimes ad-libbed things that weren't in the script to make their lines funnier. My experiences at the Royal Shakespeare Company and the National Theatre had been intense and serious. Naturally we enjoyed a bit of levity, but in general, we knew our time was limited and didn't fool around. On the *TNG* set, I grew angry with the conduct of my peers, and that's when I called that meeting in which I lectured the cast for goofing off and responded to Denise Crosby's "We've got to have some fun sometimes, Patrick" comment by saying, "We are not here, Denise, to have *fun*."

In retrospect, everyone, me included, finds this story hilarious. But in the moment, when the cast erupted in hysterics at my pompous declaration, I didn't handle it well. I didn't enjoy being laughed at. I stormed off the set and into my trailer, slamming the door.

After I'd been sulking for a while, I heard a gentle knock. I opened the door to find Jonathan and Brent standing there. "Hey, come on, let's talk about this," Jonathan said.

They were so wise and tactful in educating me, especially given that I was the senior actor in the cast. "Everything's okay. People respect you. But I think you misjudged the situation here," Brent said.

He and Jonathan acknowledged that yes, there *was* too much goofing around and that it needed to be dialed back. But they also made it clear how off-putting it was—and *not* a case study in good leadership—for me to try to resolve the matter by lecturing and scolding the cast. I had failed to read the room, imposing RSC behavior on people accustomed to the ways of episodic television—which was, after all, what we were shooting.

Over the years, I have learned so much from my *Star Trek* friends—about acting for television and simply being a good colleague. Jonathan Frakes was principally responsible for this, and it's no surprise that he evolved into an excellent director. His manner on set is always relaxed, with a twinkle in his eye—he so enjoys the work even as he goes about it seriously. I did my best to emulate his approach, because I recognized that one of my problems was that I had an anxious desire not only to work seriously, but *to be seen as working seriously.*

It took me that entire first season to relax and thaw out from being an uptight Englishman to a loose, amiable colleague given to quasi-American behavior. But bit by bit, I got there. Chance had thrown me into a company that was as generous and funny as it was talented. Our mutual respect grew over time into friendship and ultimately a feeling of family—and this feeling only gets stronger as we get older.

Our innate sense of camaraderie became especially apparent to me on Friday nights. That's when we were all exhausted and keen to wrap the week and go home. On these nights, we were usually shooting on the *Enterprise* bridge. Our custom was to shoot the whole set first, the wide shots. Gradually the shots got closer and tighter as the camera moved from the big viewscreen in front of the helmsmen's stations to the control panels at the rear. Those of us positioned in the front and middle of the bridge were able to shoot our coverage, go back to our trailers, change into our street clothes, and then play our lines off camera to the actors who were still in the shot. Poor Michael Dorn, as Worf, was always the last character with dialogue to stay in uniform, because he had to stand in front of his security panel at the very back. What's more, he had to stay in his ridged, heavy Klingon makeup, which took hours to apply and had inspired Frakes's nickname for him: Turtlehead.

Michael is the *TNG* actor perhaps the least like his character— a sweet, extraordinarily handsome man who plays a scary, martial, grumpy alien. We discovered that he could very easily be made to laugh and fall out of character. In the UK we call this "corpsing," and in the US, the more common term is "breaking up." So, on those Friday nights, we took it upon ourselves to make Michael break, pulling funny faces and saying our lines in silly voices. The Klingon makeup only made his breaking funnier, because Michael's laughter stretched his upper lip and caused his mustache to become unstuck—and then we were the ones laughing at the sight of him desperately trying to hold on to his mustache while remaining in character. Soon enough, it wasn't me but the director who played disciplinarian, clapping his hands and saying, "Okay, enough, cut it out! Let's get this wrapped!"

Michael's character, Worf, was also the basis for one of our cherished inside jokes. Worf is a Klingon who prides himself on his self-discipline—but precisely because he is of the warrior Klingon race, he can't help but occasionally lose his temper and fly into violent rages. Thanks to this disparity, we began using the term "Worfland" to describe any situation where things were spiraling out of control or one person was in a bad mood and therefore emotionally unpredictable. "Look out, it's Worfland!" became our shorthand for *Proceed with caution.*

My own little means of blowing off steam was performing my semi-regular line "Do your duty, Mr. Data" in a coarse Brooklyn accent: "Do yer doodi, Mister Datta!" This never failed to unsettle Brent, which was precisely what I took pleasure in doing. Brent and Jonathan, meanwhile, had a penchant for adding the non sequitur "I hate my space suit" to their dialogue.

At the end of the week, if our Friday workday hadn't gone too late, a group of us, mostly the guys, congregated right afterward at Nickodell, a faded old bar and restaurant on Melrose adjacent to the Paramount lot. The barman got to know us so well that he started making our drinks as soon as we entered: a Stoli martini on the rocks for Jonathan; a Belvedere martini up with an olive and a twist for Brent; Bushmills Irish whiskey for LeVar; single-malt scotch on the rocks for Gates; and Macallan scotch on the rocks for yours truly.

We all loved that place, which reeked comfortably of old Hollywood, and we were all equally saddened when, late in *The Next Generation*'s run, it closed its doors for good and was soon thereafter demolished in order to create VIP parking spaces at Paramount. Evidently the entire contents of Nickodell's were auctioned off—the ancient leather booths, the art on the walls, the lamps and chandeliers, the stools, even the bar itself. We of the *Enterprise* were unaware of the auction and still lament that we missed it. I would

have wanted the booths, for all they held: memories of a more glamorous time and the bums of Hollywood's most beautiful people.

Even as I acclimated to my new colleagues, though, those first few
months of shooting before we made it to air were full of anxiety. After
we completed filming "Encounter at Farpoint," I was still hearing
murmurings that the plug was going to be pulled at any moment.
The conventional wisdom in the industry was that we were a folly: an
ill-considered attempt to replicate the *je ne sais quoi* of something that
couldn't be replicated, and in syndication, no less, since Paramount
had not made a deal with a major network to air our show.

We never stopped working, though. After the pilot, we continued full steam ahead, shooting a further twenty-four episodes. And
good Lord, the next episode we did made me cringe. It was called
"The Naked Now"—a direct sequel to the Original Series episode
"The Naked Time"—and it played as a sex farce. Some crew members are infected with a virus that makes them act like they're intoxi-
cated: sweaty, giggly, and horny. Dr. Crusher gets horny for Picard,
Picard gets horny for Dr. Crusher, and Tasha Yar gets horny for nearly
everyone before focusing on Data. Denise's and Brent's dialogue has
become notable in *Star Trek* lore. Tasha, writhing in a midriff-exposing
outfit, asks Data if he, being an android, is "fully functional." He re-
sponds, "I am programmed in multiple techniques—a broad variety
of pleasuring."

A lot of people enjoy "The Naked Now," but to me, it smacked of
desperation, as if we had been on the air for years and the writers had
already emptied the cupboard of good ideas. But Gene, it is well
known, was a fan of cheesecake—he had Marina wear a minidress
and go-go boots in the pilot, as if the 1960s had never ended, and
had contemplated giving Deanna Troi three or even four breasts. We
all suffered to a degree from a directive to look sexy. Our one-piece
uniforms, created by the original *Star Trek*'s costume designer,

William Ware Theiss, were made of spandex and deliberately cut one size too small so that they never wrinkled and kept our bodies on constant display.

The problem was that these uniforms, beyond their leaving little to the imagination, were constricting to the point of causing pain. When I stood up straight—a requirement of the role—my one-piece stretched tightly across my chest, thighs, and back, which caused all sorts of aches. I campaigned to Gene directly to switch to different uniforms, but my pleas fell on deaf ears. Then my agent, Steve Dontan-ville, came up with a brilliant idea: I would consult my doctor and ask him to make an appeal, as a medical professional, to change the uniforms. Steve also threw his Hollywood weight around, intimating to the Paramount execs that if the situation was not remedied, he would bring suit against them for any muscular and joint damage I suffered.

Our strategy worked. It took a couple of seasons to implement the changes, but finally, a new costume designer, Robert Blackman, sympathetically came up with a two-piece uniform made of polyester. My new getup, with a top separate from my trousers, was still snug, but it had plenty of give. Gene, however, was adamant that Captain Picard's uniform must always be unfailingly smooth. So every time I sat down in my captain's chair, I tugged on the hem of my tunic—a tic that *Star Trek* fans have named the "Picard maneuver."

We were still in the thick of shooting Season One when "Encounter at Farpoint" aired on September 28, 1987. That morning, Robert Justman, my original Paramount champion, came to the set to con-gratulate us. "Do you realize," he said to me, "that tonight, more people will see your work than the total number of people who have watched you act in your entire career?"

This was quite something to ponder, but in my anxious state, it was not entirely comforting. I wondered if Robert was tactfully preparing me for the show's cancellation, basically saying, *This will be it, but enjoy the novelty of being on American TV for at least a night.*

But he was expressing genuine optimism. And with good reason. The pilot reached an awesome twenty-seven million viewers, making it the highest-rated syndicated hour-long drama in TV history. In the Los Angeles and Denver markets, "Encounter at Farpoint" beat all network programming in the eight-to-ten p.m. time slots, even though it aired on independent stations. Our reviews ranged from dismissive to grudgingly positive, but the reviews were not what mattered. The fans were. All the skeptics around me had failed to grasp something fundamental. The *Star Trek* faithful weren't looking to pick holes in *The Next Generation*; they were looking for reasons to love it.

I first began to grasp this as my castmates returned from their weekend breaks with giddy reports from the *Star Trek* conventions they had attended.

"You were at a *Star Trek* what?" I asked Marina one particular Monday morning.

"A convention," she said. "They've been having them for the old show for years. But now they're having them for *us*. People are loving the show. You get up on a stage, you do a Q&A, you sign some autographs. It's really gratifying to see the response. You should do one, Patrick."

"I can't imagine anyone would want to see me, Mina," I said. She smirked at my ignorance.

For most of the first season, I was too committed to my monastic Picard prep to yield a weekend of my time to one of these so-called conventions. And I was fearful of embarrassment: showing up to an empty room. But finally, as Season One was nearing its end, I threw caution to the wind and agreed to appear at a *Star Trek* convention in Denver.

In the greenroom, a gracious organizer said to me, "It's wonderful that you're finally doing this, Patrick. In ten minutes, we'll be ready to introduce you."

"What's the audience like? Is anybody out there?" I asked. I was totally serious. This prompted funny looks all around.

In due time, I was escorted to the wings, where someone introduced me: "And here he is, Jean-Luc Picard himself, Patrick Stewart!"

I walked out to an audience of over two thousand people, on their feet, roaring. And I hadn't even done anything! I tried to start speaking but could not, because the roar had not abated. I was overwhelmed. At forty-seven years of age, I had stood on stages thousands of times and performed in hundreds of shows. But I had never experienced anything like this. I thought back again to that miniskirted girl outside the Royal Shakespeare Theatre in Stratford, asking me, "Are you anybody?" *Oh, if only she could see me now*, I thought.

Chapter Eighteen

Season One of *The Next Generation* was decidedly a mixed bag, but really, what first season isn't? I was finding my way as Jean-Luc Picard and an episodic-TV actor, the writers were figuring out the tone of the show, and the cast was sorting itself out. Denise Crosby unfortunately left partway through our first season, unhappy with her role. The writers killed off the character Tasha Yar, but the cast bore Denise no ill will, and indeed, she returned to the fold on several occasions, as Tasha in an alternate timeline, and then as Tasha's half-Romulan daughter, Sela.

I was gradually learning my way into the *Star Trek* universe as well. In our fifth episode, "The Last Outpost," Picard encountered the Ferengi, a shady species of small-statured beings with huge, paddle-shaped ears whose cartilage extended up and over their faces, meeting just above the bridge of the nose. This was Gene at his best, creating an alien species simultaneously scary and funny, and worthy adversaries. Armin Shimerman, the actor who played the Ferengi leader, proved so charismatic that he became the new recurring character Quark in the *TNG* spin-off series *Deep Space Nine*.

In the Original Series, Gene often conspired to get Bill Shatner and company into period costumes, and when word got around that I loved Raymond Chandler's detective novels, the writers came up with an episode for me titled "The Big Goodbye." It created a scenario in which Picard, in the holodeck, gets to play a noirish character named Dixon Hill, not unlike Chandler's Philip Marlowe. This was one of those episodes where Picard's fantasy role-play was virtually indistinguishable from my own. To find myself, in my late forties, walking onto a Paramount Pictures soundstage in a trench coat and trilby was almost too "dreams come true" for me to bear.

The producers had also brought in a ringer as my adversary: Lawrence Tierney, an older actor who had actually played a series of film noir heavies in the 1940s, including the title role in *Dillinger*. Brent and Jonathan warned me that Tierney walked it like he talked it—he had a long rap sheet for drunken brawling and was known for being an intimidating presence. He arrived on our set with a scowl on his face, like he was looking for a fight. Nevertheless, I strode up to him and offered my hand in welcome, something I always did with guest actors. Tierney didn't accept my hand. He just looked me up and down and said, "You're not American. What arya, British?"

Was this some kind of test? I affirmed that I was indeed British. To my relief, he broke into a grin and said, "Good actors, the Brits."

The penultimate episode of the first season, "We'll Always Have Paris," was notable for giving Picard an old flame from his youth, Jenice, now married to someone else. It was also notable for having Michelle Phillips play Jenice. It fell to Frakes to inform me, the pop-culture idiot, that Michelle was a famous music star, formerly one-quarter of the Mamas and the Papas. I had truly never heard of her and was overwhelmed by her warmth and magnetic beauty, to the point that it affected my performance. The writer's room complained that we lacked chemistry. I chalk this up to being on my best behavior. I was a married man and did not want to make a blushing arse of myself.

We wrapped the season under rushed circumstances because there were murmurings early in 1988 that the Writers Guild of America was about to go on strike. Which, indeed, they did, on March 7 of that year. The last few scripts were perfunctory in their execution, but we did our best to make them sing. And then, as fast as you can say "Engage," it was springtime and I was on a flight back to Heathrow.

Returning to England was strange. Partly because it wasn't any different—it had always been my home. But after the events of the last several months, *I* felt different. I found myself uncomfortable driving on the other side of the road, not wearing shorts every day, and not having to get up at five a.m. most mornings.

Yet there I was, back in our semidetached house on Park Road, close to the Chiswick railway station. A very typical, quiet, middle-class neighborhood in West London. Sheila and I were the only ones at home at this point. Daniel was now a student abroad, a freshman at the California Institute of the Arts. Sophie was a teenager in boarding school in the beautiful countryside south of London, and at home only every other weekend. They had grown up so fast.

In those pre-internet days, news didn't travel nearly as quickly as it does now, and the name Jean-Luc Picard didn't mean much to anyone locally. When I ran into old friends, more than one of them said something along the lines of "Crikey, because you weren't around, I assumed you were doing a season with the RSC in Stratford."

My relatives in Yorkshire were wiser to my situation when I visited them, but that's because I had kept them abreast of my career. Several told me they were making plans to visit me in LA, but I tried not to give their plans too much encouragement because the Writers Guild strike was still underway in Hollywood and we didn't know if there would be a Season Two of *Star Trek: The Next Generation*.

Yes, after twenty-six episodes, all that work, those terrific ratings, and those two thousand people on their feet at the convention I attended, we were still in limbo. And not just in my perpetually worried mind. Ours was an expensive show to produce, and the longer the strike went on, the more momentum we lost, and the more likely it became that Paramount would cut its losses and make *TNG* a one-and-done show.

The strike did indeed drag on, all the way into August 1988, and we came closer to being canceled than most people realize. During our hiatus, Paramount invited me to attend a TV convention in Cannes, the French Riviera town famous in part for its film festival. Sheila joined me, and for a moment, all was right in the world. We met an officer from the US Navy whose ship was moored in the bay, and he informed us that *TNG* was watched religiously on board. Even better, he invited us to an event on the ship the following evening. We were picked up at our hotel, driven to the dockside, and ferried across the bay to the ship, where we were greeted as heroes and feted with music and drink.

But at a subsequent dinner with some senior Paramount people, one of them confided to me in hushed tones that *The Next Generation*'s cancellation was all but certain. Right then I did not feel unduly disappointed. In the weeks since I had returned to England, I had resumed many of my old routines, and it had all been a bit of a dream, those days in Southern California. Maybe it was *Yonadab* time after all.

But no more than a few days after we got back from Cannes, the strike came to an end, and Steve Dontanville was on the phone telling me that I was due back at Paramount in ten days.

During Season One, I had relied on the kindness of friends for lodging. But this time, I returned to LA with no place to live. I stayed in the Beverly Hills Hotel while I searched for rentals and found a small apartment located in West Hollywood, conveniently close to work.

Well, let's be honest about this place. It was not in an apartment building or even in a subdivided house; it was a studio above someone's garage. There was a sitting room, an open kitchen to one side, and, in a partitioned corner, a bedroom and tiny bathroom. It was far from being at all fancy, and in fact, I was so uncomfortable about it that I never invited anyone over. This aroused suspicion among my castmates, some of whom had the notion that I was secretly living with a girl they had never met. That wasn't the case. It was just me, my ascetic devotion to the show, and my so-called poverty mentality.

One change noticeable as we began Season Two was evident in the parking lot. Each older car with thousand of miles on it had been replaced by a brand-new Audi or Mercedes and such. Michael Dorn, a licensed pilot, even bought himself a small plane. Me? I drove a Honda in London, so I went to the Honda showroom in Beverly Hills and selected a brand-new silver Prelude. I drove it proudly onto the Paramount lot, thinking it just the kind of classy car the leading actor in a TV series should have. Instead, I was roundly mocked for my purchase. When we went out together for dinner and the valet brought my Prelude around, my fellow actors pretended to be so embarrassed that they turned their backs to it and me so that other people did not think I was part of their party. Frakes was the worst offender.

As it happens, my current home is only a few blocks away from that garage-top nest, though it is considerably more comfortable. But every time I drive past my old place, I am reminded of those days, which helps keep me humble. Stop laughing, Jonathan.

Snug in my perfectly acceptable studio, I came to realize that *Star Trek: The Next Generation* was not about to go away, and that it might go *all* the way, as in the full six years of my contract. This induced a mild panic attack, for as much as I wanted the show to succeed, I had never envisioned the future I now found myself living in. Given the intensity with which I approached my episode prep, and given that *Star Trek* would take ten months a year and more than twenty episodes per season, I would not have the bandwidth concerning the stage for a *loooong* time.

I never did get to revive *Yonadab*.

Seasons Two and Three saw our show get progressively better with episodes such as "The Measure of a Man," "Yesterday's Enterprise," and "Sins of the Father," as the writers got the hang of our world and were less inclined to echo certain plotlines from the original *Star Trek*. We also got a huge lift as an ensemble when we were joined in the second season by Whoopi Goldberg, who played the alien barkeep Guinan in the *Enterprise*'s newly invented cocktail lounge, Ten-Forward. Whoopi was already a Broadway and movie star, and we couldn't believe that she would take such a role on our program.

During her second day on set, I found Whoopi sitting alone, and I asked if she minded if I joined her. We had a delightful chat, and eventually I felt comfortable enough to ask her why, at this towering moment in her career, she would choose to play a supporting role in a syndicated sci-fi TV series. She at once began to tell me about her childhood in a housing project in a tough neighborhood of Manhattan. She had watched and loved the original *Star Trek* series. A big reason she was so taken with the show, she explained, was because there, in the middle of her TV screen, was a Black actress, Nichelle Nichols, playing Starfleet officer Lieutenant Nyota Uhura. Whoopi said that watching Nichelle gave her hope and pride. "I thought, 'Well, one of us made it to the future, and into space,'" she said.

This marked the beginning of so many wonderful times I would spend with Whoopi. She fit right in with our cast and crew, lending humor to our episodes and, in carefully selected moments, a gravitas that only she could pull off.

There was one major downside to the start of Season Two: Gates McFadden had been fired. I knew that she had been restless and critical of some aspects of how her character, Beverly Crusher, had been written, but I thought that forcing her to leave was an extreme measure and a harsh move on Gene Roddenberry's part. I asked Gates just recently what had happened, and she clarified that she always got along well with Gene. It was Maurice Hurley, the original head writer and showrunner for *The Next Generation*, with whom she'd butted heads, and it was Maurice who engineered her ousting.

Diana Muldaur came aboard as the *Enterprise*'s new chief medical officer, Dr. Katherine Pulaski. Diana is a fine actress who had
been twice featured in the Original Series, but she never established much in the way of a rapport with me, and seemed to function at a remove from the rest of the cast. Our one memorable
moment came on a day when Diana was assigned a rather complex
speech to deliver to Picard. She was given only a couple of hours to
learn it. We didn't have teleprompters on *The Next Generation*, so I
kindly offered to tape a printout of her dialogue on my hairless
forehead. Diana played the scene without a hitch, grateful to me for
serving as her flesh-and-blood teleprompter. By season's end, however, it was evident that she was not a good fit for *TNG*, and Diana
left the show. Fortunately, the departure of Maurice Hurley after
the second season cleared the way for Gates to return. At the invitation of Rick Berman, she rejoined us for Season Three.

Story-wise, the biggest development of the second season was
that Picard and the *Enterprise* crew finally got a truly frightening
adversary—the Borg, a collective of cybernetic drones linked to a
central hive mind. The Borg members' scary appearances were the
result of a brilliant collaboration between our costume designer,
Durinda Wood, and our makeup chief, Michael Westmore. Durinda
came up with the Borg's overall look of the exoskeletal bodies covered with intestine-like tubes, while Michael did the head design,
devising the pale, zombie-like base makeup and the face applications
made from disassembled electronics. The result was truly unsettling,
especially when Picard himself was temporarily "assimilated" into
the collective, and my own head got slathered in tubes and gaskets—
part of what is widely considered some of our most cherished work:
the two-parter "The Best of Both Worlds," a cliff-hanger moving us
right into Season Four.

I was throwing myself so thoroughly into my work that when
Sheila and the kids visited, I wasn't much fun. Dan and Sophie loved
frolicking on the beach, certainly, and sometimes Sheila and I enjoyed a nice dinner out. But Sheila had a career, too, and a busy one
at that. And it was in London. And for all my hopes that she might

change her tune, she never warmed up to the idea of living full-time in Los Angeles.

The strain on our marriage was alleviated somewhat when I finally took the plunge and bought a proper house for us in LA. With a Realtor's help, I found us a place in Silver Lake, a neighborhood that is now expensive but was then only on the cusp of being fashionable. I loved it at first sight—it had been developed in the 1920s, so the housing stock was old, and many of these homes were built into hillsides, so they offered great scenery. Our house, on Moreno Drive, had an end-to-end view of the actual lake (which is, in fact, a reservoir) and, beyond it, a panoramic view of the San Gabriel Mountains, including Mount Baldy. My wife and kids marveled at all this when they came for Christmas in 1988, though Sophie did complain about the Eastside location. "What's the point of living in California if you can't see the ocean?" she said.

But the fact remained that Sheila and I were living and working in two cities, and neither of us wanted to budge. Inexorably, and unfortunately, we drifted apart. I slowly grew accustomed to living alone, going to my LA Philharmonic concerts on Saturday nights and grabbing an occasional dinner with one of my fellow transplanted Brits.

And then, during the third season of *TNG*, I met someone.

For some time, I had been grousing to the *Trek* writers that Riker got all the action with the ladies. Jonathan Frakes was the show's latter-day Captain Kirk figure, with no shortage of flirtations and romantic interests (Riker and Deanna Troi were even old flames), whereas I was the solitary old buzzard who experienced only poignant reunions with ex-girlfriends and storylines that concluded with wistful what-might-have-been endings.

"Why can't we have an episode where we actually see Picard fall for someone?" I said. "We could see their relationship develop in real time and then, presumably, it would fall apart."

To my relief, the writers proved receptive to my pitch, and one of them, Ira Steven Behr, wrote a charming script called "Captain's Holiday" that checked all of these boxes. Jean-Luc, overworked, is urged to pack his bags and leave the *Enterprise* for a vacation on Risa, a so-called "pleasure planet." He puts on his leisure wear, which includes a deeply plunging powder-blue V-neck tunic, and off he goes.

Ira provided Jonathan and me with one of our funniest bits in the whole series. As Picard is leaving, Riker casually asks him to bring back a souvenir called a Horga'hn. Picard says, "Consider it done," and unquestioningly purchases one soon after he arrives on Risa. What he doesn't know is that a Horga'hn, which looks like a hand-carved Mayan phallus, is an indigenous symbol of fertility and carnal pleasure. Picard, sitting poolside, unthinkingly places his Horga'hn next to his lounge chair and opens a book, growing exasperated as one barely dressed woman after another propositions him. Finally, one of them explains to him why this keeps happening.

"The Horga'hn is the Risian symbol of sexuality," she says. "To own one is to call forth its powers. To display it is to announce you are seeking *jamaharon*. Do you seek *jamaharon*?"

Picard does a slow burn before muttering, "Riker!"

I was not, at the time, seeking *jamaharon*. Nor was Picard. But in the course of "Captain's Holiday," through a series of plot developments, Picard falls for a beautiful archaeologist named Vash. Their romance doesn't last, but it is nonetheless an experience that Picard clearly enjoys before he rejoins his crew on the *Enterprise*.

On the second day of shooting the episode, the call sheet indicated that Jennifer Hetrick, the actress playing Vash, would be working that morning. As I have noted earlier, it was always my policy to personally welcome guest actors to our show. So, when I arrived on the lot, I asked after Miss Hetrick and was told she was already in the makeup trailer.

The makeup trailer was only five paces from my own. I dropped my stuff in it, turned on my heel, walked two steps, and then, for some reason, stopped. I can't explain it—some force halted me in my tracks. I stared at the ground for fifteen or so seconds and then returned to my trailer. But again, I just stood still, as if frozen. A minute or two later, I shook my head and headed back out the door.

When I entered the makeup trailer, I was greeted by the usual boisterous morning scene, with every seat filled and Frakes offering his customary "Morning, Number One!" to which I responded with the same three words. ("Number One" was, of course, how Picard addressed Riker on the bridge of the *Enterprise*. As for Jonathan, he called me Number One because I was listed first on the *TNG* call sheet.) The only face I didn't recognize was that of the woman sitting opposite the door. I made eye contact with her through the mirror. She was lovely and smiling brightly at me.

"Hello, Jennifer, welcome to the show," I said, offering my hand. Unlike Lawrence Tierney, she was happy to shake it.

Right away, my colleagues were on my case, saying, "Ooohhh, watch out, Jennifer, this guy's trouble. Don't fall for the accent, it's a fake." This sort of workplace innuendo was customary in those days, but perhaps it would not happen today.

Playing along, I said, "Jennifer, if any of these guys give you problems or trouble of any kind, at *any* time, you tell me and I will deal with them, you understand?"

Michael, Frakes, Brent, and Marina responded with hoots of derision. Jennifer just laughed. "I think I can take care of myself, but thank you, Captain," she said.

We had a good day of work. Everyone was happy with the shoot and enjoying the company of our guest actress. It was not until I was driving home that evening that I found myself thinking about that moment when I had stood frozen between the trailers. What had happened? Why did I stop and go back? It was some kind of weighty feeling, but not one that could necessarily be articulated. So, I put the thoughts aside and went home to supper and bed.

The week went by swiftly. Jenny (as she liked to be called) and I found a good rapport, and we both had a fun time in our romantic playacting together. She was a pleasure to work with, and there was no doubt I felt very attracted to her, but that was the extent of it. I was not concocting any plans.

My colleagues were on their best behavior, though once or twice, in confidence, I received the comments "You're a lucky man, she's good" and "Wow, she's a beauty." All true.

On our final day of shooting "Captain's Holiday," Jenny and I worked quite late. When we finally wrapped, she said she would stop by my trailer to say goodbye after she had changed. I replied that it would have been nice for us to go for a drink somewhere, but it was getting so late. "I do, however, have a bottle of wine in my trailer, so come by for a glass," I said.

That's exactly what happened. Before we knew it, an hour had passed, and I admitted to Jenny that I was attracted to her.

I invited her out for dinner the following Saturday and she accepted. We had a delightful Saturday evening, and after dinner, I drove her back to her apartment.

And then it was really happening: *jamaharon*, if you will.

I was pleased to be with Jenny but also anxious and uncomfortable. There was no way around it—I was cheating on my wife. Jenny and I kept our heads down for a long time. But when I told Brent and Jonathan that I was seeing her, neither seemed surprised. They were both very supportive but advised me to take things slowly and not get caught up in drama.

A difficult time lay ahead. Easter was coming, and Sheila and Sophie were flying in to stay with me for two weeks at the Silver Lake house (Daniel, being in college, was already in California). I saw Jenny one more time and told her the situation, explaining that I could not be in touch while my family was in town, and she seemed okay with that.

Sheila's two-week visit was very difficult. We were both struggling emotionally and reading the writing on the wall. Toward the end of her stay, we were to meet with our financial adviser, whose office was in Santa Monica. We were driving west on the 10 freeway when Sheila suddenly said, "You're seeing someone, aren't you?"

I still remember exactly where we were on the freeway at that moment, and I get a shiver every time I'm there.

I was totally unprepared for Sheila's question. I remained silent for a long moment, staring at the road in front of me. But finally I nodded my head and quietly, barely got the word out: "Yes."

It was Sheila's turn to be silent for a moment. And then she said, "Yes, I knew it."

We quietly drove on, me in a state of shock. We found a meter close to the office. I got out, fed the meter, and opened the door for Sheila to get out. She didn't move. She announced that she would rather wait in the car.

Standing on the sidewalk, I looked for a long time at her face in profile.

I got through the financial meeting as quickly as I could and returned to the street. As I rode down the elevator, it dawned on me that Sheila might not have waited. It was possible she'd walked away and hailed a cab. But there she was, still in the car.

I got in and said, "Sheila, we must talk, don't you think?"

I knew that we could not go straight home because sixteen-year-old Sophie was there. So I drove east on Wilshire Boulevard until I figured out what to do. There was a hotel in Westwood Village, near UCLA, with a secluded bar. It was four in the afternoon, a dead time, and I knew the bar would be quiet and private. We sat in a corner and I ordered wine. We both needed it.

I told her I was sorry, and we talked about what to do. Sheila asked me if I wanted a divorce. I told her I didn't know—a pathetic response, but true to how I felt.

I talked about being alone in LA, and she talked about being busy with her work in London. We both calmed down and spoke intimately, probably abetted by the wine. After an hour or so, we got back in the car and drove to our house in Silver Lake.

Never doubt the perceptivity of kids. Sophie sensed right away that something was wrong. Sheila put her arms around our daughter and held her close, assuring her that everything was fine. The last couple of days they were there, however, were ghastly for all of us. When the day arrived for Sheila to return to England, I think that she and I were both feeling relief. At least our issues would now be out in the open.

Case in point: There was a moment that final day when I was walking up the stairs and Sheila met me on the landing. She commented, "That's the first time I've heard you sing in days." I hadn't even been aware that I *was* singing.

I went on working after Sheila and Sophie left. It was tough to give myself over to the *Star Trek* world, but also a blessing. It kept me occupied and in the company of friends. I told Brent and Jonathan what had gone down over Easter, and they were considerate, supportive listeners.

I didn't contact Jennifer for a few days. Rather, I spent a lot of time thinking about where I was, what was happening to me, and *what did I want?* The rational part of me told me to stop seeing Jenny. The emotional part of me told me that was nonsense and I should give her a call. But I didn't; rather, I called Sheila in London to further discuss our situation. Suffice it to say, our chats did not go well.

Right at this time, fate and Paramount provided me with a three-day break from shooting. I took the opportunity to go away on my own and ponder my future. I drove some way up the Pacific Coast Highway, found a pleasant small hotel near the beach, and walked for miles every day. I was glad to be alone because I had the space to reflect not only on my relationship with Sheila, but on the impact that my relationship with Jennifer was having on it. Before I headed home again, I came to a very sad but firm conclusion: My marriage was over.

In fact, if I was being honest with myself, it had been over for quite a while, well before I met Jenny. I believe that Sheila and I had been happiest in the years when I was a full-time member of the Royal Shakespeare Company. It was the closest thing a professional actor can have to a regular job in a regular workplace. Sometimes we had to be in Stratford and sometimes in London, but that aside, I was locked into a routine, like a commuting salaryman. But as I got rest-less in the 1980s, curious to see what else was potentially out there for me, be it onstage, on TV, or in film, I got the sense that Sheila wasn't so keen on me pursuing this curiosity. This is, of course, not to villainize her, but to illustrate that our visions of life together had begun to diverge well before *Star Trek* and Los Angeles beckoned.

I wrote a letter to Sheila to tell her of my decision and followed up with a phone call. Her reaction at first was very matter-of-fact, resigned but distant. That didn't last, though. She decided to fly back to LA to have it out with me face-to-face.

Sophie and Daniel were also upset with me. I couldn't blame them: I had moved far away for work, I had fallen for another woman, I was breaking up with their mom, and it wasn't even close to an amicable split. But while she was in town, Sheila and I agreed on one thing: We would indeed move forward with a divorce. She went back to London to seek legal advice and I did the same in Los Angeles.

I called Jenny and asked if we could meet. I told her everything. She was very sympathetic and asked me if I no longer wished to see her. I assured her that I very much did.

When we wrapped the third season, in April 1989, she and I went away for a couple of days, keeping a low profile; I had learned in the meantime, to my horror, that my new celebrity status meant the Brit-ish tabloid press had found out about my pending divorce and had been harassing Sheila, knocking on the door of our London house and lingering by the front gate—an indignity she did not deserve. A bad situation had grown worse.

I, meanwhile, had taken to spending the occasional night at Jenny's apartment in West Hollywood. When I stayed there, I was careful never to park my car near her building but a block or two away, in the belief that I could more stealthily enter and exit her place that way. Bad decision. One morning as we stepped out onto the street, a man sprang out in front of us on the sidewalk, pointing a camera with a long lens in our faces. "Oh, fuck," I remarked to Jenny.

I turned with her in the other direction, but the photographer followed us. I put up my dukes and prepared to slug the man (potentially another bad decision), but Jenny wisely held me back. "The car isn't far, let's just go around the corner and get to it," she said.

But when we did turn that corner—*wshtt, wshtt, wshtt!* That oppressive noise of paparazzi snaps surrounded us, like a plague of insects. There were two more photographers directly in front of us. We'd been besieged by a team.

We got into the car and started driving down 3rd Street. I made it about four hundred yards before another car swerved in front of us, blocking our way. It was an accomplice of the photographers. So I put the car in reverse, only for a second car to swerve into our path. We were trapped.

Luckily, a police car happened to be passing by, and I flagged it down. As it approached, the two camera cars sped from the scene. Jenny and I were free, but deeply shaken and violated by the experience. I had read of such tabloid-press sieges, but I never imagined that I would be at the center of one.

Jenny and I continued to see each other for a while, but we had to do so furtively, away from lurking cameras. Such was the extent of our caution that I had a friend book us a stay at a small, extremely private estate on an island off the east coast of Fiji, way down in the South Pacific, as remote as it got. And even then, Jenny and I traveled separately; she arrived two days after me. We tried our best to relax and enjoy ourselves, but one morning, Jenny told me that the strain was simply too much. It couldn't go on like this and she wanted to go home. I understood and escorted her to the airport. We said goodbye with sadness but no rancor.

Jenny returned to *The Next Generation* for a second episode as Vash and also reprised the character on *Deep Space Nine*. She later married and had a daughter, news that gladdened my heart.

But alone on my Fijian island, where I spent five joyless days after Jenny left, I felt like a failure. The unknown British Shakespearean actor had somehow been transformed into paparazzi and tabloid bait. His career was taking off, but his family had fallen apart. How had it come to this?

Chapter Nineteen

A small mercy: My return trip from Fiji provided me with an unforeseen spirit-boosting experience. In the private departure lounge, a man came up to me and very politely let me know that he was a fan. His name was Peter Douglas. When we were airborne, he introduced me to his wife and explained that they were coming home from their honeymoon. His father, he said, was Kirk Douglas.

The legendary Kirk Douglas was one of my childhood heroes, his movies—among them *Ace in the Hole*, *Lust for Life*, and *Detective Story*—a mainstay of my visits to the cinemas of Yorkshire. I told Peter this, and he graciously offered to make an introduction— Kirk and his wife, Anne, were soon to host a party, so Peter made sure that I received an invitation.

I felt out of place among the old-Hollywood types at the Douglas house, but Kirk was so welcoming and generous that he put me at ease. I can't say that we became close friends, but we kept in touch thereafter as friendly acquaintances (including one moment to come that I shall never forget), an unimaginable outcome for the Mirfield boy I had once been.

A few decades later, in 2016, it came to my attention that Kirk had just celebrated his hundredth birthday. I let Peter know that I would love to see his father again. He set up a time for us to meet, and along with Sunny, to whom I was by then married, I went to have tea with Kirk. He was quite frail by then but happy to see us both, and, it must be said, clearly delighted to be in the presence of my charming, beautiful wife. I was able to ask Kirk a few questions about his career, and he stunned me by saying that there were only three of his hundreds of films of which he was proud. I asked him to tell me which three, and he did, but on the condition that I never tell anyone else. So forgive me—a promise is a promise.

I returned to LA back in 1989, and my empty house in Silver Lake. With no wife and no girlfriend, I went through a rough time. Back at work, I found myself dependent on sleeping pills to get me the hours of restoration I needed to do my job properly. When we finally reached a break in filming after eight weeks, I quit the pills, but sleep became almost impossible. I often woke in the early hours with a full-body feeling of panic, my legs sweating profusely, which had never happened before and hasn't since.

I think this was the toughest period of my life. As a child, when I was being exposed to my father's fury, I was unambiguously a victim, along with my mother and brother. But with this separation and pending divorce from Sheila, I was the one responsible. Yet I also felt that getting divorced was ultimately the most responsible thing I could do. This confusion of feelings simply dragged me down. Also, both of my children were angry with me, particularly Sophie, and I sense that her fury has never entirely gone away.

My house, formerly a source of solace and pride, was also becoming problematic. I never stopped loving its views, but its setting had inspired some odd layout choices by the architect. It was a small residence on three floors. The bottom two floors, where the common areas were located, were embedded into the steep hillside. The bedroom was on the street and garage level. As such, the

door at the back of the garage opened directly onto the master bedroom.

But that was the least of it. As I have mentioned, I had never
sought out or particularly believed in paranormal experiences. The
mist and glow around the paintings in my drama teacher Ruth Wynn
Owen's house caused me more distress than wonder. So I was more
wary than thrilled when weird things started happening on Moreno
Drive. Returning home from the Paramount lot one evening, I
opened the door to the master bedroom and immediately my nostrils filled with the smell of something roasting in the kitchen, one
floor down. I thought that I must have left the oven on when I went
to bed the night before, so I hurried down the stairs to the kitchen,
where the smell was even stronger. Yet the stove was not even turned
on, and the oven was cold and empty.

In another instance, Daniel was staying with me, and when I got
home from work, he was clearly freaked out. When I asked him what
was wrong, he led me down into the living room, where the floor was
scattered with books that had obviously come from the shelves lining the wall. An earthquake? No. Dan told me he had been watching
TV when the books suddenly flew across the room, as if thrown with
great force. The incident scared him so badly that he left the house
and returned only when he knew I would soon be home. He would
never again spend a night in the house alone.

Then the noises began: the sound of voices coming from a room
that was empty; the sound of footsteps on the stairs when nobody
was using them. At bedtime, I had a ritual of turning off the lights
and switching off whatever else needed shutting down, progressing
bottom to top. Every night as I crossed the second-floor hall to go
upstairs to the bedroom floor, at a point just before the first step, the
temperature of the space abruptly turned icy. As soon as I put my
foot on the first step, it went back to normal. I had an urge to look
over my shoulder, but I never dared.

All of this prompted me to think of selling the place and finding somewhere else to live. The housing market was not strong at
that moment, however, so I went for the other option of renting it

out. A deal was done very quickly thanks to a delightful young couple with a child. They were clearly enchanted by the place, and I had already found a house of my own to rent in Beverly Hills. I moved out like a shot and immediately felt much safer in my new home, a modernist structure of concrete, glass, and steel. And not just safer—*alone*.

A few months later, I got a call from my tenant family, specifically the mother. There were a couple of routine problems with the washer-dryer, and she asked me to address them. We chatted pleasantly for a while, and just as I was about to hang up, she said, "Oh, by the way, you never told us about the *other things* that came with this house."

I asked her what she meant, and she described experiences similar to those I have mentioned. With guilt rising inside of me, I asked her if they had ever seen anything like Dan's book incident. She said that she had not, but her daughter had—as well as a shadowy male figure standing in the hall, just at the foot of the stairs. I am indebted to that family for clearly taking these things in greater stride than I did.

About a year later, I put the Moreno Drive house on the market. In California, there was a law dictating that any problem known to a property's seller must be declared to prospective buyers, *including paranormal incidents*. This came as a surprise to me, as in the UK, real estate contracts came only with a boilerplate paragraph that essentially says *Buyer beware*.

I ignored the California requirement because in my final chat with my Moreno Drive renter, she told me that one day, while she was trying to take a nap, she got so sick of the disembodied voices and footfalls on the stairs that she walked out onto the landing and screamed, "Whoever you are, fuck off and leave us in peace!" The disturbances stopped at that very moment, she said, and had not returned—which was why I felt I did not need to confess my experiences to the family that purchased the house from me.

To my relief, I never heard anything from my buyers afterward. However, I did unexpectedly run into the couple who had initially sold me the house at a film-premiere event. When I went over to greet them, they were clearly uncomfortable and beat a retreat from me almost immediately. I got the distinct impression that they had something to hide.

What saved me from the darkness of this period was work. In *Star Trek: The Next Generation* I had found a company as dear to me as the RSC, and fortunately, we were hitting our stride in the third season. In our tenth episode, "The Defector," one of our top writers, Ronald D. Moore, playfully nodded to my background as a now rather well-known Shakespearean actor. His script opens with Data in the holodeck performing Act IV, Scene 1, from *Henry V*, in which the king, on the eve of battle, visits his soldiers in their camp and quarrels with one of them, a cantankerous man named Williams.

Brent, as Data, played King Henry, while I played Williams, heavily disguised in prosthetics, a wig, and a beard. I milked this opportunity for all it was worth, delivering my lines in a growly voice and crudely comic London accent: "But iff the cawse be not good, the king 'imself hath a heavy reckoning to mayke; when awwl those legs 'n ahms n' 'eads, chopped off in a battle, shall join together at the latter day, and cry awwl, 'We *doiyed* at sooch a playce!'"

At the end of the holodeck scene, I appeared as Picard, offering my Peter Hall–like notes to Data: "Data, you're here to learn about the human condition. And there is no better way of doing that than by embracing Shakespeare. But you must discover it through your own performance, not by imitating others." It was all a little cute and self-referential, but I appreciated the opportunity to have fun with Brent and play around a bit in Michael Westmore's makeup. It was a relief to regard work as a place for *fun*.

That season ended with part one of "The Best of Both Worlds," the acclaimed two-parter whose second chapter would open the fourth season. It's in this episode that Picard is assimilated into the Borg, who assign him the name Locutus as their emissary to humanity.

The process of attaching all of Locutus's prosthetics to my head and body took about three hours, and their removal at the end of the day another hour; now I understood why Michael Dorn, despite his congenital good cheer, often looked so miserable.

But it was an aptly intense storytelling journey for me, too. Locutus knew that Jean-Luc was alive inside him but helpless and trapped, which really resonated with me—the "celebrity" I had become knew that the normal jobbing actor I'd been for most of my life was still there and was the "real" me. Doing those two episodes was emotionally close to home and at times quite painful.

This same period is when I fully grasped how popular our show had become. Given that the first part of "The Best of Both Worlds" aired on June 18, 1990—with the galaxy on the cusp of being Borgified—and the second on September 24, we had left viewers with quite the cliff-hanger. Would Picard and the *Enterprise* crew find a way to escape the Borg's grasp? A lot of viewers were irritated with us for leaving this question unresolved. I got a taste of just *how* much one day when I was driving in LA. As I waited at a red light, a car pulled alongside me and the passenger window opened. The driver leaned across his front seat to yell at me, "You have ruined our summer!"

When Gene Roddenberry died suddenly in October 1991, shortly after his seventieth birthday, I was deeply saddened. And as we continued with *TNG*, I found myself missing his presence. For all his wariness of me, he had created the magnificent *Star Trek* universe of which I was now privileged to be a part, and his guiding hand offered me reassurance.

In a way, I felt sorry for Gene where I was concerned. Jean-Luc Picard was his creation, and he had been pressured to cast someone who didn't jibe with his vision of the character. I thank Robert Justman and Rick Berman every day for prevailing in that particular struggle, but I do wish that Gene had lived long enough to see how *Star Trek* and Picard himself have continued to deepen and grow.

Fittingly, one of the last *The Next Generation* episodes overseen by Gene, the Season Five two-parter "Unification," brought one of the Original Series' stars, Leonard Nimoy, into our world. Now-Ambassador Spock has engaged in a rogue diplomatic mission to bring peace between his Vulcan race and the Romulans, and Picard and Data are deployed to find him. The writing was splendid, with scripts by two of our most trusted veterans, Jeri Taylor and Michael Piller, from a story by Michael and Rick Berman.

I loved working with Leonard, who was so warm toward all of us and inhabited Spock with such impressive conviction and subtlety. There is a wonderful scene in which he and Brent Spiner have the closest thing that a half-Vulcan and an android can have to a heart-to-heart chat: "As you examine your life," Data asks Spock, "do you find you have missed your humanity?"

"I have no regrets," Spock says.

"No regrets," Data says, pausing for a moment, puzzled. "That is a human expression."

"Yes," says Spock, dispassionate as ever. "Fascinating."

We all missed Leonard when we wrapped those two episodes, as we still do today. I am honored that the writers gave him a speech in which Spock pays my character tribute. "He intrigues me, this Picard," Spock says to Data. "Remarkably analytical and dispassionate . . . There's an almost Vulcan quality to the man."

The end of that season brought what remains to me perhaps the most moving *TNG* episode of all, "The Inner Light." Its co-writer, Morgan Gendel, based it on the Beatles song by George Harrison, whose lyrics are themselves based on the words of the classic Chinese philosophical text the Tao Te Ching. Our episode was unique in that most of its action takes place inside Picard's mind—without going out of his door, as Harrison's song says. While on the bridge of the *Enterprise*, Jean-Luc is knocked unconscious by an alien probe. He awakens in another world, a water-deprived, relatively primitive planet called Kataan, where he discovers that everyone knows him as Kamin, an "iron weaver," and that he has a loving wife, Eline, played with heartrending tenderness by Margot Rose.

Angry at first at his displacement, Picard gradually resigns himself to being Kamin and eventually warms to his alternative life. Over a span of forty years, Kamin has children and grandchildren and sees his adored wife pass away. We do not learn until the end, after Picard comes to on the bridge, that the captain has been out for only twenty-five minutes. The probe that walloped him came from a civilization that died out a thousand years ago—it was their last will and testament, and Picard is the vessel through which their story will be remembered.

The great treat of "The Inner Light" for me was that Kamin had two children with his wife, a girl and a boy, and when the boy grew up into a young man, he was played by . . . my own son, Daniel, who had by then become a professional actor. Dan looks good today, but there is a boyishness about him in that episode that brings a lump to my throat when I watch it now. I take comfort in knowing that "The Inner Light" will always be there, allowing me to access that precious time when he and I worked together on *The Next Generation*.

Though I was sadly estranged from my daughter, Sophie, in the aftermath of the split with her mother, Daniel was someone I continued to see regularly. We benefited from having acting in common. And he proved invaluable in helping me get back on my feet as a stage actor, when I stumbled into the idea of performing a one-man version of Charles Dickens's *A Christmas Carol*.

I'm getting a little ahead of myself. By 1988, when it became evident that *Star Trek: The Next Generation* was going to be my full-time job for the foreseeable future, I realized that there was no way that I could do a proper play for a long time. Even with a summer break, there would never be sufficient time to rehearse, go into tech and previews, and then perform eight times a week. But I still yearned for the stage, for it is my first love and keeps me sane. So after one of my Saturday morning poverty-mentality laundry sessions, I sat down with my coffee and contemplated the possibility of doing a solo show.

The first thing that came to mind was Charles Dickens's *A Christmas Carol*. I had done a version as a reading a few years earlier, when my parish church in Mirfield invited me back for a night to perform at an event raising funds for restoration work. I'd done an edit of the story, but it turned out to have been nothing like enough—I was up there behind the lectern for over two hours. Still, the audience seemed to like it. I expected people to start leaving in droves as I went on, as it was December and the church nave was not the warmest place to be. But to my amazement, nobody left. This made me reflect on the enduring power of that story, which people love to hear even though they already know it so well, and especially how it ends.

Wasting no time, I went out that Saturday and bought myself a new copy of *A Christmas Carol* at an LA bookshop. I spent the remainder of the weekend doing a re-edit, becoming more and more excited with every turn of a page. I decided that in my next version, I wouldn't be pinned behind a lectern, nor would I be reading. This time, I would commit to memory every line of my script and *act*, playing each and every character.

Then I called my UCLA pal David Rodes and one of his colleagues in the English Department, Al Hutter, seeking suggestions on next steps. Al had a ready answer. "Simple," he said. "You'll do a performance one evening at my house and I'll invite other members of the department, and maybe a few of our students as well." Done, perfect.

Two weeks later, we tried it out in Al's living room. I couldn't get off-book in that short amount of time, but the whole thing went well. Just like my audience in the church, the invited guests responded with genuine emotion, laughing and applauding at the funny parts, sitting still with pregnant silence in the somber moments. One woman told me that during the last few minutes, when Scrooge undergoes his redemptive reevaluation of his life, she had to wipe her eyes more than once.

Flush with momentum, we scheduled a Saturday evening performance not long thereafter at the Wadsworth Theatre on the UCLA campus. I would like to tell you it was a triumph. But it was not—it was ghastly. First of all, we were going through that rarest of things, a cold night in LA, and the theater's heating system broke down. Someone from the university suggested that I not go through with the performance, given the heating situation and the poor turnout. I was outraged. With rising indignation, I said, "I would do the performance for one person if that's all there was!" What a pompous ass.

In the end we had about forty people there, but the performance came to be known as the "two old men and a dog" show. A British actor's way of saying "Nobody came." They all did their best to support me, but everyone was cold and I was still reading a script. I went home massively discouraged.

But a year later, as the Christmas season approached once again, I had regained some of my confidence. By this time, I had most of the script committed to memory and had teamed up with Fred Allen, a lighting designer associated with UCLA, who suggested that his wife, Kate Elliott, join us as the show's stage manager. Kate helped me set up four performances, two apiece at the Wadsworth and at UC Santa Barbara. Fred did a marvelous and unexpectedly complex job with the lighting that made everything more dramatically effective: the atmosphere, the moments of intimacy, and the revelations. Kate proved outstanding in handling the show and other people, becoming, as we got deeper into this project, my rock, my adviser, my protector, and my dear, dear friend. At the end of a performance, as soon as I was done with the curtain calls—which she also supervised perfectly—Kate was there in my dressing room opening a bottle of wine and filling two glasses for us both.

To my pleasant surprise, our Southern California performances played to full audiences and roaring applause, even though I still wasn't totally off-book and had the script onstage with me. My pals from *TNG* came to UCLA for the Sunday matinee, and afterward, we shared a champagne toast backstage. They told me that what I was doing was innovative and promising, and they swore they weren't playing a prank on me, not even Jonathan.

Hmm, maybe this is really going somewhere, I thought.

By 1991, Kate and I were getting more ambitious about *A Christmas Carol*. We spoke of booking an autumn tour of West Coast venues followed by a two-week residency in a Broadway theater. Rick Berman was looped into these conversations because he was *The Next Generation*'s producer-in-chief and had to sign off on the idea of me spending weekends on my Christmas show while *TNG* was very much in the thick of shooting.

Fortunately, Rick proved accommodating, and, miracle of miracles, the Eugene O'Neill Theatre in New York had just the right window for our show—and wanted it! The moment we signed the deal, though, I had a bit of actor's remorse. What was I thinking? I had a full-time job, my show had neither a director nor a set, and I had gone ahead and committed to playing fifteen performances in a thousand-seater Broadway house!

I needed dramaturgical help. And that was where my son, Daniel, came in. He had studied theater at CalArts, so I trusted his judgment. I asked him to sit with me in the rehearsal room as I performed the piece in its entirety. He was fantastic. Often, he'd stop me in the moment to make a staging suggestion or an improvement on a line interpretation. His notes were incisive and improved the show immeasurably.

We had never been in such a situation before. In the past, it had always been me watching him in a school or college play. It felt wonderful to experience this new dynamic with my son: without a doubt, one of the best rehearsal-room memories of my sixty-plus years of working in the theater. Daniel was now part of my show, and I made sure to let him know that when I opened on that Broadway stage, he would be standing beside me in spirit.

I could not have anticipated more generous reviews than I got in New York. My favorite came from Clive Barnes, formerly of the *New York Times* and by then of the *New York Post*, who confessed up front that he found the concept of a one-man, bare-stage *Christmas Carol* worthy of a "Bah, humbug!" But he was won over by our "unexpectedly beautiful and thrilling" production featuring an actor he knew from the Royal Shakespeare Company, "the troupe with which Stewart was so long an ornament."

But Barnes's kicker was delicious and, to me, rewarding. "Obviously many of the people currently crowding the O'Neill Theater are going to see Stewart because he plays the apparently valiant Captain Jean-Luc Picard in *Star Trek: The Next Generation*. Not me. How selectively out of it can one get? No Trekkie I. Until the other day I didn't even know he had a TV series . . . For about five years I have idly wondered whatever became of him. Now I know. He was rehearsing for 'A Christmas Carol.'"

I never became complacent as a result of these reviews, though. Kate, Fred, and I continued to tinker with the production as we reprised it every year as the holidays neared. And in 1993, we booked it into a place I'd never imagined playing back when it began in Al Hutter's living room: the Old Vic Theatre in London.

We started out with another warm-up tour in the States, with me performing weekend dates in Cerritos, Santa Cruz, Santa Barbara, Telluride, La Jolla, and Pasadena. I was already fifty-three years old, and I honestly don't know how I did it, shooting the seventh season of *The Next Generation* at the same time. It helped that *A Christmas Carol* had no set, which meant that every theater was basically the same, with the stage walls obscured by black curtains.

Kate also took care of nearly everything related to each date so that I didn't have to worry. During performances, she positioned herself close to the proscenium arch but out of view of the audience. This was important for me because I had discovered that doing a solo show can be lonely, full house or not, and I needed a friendly face to turn to. Sometimes when I glanced offstage into the wings, Kate returned my look with an obscene gesture. If it made me laugh, I had to find an instantaneous way of incorporating the laugh into the content I was performing. I adored that, because she kept me on my feet while also vanquishing my longing for another actor to walk onto the stage.

In Pasadena, I experienced a confidence boost like no other in my *Christmas Carol* journey. After a Sunday matinee, I was showering in the locker room under the stage, as every performance left me drenched in sweat and my dressing room didn't have a private bathroom. I was unexpectedly interrupted by a pounding at the door. It was Kate, saying, "Patrick, you've got to come quickly. Kirk Douglas and his family are in your dressing room and want to see you!"

I toweled off as fast as I could, wrapped myself up in my old dressing gown, and shot upstairs. My modest room was crowded with Douglases, and there, in the middle of the group, was Kirk himself. I received a round of applause as I entered, but then Kirk, the boss and the patriarch, held up his hand. Everyone went silent.

I was aware that Kirk was in poor health at the time, with severe throat problems. So right away, I moved to stop him from any speechifying on my behalf. "Please, Kirk, you mustn't speak, it's okay," I said.

But he moved close to me, pulling me in with both arms so we were nose-to-nose. Then, mustering all of his will to speak, Kirk said, "Patrick . . . You . . . are . . . my . . . in-spir-a-tion." I saw that his eyes were moist, and within a moment, so were mine. This actor, one of my heroes and inspirations since I was fourteen, was paying me the finest compliment I had ever received.

So, to assess: I had succeeded in entertaining a lot of people over the past few Christmases, many of whom, including a childhood idol, had said they felt changed by what they had witnessed. This gave me enormous satisfaction. The story and text of *A Christmas Carol* are so familiar, yet I had found a way to engage people with the material in an entirely new way.

But I knew I would have to do better still for the Old Vic. It's important for you to understand what a huge career moment this was for me, performing my one-man show there. I had seen Shakespeare in that theater when I was a student in Bristol: the best Shakespeare I had ever seen in my life to that point. My audition for the tour with Vivien Leigh had taken place there, back when I was a nobody and a plaything for the mean-spirited Douglas Morris. The stakes were high.

I needed the insights of an outsider, someone who could view the play afresh and offer unvarnished critiques of the show and suggestions for how it could be better. There was one man I believed was perfectly qualified for this role, and fortunately Roger Rees was already in Los Angeles.

You'll recall that Roger had joined the Royal Shakespeare Company one year after me. In the twenty-six years that had passed since then, he had done some beautiful work as an actor and director, becoming the toast of Broadway in 1981 when he starred in the eight-and-a-half-hour RSC production of *The Life and Adventures of Nicholas Nickleby*. The man had serious Dickens cred. He was also a very gentle and empathic person, which was what I needed. I wanted feedback but not bombast, and I didn't want to be told that my approach was fundamentally wrong.

I called Roger, and after a bit of catching up, I told him what I was up to. He said he would be happy to help out and agreed to see the Sunday matinee of my show the weekend it was in Santa Barbara. When the afternoon of that performance came around, I found myself in my dressing room early, looking through the script and trying to quiet my nerves. I was nervous, wondering if inviting Roger had been a good idea.

Kate came into my dressing room and notified me that Roger was in the front-of-house bar having a coffee. I asked her if he had a notepad with him. She said he hadn't. I asked her to get hold of a pad and pen, find Roger, and offer them to him. Shortly she was back and said Roger had no pad and didn't want to take notes. I was disappointed by this news, as I was looking forward to lots of help from him, but . . . hey-ho. I guess a genius has his methods.

After the performance, Roger came backstage, gave me a fierce hug, and said, "Beautiful, Patrick, beautiful. Now, what are you doing tomorrow?"

I said that I was free until lunch and then needed to report for work at the Paramount lot. He said he would come by the following morning at nine o'clock, then quickly left.

You know that feeling of having turned in the test, but the teacher hasn't graded it yet, so you have no idea how you did? That's what this was like. I awoke the next morning and for the first time in two years, I was anxious about *A Christmas Carol*. What if I ended up being undermined by Roger's criticism? What if I disagreed with everything he said? What if I got so upset that I would have to ask him to leave?

Roger was at my front door bang on at nine o'clock and started talking about the show right away, while I was still making us coffee. He commenced with the opening of the show. The way I did it was very simple. I walked onto the stage as the lights came up, smiled at the entrance round of applause, and then said half of the first line directly to the audience: "Marley was dead . . ."

I then turned away, my back to the audience, to begin miming the setting out of furniture, and looked over my shoulder and said the other half: ". . . to begin with." That always got a nice laugh, which was encouraging at the very top of the show.

Roger said, "Patrick, that's funny, but what if you said it as a warning? Let them greet you as a friendly storyteller but then you set them straight, letting them know that this will be no feel-good fairy story."

I immediately replied, "Roger, I think it could be both."

"Yes," he said excitedly, "you've got it!" And off we went. For the remainder of the morning, he gave me notes on every single page, literally—he borrowed a pen and marked up my script. Except they were not really notes, more like reflections, conjectures, maybes, possibilities. Pure uplift and no undermining. I was most animated by how Roger alerted me to multiple ways of playing a line or a scene. Charles Dickens was a brilliant writer, and yet it was Roger, steeped in *Nicholas Nickleby*, who made me realize that Dickens was more brilliant than I had ever understood.

When we wrapped three hours later, I noticed that Roger had not even finished the coffee I had poured him. He just said, "Gotta go," and disappeared, like a superhero acting coach.

I also enlisted once again my son, Daniel, who was still attending CalArts. Paramount had been supportive of my *Christmas Carol* habit, and now the studio was generous in letting us use one of their free soundstages. The one they lent us turned out to be the biggest on the lot, and it was entirely empty except for my stage furniture. Daniel and I marveled at our surroundings, speculating about which of the movies we loved had been filmed right where we were sitting. Then we got to work.

I had a list of scenes I still needed help with, so Daniel put me through my paces, isolating the problems we encountered. Then, after lunch, I ran the entire show for an audience of one: my son. Daniel and Roger got me in the right place, ready to fly to London and face a potentially unforgiving UK theater audience for the first time in five years.

Because of my divorce, I no longer had a home in London proper, so I went for total indulgence and booked a suite at the Dorchester hotel in Park Lane, the very place where my father had once been offered a job as a doorman. My suite was gloriously comfortable and looked out onto Hyde Park. If only Alf Stewart could have seen me.

I'd arrived in London early on a Saturday, but because there was a show playing at the Old Vic that weekend, Kate, Fred, and I could not get up on its stage until Sunday evening. When that finally happened, the three of us shared a long embrace in the center of the stage; Kate and Fred knew how much this engagement meant to me, and they'd been with me from virtually the beginning of my Dickens adventure. The next few days of rehearsal and tech were hectic, but I knew enough to step back occasionally and revel in the fact that this magical place was, for the next fortnight, my home.

The only unease I had concerned the London critics. In the UK, we have something called "tall poppy syndrome," wherein those who have risen from humble roots to great success are, by cruel ritual, cut down for being successful. Following my paparazzi encounters, a part of me was resigned to the notion that my head was on the block, the next to be chopped off. SPACE-CAPTAIN YORKSHIREMAN PLUMMETS TO EARTH IN DIRE DICKENS FOLLY. The headlines wrote themselves. I began to dread the mockery and derision of my countrymen.

Thank goodness for Fred and Kate. They were nothing but positive, which kept me steady. The first two shows of our run were essentially previews, but the performances were sold out, so as far as I was concerned, it was go time.

But within minutes of the first performance commencing, I felt something new, a feeling I hadn't experienced doing the show in America. An uncommon audience alertness. An instinctive tuning in to the characters and the language.

Then it hit me: *Of course.* This was not just a British audience, but a *London* audience. This play was about their town, their people. For Americans, my *Christmas Carol* must have at times felt as if it took place in a dark fairy-tale world, completely divorced from reality and lived experience. But this London audience knew the streets of which I spoke, the particularly drafty winters of which Dickens wrote: "The fog and darkness thickened. And the cold became intense. Piercing, searching, biting cold."

Sensing my audience's sensitivity to the material, I began to relax. I felt a warmth spreading through the house, an emotional connection to the situations and the people in them. It had never been like this before. I decided to let Patrick Stewart explore and investigate the narrative in new ways, as Roger Rees had encouraged me to do. Each page felt like a new one whose language and emotions were coming from *my* heart, *my* head, *my* gut.

And, of course, from Mr. Dickens. For the first time, I felt toward him as I did Shakespeare in my most transcendent moments onstage: He was inside me, and his responses were part of me.

The performance seemed to fly by. Suddenly, I was on the last page and speaking the final lines of this awesome story: "It was always said of Scrooge that he knew how to keep Christmas well, if any man alive possessed the knowledge. May that be truly said of us, and all of us. And so, as Tiny Tim observed: God bless us, every one."

To my astonishment, I heard people speak those final five words with me from all over the auditorium. Some spoke them in a murmur, but others declaimed them joyfully, triumphantly. I had never experienced anything like this onstage: audience and actor fused into one. I was overtaken by emotion and silently thanked Fred for going to a complete blackout after that last line, giving me a chance to wipe the tears from my face before the curtain-call lights came up.

But the tears came anyway at curtain call because everyone was on their feet, applauding and shouting. Extraordinary. I don't recall how many curtain calls I took, but for the final one, I pulled Kate and Fred onto the stage. They were adorably confused, and most of the audience had no idea who they were, except that I was making it plain they had played a vital part in what had taken place.

Fred had laid out champagne in my dressing room, and when I got there, I made a dive for the bubbly. Immediately there was knocking on the door. I put down my glass and it was half an hour before I lifted it again. For the smallish room rapidly became jammed with friends and well-wishers, including Mary Tyler Moore, Arthur Miller, Ben Vereen, André Previn, and Joel Grey.

What's more, the UK critics surprised me by not plunging their knives into me—they actually had nice words for the show and my performance. Paul Taylor, writing in *The Independent*, wrote that "even the most confirmed non-Trekkie would have to grant that Stewart—on leave now from the Starship *Enterprise*—has, in the flesh, a spry agelessness that suits the multiple role-playing this piece demands."

A few months later, *A Christmas Carol* was nominated for an Olivier Award, the highest honor in the British theater, our equivalent to the Tony. Rick Berman granted me a few days off from *Star Trek: The Next Generation* to travel to London, and I invited Kate and Fred to join me. Win or lose, we were proud to be recognized in my home country. And then *A Christmas Carol* actually *did* win, in the category of Best Entertainment.

When I returned to the *TNG* set the following Tuesday, I brought the Olivier Award statuette with me. I held it up to cheers and applause, and everyone in the cast and crew took their turn holding the trophy. For the first time, I felt that I could live a life that comfortably accommodated both the theater and Hollywood.

A few days later, a card arrived in the mail. It was from Roger Rees, and on it was written only one word: "Bravo."

Chapter Twenty

I t is extraordinary, the reach of *Star Trek*. If I entered into its universe a stranger to its customs, I neared the end of my time on *The Next Generation* recognizing that I was a custodian of something held dear by millions of people, probably hundreds of millions.

I have been approached by so many strangers who freely confess to me that they endured difficult childhoods and that the one thing that they could hold on to—that pulled them through by giving them something to look forward to—was our show. I have observed that a significant proportion of the fans who approach me in America are Black. The precise reasons for this are not for me to articulate. But I suspect that what Whoopi Goldberg said to me rings true with many people of color: that *Star Trek*, in its different incarnations, presents an aspirational future preferable to our present—a future where inclusivity is a given rather than an effort.

Then there are the famous fans. Tom Hanks has told me he knows all the *TNG* episodes by name, so obsessively has he watched them. I have it on good authority that Frank Sinatra, of all people, was a devoted viewer. I only wish I could have heard his reasons why.

And it's always a strange feeling when I am talking to some enormously accomplished person and I suddenly realize that they are behaving a little oddly because they're hanging out with Captain

Picard. This happened when I met novelist Salman Rushdie. I was intimidated by him to the point of inarticulacy, so reverent am I toward his books and intellect. Then I noticed that he was acting the same way toward me—shyly, haltingly asking me half-formed questions about the *Enterprise* and the Borg. *Ohhh, I get it*, I thought to myself, *he's a fan.*

For the purposes of this book, I rewatched nearly all the episodes of *Star Trek: The Next Generation*. What an emotional roller coaster! Allow me to share some additional random musings on our show to perhaps keep in mind for your own possible rewatch.

Some of the earliest episodes make me cringe. Our fourth-ever show, "Code of Honor," traffics in hideous racial stereotypes of Black people as primitives, with Tasha Yar abducted by a people called the Ligonians, the head of whom makes her engage in an excruciating cage fight with his "first one," or primary lover.

I was much happier to revisit our fifteenth episode of Season One, "11001001," in which the *Enterprise* is briefly hijacked—for what turns out to be a benign purpose—by a race of tiny, chittering humanoids called the Bynars. The producers wanted to cast children to play them, but there are strict limits on the hours that child actors can work, so the Bynars were instead played by petite women. Makeup artist Michael Westmore fitted them in elongated bald caps and I found them adorable. The spirit of this episode was very Original Series *Star Trek*, more like something you might have seen in the 1960s, but I enjoyed making it and was sorry to say goodbye to the Bynars; unlike Jean-Luc, I like kids and kid-like creatures.

As I get to the third season, though, I see *TNG* finding its own footing. In "The Offspring," the first episode that Jonathan Frakes ever directed, Data creates an android child whom he names Lal. She assumes the form of a teenage girl, movingly played by Hallie Todd, but she is literally not built to last, and Data musters something close to genuine human emotions as he watches the life drain out of her. Brent Spiner's performance is staggeringly good—he found new depths to his character's Pinocchio-like predicament of being a human invention who wishes to *become* human. It's a major injustice to me that Brent has never won an Emmy for playing Data, not to mention the androids Lore and B-4 and the bizarre Soong family of mad scientists.

Reviewing the old episodes also reminds me of how, as our popularity grew, we attracted prestigious visitors. In Season Two, Mick Fleetwood, the founder-drummer of Fleetwood Mac, petitioned to be on our show, no matter how onerous the conditions. So our producers cast him as a fish-headed alien whose facial prosthetics required Mick to shave off the beard that he'd had since 1977. He happily did so, all to appear unrecognizably in the episode "Manhunt" for a few minutes, with a single spoken line: "Food-food-food."

While we were filming the finale of Season Four, "Redemption, Part 1," Rick Berman came down to the soundstage to inform us that Ronald Reagan, two years past his presidency, was a big fan of the show and had requested a set visit. I had already played host to Reagan's chairman of the Joint Chiefs of Staff, William J. Crowe, who had come to the bridge and asked me shyly if he could sit in the captain's chair. I'd told him he outranked me and didn't need to ask.

As for Reagan, our politics didn't align, but the young moviegoer in me was thrilled to meet someone he had seen in *Cattle Queen of Montana* and *Prisoner of War*. When the former president arrived, I gave him a tour of Stages 8 and 9, where the bulk of our show was filmed. He couldn't have been more pleasant, but he was quiet and at times seemingly confused by his surroundings— which made more sense when, three years later, he announced he had Alzheimer's disease.

The Season Six finale, "Descent, Part 1," opens with Data in the holodeck, playing poker with holographic representations of Albert Einstein, Isaac Newton, and, playing himself, Stephen Hawking. Maddeningly, I didn't get to meet the great physicist. I was not on the call sheet for that morning, and Hawking's appearance was both a

last-minute request—he happened to be visiting LA from England—
and a closely guarded secret. I was at home learning my lines, so I
only found out about his cameo after the fact. Brent told me that
Professor Hawking clearly had a blast doing the scene, in which he
vanquishes his fellow geniuses, but I so wish I could have given him a
tour of the bridge.

And it would have been nice, too, to meet the actor who played
Sir Isaac Newton: John Neville, the devastatingly handsome English
actor whom I had watched, enthralled, back in 1956, when he played
Romeo on the stage of the London Old Vic. Even in a silly Isaac
Newton wig, he looked as dashing as ever.

Upon reflection, I would say that our show peaked in its fifth and
sixth seasons. The latter presented me with a fantastic experience
that I would have earlier placed strictly within the realm of fantasy:
acting opposite David Warner on television.

Ever since I'd seen him in that 1965 production of *Hamlet*, I had
thought of David as one of acting's untouchables, a prodigy with
whom I was privileged simply to share the same stage. Yet there we
were for one week on the Paramount lot, the Player King and Hamlet
reunited. This was for a two-part episode titled "Chain of Command," in which Picard is taken prisoner by a militaristic race of
aliens known as the Cardassians (please note, no relation to the reality-
television family). David played the Cardassian officer Gul Madred,
whose goal is to pry Federation secrets out of Picard via torture.

I had not known that David was under consideration for the role
of Gul Madred, and I never would have imagined that he would
deign to accept it. So when Rick Berman slipped me the news one
day that David was to join us, I was beside myself. All but one of my
scenes in the episode were to be with him, and he was going to torture me! I didn't feel worthy.

When he arrived on the set, David was an absolute sweetheart, clearly delighted to be in *Star Trek: The Next Generation*. I'll admit that it all felt a bit wrong, this dynamic. Through a strange and unlikely chain of events beginning with a last-minute invitation from David Rodes to perform at a UCLA event, I had become, in my forties and fifties, the leading actor in a major TV series. Now, here was the greatest star of the British stage when I was starting out, thrilled to be a guest actor on my show. Life is indeed strange.

David had been hired on such short notice for "Chain of Command" that there was barely any time for him to learn his lines. Indeed, he worked off of cue cards for much of the two episodes, but you would never know this from watching him—that's how great he was as Gul Madred, and how naturally he inhabited every character he played, always delivering a performance that was truthful and real.

David, I am pleased to say, enjoyed a long, terrific, and decorated career, working nearly to the very end of his life in 2022. Observing him in action was astounding—the way he virtuosically switched between a near whisper and a bellicose shout as he circled me in his Cardassian armor and spiny facial prosthetics. "Chain of Command" is beloved by the *Trek* faithful, and I think that our scenes together are a big reason. Gul Madred violates every human rights convention, having Picard stripped bare, hung from a rack, and implanted with a pain-inducing device. He engages in Orwellian cruelty, promising Picard relief from pain if the captain grants that there are five lights shining in his face—when, in reality, there are only four. Picard, defiant, keeps replying "There are four lights," ensuring a new round of torture. When, finally, Madred is compelled to release Picard, the captain dramatically shouts at his tormentor, "There . . . are . . . *four* . . . lights!"—a line now entrenched in *Trek* lore.

When I rewatched "Chain of Command," I smiled the first time that Picard uttered the "four lights" line, but I grew more tense each time it was repeated, with higher doses of pain administered to Picard as punishment. But by the time the episode concluded, I needed a moment to collect myself and let a range of emotions pass through me—pride in how good we were, exhaustion at how wrenching the material is, and sadness over how much I miss David.

By the seventh and final season—yes, we went one more than my original contract called for—I was getting very, very restless, and I felt that the scripts did not scale the same heights as before. To be honest, I was happy that the show was coming to an end. I know this sentiment was not shared by many of my fellow cast members, and that Paramount might have let the show carry on for a few more seasons had I been amenable. But I needed a change. Seven years was plenty, and I had developed a fear of losing out on film roles because Hollywood would only ever see me as the *Star Trek* guy. This was more than just paranoia. A major director said, to my face, "Why would I want Jean-Luc Picard in my movie?"

This prompted me to issue a directive to Steve Dontanville, my agent, to get me a role as far away from Picard as possible. My word, did he listen. The first non–*Star Trek* movie I signed on to do as we wound down the TV show was *Jeffrey*, based on Paul Rudnick's stage comedy about gay romance in the time of AIDS. I played an older gay gent, Sterling, and Bryan Batt played my HIV-positive partner, Darius, an actor-dancer and long-standing member of the company of *Cats*. I embraced Sterling and the opportunity to work with Bryan, Steven Weber, Christine Baranski, Sigourney Weaver, and Victor Garber, among others in the impressive cast. I am not so sure that I would play a gay man now, however, given current sensitivities and the fact that I am heterosexual. At the very least, I would hear out those around me to gauge their feelings.

But making the movie was a joy, full of trust and laughter. *Jeffrey* was given a limited release and reached only a small audience, but it got good reviews. I have some wonderful mementos from the film, too. For the purposes of the set, which required convincing evidence of the characters' home lives, Bryan and I spent a day out and about in New York City, getting photographed in romantic locations as a blissful couple. I cherish these photos to this day.

As for *Star Trek: The Next Generation*, I am pleased to say that our writers rose to the occasion for our last hurrah, the aptly titled "All Good Things...," whose two parts, the 177th and 178th (!) episodes of our program, closed out our epic run. Picard becomes unstuck in time, hopping between three different periods: the past, specifically a short time before the events of *TNG's* pilot, "Encounter at Farpoint"; the present; and twenty-five years in the future, when Picard faces a debilitating disorder akin to dementia, and Riker looks somewhat like Jonathan Frakes really does now. Picard must reconcile a disruption to the space-time continuum in all three eras in order to prevent the destruction of humanity.

This turns out to be a puzzle devised by the Q Continuum, which meant, for us, that John de Lancie not only returned as Q but did so in his famous inquisitor costume from our pilot episode, bookending the entire series. It will not surprise you, if you somehow missed the episode, to learn that Picard does indeed stave off the destruction of humanity. And when the drama is all over, he is the only officer on the *Enterprise* who has any memory of the temporal anomaly. The final scene depicts the senior officers—Riker, Crusher, La Forge, Worf, Troi, and Data—playing their routine poker game. They are surprised when the captain, in an uncommonly good mood, elects to join them for the first time.

Picard is given the honor of dealing the cards. It was Brent Spiner, rather than the writers, who came up with the final line of scripted dialogue, so brilliant in its larger resonance. As he deals, Picard says brightly, "So: five-card stud, nothing wild. And the sky's the limit."

The last day of shooting, however, on April 5, 1994, was devoted not to that scene but to a two-pager between de Lancie and me. As we began, the set was crowded with visitors, but by the time the first assistant director announced, "Aaaand that's a wrap," only a dedicated crew was still there, and there was just a smattering of applause. Rick Berman was on set, though, and gave me a hug, holding me in his embrace as he thanked me for my service.

We knew this wasn't a hard goodbye, as we had already begun transitioning *The Next Generation* into a movie franchise along the lines of the original *Star Trek*. In fact, it was only eight months later that our first film, *Star Trek Generations*, was released. However, I wish that *Generations* had been more differentiated from what we were doing in Season Seven; to me, it plays like an extended, expensive episode rather than a feature film.

But it does highlight the notable pairing of Jean-Luc Picard and Captain James T. Kirk, who, by some writerly trick of extradimensional logic, is allowed to coexist with his successor in his full, brown-haired, middle-aged virility. Up to this point, Bill Shatner had been relatively cold to *TNG*, professing to the press that he'd barely watched any of it, and I was a little disappointed that the producers and writers had decided to insert Kirk into our first movie—it made me feel that they didn't trust the *TNG* cast to carry a film by ourselves.

Yet I ended up eating my words, for Bill was a pleasure to work with, open and generous, and his death scene is moving. In the film, Picard and Kirk team up to foil a plan by the movie's villain, Tolian Soran, who was played by Malcolm McDowell, a long way from his days as a Royal Shakespeare Company walk-on background actor. Kirk and Picard succeed in locking down Soran's deadly space probe, but not before Kirk makes the ultimate sacrifice to do so, incurring fatal wounds.

With me standing over him, Bill gave Kirk a perfect send-off, mustering one last trademark smirk before saying, "It was . . . *fun*." Then his facial features subtly rearranged themselves into a wary middle-distance stare, and he said Kirk's last words: "Oh, my." Our fans loved that Kirk died virtually in Picard's arms, even as they grieved for their original captain.

Between *Star Trek Generations* and the second film with the *TNG* cast, *Star Trek: First Contact*, I was offered the role of Prospero in the Public Theater's 1995 Shakespeare in the Park production of *The Tempest*. I had played the smaller role of Stephano in the Royal Shakespeare Company's 1970 production, which starred the great Ian Richardson. Watching Ian's inspiring approach to Prospero made me fantasize about one day having a crack at the role myself. Now that day had come—and it was to happen on the open-air stage of the Delacorte Theater in Central Park, in front of 1,500 people.

This production of *The Tempest* was directed by the dynamic young visionary George C. Wolfe, then the Public's artistic director. George, I was surprised to learn, had never before directed Shakespeare, but I found that inspiring rather than concerning. We proved a good match. I loved his fresh approach to the material and his flair for experimentation.

We had a wonderful cast, too: Aunjanue Ellis as Ariel, Carrie Preston as Miranda, Teagle F. Bougere as Caliban, Bill Irwin as Trinculo, John Pankow as Stephano, and Larry Bryggman as Alonso. A disparate troupe from a variety of backgrounds, but it worked brilliantly. The critics loved us, and the free tickets for the entire summertime run were gobbled up within hours of when they were made available.

The Tempest represented my return to live Shakespeare after years of being primarily a film and television guy, and I knew that I bore a certain responsibility. A lot of people in the audience were *Star Trek* fans, coming to see me mainly because they knew me as Jean-Luc Picard. For many of them, this would be their first-ever Shakespeare play. I wanted it not to be their last, and for them to cherish the experience the way I did. I think we as a company succeeded in this regard. The audience engagement was electrifying to those of us onstage, and that fall, the production rolled into the Broadhurst Theater on Broadway for a sold-out limited run that was received every bit as ecstatically.

Star Trek: First Contact, the *Next Generation* cast's second motion picture, came out in 1996. I consider it to be the best *Star Trek* work that our team ever did.

First Contact marked Jonathan Frakes's debut as a feature-film director. We had all loved being directed by him during the show's run, but here he really elevated his game. Jonathan is a funny, lighthearted man who always creates a positive atmosphere on the set, but this time, he sharpened our focus, demanding of us an emotional authenticity beyond what we'd given on the show. This was the big leagues, after all.

The movie's title alludes to a historic moment in the year 2063 when, in canonical *Star Trek* lore, human beings first encountered an alien species, specifically the Vulcans, leading to the eventual creation of the United Federation of Planets. The *Enterprise* crew is compelled to travel back in time to 2063 because the Borg have already done so, and are trying to change the course of history by assimilating humanity before the Vulcans' arrival. Everything hinges on preserving the timeline in which Zefram Cochrane, a twenty-first-century American inventor, successfully pulls off the first-ever flight at warp speed in his vessel, the *Phoenix*, thereby attracting the attention of a Vulcan survey ship and precipitating their outreach to human beings on Earth.

The screenplay, by Rick Berman, Brannon Braga, and Ronald D. Moore, was first-rate. They took a big risk in giving our principal cast members unexpectedly raw, relatable feelings to work with, almost unbecoming of Starfleet officers. Picard's edgy scenes with the Borg Queen reveal him as a fallible character rather than the noble, spacefaring hero that *Star Trek: The Next Generation* previously set him up to be—his lingering PTSD from his prior assimilation into the Borg has made him vengeful and short-tempered. That took courage. So did the movie's liberal use of humor, which made Riker, Data, Geordi, Troi, Dr. Crusher, and Worf seem more like exasperated, stressed-out coworkers in the real world—which, given that much of *First Contact*'s action takes place in our current century, they basically were.

Our cause was helped immeasurably by a trio of amazing guest actors: on the human side, two Oscar nominees, James Cromwell as Zefram Cochrane and Alfre Woodard as his deputy, Lily Sloane; and on the Borg side, Alice Krige as the collective's serene, merciless queen.

James, playing a character whose historic image as a hero turns out to run somewhat counter to reality, gave a performance of intelligence and wit; his emotional journey in the final moments, in which this disparity is bridged, is a tour de force. Alice, done up in an elongated, glazed head bulging with Medusa-like extensions—the work of our makeup maestro Michael Westmore, in peak form—was at once terrifying and sexy; I can't blame Data for succumbing, however temporarily, to her charms.

As for Alfre, she brought the heat, knocking some twenty-first-century sense into Jean-Luc to disabuse him of his lofty twenty-fourth-century pretensions. In a climactic scene in which the Borg have infiltrated the *Enterprise*, Lily, in an act of insubordination unfamiliar to Picard, chides him for his egotism and bloodlust. He refuses the obvious course of action—blowing up the *Enterprise* to destroy the Borg invaders—because he has made the situation all about him. As Lily says with withering sarcasm, "I'm sorry, I didn't mean to interrupt your little quest. Captain Ahab has to go hunt his whale."

Oh, does that set off Picard. He snaps, howling primally and shattering the glass of a display case. He seethes with fury, declaring to Lily that he will never again give an inch to the Borg.

The moment we read the script, Alfre and I recognized how explosive the scene was going to be. Jonathan supported the line we took, making us feel safe in committing so deeply to our characters' feverish energy. This scene shows Jean-Luc at his most vulnerable, his anger and aggression boiling over into frightening rage. Under the spell of these emotions and Alfre's intensity, I spat out the words "The line must be drawn here!" like venom: "The line must be drawn *h'yah*!"

We all felt good about the scene after we shot it, but it was Jonathan who recognized instantly that my eccentric pronunciation was bound to achieve traction. He started saying "The line must be drawn *h'yah!*" in my voice, in all sorts of situations. Sure enough, it has become a pop-culture trope, oft quoted and parodied. I am all too pleased about it.

A word here about Jonathan's direction. Beyond his deft handling of the cast, he also demonstrated technical mastery, his camera capturing the intimacy of the film's emotional scenes without being intrusive. *First Contact* was also the best-looking *Star Trek* film to date, a tribute to its excellent lighting design and sets, as well as Jonathan's choices regarding camera movement and color palette.

Watching myself in *First Contact*, I'm inspired. Technique is a slippery thing for an actor, something you struggle to maintain at a high level. The 1996 Patrick Stewart reminded me how it's done.

When *Star Trek: First Contact* came out, I was convinced that we were on the threshold of establishing a potent movie franchise. Unfortunately, the two films that followed it, *Star Trek: Insurrection* and *Star Trek: Nemesis*, were both a letdown. And *Nemesis*, which came out in 2002, was particularly weak. I didn't have a single exciting scene to play, and the actor who portrayed the movie's villain, Shinzon, was an odd, solitary young man from London. His name was Tom Hardy.

Tom wouldn't engage with any of us on a social level: never said "Good morning," never said "Good night," and spent the hours he wasn't needed on set in his trailer with his girlfriend. He was by no means hostile—it was just challenging to establish any rapport with him. On the evening Tom wrapped his role, he characteristically left without ceremony or niceties, simply walking out the door. As it closed, I said quietly to Brent and Jonathan, "And there goes someone I think we shall never hear of again."

It gives me nothing but pleasure that Tom has proven me so wrong. He has flourished in such blockbusters as *Inception*, *The Dark Knight Rises*, *The Revenant*, *Mad Max: Fury Road*, and *Legend*, not to mention the TV series *Peaky Blinders*. My favorite of his movies, though, is *Locke*, in which he is the only actor on-screen, driving for nearly the entire duration of the film while taking calls from characters voiced by such actors as Olivia Colman, Ruth Wilson, and

Tom Holland. I would love to have dinner with him someday and get to know what's going on inside that brain.

But *Nemesis* was a dud, as far as I was concerned. By the time it had come and gone, I wanted no further part of sci-fi, uniforms, or anything to do with outer space. I was convinced that my time as Jean-Luc Picard was consigned forever to the past.

Meanwhile, in real life, I had struck up a romantic relationship with a wonderful woman named Wendy Neuss. We had been friends for ages, since the second season of *Star Trek: The Next Generation*, when she joined the series as a member of the postproduction sound team. Wendy was in charge of running our ADR sessions, which are also known as "looping"—recording additional dialogue after shooting has been completed.

Such sessions can be tedious, but Wendy won over the cast with her infectious wit and enthusiasm. I had more ADR sessions than anyone else, because no matter what, I would have to record the "Captain's Log" voice-over that opened nearly every episode. I also had to record brief bursts of vocalized emotion: shouts, sighs, groans, laughter, labored breathing, you name it. We had a ball recording these together, and I enjoyed Wendy's acerbic commentaries on the industry we worked in. "Losing after being nominated is bullshit," she'd said, "and so is winning."

That kept me on my toes. As did her jibes about my messy eating habits. "Patrick looks good in everything he eats," she was fond of telling people.

Best of all, Wendy was a fellow fan of live theater and classical music. Whereas Gates McFadden had been the only taker when I invited my castmates along to hear the LA Philharmonic play, Wendy became my steady concert companion.

I had found Wendy attractive from the day I met her, but for several years, we were friends and nothing more. As time passed, however, I found myself falling for her. We had so much in common and loved each other's company. I'd thought that was the secret to a good marriage. Alas, I would eventually discover this alone is not sufficient. But in the late 1990s, Wendy was the woman with whom I wanted to spend my life. So I proposed to her, she said yes, and we were married in 2000.

In this same time span, if you can believe it, yet another major development in my life sprang from a looping session. In 1997, I played the bad guy opposite Julia Roberts and Mel Gibson in a thriller called *Conspiracy Theory*, directed by Richard Donner. I had just finished an ADR session for that film when an assistant rushed into the studio and presented me with an envelope. On its front was written my name and the words READ NOW.

I opened it up and found a piece of notepaper with the name LAUREN SHULER DONNER printed on the top. I knew Lauren to be Richard's wife and a successful, highly regarded film producer. We had met once before and hit it off. The note requested that I stop by her office when I finished recording.

Her door was open, but I politely knocked nevertheless. I was still mildly traumatized by that first meeting with David Lynch all those years ago in Mexico City, worried that this might be some kind of mistaken-identity situation. But when I entered, I quickly realized that Lauren knew exactly who I was. Seated behind her desk, she greeted me by proferring a mocked-up photographic image of someone who looked like me, sitting in a wheelchair.

"What on earth is that, Lauren?" I said.

"Ha!" she said triumphantly. "It's you, six months from now. You were born to be Professor Charles Xavier."

"Who on earth is that, Lauren?" I said.

"He's the leader of the X-Men," she said.

This conversation made about as much sense to me as the one

I'd had with Steve Dontanville all those years ago in which he asked me why Gene Roddenberry wanted to meet me. Charles Xavier? The X-Men? I hadn't a bloody clue what was going on.

Lauren patiently explained that *X-Men* was to be a big-budget film based on a Marvel Comics superhero team. Charles Xavier was the creation of comic book legends Stan Lee and Jack Kirby. He is a telepath and paraplegic who exists in a world where mutants represent the next phase in human evolution, but face discrimination and bigotry because of their superhuman powers. He oversees an academy called the Xavier School for Gifted Youngsters and a strike force of do-gooder fellow mutants called the X-Men. He is the guy who puts the *X* in X-Men.

Oh, and Lee and Kirby's physical inspiration for the character was the original sexy bald man, Yul Brynner.

Lauren said that Bryan Singer, whose Academy Award–winning movie *The Usual Suspects* I had loved, was going to direct the film. He was awaiting a signal from Lauren to ask me out to lunch.

My thoughts at the time? *No. No more fantasy. No more sci-fi. No more telepaths. No more actors zipped into formfitting costumes. I'm done with all that. Thanks for thinking of me, but—no, absolutely not.*

Chapter Twenty-One

Needless to say, I soon thereafter found myself having lunch with Bryan Singer. A confident young man, he patiently heard my issues as I laid them out, never once interrupting me. But when he knew that I was done speaking, he presented his case. Bryan passionately argued that there were no major similarities between Jean-Luc Picard and Charles Xavier, or between *Star Trek* and *X-Men*. One was a legacy sci-fi franchise and the other part of the burgeoning industry of big-budget comic book adaptations—totally different in style and content. He said he had studied the work I had done over the past ten years, and *X-Men* related to none of it. With bravado, Bryan said this was going to be totally new territory for me, and the whole world would see my work.

I could feel that I was being won over. Even though I was doing my damnedest to play it cool, he had already hooked me. The next day, I had my agent call Lauren Shuler Donner's office and start negotiations.

It took some time to work out the details, but by 1999, I was swept up into the *X-Men* franchise. In the intervening years, I had studied up on Charles Xavier, or Professor X, to use his mutant honorific. He is the white hat of the mutant tribe, a leader who believes in a world where human beings and mutants may peacefully coexist. This places him in contrast to fellow mutant Erik Lehnsherr, the black hat. Lehnsherr is a survivor of the Auschwitz concentration camp and a former ally of Xavier's, who takes a dim view of humanity and has organized his own task force, the Brotherhood of Mutants, to advance the cause of a world dominated by his kind. Because he is able to generate magnetic fields for any use, he is known by the alias Magneto.

I did not know until late in the casting process that Lehnsherr/Magneto was going to be played by Ian McKellen. What a coup! Ian and I had barely worked together—never in our days in the Royal Shakespeare Company and just once in London, in Tom Stoppard's play *Every Good Boy Deserves Favour*, which had an extremely limited run. So while Magneto and Professor X have a long, complicated relationship encompassing friendship and animus, Ian and I really did not know each other well at all. I was looking forward to seeing this situation change—and did it ever, as I would see.

When we arrived in Toronto to begin the shoot, I met Halle Berry and James Marsden, who were playing, respectively, my allies Storm and Cyclops. But on the cast list, there was a blank space next to the name of Wolverine, the main protagonist of the *X-Men* series. We were told that the actor Dougray Scott had been cast, but he was making the movie *Mission: Impossible 2* with Tom Cruise, which was running over schedule, and he could not be released. So we started production without a Wolverine, working on scenes that didn't involve the character.

On the second day of shooting, while Ian, Halle, James, and I were sitting around drinking coffee and waiting for a lighting setup to be completed, a production assistant escorted a young man onto the soundstage and introduced him to us. He was a handsome, dark-haired fellow with a relaxed, amiable manner, and he explained that he had come to meet Bryan and be put on camera for a screen test.

We all took to him at once, and when he was called onto the set—for what turned out to be an audition for the part of Wolverine—each of us shook his hand and wished him well. In his absence, we discussed the new guy, who had asked us to call him Hugh. We were all rooting for him—he had that intangible star quality. But he also had a thick Australian accent. Would that disqualify him? We wondered if he would be able to cover it up, maybe by working with a dialogue coach.

About half an hour passed before Hugh returned. This time, his air of easy confidence was gone.

"How did it go?" someone tentatively asked.

Hugh shook his head mournfully. "Well, you guys are never gonna see me again," he said.

We let out a collective groan and rose to console him. But right at that moment, Hugh was summoned by one of our producers into another meeting. "Poor guy," I said. "I bet they're going to offer him a bit part as consolation."

We sat in gloom for a few minutes, pondering how brutal our business is. Then the same poor guy returned to our cluster of chairs with a dazed look on his face. The producer escorting him said to us, "Ladies and gentlemen, meet Wolverine!"

Well, there was uproar—everyone on their feet, hugging him and slapping him on the shoulder. Hugh Jackman, until then primarily an actor in stage plays and musicals, was now one of us, a fellow mutant. He told us later that he had been about to head straight for the airport when he emerged from his audition with that disconsolate look on his face. Instead, he was whisked off to the wardrobe department for an urgent costume fitting. Our business is not only brutal, but at times quite insane.

Soon thereafter, I met the rest of the cast: Famke Janssen, Rebecca Romijn, Ray Park, Bruce Davison, Tyler Mane, and seventeen-year-old Anna Paquin, whom I vividly remembered from Jane Campion's extraordinary film *The Piano*, in which she played Holly Hunter's daughter. For that role, she became, at eleven, the second-youngest actress to win an Oscar. Quite a group, this *X-Men* cast.

The filming experience was positive on the whole. Our cast got along famously, though Bryan Singer was so fixed in his vision for the film that his demeanor sometimes bordered on authoritarian.

Still, he kept his promise to keep our stories rooted in humanity rather than superhero hyperreality. Almost as soon as we wrapped the original *X-Men* film, I learned that a sequel, *X2*, was in the works. It was clear that I had gotten myself caught up in another major franchise.

But unlike the *Star Trek* TV series, the *X-Men* movies allowed me the space to work regularly in the theater again. I took advantage and did lots of good stuff. I finally played George in *Who's Afraid of Virginia Woolf?* again, at the Guthrie Theater in Minneapolis, with Mercedes Ruehl doing a fantastic job as Martha. On Broadway, I performed in Arthur Miller's *The Ride Down Mt. Morgan*, a production I absolutely loved . . . though I landed in hot water when, during a curtain call, I criticized our producers, primarily the Shubert Organization, for not doing enough to promote the show.

Specifically, I said: "There are many elements that go into making a Broadway play a success. The casting, the direction, the design, the acting, the play. And in *The Ride Down Mt. Morgan*, we know we have an extraordinary, provocative, and vastly entertaining play. What is also needed is promotion and publicity. People need to be told that a play is out there. Arthur Miller and I no longer have confidence in our producers' commitment to this production—especially the Shubert Organization—or their willingness to promote and publicize it."

This was after a Saturday matinee. Within an hour, I took a phone call from a furious Gerald Schoenfeld, the chairman of the Shubert Organization. He insisted that after the evening's performance, I should again speak during the curtain call, this time to retract my complaint and offer a public apology to the organization. I told him I would not and I hung up.

Then Arthur Miller himself called, telling me that he supported my action one hundred percent. He said he wished that he could join me on the stage that night, but he had an engagement he could not abandon. I was enormously calmed by this. If Arthur Miller, a giant of American theater, had my back, what harm could come to me?

When, after the evening performance, I stepped forward from the curtain-call lineup and started to make my protest speech, I immediately sensed an energy in the theater different from what I'd felt in the afternoon. Now there were people in the audience who expected my conciliatory speech to happen, and there were boos as well as a smattering of applause. It didn't feel good, and I wished like hell that Arthur had been at my side.

The following morning, my protest had blossomed into a news story. But it was not until Monday that I received a call from the head of the American Actors' Equity, informing me—quite sympathetically—that a complaint had been lodged by the Shubert Organization and that I would be required to attend an investigation.

The hearing began with Gerald offering a litany of the contractual rules I had disrespected and the false accusations I had made about him and his production company. Then it was my turn. I began by admitting that everything Gerald had said was correct. I was aware that I had indeed broken my contract, but that I did so in an attempt to save the production, which would have been to everyone's benefit. I also made it clear that no other cast members had been involved or consulted with regard to my protest. The only person who expressly offered me support was our playwright, Arthur Miller.

The meeting concluded, and we were all told to take an hour's lunch break and then return to hear the verdict. I expected to be found guilty and perhaps fined. But I did not want to be kicked out of Equity. That's pretty much how things turned out—I was found guilty of breaking the terms of my contract, fined a modest amount, and required to offer a public apology to Schoenfeld and his production company. I kept my Equity status. In fact, the head of the union's board told me later that many in the union were hoping for a not-guilty verdict. Still, this controversy ended my good relationship with the powerful Shubert Organization, and that was the biggest price I paid. Nowadays, I might handle such a situation more delicately, but at the time, I did what I felt was best for our show.

In 2003, an offer came my way that I couldn't refuse: to return to London's West End to play Halvard Solness in Henrik Ibsen's *The Master Builder*. In this great play, Solness is a driven, ambitious architect with a roaringly successful career but a cold, passionless marriage. A young woman, Hilda Wangel, shows up on his doorstep and reminds Solness that they met ten years earlier, when she was a child. She had fallen in love with him then, and ever since has maintained a determination to reenter his life. Solness rapidly falls under Hilda's spell. However, as you can imagine, it does not end well.

Ibsen based the plot in part on a brief affair he had with an eighteen-year-old Viennese student when he was in his sixties: art imitating life. In my case, though, life imitated art. As we rehearsed the play and toured it in other English cities before opening in London, I found myself increasingly attracted to Lisa Dillon, the actress playing Hilda. She was twenty-three years old and only two years out of the Royal Academy of Dramatic Art, with a bright sense of humor and grasp of technique beyond her years.

I was no dummy. I remembered the warning I had received from an older actor decades ago, that if you keep saying "I love you" to someone in a play, you can drift into believing the sentiment to be true, which makes the performance more convincing but the personal ramifications more dangerous.

Sure enough, in London, as we began our limited run at the Albery Theatre, Lisa and I became a couple. This was indeed a dangerous situation, because Lisa already had a boyfriend and I was married to Wendy.

As with my marriage to Sheila, I had already found myself in a state of unhappiness when I began a relationship with another woman. Working together on *Star Trek: The Next Generation* and some feature films we produced, Wendy and I were a formidable pair. Going to concerts together, we had a wonderful time. But we simply weren't simpatico as a cohabitating couple, and there were strains in our marriage almost from the start.

Halfway through the run of *The Master Builder*, Wendy joined me in London. It was a sad replay of Sheila's visit to Los Angeles the time that things came to a head on the I-10 freeway. I had managed to keep my affair hidden, but Wendy and I had a series of rows, our chemistry gone. And when the play's run ended and I told Wendy that I thought our marriage had been a mistake, she asked me if there was someone else. I confessed that there was. She asked me if it was Lisa. I responded in the affirmative.

And so, another divorce. I felt stupid and responsible. My twenty-three-year marriage to Sheila wasn't a mistake but a case of a loving couple growing apart. However, I didn't feel the same about my three-year marriage to Wendy. Still, I had cheated on my wife with a younger woman—again—and there is no getting around that. And just like my affair with Jenny Hetrick, my time with Lisa Dillon would also prove to be relatively short.

I needed to do better by the women with whom I was romantically involved. In a life chockablock with joy and success, my two failed marriages are my greatest regret.

Chapter Twenty-Two

The fame afforded me by the *Star Trek* and *X-Men* franchises opened up possibilities and opportunities for me well beyond my early dreams as an actor. In the 1990s and early aughts, I found myself in high demand for comic roles, largely, I suspect, because Jean-Luc Picard and Professor X carry themselves with such gravitas and speak with such Shakespearean eloquence that people thought it would be fun to see me play against type.

It all began in 1994, when I was asked to host the late-night sketch comedy series *Saturday Night Live*. This should have been one of my crowning achievements, as it is for many of the actors, comics, and athletes who get to host the show. But I wasn't as loose then as I am now, and I found the whole experience incredibly stressful. My opening monologue was one of the more awful ones in the history of the show, full of lame *Star Trek* jokes that I failed to land, and I just didn't connect with *SNL*'s cast, as talented a group as they were.

The one exception was Mike Myers, with whom I found myself in a sketch in which he played an irritable Scotsman who runs a Scottish paraphernalia shop and uses the catchphrase "If it's not Scottish, it's craaap!"—something that Sunny and I still like to say around the house. My most lasting impact on *SNL* history, though, was my full-throated announcement of that episode's musical guest, Salt-N-Pepa, around which the comedian John Mulaney, a former writer for *SNL*, built an entire stand-up segment.

Things changed for me, however, when I fell into the embrace of Seth MacFarlane, the wunderkind behind the animated series *Family Guy* and *American Dad!* In 2005, he recruited me as a roving guest voice for both programs. Seth is a sweet man with movie-star looks but the heart and soul of a kindly sci-fi nerd. I love him for that.

Needless to say, he is also a hard-core *Star Trek* fan. Sometimes he had me play myself or a version of Jean-Luc Picard, blurting out something inappropriate like "Commander Worf's head looks like a fanny!" (Michael Dorn, guesting as himself as Worf, told off Frakes and me by saying, "You can both suck my ridges!")

I am still part of *American Dad!*, in which I voice series regular Avery Bullock, the boss of the main character, CIA agent Stan Smith, performed by Seth. I enjoy being Avery, who is monstrous, self-obsessed, and manipulative. My favorite aspect of him is his very English accent, which is completely inappropriate for a US intelligence operative. What I love is that nobody working for him seems to have noticed. The show's producers long ago assured me that when the series finally winds up, one of the stupid people to whom Avery reports will say something like, "Hey, have you guys ever noticed what a weird accent Deputy Bullock has? What is it, Australian or Irish or something?"

Perhaps my most celebrated comic turn came in a 2005 episode of the TV show *Extras*, in which I played myself. Or, rather, a fictitious, deranged, sexually perverted version of myself. It all started early one evening when I was shopping for groceries in my local supermarket and my cell phone rang. The voice on the other end announced himself to be Ricky Gervais, whom I knew as the star and co-creator of the original UK version of the smash TV comedy *The Office*. On the phone, he moved straight into a pitch for me to be a guest on his new show, in which he played a struggling writer-actor who encounters notable thespians while he works as an extra in their films.

I thought for sure that this phone call was a prank, for I have a friend who enjoys playing tricks on me in this manner. But when I challenged the caller, he kept insisting he really was Ricky, and his protestations were so convincingly Gervais-like in their desperation that I decided to hear him out. Ricky—for it was indeed him—explained that he had already booked Ben Stiller and Kate Winslet to appear and wanted me for the new show's sixth and final episode of its debut season. He told me no more, asking only if I was interested.

I had never before had a role offered to me in this fashion, standing in a store aisle with a box of Raisin Bran in my hand. I asked Ricky if we could meet and discuss the role in more detail. He said that we couldn't, because he and his producing partner, Stephen Merchant, would not start writing the script until I agreed to do it. I carefully put the Raisin Bran back on the shelf, took a deep breath, and said, "Fine. Yes." Ricky said, "Great!" and hung up. I still don't know how he got my cell number.

The next morning, my agent, Steve Dontanville, called me and asked what was going on with Ricky Gervais, whose office had just been in touch. Luckily, Steve knew about *Extras* and approved my signing on for it. I would rehearse and shoot it in a week's time. But . . . I still had no idea what I was doing in the episode. This was an absolute first—agreeing to play a role whose nature had yet to be revealed to me.

At last, a script arrived and I instantly loved it. All that was required was that I be Patrick Stewart . . . but this version of me obviously has problems. He is starring in a film adaptation of *The Tempest*, and Ricky's character, Andy, manages to sneak his way into this Patrick's trailer to see if the esteemed actor can pass along Andy's spec script to anyone of importance. Patrick Stewart reveals to Andy that he himself has written a script for a project he is developing—all of it predicated on the main character's ability to use mind control to make women's clothes fall off. "I'm walking along," Patrick says, describing a typical scene in his screenplay, "and I see this beautiful girl and I think I'd like to see her naked. And so all her clothes fall off. And she's scrabbling around to get them back on again. But even before she can get her knickers on, I've seen everything, you know. I've seen it all."

"It's a comedy, is it?" asks Andy.

"No," says Patrick, mildly affronted by the question.

Ricky and Stephen's script just escalated the absurdity from there, making Patrick a bigger and bigger creep as it went along. I knew the end result would be incredibly funny.

But the day of the actual shoot proved bumpy. Ricky and Stephen had never actually heard me say these lines until I performed them. And when I did, with the Andy and Patrick characters sharing a couch in the latter's trailer, Ricky burst into peals of laughter that he simply couldn't bring to a stop. "Knickers" was the specific word that first set him off. But soon it was anything I said. The more seriously I behaved, the more Ricky laughed.

After a time, Stephen came into the trailer and told Ricky to get a grip. Ricky, apologetic, said he would, and put on a very serious face. But before I could even complete the setup to the "knickers" line, he started shrieking anew. By this point, I couldn't help but join him.

Stephen came in again, quite cross. He told Ricky to leave the trailer, explaining that he, Stephen, would read Ricky's lines offscreen, and they would stitch the scene together later in the editing room. Ricky looked sad and irritated at this development.

Stephen and I performed the scene without breaking, but it just wasn't the same. Something was missing, and that something, clearly, was Ricky. Adopting a more encouraging tone, Stephen escorted Ricky back into the trailer, saying, "I know you can do it this time." Ricky and I did indeed complete a usable take, and that is what was seen on TV.

The two hours I spent with those guys, though, were one of the most fun times I have ever experienced in show business. I love that people still happen upon that episode of *Extras* and have a *What the hell?* reaction to my appearance in it.

What's more, for my efforts, I received an Emmy nomination for Outstanding Guest Actor in a Comedy Series!!!!

I was having fun professionally in the early aughts, but I was not so successful in the romance department. Thank heavens I fell into what the public has deemed my greatest bromance.

During the making of any given blockbuster Marvel film, there is a lot of downtime for the actors. And so, as the *X-Men* films consumed so much of my filmmaking life in the first decade of this century—with the original coming out in 2000, *X2* in 2003, and *X-Men: The Last Stand* in 2006—I found myself spending much of my days idling in a luxury trailer adjacent to Ian McKellen's.

Ian and I, born a year apart, made the most of it. Over tea in the morning and wine in the evening, we began a conversation that has continued, more or less without pause, for twenty-three years. There is a perception that Ian and I have been best buddies since we were infants during the Blitz, but the truth is that only after mutating into Magneto and Professor X did we become the dearest of friends, something that was meant to be.

But we had yet to take the stage together in any significant way. That all changed in 2008, when I was on holiday by myself in Italy and my phone rang. I happened to be in Florence, standing on the very narrow walkway that surrounds the top of the dome of the Santa Maria del Fiore cathedral. There were spectacular views in every direction and I was annoyed at my phone for ringing, but since it was my London agent, I decided to take the call.

"Sean Mathias is directing a new production of *Waiting for Godot*," he said. "It'll begin with an eight-week tour of the UK, followed by an opening in the West End, theater to be determined. They want you for Vladimir. Ian McKellen is already in as Estragon."

From my high, scenic perch in Florence, I said without hesitating, "I'm in."

There's a common misperception that *Godot*, like the rest of Samuel Beckett's plays, is hard, challenging, complicated, and obscure. Well, it *can* be, in the wrong hands, but it *needn't* be. Vladimir and Estragon are poor, homeless characters who meet every evening in the hope that Godot will keep his appointment with them and take them under his wing. Their counterparts Pozzo and Lucky are also homeless, but while Vladimir and Estragon are passively waiting for life to happen to them, Pozzo and Lucky are, in their own dysfunctional way, actively searching.

I was initiated into the peculiar charms of *Waiting for Godot* decades ago, seeing it in my first semester of drama school, with Peter O'Toole as Vladimir, Peter Jeffrey as Estragon, David King as Pozzo, and Barry Wilsher as Lucky. I was only seventeen and barely educated, but I had no difficulty understanding what was going on.

If anything, I enjoyed myself *too* much. As students, we were allowed only to attend the dress rehearsals and to sit in the gallery, with firm instructions to remain absolutely quiet and still, with no applauding, commenting, or laughing. O'Toole, however, knew about this draconian edict and took pleasure in toying with us, going out of his way to do flamboyant stuff aimed only at us students. When we couldn't control our laughter, he theatrically interrupted the rehearsal to shout in our direction, "Shut the fuck up or get out!"

At first glance, the script of *Waiting for Godot* is a wild jumble, a lake of language. But as you read it closely, you discern a pattern of ripples and bubbles in this lake, the words taking on meanings and intentions that clue you in to Vladimir and Estragon's objectives. In preparation for doing the show, which had its London premiere in 2009 at the Theatre Royal Haymarket, I spent every day with my head in the script, trying to absorb this material into my brain and body so I could bring it to life on the stage. Only with Shakespeare and Dickens had I experienced such a complete union with a writer's words—and, in Beckett's case, stage directions. Look at this dialogue:

> **Estragon:** (*Anxious*) And we?
> **Vladimir:** I beg your pardon?
> **Estragon:** I said, And we?
> **Vladimir:** I don't understand.
> **Estragon:** Where do we come in?
> **Vladimir:** Come in?
> **Estragon:** Take your time.
> **Vladimir:** Come in? On our hands and knees.
> **Estragon:** As bad as that?
> **Vladimir:** Your worship wishes to assert his prerogatives?
> **Estragon:** We've no rights anymore?
>   *Laugh of Vladimir, stifled as before, less the smile.*
> **Vladimir:** You'd make me laugh if it wasn't prohibited.
> **Estragon:** We've no rights anymore?
> **Vladimir:** (*Distinctly*) We got rid of them.
>   *Silence. They remain motionless, arms dangling, heads sunk,*
>   *sagging at the knees.*

On a first reading, this back-and-forth might come off as gibberish. But as you familiarize yourself with its peculiar rhythms and subtle courtesies ("your worship," "take your time"), you discover a tenderness in the two men's shared desperation. All the more so if your sparring partner happens to be Ian McKellen.

I wish Ian were here with me right now to perform this dialogue.

We opened in London to an enthusiastic audience and perhaps the best reviews I had ever received from the British press—a milestone moment in itself. We played every single show of our run to a sold-out house. And at the opening-night party, two distinguished bassists showed up to congratulate us: Sting, the one who played with a policemen's band, and Paul McCartney, the one with the flashy Aston Martin.

For the first time in my life, at an advanced point in my career, I was part of a double act. Sean Mathias wasted little time in pairing Ian and me again, this time in Harold Pinter's *No Man's Land*, a similarly cloistered drama open to a wealth of interpretations. I was Hirst, a famous and affluent writer whose smug affect and Savile Row suits are a cover for his inner insecurity, while Ian was Spooner, a struggling poet who initially behaves sycophantically toward Hirst but gradually gets the better of him. Shuler Hensley and Billy Crudup joined us as Hirst's manservants, Briggs and Foster, who carry an air of menace.

We did a pre-Broadway run in 2013 in Berkeley, California, a charming city in which to spend a month. And then, in a bravura move for a pair of guys in their seventies, we brought to Broadway not only *No Man's Land* but also *Waiting for Godot*, with Shuler and Billy taking on the Pozzo and Lucky parts. We performed the two shows in rep at the Cort Theater, alternating between *Godot* nights and *No Man's Land* nights—and, on Wednesdays and Saturdays, doing both on the same day.

Ian had the toughest deal in this arrangement, because Estragon and Spooner never leave the stage. I, at least, had two scenes off in the Pinter and a minute off in the Beckett. However, Ian did get to take an onstage "nap" toward the end of *Godot*. On a couple of occasions, I actually had to wake him up—he had a reputation of falling asleep in such moments. He always looked at me angrily, as if he resented being woken up, which, of course, was just perfect for Estragon.

Without a doubt, this one-two punch of Beckett and Pinter was, to date, the high point of my stage career. To be performing in these plays with Ian, Shuler, and Billy, arriving at the Cort's stage door every day knowing what joys lay in store—and, equally, *not* knowing what joys lay in store—was everything I had always wished for in my career. I was truly blessed. We played for four and a half months, closing at the end of March 2014. At the final curtain call, looking out at the audience, I noted a lot of familiar faces: not of celebrities, but of repeat visitors, people who had enjoyed both shows so much that they came back for more.

After the curtain call, backstage, I couldn't find Ian. Someone told me that he had walked offstage and vanished, so I went looking for him.

I found him sitting in a stairwell, his head buried in his hands, sobbing. I lowered myself beside him and wrapped my arms around him, holding him until his crying abated. I searched for a few words of love and support, but when I offered them, he batted them away. "No, no, it's not that," he said. "It's that everything is done. This is the end. There'll be no more."

He meant his acting career, this crowning moment, but as we all know, that hasn't happened.

Chapter Twenty-Three

I have until this point withheld another Ian story, concerning his sage advice when I was playing Macbeth in the 2007 production of the play directed by Rupert Goold. We opened at the Minerva Theatre in Chichester and then transferred to the Gielgud Theatre in the West End. One day, while I was in rehearsals in London, I bumped into Ian on Charing Cross Road. He asked me how things were going with the production.

Now, Ian had been the most important Macbeth of my generation, renowned for starring in Trevor Nunn's gold-standard RSC production of 1976, which costarred the equally astounding Judi Dench as Lady Macbeth. I was, to be honest, rather intimidated by Ian's question, so I answered with a neutral response.

Then Ian leaned in. "Patrick," he said, "there is just one thing I have to say to you. The line 'Tomorrow and tomorrow and tomorrow'? The most important word is 'and.'"

I needed a moment to process this, but then I realized exactly what he meant. Macbeth, in that famous soliloquy, sees in his future nothing but a weary despair that will never leave him—that will, in fact, haunt him day after day. "Tomorrow *and* tomorrow *and* tomorrow . . ." Ian's note had a huge impact on my approach toward the second half of the play. Without it, the play's ultimate act of self-slaughter would have meant so much less. It also reminded me of something that I already knew but have occasionally overlooked: Such is Shakespeare's mastery of the English language that sometimes his most ordinary words serve to express his characters' most extraordinary thoughts.

The other reason Ian's note so resonated with me was that my own mindset at the time was a little too close to Macbeth's for comfort. Let me give you the whole thing:

> *Tomorrow, and tomorrow, and tomorrow,*
> *Creeps in this petty pace from day to day,*
> *To the last syllable of recorded time;*
> *And all our yesterdays have lighted fools*
> *The way to dusty death. Out, out, brief candle!*
> *Life's but a walking shadow, a poor player,*
> *That struts and frets his hour upon the stage,*
> *And then is heard no more. It is a tale*
> *Told by an idiot, full of sound and fury,*
> *Signifying nothing.*

Imagine what it felt like to be living Macbeth's life onstage, comparing oneself to a pitiable actor, when a pitiable actor is what I felt like I was, in any case. I was in a bad way personally, which helped the performance but not my mental state. I was living alone, without a partner, and the play was all I had for support. Well, that and alcohol. My time in rehearsals and onstage was heaven, but as the weeks passed, the role swallowed me up, messing with my head even when I was off duty. It wasn't fun to bring the murderous King of Scotland home with me.

Still, Rupert's approach to the play was exciting. We were in semi-modern dress—meaning we wore clothing appropriate to the World War II era—and Anthony Ward's set was cold and clinical, more like a barracks in a Stalinist totalitarian state than a Scottish wood.

Rupert is justly lauded as an inventive director, and we seemed to agree on nearly every choice. I was given a say in casting Lady

Macbeth, and when we discussed the matter with Jonathan Church, the Chichester Festival's artistic director, I raised the name of Kate Fleetwood. Rupert was clearly uncomfortable discussing her because she was and is his wife. But I had seen Kate's work and thought she was perfect. Jonathan pointed out that Kate, then in her thirties, might be too young for the role, given that I was on the older side to be playing Macbeth. But that was my point, or part of it. Lady Macbeth *should* be much younger than Macbeth. To me, her influence over her husband in the first third of the play makes even more sense if he is besotted by his beautiful, ambitious bride. When Macbeth's life falls to pieces, he feels an even more acute pain at her loss. Once again, perhaps my own personal experience—in this case, my poor record with relationships—was coming to bear on my approach.

Rupert insisted that he and I should audition Kate, just as we would anyone else. As I'd suspected, she was amazing, darting from softness to steel in the quicksilver way of a person truly on the precipice of madness. The critics would later note this ability, too, in their raves over her performance.

Then there was the issue of my mustache. I grew a thick one, almost a push broom. This was not something I ever discussed with Rupert; I just instinctively did it. Given the period in which we were setting the play, it seemed appropriate. Oddly, I didn't consider the example of my father, a military man who served in the 1920s, '30s, and '40s, and wore a mustache the whole time. His was thinner and more tidily groomed, a sergeant's mustache.

But subconsciously, I must have been thinking of Dad. The effect on my face was transformative. At the first tech rehearsal in which I wore my costume—a full uniform, an overcoat, and a military cap, with a rifle slung over my shoulder—I happened to look in a mirror. I was startled to see my father looking straight back at me. Startled, but not upset. I found it stimulating, the prospect of channeling Alfred Stewart—but only a *bit* of him—into Macbeth.

We all sensed in rehearsal that we had a special show on our hands. Rupert and I shared a desire to dig deeply into the subtext of the play, adding gestures and actions not in the actual text but appropriate to it. The best example of this is what came to be known as "the sandwich scene." Specifically, I am referring to Act III, Scene 1, which finds Macbeth questioning two men who are identified only as First and Second Murderer. It's a long scene in which Macbeth is attempting to corrupt them into agreeing to kill not only Banquo but also Fleance, Banquo's young son. One day in rehearsal, I stopped in the middle of a long, complex speech and said, "Damn it, Rupert, I wish I had something to do in this scene—some action to illuminate what I'm saying."

Rupert furrowed his brow for a moment and then said, "You're right. So why not make a sandwich?"

Everyone in the room laughed except me. I said, "A sandwich? Why?"

"I don't know, but let's try it," he said.

An assistant was dispatched to buy a loaf of bread—*not* sliced— along with butter, boiled ham, pickles, and a bread knife. Rupert placed the bread on a small table off to the side and told me to pretend the butter and sandwich fillings were in a small fridge. We restarted the scene.

In that moment, I decided that Macbeth should be a really efficient sandwich-maker. At the start of my second long speech in the scene, feeling that I wasn't getting through to the two men, I paused, walked over to get the loaf and knife, and carried them to a table in the middle of the room.

I cut two slices very carefully, trying not to create any crumbs, as I continued my speech. I added the butter, layered on the ham and pickles, placed the second slice of bread on top, cut the sandwich in half, and cut one of the halves into quarters. I handed the quarters to the two guys, picked up the second half for myself, and took a big bite out of it. As the three of us ate, we talked our way through to the end of the scene, with Macbeth saying he wanted Banquo murdered:

> ... *and with him,*
> *To leave no rubs nor botches in the work,*
> *Fleance, his son that keeps him company*

Whose absence is no less material to me
Than is his father's, must embrace the fate
Of that dark hour.

Right at that moment, I popped the last bit of my sandwich into my mouth and shook the hands of the two men, though neither of them had finished their quarter. The scene ended to a round of applause from those watching in the rehearsal room.

As time went on and more and more people saw our *Macbeth*, the scene was no longer referred to as "the murderers scene" but "the sandwich scene." Not just in Chichester and the West End of London, but also when we took *Macbeth* to New York in 2008, where it played to sold-out houses at the Brooklyn Academy of Music (BAM) and the Lyceum Theatre on Broadway. The Lyceum crowd was particularly enthusiastic about my sandwich-making.

My full year of *Macbeth* through 2008 was incredibly rewarding, but it took a toll. As I've said, I was without someone in my life to help me come down from my nasty evenings in Scotland. I was drinking heavily. Most nights, it would begin in my dressing room right after curtain call, with a glass of wine or three. Then my driver would bring me back to the high-rise apartment I was renting in Tribeca. Once the door shut behind me, I poured myself a glass of Jameson whiskey, turned on the TV, and stared blindly at whatever was on. Rarely did I have supper, unless you consider the whiskey a supper.

Often, I woke up in the middle of the night on the sofa, discovering that I had passed out there. I would then haul myself to bed and sleep until midmorning, almost always waking up with a hangover. I recovered by reading the *New York Times*, drinking a lot of water, eating brunch, and taking a midafternoon nap, from which I always awoke feeling great: I had another shot at *Macbeth* coming up in two or three hours, which was invigorating all by itself. I got away with this regimen, but I don't recommend it at all to any aspiring actors who might be reading this. It was no way to live.

But then . . .

On the Friday of our final week at BAM, I had a friend in the audience, the legendary Joel Grey. He came to my dressing room after the show full of enthusiasm, and suggested that we have dinner. I didn't know Brooklyn well at the time, but Joel said there was only one place to go, Franny's on Flatbush Avenue. I had never been there or even heard of it, so I put myself in his hands.

It was approaching eleven o'clock when we arrived, but it was packed with a Friday night crowd and there was not a table to be had. However, there were two open stools at the bar. We placed our drinks and dinner orders with the bartender. Before our food arrived, Joel went to the bathroom, and I scanned the place, enjoying the boisterous scene. My eye was caught by an attractive waitress who was serving tables toward the back of the restaurant. She was full of energy and seemed very engaged with all her customers.

After Joel and I finished eating and our plates had been cleared away, the waitress I had eyed earlier was standing directly behind us, saying something to the barman that I didn't catch. Then she turned to us, telling us that the restaurant wished to offer us dessert on the house and that her name was Sunny.

It was not until weeks later that I learned what lay behind the moment described above. Sunny had seen me and Joel arrive. Joel was a regular and she already was fond of him. She also recognized me, which threw her into an uncharacteristic tizzy. She and her family had watched every episode of *Star Trek: The Next Generation* together and were big fans. The restaurant's front-of-house manager noticed that Sunny was behaving a bit oddly and asked her what the deal was. When Sunny explained, the manager said she understood, but having seen Sunny wait on many well-known people, she knew her behavior was out of the ordinary.

So the manager ordered Sunny to pull herself together and offer us dessert on the house. Sunny protested that she didn't want to do that, but the manager said that she would do as she was told or be fired. So that was what brought this exuberant young woman our way.

I also learned later on that she assumed that Joel and I were a couple—which I took as a compliment.

By the time she arrived back with our dessert order, Sunny was a little calmer. She told me that she had wanted to see *Macbeth* at BAM, but it was already sold out. I told her that we were transferring to Broadway and that I would be happy to arrange tickets for her if she could just let me know what performance she would like to see. And then—I don't know what had gotten into me—I went ahead and gave her my phone number, something I would never do ordinarily. She thanked me and said good night.

During the break between BAM and Broadway, I had five days off, and I took a mini-vacation in the Caribbean. Telephone service was poor where I was staying, and it was not until I was en route back to JFK that I found a message from Sunny Ozell Michelson—for that was her full name—saying she was grateful for my offer for tickets and had a date that worked for her.

I called her back when I landed, and I asked her how many tickets she would like. After a moment of hesitation, she said, "Oh, just one, please."

This delighted and intrigued me, the thought that it was to be only her. I asked Sunny to come backstage afterward and join me for a glass of wine.

At the end of the performance on the night she came, I worried that she might not come around, so I sent someone to find her in the auditorium and escort her back. He caught her on the way out and guided her to my dressing room.

Sunny had been ready to bolt, she has since admitted to me. She was a bit frazzled after what she had just witnessed at the play's end: my severed head held up on a spear, bleeding. This was not an unusual reaction. My son Daniel's mother-in-law had come to see the play and was so upset by the experience that she couldn't face me afterward, making a beeline for a bar across the street instead. I wasn't going to let Sunny go, though—I had a nice bottle of wine open, after all.

Following a glass of the wine, I offered her a ride back to wherever she wished to be dropped off, which she accepted. In the car, I said, "Hey, I know it's late, but I'm hungry. Would you care to join me for supper at the Odeon in Tribeca?" (*Steady on, Patrick, you might be pushing your luck.*)

But Sunny, who had never been to the Odeon, told me she was only too happy to dine with me. We talked for hours, until we realized we were the last ones in the restaurant and the place was closing up. I suggested that my car could drop me off in Tribeca and then drive her home to Park Slope, Brooklyn, to which she readily agreed.

En route to Tribeca, I asked Sunny if she would like to come up for a glass of wine.

Fortunately, and consequentially for my future, she said, "Yes." I told my driver that he could go home.

For our second date, if indeed her night at *Macbeth* had been our first, we went to a Monday night benefit concert called "The Ladies Who Sing Sondheim." It was a glorious evening. Raúl Esparza had stepped in as an understudy at the last moment, and he sang "No One Is Alone" so beautifully that we both wept. This time we had dinner at Balthazar, another "late-nighter." It was there that I learned Sunny was a singer-songwriter, something she had not indicated before; I was so impressed by her modesty. Professionally she went by Sunny Ozell, dropping her surname. I asked her if she had any gigs planned, and she shyly told me that she did, the following Monday night, but her slot was at eleven p.m. That jolted me, but . . . fine. She was worth it. Date number three.

Sunny has since told me that she could not believe that I agreed to turn up alone at a music venue at eleven p.m. She was accompanied by brilliant New York guitarist Jim Campilongo, and they were fabulous.

That Sunny is a musician has brought changes into my life. Not just because I listen to more than I used to, but because I grew accustomed to socializing with her musician friends. I used to be intimidated by anyone proficient at music, but the ones I was now meeting were warm, friendly, smart, generous, and funny.

It so happened that Paul Simon was doing a residency at the Brooklyn Academy of Music right on the heels of my *Macbeth*, so I was able to get us great seats and passes to the post-concert parties. Sunny, I was to learn, is uncomfortable with backstage scenes, even where my shows are concerned. But after a show in which David Byrne and Ladysmith Black Mambazo had appeared as Paul's guests, I persuaded Sunny to go to the party with me, where I noticed Paul standing in a corner, looking a bit bored.

I took Sunny by the arm, almost dragging her across the room so we could introduce ourselves. Paul was at first a bit subdued. But after a few minutes of chatting, Sunny asked him about a horn arrangement on a song off an album of his, *The Rhythm of the Saints*, that she said had altered the course of her life. Paul's interest level shot up, and at once the terminology became too complex and musical for me, so I eased myself away and just watched them, their heads close together, both clearly enjoying a genuine conversation. At some point, the Ladysmith guys broke out in song, which swirled magically over our heads in the small, packed room. Afterward, a couple of the members introduced themselves to me as big fans of *Star Trek*. How much better can a night go?

We quickly got serious as a couple, and I grew accustomed to staying some nights at Sunny's place, a 365-square-foot apartment of which she was house-proud. She had saved me from mentally falling apart those last few weeks on Broadway, and has basically continued to do so ever since.

That winter, our relationship became transatlantic, because I had to be in England for Rupert's film version of our *Macbeth*. The cast and crew were put up in a shabby motel in the Midlands. I awoke very early one morning for my call, shivering from the chill. I knew I would need my warm overcoat, so I went over to the creaky cupboard where some of my clothing was hanging.

As I was about to close the door, I noticed on the floor in a corner a plastic carrier bag from Sainsbury's, the British grocery chain. I knew at once what was in it: all the mail I had found stacked in my London flat, where I'd spent a single night before heading off to the film location. I had meant to review my mail when I had a free moment. That was a week ago.

I had a few minutes to spare before heading off, so I emptied the bag's contents onto a small table. A few pieces of mail slipped onto the floor, and the first one I picked up was a brown envelope with the words CABINET OFFICE printed across the top. Why would someone from the government be contacting me? I quickly tore it open. Inside was just a single sheet of paper with two paragraphs of print. I raced through it, then read it a second time a little more slowly.

I was being offered a knighthood in the coming New Year Honours.

What?

My first reaction was that someone was having a joke. I do have friends, or perhaps enemies, with a predilection for such stunts. But there was nothing about the note's contents or letterhead—once again reading CABINET OFFICE—that hinted at a prank.

Oh my God, I realized, *this is for real*. I slumped down onto my unmade bed and stared at the dull brown wallpaper. *Me?* A knighthood? My chest was tight with turbulent emotions: amazement, delight, fear. But I pulled myself together. I knew I could handle this. Damn it, I had been called "Your Majesty" often enough!

I had to share my news with someone. There was a sentence in the letter about confidentiality, but there was someone I knew I could trust. So I called Sunny. She answered and I spluttered out my news, which at first she didn't comprehend. Then she asked if I was being funny. I assured her I was not. And I had to report to the set. I was running late, so I said, "We'll talk more later." I was now so flustered that I forgot to lock the door.

That day was a tumult of feelings. We were shooting a scene in which nearly the entire cast was involved, and more than anything, I wanted to blurt out, *Excuse me, everyone, there is something I want to share with you!*

But I couldn't. Earlier in the day, I had called the phone number included in the letter, and the representative on the other end of the line confirmed the veracity of my pending honor. However, I was asked to put my acceptance in writing, which I did that evening. When I called Sunny back to fill her in on the details and tell her she was invited, she said, "This is so fucking weird—I am going to go to Buckingham Palace and my boyfriend is going to be a knight. What the hell am I going to wear?"

The ceremony was held on June 2, 2010. We were joined by my brother Trevor and his wife, Pat. To have a close member of my family to share in this event, someone who had literally known me my entire life, was wondrous. The boy from Mirfield, knighted. I am still in disbelief.

Before the ceremony, I was put through a rehearsal at Buckingham Palace with another person who was being knighted, a businessman. We were surprised to learn that we were to be the first ones called up for the Honours, with me going second overall, because otherwise, the awards were to be distributed alphabetically and by degree of honor. The way the investiture worked, we were instructed, was as follows: You were presented to the Queen while kneeling on a little upholstered "knighting stool" designed for precisely this purpose. Then Her Royal Highness would stand up and perform the knighting, tapping you on each shoulder with a real sword. Then she would engage you in a very brief chat, at the conclusion of which you were to walk away backwards, including down a step, before exiting stage left.

It all went as planned, thank goodness. I remained upright, avoiding my greatest fear of tripping and falling. The Queen was as gracious as I had imagined she would be, though I am not entirely sure if she knew who I was. During our "small talk" moment, she asked of me, "And how long have you been doing this?"

"Oh, Your Highness, a very, very long time," I replied.

"Oh, really?" she said.

And that was it.

When I joined Sunny and my family in the audience to watch the remainder of the ceremony, where a further fifty or so people were given awards, I noted that the Queen took a more avid interest in another honoree, a woman. "I'm told that you are interested in horses," said Her Royal Highness. When the woman replied in the affirmative, they proceeded to chat for several minutes.

I am convinced, however, that King Charles is a *Star Trek* fan. As I've said, I met him several times when he was the Prince of Wales, and though he never broached the topic, I got a sense that he was familiar with the show. I would love to find out for sure if he is.

The fun part of the day came next. Lady Susie Sainsbury, a friend and a major UK philanthropist of the arts (who is married to a scion of the supermarket family), had asked me if she could organize a celebratory lunch, an offer I gladly took her up on. Among those who joined us were Trevor and Pat and my old dear pals Gawn Grainger and Brian Blessed. But the guest of honor was my childhood English teacher, Cecil Dormand, the man who had started all of this. To have him there with his wife, Mary, was beautiful—almost the same as having Mam and Dad.

Toward the end of lunch, Susie invited everyone at the table to say a few words in tribute to me, which I was not expecting. It was emotionally overwhelming and I choked up several times. The best moment of all, though, came when Cecil spoke. He offered a marvelous testimonial and concluded by noting that, in the fifty-eight years he had known me, I had always called him "Sir."

"So, what the hell are we going to do now, Patrick?" he remarked.

A final note on becoming Sir Patrick. At the time of my knighting, I had become a familiar face in Brooklyn thanks to my frequent visits to Sunny's place. Indeed, I was a regular at a wonderful old pharmacy on 7th Avenue in Park Slope, where she'd first introduced me to the proprietors. At my increasing age, I was going there a lot, forever topping up my prescriptions. I became particularly well acquainted with a pharmacist named John, a voluble, lovable man.

On my first morning back in Brooklyn after my investiture, I paid a call to the pharmacy. As I walked to the counter, John poked his head around the transparent divider screen and said, "Hey, Sir Patrick! *Sir* Patrick Stewart. So, whadda we have to do now— *coytsy?*"

Sunny and I enjoyed our share of travel together. First she came to visit me when I was in the UK for the Royal Shakespeare Company's latest production of *Hamlet*, with David Tennant in the title role and me as Claudius. I reveled in her wide-eyed joy at encountering the English countryside for the first time as we drove from London to Warwickshire. And she made me see Stratford, a town whose center I had come to regard as tiresomely touristy, through fresh eyes.

As we faced the altar in Holy Trinity Church, I pointed to what was inscribed on a stone right in front of us.

"Wait, what?" she exclaimed. "William Shakespeare is buried here? *No!* How is that possible?"

I also showed her the tree that had been planted in memory of Buzz Goodbody shortly after she had died. Sunny had not heard Buzz's story and was moved by it, as were both of us by the sight of the tree, now thirty-odd years old and flourishing.

I also introduced Sunny to Paris, staying at a friend's apartment on the Île Saint-Louis in the middle of the Seine, and to my beloved Mexico. We hit Mérida, in the northwest of the Yucatán Peninsula, climbed an ancient pyramid in the recently excavated Zona Arqueológica de Ek Balam, and drank the best margaritas of our lives, spiked with Xtabentún, a Yucatán liqueur made from fermented honey and anise seed.

At the end of this trip, we parted ways in Mexico City, with

Sunny returning to Brooklyn and me to London. We found ourselves in a kind of relationship limbo. We knew we wanted to be together, but we hadn't figured out how. Sunny had moved on from waitressing to a dream position, applying her knowledge of food and cookery to being the assistant to Melissa Clark, the renowned cookbook author and cooking columnist for the *New York Times*. I was still living my peripatetic life as an actor.

One indication of how serious we had become was that I was invited to Reno, Nevada, to meet Sunny's parents, Bill and Judy Michelson. With them, we drove up to their ranch in the foothills of the Sierra Nevada, where they keep four horses. This meant that we could all ride together. But Bill had laid out a plan for us to ride together, just him and me, along the summit trail. I had ridden quite a lot in England, usually in the cause of a film or TV project, but never Western-style. The saddles and horsemanship are completely different, and I slept anxiously the night before our outing. Was this Bill's Robert De Niro–*Meet the Parents* test of my manhood?

I was relieved to discover that Bill only wanted to show me the spectacular views on either side of the trail—and also to learn that he was the director of the ER at Saint Mary's Regional Medical Center in downtown Reno, because I had never been more saddle-sore in my life when I dismounted, and if my back gave out, I was at least in the company of a first-class physician. Judy had packed us beers for this excursion and Sunny had made us sandwiches, and in truth, it was a lovely introduction to her family, sore bum and all.

I also spent Christmas with the Michelsons. They have a ski cabin in Alpine Meadows near Lake Tahoe. I did not ski, but the scenery was lovely around their cabin, and I looked forward to going for walks, tending the fire, and reading a good book. The Michelsons are passionate skiers, and I learned something new about my girlfriend, that she had competed in downhill skiing at the state level in her teens. "I'd so love to join you all on the slopes," I told my hosts, "but I do not ski, and at my age, the time to learn how has passed me by."

Little did I know that the Michelsons had already made plans for me. Judy took me to town to buy a ski outfit, and Bill announced, "Your first lesson is at eight on Monday morning."

I protested, "It's too late, I'm too old. I'll kill myself!"

"Yes, it *is* too late," Bill said. "So you have four four-hour training sessions booked and you have a wonderful instructor. She will be with you at all times and it's one-on-one lessons." At least I would only make a fool of myself in front of one person.

My teacher was a kindly middle-aged woman who patiently showed me how to position myself, keep my balance, hop onto a chairlift, push off a chairlift, and give myself over to the slope. That evening, I told my hosts how pleased I was with my progress, and the three Michelsons confessed to having spied on me, as if I were their ten-year-old, and how proud they were of their boy Patrick. After my fourth lesson, I skied on my own for the first time in my life, from the top of the highest lift down to the clubhouse. It was exhilarating. I thanked my hosts profusely for pushing me past my fear and complacency.

Unfortunately, my next visit to the cabin, just a few weeks later, was the opposite of December's perfect Christmas idyll. Judy and Bill were as lovely and welcoming as ever, but there was a cloud hanging over Sunny and me. Two nights in, the tension snapped and we had a serious falling-out. It was about the long-distance, see-you-when-I-see-you way we were living. Our lives were in so much temporal and geographical misalignment that our relationship didn't seem to be building, but drifting aimlessly.

It was painful, but we agreed to break up. I would leave the next morning, after we had explained the situation to Sunny's parents. We slept in different bedrooms that night.

In the morning, we shared our sad news with Judy and Bill. I say "we," but Sunny has reminded me that I did most of the explaining because she was crying too much. I booked a flight to LA for later that morning and Bill offered to drive me to the airport. I have a feeling that Sunny's parents had talked about the situation and decided that Judy should stay with her daughter, leaving Bill and me to talk in the car, should I want to.

We did speak, but just a little. At the departure door, Bill and I embraced, both profoundly upset. I felt I had just said goodbye to wonderful people whom I wanted in my life but would never see again. I had quite a long wait for my flight, so I spent that time just sitting in a chair at my gate, gazing out through a big window at the airfield as planes came and went. It felt like a metaphor for my life.

When I got back to LA, I was in no mood to see anyone and had nowhere to stay. So I called the San Ysidro Ranch, a resort near Santa Barbara, and booked myself two nights. I needed to be alone and think hard about what had just happened. About twenty years earlier, I had driven up to that same hotel off the Pacific Coast Highway to contemplate my marriage to Sheila: a solitary man, mourning the end of a relationship. Was I destined to play this script over and over?

In February I flew back to London to prepare for Rupert Goold's RSC production of *The Merchant of Venice*, in which I was to play Shylock. During rehearsals, Sunny and I started reconnecting by phone. The mere sound of her voice brought me a calm and hopefulness that my life was otherwise lacking.

We talked, intensively, about our wants and needs. In June, Sunny agreed to come see me in England, our first in-person contact in five months. In my ledger of the week she visited, those six days are blank, with no reference to what we did or where we went. We were just . . . together, and rediscovering that this was the state we wanted to be in.

We were back on track but still leading separate existences, usually in separate countries. But that changed when, in April 2012, I booked us two seats on the Orient Express to Venice. In that most romantic of cities we finally discussed marriage. What's odd is that I'm pretty sure I never proposed to her; we simply arrived at a shared conclusion, Sunny's memory of which I present to you here in her own words:

> Patrick, we had already talked about this before you formally proposed to me at a fancy restaurant in Venice on Easter Sunday. I have never understood women who get proposed to as a total surprise, and who are then delighted with that surprise. Like, what the hell is that? It is one of the biggest decisions one can make in life, and someone is just going to POP THE QUESTION, and you, the woman, are supposed to just be DELIGHTED??? That is not how it went with you and ME. I know we had loving but sober and frank conversations about just what it was we were envisioning by marrying each other: what it meant for me and what it meant for you. It was a lot to talk about, as it should be. So by the time you proposed to me in Venice, it was a foregone conclusion and truly not some big event. There was no ring, no getting down on your knee. I mean, Jesus.

Our stampede toward connubial bliss coincided with the Berkeley–to–New York trajectory of *No Man's Land*, the Pinter play I was doing with Ian McKellen. Ian took to Sunny, and vice versa, with such immediacy and ferocity that I can only say that I am lucky they haven't run off together.

In the period between the Berkeley and Broadway productions, Sunny and I repaired to her family's ski cabin. One afternoon, we dipped modestly into some of the MDMA that Sunny had on hand; I'm not generally into such things, but Sunny is a dabbler. The result, filmed by Sunny on her phone, was my lecture on and demonstration of "the quadruple take." You've heard of the double take and the triple take, certainly. But as I made clear in my lecture—in which Sunny's painted toenails are visible in the frame, her feet pressed against my knees—the quadruple take, unlike the single, double, or triple, is based not in naturalism but in stylized, cartoonish movement.

We sat on the video for twenty-four hours after we filmed it, as we weren't confident that it was anything worth posting. But by the next day we decided there was no harm in sharing it. Released into the ether, it went viral with a fury neither of us anticipated. I was delighted. Moments like this offer a different look at who Sir Patrick Stewart is. For too long a time, I was reluctant to share my unserious side, but these days, that fear has been dispelled. Indeed, I think having comic chops benefits my more serious work, affording me a wider range of choices when I am performing.

Finally, on September 7, 2013, Sunny and I were married. The location was the Thunderbird Lodge, an old waterfront estate on the east shore of Lake Tahoe. The officiant was none other than Sir Ian McKellen (himself having been knighted), who, for the occasion, had been licensed online by the Universal Life Church to perform his duties. Our guests came from everywhere: Los Angeles, San Francisco, New York, Chicago, and the UK. They included my son, Daniel; my brother Trevor and his wife, Pat; and Sunny's parents.

Sir Ian began the ceremony with a welcoming speech, followed by a sincere address to Sunny and me about his love for us both. When he was done, there were many tears being wiped away, including Sunny's and mine.

The music at the reception was provided by Sunny's band and the bride herself. My first waltz with Lady Stewart, however, was stolen from me. As the intro began, LeVar Burton grabbed my wife by the hand and swept her onto the dance floor. Magnanimous guy that I am, I let him do it.

What nobody knew this glorious night, except for the two of us, Ian, and our *No Man's Land* costars Shuler Hensley and Billy Crudup, was that Sunny and I were already married.

Here is what happened: While *No Man's Land* was still in the midst of its run at Berkeley Rep, Sunny discovered that the state of Nevada would not accept a ceremony presided over by an online-ordained minister—even one with a knighthood and the ability to create magnetic fields or repel an orc army—as legally binding. But by the time she made this discovery, the wedding invitations had already gone out and it was too late to switch to a different venue. Aaaargh.

However, the state of California *would* accept a marriage presided over by our designated officiant. Ian, Sunny, and I put our heads together and came up with the idea of a secret ceremony, which, in order to remain just that, needed to happen right after a performance. We knew of a Mexican restaurant just around the corner from the theater that stayed open late and would be quiet around eleven p.m. Perfect. We invited Billy, Shuler, and our director, Sean Mathias, who happened to be in town, to serve as our formal witnesses. But we didn't tell them of their purpose—to them, it was just a post-show dinner invite.

Thankfully, the restaurant was indeed quiet when we arrived. We ordered glasses of champagne for our party. As soon as they arrived, Ian whipped out of his bag a ceremonial cloak, which he draped around his shoulders. There was puzzlement on our witnesses' part until Ian fetched a ring out of his pocket.

The first to figure out what was going on was Billy, who let out a loud squeal of excitement, which turned the heads of the servers and the few remaining customers. Ian explained to Billy, Shuler, and Sean that the three of them were important and necessary witnesses to what was about to take place. He produced the legal forms that Sunny and I had collected during a private visit to an Oakland courthouse and began his own version of a marriage ceremony.

At this very moment, a waiter appeared and said, "May I take your order?"—looking suspiciously at Sir Ian's cloak. Ian waved him off, saying, "In a moment, in a moment," and continued the proceedings. Again, he was interrupted by the waiter, who said, this time with some indignation, "If you don't order now, the kitchen will close."

Ian was equally annoyed. "All right, all right, be patient," he scolded the man. But Shuler said, "Let's just order something, anything." So we all reeled off some favorite Mexican dishes— "Tamales! Tacos de carnitas! Chile relleno!"—and Ian hastily wrapped up his marriage ceremony. I took the ring and put it on Sunny's finger, and the rest of our table cheered and applauded. A fraction of a second later, our supper arrived. But we had all finished our champagne. We had just enough time to order one more round. I suspect the tired staff were happy when we finally paid our bill and left. Truly a night to forever remember.

Chapter Twenty-Four

I t was not lost on me that in some quarters, eyebrows were raised at me marrying a woman younger than my own children. "He must be delusional," "She must be a gold digger"—I heard snide comments like that. Tabloid fodder. Of course nothing could be farther from the truth. The fact that Sunny and I have just celebrated our tenth wedding anniversary is a testimony to our enduring and very real love.

Age, by the way, is a strange concept for me. I am often told that Jean-Luc Picard seems to have barely changed in appearance since the days of *Star Trek: The Next Generation*, and while that is largely down to the strategic advantage of premature baldness, it's also reflective of my lifelong refusal to be defined by my chronological age. As a child, I was comfortable playing sports with older boys and participating in amateur dramas with adults. In my twenties, I married a woman in her thirties, Sheila. And now, I can't quite believe that I am in my eighties, even though I know it to be true. How on earth did that happen? For a long time I've felt more like mid-forties—as if I were already middle-aged when I was young and remain so now.

As for my marriage, it's an enormous credit to Sunny that the public has been on our side. She has a better grasp of social media than I do and has been masterful in showing people how much fun we have. She was my cameraperson for my viral "quadruple take" and "New York slice" moments. She is also partially responsible for one of my most out-there comic endeavors, a fake ad for a fake album called *Patrick Stewart's Cowboy Classics*. One day, her drummer and producer, Ethan Eubanks, overheard me singing one of my cherished cowboy songs. He asked me how I knew the song, and I told him all about my long-ago days listening to *Children's Choice* on BBC Radio.

Ethan suggested that I try recording some of these old songs with his and Sunny's band. I rejected the notion at once. But Ethan persisted, and once I started practicing, I realized I was having too good a time not to move forward. So we did indeed record a set of these songs. Then Sunny, the musicians, and I dressed up in Western outfits and shot some green-screen footage at Arlene's Grocery, a music club on Manhattan's Lower East Side. You can find the resultant video short, hawking music by the man "long known as England's premier cowboy singer," on YouTube. You might not ever respect me again, but I had quite a lot of fun doing it.

Sunny was also invaluable in advising me and Ian McKellen when we were trying to come up with promotional plans for our *Waiting for Godot–No Man's Land* double whammy in New York. She and I were by then living in Park Slope, having at last purchased a home to share as our own.

Ian and I had a top-line publicity team, and they were pitching an array of proposals for local press, TV, and personal appearances. But it all began to feel too ordinary, too conventional, for a project as unusual as ours. One day, I think as a result of my relentless whining, Sunny presented an idea that she had been brooding on for a long time, which she called "Gogo and Didi Do NYC"—Gogo and Didi being Estragon's and Vladimir's nicknames in *Godot*.

Sunny's scheme was that, together, the three of us would spend a Saturday visiting all the famous landmarks of Manhattan, with Ian and me in our ordinary clothes but wearing the beaten-up bowler hats our two characters wore all through the play. We would not employ a professional photographer; rather, Sunny would take photos on her phone, giving the pictures a relatable "tourist" feel. I loved the idea, and Ian was equally keen.

On the appointed Saturday, we enlisted my longtime driver and dear friend, Rudy Gonzales, to chauffeur us around for the day and also act as security, as we were working guerrilla-style and didn't want to attract fans with their own cell phone cameras—we couldn't allow leaks. To pull this off, we had to work very fast: out of the car, onto our marks, snap the photos, and quickly get back in the vehicle and speed off to the next location.

By late afternoon, we were wiped out, having traveled almost the length of Manhattan Island. Ian and I looked at Sunny's pictures in the car and we loved them. She had suggested that we change clothes often, to make each photo look as if it were a unique event. This entailed stripping down to our underwear in the back of the car. Rudy guarded the doors both as a measure of protection and to save two knights from being charged with indecent exposure.

Our plan was to let these photos come out in a slow drip, building up anticipation for our two-show bill. We faced some resistance from our PR people, who thought it was beneath me and Ian to be going around New York dressed as tramps and taking quickie photos. But we forged on. Indeed, Sunny, Ian, and I decided that we should do one more weekend of shooting, this time in Brooklyn. As it turned out, we spent most of our second day out in Coney Island, hitting the most famous spots: the Skee-Ball arcade, the Wonder Wheel, the boardwalk, and, of course, Nathan's Famous Hot Dogs.

In a mighty stroke of kismet, at Nathan's we encountered none other than Leonard Nimoy, who was enjoying a hot dog and, bless him, agreed to be photographed with us. From Coney Island we headed to Dumbo, strolled along the Brooklyn Heights promenade, and finished the day by walking across the Brooklyn Bridge.

Our PR strategy was vindicated when the Gogo-and-Didi photos took off on social media like wildfire. Sunny wisely knew that the key was not to overexplain things, piquing the viewer's curiosity. For instance, the photo of us on the Empire State Building's viewing deck read simply, "Empire State! #gogodididonyc @TwoPlaysInRep." The media began picking up on our campaign, so our photos were seen not only on social media but also on TV. *Good Morning America* featured our local adventure, and our ticket sales spiked.

Inspired by all of this, in October 2013, Sunny procured a ridiculous adult-sized lobster costume and took a photo of me wearing it as I lay in our empty bathtub. The caption read simply, "Happy Halloween." As it turned out, me as a lobster proved an even bigger global story than me enjoying a slice of pizza. And Sunny proved me to be a greater comic ham than I ever thought I was capable of.

The Patrick Stewart of yore, the serious one who declared that actors on set weren't there to have *fun*, would have been taken aback, but I love doing comedy. In the mid-teens of this century, the novelist and playwright Jonathan Ames and I held a series of conversations about the possibility of me starring in a half-hour TV comedy he was writing about an arrogant, outspoken ex-soldier and journalist who hosted his own interview show on cable television. I loved the idea, and when Jonathan mentioned that this character needed a name, I instantly replied, "Walter Blunt"—none other than the very first role I played as a member of the Royal Shakespeare Company, in *Henry IV, Part 1*.

Jonathan laughed, appreciating both the backstory and how apt the name was. "We could call his show *Blunt Talk*," he said.

My comedy godfather Seth MacFarlane came aboard as the executive producer, and we got the green light from the Starz cable network and put together a crackerjack cast of comic actors, including Jacki Weaver, Adrian Scarborough, Dolly Wells, Timm Sharp, Karan Soni, and Mary Holland. We made two seasons and twenty episodes of *Blunt Talk*, as the parent show of the fictitious show was also called, but just as we were finding our audience, the plug was pulled on us. I was never provided with an explanation. So much for my comedy career.

I had little time to brood, though, for I had committed to participating in one final *X-Men* movie, my sixth. I wasn't particularly keen on doing more work in that world until I learned that the new picture was going to be directed by James Mangold, the man behind such literary films as *Heavy* and *Girl, Interrupted*, not to mention *The Wolverine*, an *X-Men* movie in which I made only a fleeting appearance. I admired James's work, and when he met with me, requesting my return to playing Charles Xavier, he assured me that this new film was going to be very different from the prior *X-Men* movies.

Even with this assurance, I was entirely unprepared for *how* different it was. In March 2016, I was sent a script labeled "Natchez," a dummy title devised to keep the film's actual title, *Logan*, under wraps. I started reading. Whoa. The year is 2029. The X-Men themselves are in steep decline, and no mutants have been born for twenty-five years. James and his co-writers, Scott Frank and Michael Green, were exploring the idea of superhero entropy—what happens when they get clapped out and old, their powers waning, the general public indifferent to them?

On page two of the script, I discovered that Logan, Hugh Jackman's character, is no longer Wolverine, scraping out a sorry living by driving a dirty limo in a Mexican border town. And Charles Xavier? He is now Logan's ward, a ninety-something shell of his former self, beset by dementia and babbling nursery rhymes and gibberish. Logan looks after Charles in some kind of wrecked factory, administering pills to prevent Charles's seizures and intravenous shots to tamp these seizures down when they did happen. For all his weakness, Charles is still possessed of superhuman telepathic powers, so these seizures are capable of causing deadly, earthquake-like disruptions.

We started filming in May 2016. Being back on a set with Hugh was thrilling and invigorating. We were joined by Stephen Merchant as the mutant Caliban—"that fucking albino," as Charles describes him in his now unfiltered state—and child actress Dafne Keen, the most extraordinary juvenile performer with whom I have ever worked. Dafne played a new character named Laura, a feral girl with mutant DNA who has been engineered to kill, but resists this imperative because she has a conscience.

Dafne's focus and seriousness were something to behold when we were rehearsing and shooting—she reminded me of myself in my younger "We are not here to have *fun*" days. But when our work was on hold for camera and lighting setups, she was a joy: a smart, normal, very funny eleven-year-old.

James directed the movie with such care and sensitivity, accepting creative input from the actors and heightening our performances with his own input. I want to work with him again, and I was desolate when my time on *Logan* was up. I had another commitment to dash off to, so all of my scenes were completed early in the shoot. Saying goodbye to James, Hugh, Stephen, and Dafne was hard.

Hugh and I didn't meet again until *Logan*'s world premiere at the Berlin Film Festival in February 2017. We were presented onstage and then seated side by side in the center of the auditorium. I had not yet seen the film and was unprepared for the impact it had on me—and on Hugh. After (spoiler alert) Charles Xavier dies, during a scene in which Logan and Laura stand by the pile of earth that marks his grave, I noticed out of the corner of my eye that Hugh had lifted a hand to his cheek to wipe a tear away. There was nothing I could do except take his hand in mine. He smiled at me, and we held hands until the credits ran.

Not long after that, my agent informed me that two acclaimed screenwriters, Alex Kurtzman, who had co-written the *Star Trek* movie-franchise reboot starring Chris Pine, and Akiva Goldsman, an Oscar winner for Ron Howard's *A Beautiful Mind*, wanted to meet with me about a new TV series they had in mind. Its premise? It revisited Jean-Luc Picard as he was now, in his later years. My instant reaction? "No, definitely not interested. Sorry."

Fifteen minutes later, perhaps hedging a little, I called my agent back and told him that I would meet with Alex and Akiva, but only to explain why I was not interested in reentering the *Star Trek* realm. It was the polite thing to do, after all.

I met with Alex at the Hotel Bel-Air for lunch. For some reason, Akiva was not present, but Alex had brought with him Kirsten Beyer, a prolific author of *Star Trek* novels, and screenwriter James Duff, who co-created the Kyra Sedgwick show *The Closer*. I sighed inwardly—clearly, I was about to be pitched.

By way of a preamble, I made it clear to my lunch hosts that I was proud of the work we had done on *The Next Generation* and the four feature films that followed. I had very much enjoyed being Jean-Luc and kept him close in my heart. But. I was done with him. I had said everything I wanted to say about him. His journey, as far as I was concerned, was complete, and for the remainder of my life, I was eager to find work as far away from *Star Trek* as possible, to keep moving forward as an actor. I thanked Alex, Kirsten, and James for their time and interest, but that was that.

It will not surprise you that they pushed back.

They all said, in different ways, that they did not feel that Picard's story was over. Seventeen years had passed since *Nemesis*, the final movie featuring *The Next Generation* cast. That was a long time ago, but Picard's life had not ended. In fact, his life might very well have taken a radically different course post-*Nemesis*.

"How so?" I asked.

My hosts were ready for this and bombarded me with questions. Was Picard still a captain? Was he still in Starfleet? Had he been promoted? Had he retired? Did he still have his château in France? Did he have a wife or partner? What was his relationship with the Borg after all this time?

But mostly, they raised questions about Picard's emotional state. He was an older man now—was aging changing him, as, perhaps, it was changing me?

Whew. I needed to think about all of this.

When we adjourned, we agreed that they would get me a memo presenting their ideas and that I would give it some consideration.

The memo that arrived was over ten pages long, and I studied it very carefully. I had a series of talks with Sunny because committing to such a project would have a big impact on us, tethering me to a fixed schedule and a return to LA after our wholehearted embrace of Brooklyn.

We decided that revisiting Picard was worth considering, and I asked for another meeting. This time, Akiva Goldsman was in on the discussion. He spoke compellingly of his personal vision for a new series and mentioned that he was keen to involve Michael Chabon, whose Pulitzer Prize–winning novel *The Amazing Adventures of Kavalier & Clay* I had loved. That really got my attention.

I told Akiva and his team that I would return for *Star Trek: Picard,* as the series was to be called, if they met the following conditions:

1. The series would not be based on a reunion of *The Next Generation* characters. I wanted it to have little or nothing to do with them. This was not at all a mark of disrespect for my beloved fellow actors. Rather, I simply felt it was essential to place Picard in entirely new settings with entirely new characters. Perhaps Picard might encounter Riker or Dr. Crusher in the second season, but such encounters were not to be the series' raison d'être.

2. Picard would no longer be serving in Starfleet, and he was *not* to wear any kind of uniform or badges.

3. The series would run for no more than three seasons.

It was clear to me that the writing team was not entirely thrilled with these conditions, but basically, they were all agreed to. The no-uniform rule was the toughest one for them to stomach, for some reason, and more than once, I was asked to reconsider my hard line. I stuck to my guns.

But once I committed to being Jean-Luc again, I committed fully. I told the new program's producers that I wanted to announce *Star Trek: Picard* with a splash—by making a surprise appearance at the 2018 edition of the annual *Star Trek* Las Vegas convention. So much for the convention-shy Pat Stew of 1987!

I wanted it all kept hush-hush, with no mention whatsoever of my being in Las Vegas. Somehow, the secret never leaked. When I strode out to center stage, dressed casually in a T-shirt and jeans, I was greeted with a thundering round of applause that I consciously took a moment to enjoy. No more sheepishness, no more embarrassment—I *like* being liked. I told the audience a few familiar stories of my early days on *Star Trek: The Next Generation*, which were received appreciatively. I talked about how I had long thought that our four feature films marked the end of the line for Jean-Luc. That elicited a few groans.

Then I sprang it on 'em: "Jean-Luc Picard is back." *Whoooo!* Hoots of joy, more applause, lunatic shouts of glee. That moment alone made returning to the *Star Trek* universe worthwhile, and we hadn't yet shot a scene.

Once we started filming, I was relieved and pleased to find myself discovering a new gear in which to play Jean-Luc. Having reviewed my work in *Blunt Talk*, I'd come to recognize that at times I was being a bit heavy in my delivery, hitting words too firmly and delivering my lines too theatrically. I was determined to remedy that. Also, my voice has grown more ragged with age. So for the Jean-Luc on the precipice of turning eighty, I found a tone that was softer and gentler, and it really worked.

My whole career had been, to a degree, defined by my speaking voice and its power. Yet now, in acknowledging the limitations that Picard and I faced as older men, I found my voice more full of expression and spontaneity than before. I could also hear my brain and my feelings connecting to this voice, bringing forward a nuanced, autumnal Picard who was new to me and, I hoped, the show's viewers.

The writers did a remarkable job of inventing new characters, such as Picard's former Starfleet first officer Raffi Musiker, who struggles with substance abuse, and Agnes Jurati, a cybernetics expert who ultimately gets assimilated into the Borg. The producers did an equally fantastic job of landing the blue-chip actors Michelle Hurd to play Raffi and Alison Pill as Agnes. I couldn't wait to share our show with the world.

Our euphoria over the prospect of launching *Star Trek: Picard* was blunted somewhat by the onset of the Covid-19 pandemic early in 2020. We were still scrambling to finish up our first season when the virus reared its head, wrapping just under the wire before the whole world locked down. If nothing else, we had a captive audience that was grateful to have a new *Star Trek* show to watch.

But it was a frustrating time professionally for Sunny and me. I was looking forward to moving right along into the next season, while she had a new album of original songs, *Overnight Lows*, ready for release, with several concerts and promotional appearances lined up—all of which were canceled. Covid had arrived and we were about to enter a lockdown, something most people had never experienced before. Her album came out, but with barely any promotion behind it.

We were not oblivious to our privilege, though. We had recently moved to a house in a lovely section of Los Angeles that was convenient for work, with a swimming pool, citrus trees, and a wood-paneled study with a fireplace. There are worse places to spend a global pandemic than Southern California, and we knew how fortunate we were. We rented out our Brooklyn home, and LA has been our place of permanent residence ever since.

One day early in lockdown, as Sunny and I were out walking, I started to recite Shakespeare's Sonnet 116: "Let me not to the marriage of true minds admit impediments. Love is not love which alters when it alteration finds, or bends with the remover to remove."

"I love that," said Sunny. "Can you do the whole thing from memory?"

Indeed I could! And did. Sunny found this exercise so uplifting amid the gloom of the pandemic that she suggested that we record a video of me reading Sonnet 116 and post it to my Instagram account. Maybe it would brighten the day of some of our fellow housebound human beings.

Little did we know how popular this post would be. Within a week it had been viewed over four hundred thousand times, with appreciative comments piling up in the thousands. So, Sunny suggested, why not read *all* of Shakespeare's sonnets, posting one a day? I proceeded to do just that over those fraught months of 2020 when the terms "social distancing" and "contact-free delivery" became part of our lexicon. It was a big commitment, as I never once recited a sonnet cold. Each social media post was preceded by much study and rehearsal—I was determined to make Shakespeare's verse flow as mellifluously and joyously as possible.

To be honest, I was happy when I read the last of Shakespeare's 154 sonnets. It was hard work delivering new content day in and day out, and it took a lot out of me. But I am proud of what Sunny and I achieved during lockdown. Not a week goes by in which I don't encounter a fan who says, "Thank you for the sonnets—they pulled me through." And amazingly, the sonnets are all that these fans mention—not *Star Trek*, not *X-Men*, not *American Dad!* As a lifelong champion of Shakespeare, I find this tremendously gratifying.

There was one more aspect of lockdown that produced an unlikely positive outcome. Earlier on, I mentioned the sad story of the squirrel whose death I witnessed at the age of seven. That memory had weighed on me for more than seventy years, sitting in my subconscious and occasionally rising to the surface and traumatizing me all over again. But that pain began to dissipate during the pandemic, thanks to the fortuitous appearance of a consoling creature: another squirrel.

Soon after we moved into our house in Los Angeles, Sunny and I became aware that we had a daily visitor to our backyard—a squirrel looking for nibbles. At first, we presumed the creature to be male, and we gave it the name Cyril the Squirrel. But it quickly became evident that Cyril was pregnant, and eventually, she welcomed two babies. Even before that momentous event, however, our squirrel—now renamed Cheryl—developed a special rapport with my wife.

Speaking to Cheryl in a tender, high-pitched voice, Sunny won the squirrel's trust. Cheryl came to understand that if she was patient, she would get to enjoy tasty treats, primarily roasted peanuts still in their shells. Like everyone else living through lockdown, we had ample time on our hands and a desperation for some diversion. With every passing day, Cheryl became more at ease in our presence, accepting the offerings we laid on the patio outside our back door. Finally, on one thrilling morning, when she might have been unusually hungry, Cheryl took a fragment of a walnut directly from Sunny's fingers.

That evening, I toasted Sunny and Cheryl with a glass of champers, celebrating their friendship but never imagining that I, too, would soon enjoy the rush of human-squirrel intimacy.

Cheryl grew so comfortable with us that she took to daily announcements: approaching our back door, which opens into the kitchen, and tapping its glass panes with her very sharp claws to let us know that she was present—and hungry. Sunny and I responded at once, no matter what. When one of us opened the door and stepped outside, Cheryl's custom was to back away and then, once we held out a treat, to come and get it. Sunny took to kneeling on the ground, laying the nut in her lap so that Cheryl was incentivized to climb aboard and get her food—which, indeed, she began to do. This breakthrough was followed, quite soon, by Sunny's ploy of opening the door but remaining inside the kitchen, crouched on the floor. It took a while, but after a few weeks, ever so cautiously, Cheryl walked into our kitchen to receive her daily morsel.

Nowadays, she doesn't hesitate—once we open the door, Cheryl scuttles straight into the kitchen to be fed. Only when she is certain that all of the nuts are gone will she turn on her heel and scuttle back out. And I, too, have joined the privileged ranks of Cheryl's close friends, enticing her to eat nuts while perched in *my* lap.

The milestones keep on coming. One day a few months ago, Cheryl allowed Sunny to twice stroke her head before taking off. Even more recently, as I was leaving the house through the front door, I spotted Cheryl in the lower branches of a tree and called her name. She came to me at once, even though I had no treats to offer her. I rewarded her by stroking the back of her head before she hurried away.

The trust we have engendered in Cheryl has brought us such delight. For me in particular, my lifelong guilt over the tragic events from 1947 is lifting. I like to think that I have been forgiven by the squirrel community.

We shot the second and third seasons of *Star Trek: Picard* back-to-back, making up for lost time. Little by little, as the producers wore me down, I softened on my hard-line conditions regarding how I would participate in the series. Brent Spiner and Jonathan Frakes had reprised their characters in the first season, and Marina Sirtis, whose character Deanna Troi is now married to Riker, made a one-off appearance. By our second season, Q had reared his head, meaning a return for John de Lancie, and Whoopi Goldberg put in a couple of very valuable appearances as Guinan. For good measure, throughout the series we were also joined by the brilliant, beautiful Jeri Ryan, reprising her role as the ex-Borg drone Seven of Nine from the late-1990s TV series *Star Trek: Voyager*.

For Season Three, our last, Terry Matalas, by then *Picard*'s showrunner, told me that the studio wanted a full *Next Generation* reunion. Ugh, just what I had firmly said I *didn't* want. But that had been three years ago. Now I was less resistant, having enjoyed working with Jonathan, Brent, Marina, John, and Whoopi. As an executive producer, I had a say in how we might go about achieving such a reunion. I told Terry, "I like the idea, provided that we don't bring them all back at once. Let's trickle them back in."

It was essential to me that each *TNG* character came into the picture because he or she had a specific contribution to make and it wasn't just sentimental window dressing. If Jean-Luc had changed so much over the years, so, too, surely, had the other members of the *Enterprise* crew. The writers, bless them, took this to heart.

The final season's premiere episode, written by Terry, Akiva, and Michael Chabon, found Picard in a relaxed state of post-Starfleet life, proclaiming to his Romulan minder, Laris, played by the fine Irish actress Orla Brady, "I'm going to sip Saurian brandy and think about writing my memoir." Hey, I could relate to that!

Then, out of nowhere, Jean-Luc receives a distress call from none other than his former chief medical officer and occasional lover, Dr. Beverly Crusher. Hello and welcome back, Gates McFadden!

And as he plots to rescue Dr. Crusher and ward off an unknown enemy who is keen to abduct her son, Jack—who is also, we learn, Picard's child—Jean-Luc gradually rounds up the only people he can trust: his old *Enterprise* gang. Hello and welcome back, Gates, Brent, Jonathan, Marina, LeVar, and Michael! (I especially liked Worf's pacifist reappearance with a white goatee.)

And also, a grudging hello and welcome back to Starfleet badges and uniforms. Everyone else wore them, but Terry Matalas, knowing of my reservations, worked out a compromise. Picard's outfits had the same silhouette as the Starfleet uniform but looked more like everyday street clothes, with no two-tone color scheme.

The third season came off magnificently. But its final scene, in which the reunited crew is gathered around a table with drinks, sharing a toast, is not how it was originally supposed to end. I had a different idea, which I brought to the writers a few months before we wrapped the series.

"What I'd like to see at the end of the show," I told them, "is a *content* Jean-Luc. I want to see Picard perfectly at ease with his situation. Not anxious, not in a frenzy, not depressed. And I think this means that there is a wife in the picture."

You see, the line between Jean-Luc and me has grown ever more blurred. If I have at last found true love, shouldn't he?

The writers came up with a lovely scene. It is dusk at Jean-Luc's vineyard. His back is to us as he takes in the view, his dog at his side.

Then, off-screen, a woman's loving voice is heard: "Jean-Luc? Supper's ready!"

Is it Beverly Crusher's voice? Laris's? Someone we don't know? It isn't made clear. But Sunny was set to record the lines.

Heeding his wife's call, Jean-Luc turns around, says to his dog, "C'mon, boy," and heads inside. Dusk fades to night, and Picard fades into history.

But this scene was never shot. And I am sort of to blame. Our final day of shooting Season Three was a bear, with a very long to-do list. About eight hours in, I realized we were in for a fourteen- or even sixteen-hour day. Brutal. And I was booked to fly to New York the first thing the following morning. So I made a suggestion to the production team.

"Look," I said, "the scene with the dog will take no time to shoot, but it will take hours to set up the lighting and the green screen and all that. We don't have those hours. So let's not shoot that scene today. I can come back at any time you like and take care of it. Just me and the dog."

The production team was grateful and relieved. And I was assured that we would take care of the final scene upon my return from New York.

But I never got a call. When I made a few inquiries, I kept getting put off. Finally, someone told me, "The studio doesn't want to do it. It's too expensive and they think it's unnecessary." Unnecessary? I thought it was crucial to the completion of Picard's arc. But so be it: The TV series ended with the toast, which is a warm, emotional send-off to my favorite Starfleet crew. (The Shakespeare was, I think, my suggestion and everyone liked it.) Either way, you now know of my original intent.

So is that it for Jean-Luc Picard?

Most probably, but never say never. I am gently pushing Paramount to let us do one single *Picard* movie. Not a *Next Generation* movie, as we have already done four of those. This would be an expansion and deepening of the universe as we've seen it in *Star Trek: Picard*. I've discussed this with Jonathan, Brent, and LeVar, and they are all game. Jonathan is my first choice to direct it.

Chapter Twenty-Five

I shall forever be known first and foremost, by most people, for playing Jean-Luc Picard and delivering catchphrases like "Engage" and "Make it so." There was a time when I was uncomfortable with this reality, when it seemed incompatible with my background and reputation as a serious stage actor. And it wasn't just me— an English critic once called me out in print for abandoning my craft "to zoom about television screens in a preposterous spacesuit."

But I have grown to treasure Jean-Luc. He has come a long way from the relatively stiff character introduced back in "Encounter at Farpoint." I wish I could time-travel to 1987 and inform that scared, perpetually worried English actor what my *Winter's Tale* director, Ronald Eyre, told me when he wanted me to play Leontes: "I know that he is inside you already, Patrick. All you have to do is let him out."

Like me, Jean-Luc has lived an unusual life that has taken him far beyond the bounds of normal human experience. But he is also someone who has remained true to his earthbound roots, for they are what gave him his identity. In the end, he feels the call of home, as do I.

As for earthbound roots, I am the last Stewart standing of my original nuclear family. My beloved brother Trevor died on October 25, 2022. He had been unwell for some time and had never really recovered from the death of his wife, Pat, two years earlier. The second-to-last time I visited him at his care home, in April 2022, he barely seemed to know who I was, and I sensed he was slipping away.

Trevor's four wonderful children, Ian, Anne, Robert, and Julie, assured me that they would be in contact the moment the doctors said he was nearing the end of his life. At the time, we had no real grasp of when that might be, as he still experienced moments of lucidity and connection. I was constantly wracked with anxiety, fearful that I might be thousands of miles away in the middle of a stage production or a film when he passed. Any time the phone rang late at night or early in the morning, my heart pounded with trepidation.

But when the dreaded call finally came, I was, fortunately, at the vacation home that Sunny and I keep in Oxfordshire, a three-hour drive from Trevor's care home in Yorkshire. My niece Julie was the one who delivered the news: The care home manager said that Trevor had taken a turn for the worse.

Julie told me to come quickly.

Sunny immediately called a car to pick me up—she and I had already agreed that when the time came, I would go alone to be with Trevor and his immediate family. I had brought some work to do on the way, but I did none of it. All I could do was gaze out of the window at the peaceful, pretty English countryside in early autumnal glow—a sight that Trevor loved.

The driver knew of my mission's urgency and did everything within the bounds of the law to get me as quickly as he could to Heckmondwike, where the care home was. When I got there, I found my brother propped up on pillows with just a hospital gown around his shoulders. After hugging my nieces and nephews, I sat at the edge of Trevor's bed and took one of his hands in mine. He had lost so much weight. His face had hollowed out and his mouth fell open as quick little gasps of air passed in and out of his thin, pale lips. He looked at me and frowned slightly.

I told Trevor how happy I was to see him, that I loved him very much and that Sunny also sent her love. I wasn't sure if he comprehended what I said or even knew who I was, but somehow, that didn't seem to matter.

There came a moment when he indicated that he wanted to sit up, so I gently put my arms around him, lifted him up, and held him very close. He seemed to relax a little. I placed my hands behind his head to bring it forward toward mine. When our heads were nearly touching, I saw a trace of a smile come over his eyes and lips.

He closed his mouth for a moment. Then his lips parted again. Very softly, he said, "Pa . . . trick."

A smile covered my face as I nodded my head and said, "Yes, Trevor, I am your brother and I love you so much." I lowered my forehead and rested it against his. My cheeks were streaked with tears. I felt his breath on my lips, so I made sure that he would feel mine and I kissed him.

We sat with Trevor for more than three hours before one of the nurses told us that he needed to get some sleep. As she eased him into a prone position, I put my head close to his once more and said, "See you in the morning, Trevor."

But I never got the chance. Julie and her husband, Neil, had invited me to spend the night at their place. At around 1:30 in the morning, my phone rang. It was my niece Anne. The care home had just called her to say that Trevor had passed away.

His children all went to see him one last time and asked if I wanted to join them. But I decided that I did not want to see him that way. Too many memories of dead bodies—Mam, Dad, all those poor people from when I was on the obituary beat. No, I wanted my memory to be of my beloved brother Trevor alive, sharing a bed with me at the start of my life, and my arms around him the evening before nearing the very end of his own.

Arriving home to Oxfordshire, I found Sunny waiting to take me into her arms for a good cry, which was what I most needed. Sunny comforted me and also said that because Trevor had been told that I was on my way, he had chosen not to die until he had seen me one last time. I hadn't considered that as a possibility, which was a very Sunny way to look at this. It gave me immediate comfort and peace alongside my sadness.

The funeral was held at the same parish church in Mirfield where Trevor and I had been choirboys. As Sunny and I drove to the service, we were struck by a natural wonder: the most intensely vivid rainbow either of us had ever seen, bending perfectly over Mirfield. The elements, it seemed, were acknowledging Trevor's passing.

I was glad that my children, Daniel and Sophie, attended the funeral. They loved their Uncle Trevor very much. My own relationships with them remain a work in progress—the hurt caused by my split with their mother has never fully gone away. I do get on wonderfully with their children—my four remarkable grandchildren, the eldest in his early twenties and the other three in their teens. For all the grief that my brother's death caused us, it emphatically underscored the importance of family. I am forever grateful to Trevor for bringing mine together.

Coming face-to-face with my brother's mortality has inevitably forced me to confront my own. Mark you, I am in no hurry to leave and have no plans to do so any time soon. I am fortunate to live an active life and to be in good health. But at my age, I obviously take nothing for granted.

I do the normal things, like eat right and exercise. I also do memory exercises to keep the brain sharp. As for why I do all this, and why I don't just retire and spend my days doing crosswords or playing pickleball . . . I like my job too much! Acting was the thing that made me happy when I was thirteen years old, and that is still the case seventy years later. I have so much more work to do. I am not done with the stage. I still want to try another TV comedy. I still have so many characters inside me that I need to let out. And, thank heavens, the door is still open. So why would I ever stop?

The only thing that I'm putting an end to is this book, as I think you might have got the gist of me by now.

Also, I hear Sunny calling. Supper's ready.

Acknowledgments

I would like to thank the following people for helping bring this book to fruition: At CAA: Jennifer Joel and Carter Cohen; at Anonymous Content: Sandra Chang and Tony Lipp; at Independent Talent: Paul Lyon-Maris; at ID: Kelly Bush Novak, Scott Braun, and Adryan Dillon; at Gallery Books: Jen Bergstrom, Aimée Bell, and Ed Schlesinger. Thanks also to editorial consultant David Kamp and copyeditor Mary Beth Constant. And, most especially, to my wife, Sunny Ozell, who provided encouragement, support, counsel, and love over the three years that I was working on making this book so.

Index

An Actor Prepares (Stanislavski), 126
Actors' Equity Association, British,
    163–64
Actors' Equity Association, US, 389
African National Congress (ANC),
    91–93
Ahmanson Theatre, Music Center
    (Los Angeles), 235, 238, 322
Albee, Edward, 301–2, 305, 388
Albery Theatre (London), 390–91
Aldwych Theatre (London), 217,
    222, 225, 232, 241, 257.
    see also Royal Shakespeare
    Company
Alien (movie), 272
Allen, Corey, 309, 310–11
Allen, Fred, 358, 365, 366, 367
Allott, Mr. (choirmaster), 47–48
American Dad! (TV show), 394
Ames, Jonathan, 426
Anderson, Lindsay, 224
animals
    "Blackie"/"Crab" (dog in *The Two
    Gentlemen of Verona*), 242–47
    Rover (Stewart family's pet), 8
    squirrels, 29–30, 433–35

Ann (daughter of Wynn Owen),
    73
Anne (Stewart's niece), 440, 441
Annie (Stewart's aunt), 6, 14, 16, 23,
    293
Annis, Francesca, 280
Armstrong, Patricia, 118
Arthur (Sheffield landlord), 166
Ashcroft, Peggy, 74, 91, 296
Asher, Jane, 213–15, 216
As You Like It (Shakespeare),
    233–38, 281
audience, fans, and publicity
    A Midsummer Night's Dream, RSC
    white-box production, New
    York, 253–54
    Old Vic World Tour travel and
    publicity, 182, 189
    Royal Shakespeare Theatre
    patrons, 231–32
    Sonnets (Shakespeare) on social
    media, 432–33
    Star Trek, celebrity fans of, 153,
    275, 369–70, 411
    Star Trek conventions, 321,
    331–32

audience, fans, and publicity (*cont.*)
  Star Trek fans introduced to
    Shakespeare, 377
  Star Trek fans on "Picard
    maneuver," 330
  Star Trek franchise impact, 369–70
  Star Trek paparazzi, 347–48
  Star Trek: Picard announcement,
    37, 431
  Star Trek, wife's family as fans, 408
  Stewart's early lack of celebrity,
    227, 320, 327
  Stewart's social media posts, 237,
    419–20, 424–26

Bacall, Lauren, 253
Baker, George, 276
The Bald Soprano (Ionesco), 142
Baranski, Christine, 374
Barbican Centre (London), 277,
    289–90
Barnes, Clive, 252–53, 360
Barron, Keith, 161, 169, 170
Barron, Margaret, 119
Barrowclough, Alma (Stewart's
    sister-in-law), 55
Barrowclough, Freedom (Stewart's
    maternal grandfather), 14, 15
Barrowclough, Geoffrey (Stewart's
    oldest brother), 14–16, 26, 55,
    294
Barrowclough, Mary (Stewart's
    maternal grandmother), 14
Barton, John, 210–12, 218–19,
    232–33, 260, 267
Bassett, Frank, 60, 68–69
Bates, Alan, 299, 300
Batt, Bryan, 374
BBC, 38–39, 75–76, 115, 118,
    143–44, 237, 276–77, 424
Beatles
  Beatlemania, 201–2
  "The Inner Light" (song), 355–56

McCartney, 214–15
  Starr, 215
Beaumont, Richard, 110
Beckett, Henry, 141
Beckett, Samuel, 47, 115, 142,
    397–401, 424
Behan, Brendan, 213
Behr, Ira Steven, 341
Bennett, Rodney, 273
Benthall, Michael, 174, 175, 184
Berlin Film Festival (2017), 428
Berman, Rick
  final *TNG* episode and, 375
  First Contact screenplay by, 378
  Picard character and, 354
  Stewart's *A Christmas Carol*
    supported by, 359, 367
  Stewart's *TNG* hiring and, 306–7
  on *TNG* guests and guests
    appearances, 371, 372
  as *TNG* producer-in-chief, 359
  TNG Season Three, 339
  TNG Season Five, 355
Berry, Cicely, 74
Berry, Halle, 386
Besley, Charles, 70, 71, 78, 81–83
Beyer, Kirsten, 429
Billy Rose Theatre (New York), 251,
    254
Black Dick's Tower (England), 110
"Blackie"/"Crab" (dog in *The Two
    Gentlemen of Verona*), 242–47
Blackman, Robert, 330
Black Swan (RSC "club"), 228
Bland, Marjorie, 260
Blessed, Brian
  career success of, 146
  in *I, Claudius* (BBC), 276
  Stewart's acting training with, 63,
    65, 67, 74, 76, 99, 102, 115
  at Stewart's knighting ceremony,
    414
Bloom, Claire, 132

Blunt Talk (Starz), 426, 431
Bougere, Teagle F., 377
Brady, Orla, 436
Braga, Brannon, 378
Brando, Marlon, 41, 273
"breaking up"/"corpsing," 327–28
Brecht, Bertolt, 116
Brierley, David, 218
Brighouse Children's Theatre, 66
Bristol Old Vic Theatre School,
    131–51
  Bristol, town description, 114–15
  classmates, 115, 119–20
  curriculum, 115–19, 131–32
  "Here at the school" (class song),
    118–19
  housing, 115, 120–21
  improv lessons, 124–25
  makeup lessons, 140–41
  movement training, 63–64,
    128–29, 141–42
  nurturing environment of,
    125–26
  "performing" mindset of, 126
  shows performed at, 142–44,
    145–49
  staff, 115–19
  Stewart's acceptance at, 99–104
  Stewart's balding as acting
    advantage, 136–37, 193
  Stewart's fear of failure overcome
    at, 144–45
  Stewart's first acting job after,
    150–51
  Stewart's Mirfield visits during
    attendance at, 131, 133–37,
    149, 151
  Stewart's preparation for,
    110–14
  Stewart's romantic life during,
    121–22, 136–39, 148, 149
  Stewart's Spain trip during,
    138–39
  Stewart's stage fright experience,
    46
  technique lessons, 122–24
British Actors' Equity Association,
    163–64
Brittany, John, 159
Brook, Peter, 241–42, 249–52, 258,
    260, 268
Brooklyn Academy of Music (BAM),
    251, 407, 411
Bryggman, Larry, 377
Buckingham Palace, 413–14
bullfighting, 138–39
The Buried Man (play), 197–98
Burton, LeVar, 319–21, 328, 420,
    436, 438
Burton, Richard, 143, 301
Bury, John, 218
Byrne, David, 411

Campilongo, Jim, 410
Campion, Jane, 387
Caron, Leslie, 198
Carter, Helena Bonham, 266
Cartwright, Arnold, 16–17
Chabon, Michael, 430, 436
Chandler, Raymond, 86, 334
Charles III (king of England), 414
Chekhov, Anton, 116, 161, 209
Cheryl the Squirrel, 434–35
Chichester Festival, 403, 405
Children's Choice (BBC), 38–39, 118,
    424
Chitty Chitty Bang Bang (movie), 175
A Christmas Carol (Dickens), 356–67
  on Broadway, 359–60
  California warm-up tour, 360–61
  at Old Vic Theatre (London),
    360–61, 364–67
  Olivier Award, 367
  one-man show concept for,
    356–59
  Rees's critique of, 362–64, 367

Church, Jonathan, 405
Church, Tony, 218, 219, 221, 240
Churubusco Studios (Mexico City), 280, 283–85
Clark, Melissa, 416
Clifford (Stewart's uncle), 21, 53
A Clockwork Orange (movie), 224
clothing and costumes
    for acting training, 62, 117
    Dune, 284
    Hamlet (Shakespeare), modern-dress version, 268
    for journalist work, 85–86
    Macbeth (Shakespeare), semi-modern dress, 404
    Old Vic World Tour, 170, 178
    RSC, 141–42
    Star Trek (Original Series), 333
    Star Trek: Picard, 430, 436
    Star Trek: TNG costumes, 329–30, 333–34
Cobb, Lee J., 41
Cocker, Jarvis, 159
Cocker, Joe, 159
Collymossie, Mrs. (teacher), 55–56
Colman, Olivia, 380
"Common People" (song, Cocker), 159
Community of the Resurrection (CR, Mirfield), 45–46, 91–93
Conspiracy Theory (movie), 382
Cooke, Brian, 68–69, 112–13
Coriolanus (Shakespeare), 260, 261, 267
"corpsing"/"breaking up," 327–28
council estates, 109–10
Court, Margaret, 88–89, 93, 96
Courtenay, Tom, 51
COVID-19 pandemic, 432–33
Coward, Noël, 202
"Crab" (dog in The Two Gentlemen of Verona), 242–47
The Critic (Sheridan), 146, 147

Cromwell, James, 379
Crosby, Denise, 127, 319, 326, 329, 333
Crowe, William J., 371
Crowlees Boys' School, 45–52
Crudup, Billy, 400, 420, 421

Danby, Ian, 73
Daniels, Maurice, 199, 200, 210–12
David (Stewart's childhood friend), 112–13
Davies, Howard, 270
Davison, Bruce, 387
Day-Lewis, Daniel, 260
Dear Tom (Courtenay), 51
De Lancie, John, 308, 324, 375, 435
De la Tour, Frankie, 254
De Laurentiis, Dino, 288
De Laurentiis, Raffaella, 288–90
Dench, Judi, 90, 403
"Devil Tree" incidents, 48
Dewsbury and District Reporter (England), 82–83, 85–87, 171
Dewsbury Drama Club, 99
Dickens, Charles, 204, 234, 295, 356–67, 399. see also A Christmas Carol
Dighton, John, 52, 104, 209
Dignam, Mark, 262
Dillon, Lisa, 390–91
Dirty Duck (RSC "club"), 228
Dixon, Gilbert, 6
Dixon, Lizzie, 6–7, 35–36
Doctor Faustus (Marlowe), 240
Dodimead, David, 186
domestic violence awareness, 37
Donegan, Lonnie, 153, 233
Donmar Warehouse (London), 218
Donner, Lauren Shuler, 382–83, 385
Donner, Richard, 382
Dontanville, Steve, 304, 305–8, 312–14, 330, 336, 374, 395
Dorchester hotel (London), 26, 364

Doris (Stewart's "Auntie Dolly"),
        21–22
Dormand, Cecil
    Stewart's acting training and,
        56–58, 59–62, 66, 72, 74, 78,
        80–82, 195
    at Stewart's knighting ceremony,
        414
Dormand, Mary, 62, 414
Dorn, Michael
    in *Family Guy,* 394
    personality of, 37
    as plane pilot, 337
    in *Star Trek: Picard,* 436
    in *TNG,* 129, 319
    Worf character of, 327–28, 354,
        394
Douglas, Anne, 349
Douglas, Kirk, 25, 349–50, 361
Douglas, Peter, 349–50
Dourif, Brad, 280
Duel of Angels (Giraudoux
        adaptation), 170, 175, 176, 182
Duff, James, 429
Dumas, Alexandre, 170, 176,
        179–80, 182, 184
Dune (Herbert), 277, 279, 280
Dune (movie)
    filming of, 282–88
    Stewart's casting in, 277, 279–80,
        288–90
    travel to set of, 280–82
Duplessis, Marie, 179
Dyson, Barbara, 65, 66

The Elephant Man (movie), 279
Eles, Sandor, 120
Elizabeth II (queen of England), 189,
        413–14
Elizabeth (Stewart's paternal great-
        grandmother), 17
Elliott, Kate, 358–61, 363, 365–67
Ellis, Aunjanue, 377

"Empire State! #gogodididonyc @
        TwoPlaysInRep" social media
        campaign, 424–26
England
    arts funding by, 99, 156
    Bristol, 114–15 (*see also* Bristol Old
        Vic Theatre School; Old Vic
        Theatre Company (Bristol))
    council estates of, 109–10
    dialect and accent (*see* language
        and voice)
    eleven-plus exam, 49–52
    English Football League, 319
    Mirfield (Northern England)
        lifestyle, 1–3, 5–13
    Parachute Regiment (British
        Army), 4–5, 25
    World Cup (1966), 226–27
    Yorkshire Dales, 112–14
Esparza, Raúl, 410
Eubanks, Ethan, 424
Eugene O'Neill Theatre (New York),
        359–60
Every Good Boy Deserves Favour
        (Stoppard), 386
Extras (TV show), 394–97
Eyre, Ronald, 296–97, 298, 439

failure, fear of, 144–45
Falconer, Sheila (Stewart's first wife)
    dance/choreography career of,
        207–8, 228, 260
    in Los Angeles, 240, 268
    in New York, 250
    on Stewart's career decisions, 230,
        280, 287, 295, 299, 301–3, 308,
        316, 318
    Stewart's early romance and
        marriage to, 207–8, 216, 218,
        222, 423
    Stewart's homes with, 134–36,
        217–18, 231, 232, 243, 244,
        295

Falconer, Sheila (*cont.*)
  Stewart's marriage breakdown and
    divorce, 302, 335–36, 339–48,
    350, 359, 391, 418
  Stewart's Old Vic World Tour and,
    193
Fernald, John, 168
Fernald, Karin, 167–68
Ferrer, José, 280
Festival of Britain (1951), 24, 48
film career. *see* Stewart, Patrick, film
  career
Finch, Adrienne, 119–22, 136–39,
    148, 149, 159
Finsbury Park Empire, 173, 174
Fleetwood, Kate, 276, 405
Fleetwood, Mick, 371
food
  corn beef sandwich, New York,
    254–55
  Original Tommy's, Los Angeles,
    236–37
  pizza "slice" in New York City,
    237
  "sandwich scene" (*Macbeth*,
    Shakespeare), 406–7
  Stewart's eating habits, 42, 381
  Stewart's father's food preferences,
    42
Forester, C. S., 323
Frakes, Jonathan
  directing by, 326, 370–71, 378–80,
    438
  in "Encounter at Farpoint" (*TNG*
    final episodes), 375
  Picard movie plans, 435
  on Stewart as "famous nude
    Oberon," 260
  on Stewart's "poverty mentality,"
    321, 336–37
  TNG hiring of, 319
  TNG Riker character and
    storylines, 341

TNG Season One, 321, 325, 326,
    328, 334
  TNG Season Three, 340, 343, 345
Frank, Scott, 427
Fred (childhood friend), 36–37

Garber, Victor, 374, 376
Gardner, Glenys, 119
Gaskell, Elizabeth, 273
Gee, Donald, 222
Gee, Shirley, 222
Gemäldegalerie (Berlin museum), 54
Gendel, Morgan, 355
Genet, Jean, 142
Gervais, Ricky, 394–97
Gibson, Alan, 146
Gibson, Mel, 382
Giraudoux, Jean, 170. *see also Duel of
    Angels* (Giraudoux adaptation)
Gladys (Stewart's aunt), 53
Godfrey, Patrick, 269
"Gogo and Didi Do NYC" social
    media campaign, 424–26
Goldberg, Whoopi, 338, 369, 435
Goldsman, Akiva, 428–30, 436
Gone with the Wind (movie), 178–79
Gonzales, Rudy, 425
Goodbody, Mary Ann "Buzz,"
    266–68, 415
Good Morning America (TV show),
    426
Goold, Rupert, 276, 403, 404–6,
    411, 418
Gore, Al, 141–42
Grainger, Gawn, 205–7, 208, 209,
    213, 414
Gramsci, Antonio, 267
Granger, Stewart, 118
Grant, Hugh, 74
Graves, Robert, 276
Gray, Simon, 299
Green, Michael, 427
Grey, Joel, 366, 408, 409

Griffiths, Trevor, 267
Grinling, Amanda, 162
Guthrie, Tyrone, 208

Haigh, Mr. (headmaster), 44
Half a Sixpence (movie), 228
Hall, Peter
    directing style of, 233
    at National Theatre, 238
    on stage makeup, 140
    Stewart's first year with RSC and,
        218, 223, 225–26, 227,
        229–30
    Stewart's hiring by RSC, 198–200,
        208–13, 223, 229–30
    Yonadab (Shaffer) direction by
        (1985), 298–301
Hall, Reverend (Mirfield parish
    church), 48
Hamill, Mark, 163
Hamlet (Shakespeare), 208–9, 213,
    225–27, 268
handkerchief incident, 44
The Hand (The Beast with Five
    Fingers, movie), 39
Hanks, Tom, 369
The Happiest Days of Your Life (play),
    52, 104, 213
Hardiman, Terry, 206–7
Hardy, Tom, 380
Harrison, George, 355
Hawking, Stephen, 371–72
Hawkins, Leader, 120
Haycock, Philip, 55
Hay Fever (Coward), 202
Heal, Joan, 207
Heard, Daphne, 116, 117, 124–25,
    127, 144
Hecht, Deborah, 121
Hedda Gabler (Ibsen), 268
Helpmann, Robert, 174–75, 178,
    181–84, 189, 191
Hennessy (movie), 41, 123–24

Henry IV, Parts 1 and 2
    (Shakespeare), 213, 218–23,
    277–78, 288–90, 322
Henry V (Shakespeare), 167, 194,
    199, 210–13, 223–25, 353
Hensley, Shuler, 400, 420, 421–22
Herbert, Frank, 277, 279, 280
"Here at the school" (class song),
    118–19
Hetrick, Jennifer "Jenny," 341–43,
    345–48, 391
hiccups incident, 162
Hogg, Ian, 261
Holdsworth, Bryan, 24, 67
Holland, Mary, 426
Holland, Tom, 381
Hollywood Bowl, 46
Holm, Ian, 90, 211, 218, 220–23,
    269–72
The Homecoming (Pinter), 222
Hooper, Tobe, 290, 291
Horatio Hornblower book series
    (Forester), 323
Horne, Roderick "Rod," 184–85,
    193
Housewives' Choice (BBC), 38
Howard, Alan, 238, 249, 250, 253,
    254, 257–60
Howerd, Frankie, 196–97
Huddersfield Town (football club,
    England), 319
Huddersfield University (Yorkshire),
    106
Huddleston, Trevor, 91–93
Hudson, Derek, 97, 98, 102, 110
Hudson's Furniture (Mirfield),
    97–98, 102, 107, 110
Hungarian Revolution (1956), 120
Hunter, Holly, 387
Hurd, Michelle, 432
Hurley, Maurice, 338, 339
Hurt, John, 276
Hutter, Al, 357, 360

I, Claudius (BBC), 276–77
Ian (Stewart's nephew), 440
Ibsen, Henrik, 116, 161, 268, 272, 390–91
The Iceman Cometh (O'Neill), 268–71
ICM, 304, 313
If . . . (movie), 224
"The Inner Light" (Beatles), 355–56
An Inspector Calls (Priestley), 105
The Investigation (Weiss), 241–42
Ionesco, Eugène, 116, 142
Irwin, Bill, 377

Jackman, Hugh, 387, 427, 428
Jackson, Glenda, 225, 241, 268
Jackson, Peter, 272
Jacobi, Derek, 276
Janssen, Famke, 387
Jarvis, Martin, 200
Jayston, Michael, 219
Jean-Luc Picard. *see* Picard character
Jeffrey, Peter, 398
Jeffrey (movie), 185, 374
John (Brooklyn pharmacist), 415
Jones, Anita Hartwell, 119
Jones, David, 233, 271
Jones, Freddie, 280, 285
Julie (Stewart's niece), 440, 441
Julius Caesar (Shakespeare), 262–66
Justman, Robert, 306, 330–31, 354

Kabak, Christo, 267
Kane, John, 254
Keen, Dafne, 428
Kelley, DeForest, 325
Kestelman, Sara, 249, 254, 258
King, David, 398
King John (Shakespeare), 266–68
King Lear (Shakespeare), 238–39
Kingsley, Ben, 234, 239, 254, 257–59, 267–68
Kinnear, Roy, 234–35

Kirby, Jack, 383
Kishvalvi, George, 120, 136–37
Kitchen, Gillian, 119, 121
Kohler, Estelle, 225, 242, 244, 267
Krige, Alice, 379
Kubrick, Stanley, 224
Kurtzman, Alex, 428–29

labor unions, 163–64
Lady Jane (movie), 266
The Lady of the Camellias (Dumas), 170, 176, 179–80, 182, 184
Ladysmith Black Mambazo, 411
Lambert, Norman, 63, 67, 72–73
language and voice
  "ha-ha," 43
  received pronunciation (RP), 75–76
  Stewart on his speaking voice and career importance, 431–32
  Stewart's American accent, 146–47
  Stewart's coaching for *TNG*, 310
  Stewart's early voice/acting lessons with Wynn Owen, 66–67, 72–78
  Stewart's East London Jewish accent, 204
  "t'bottom," 1–3
  Vic School vocal warm-up, 118
  West Riding phrases, 106
  Yorkshire dialect, 6, 98, 198
Lansing, Sherry, 141
Laurel, Stan, 171
Lee, Stan, 383
Lee Green Infants School, 32, 41–44
Leichner (stage makeup), 140–41
Leigh, Vivien
  characterization of, 175, 179, 183–87
  death of, 193
  Gone with the Wind, 178–79
  Old Vic World Tour acting roles of, 179–80, 183, 184, 191

Old Vic World Tour publicity, 19,
    170, 171, 182, 189
Leigh-Hunt, Barbara, 206
LGBTQ issues
    gay actors in 1940s and '50s, 147
    gay actors in Old Vic World Tour,
        184–85
    Howerd incident, 196–97
Library Theatre (Manchester,
    England), 23, 167, 193–94,
    195–201
*The Life and Adventures of Nicholas
    Nickleby* (Dickens), 234, 362
Lifeforce (movie), 290–91
Lincoln, England, 154. *see also*
    Theatre Royal (Lincoln,
    England)
Linklater, Kristin, 74–75
Liverpool Playhouse, 193, 200–208
Lloyd, Bernard "Bernie," 238,
    239–40, 297–98
Locke, Philip, 254
Locke (movie), 380
Lock Up Your Daughters (play),
    207–8
Lockwood, Miss (deputy
    headmistress), 68, 69, 70–71
Logan (movie), 54, 427–28
Lorre, Peter, 39
Los Angeles Philharmonic, 322, 381
Los Angeles Times, 320
Louis, Joe, 38
Love in the Time of Bloomers (play),
    196
Lumet, Sidney, 275
Lyceum Theatre (New York), 407
Lynch, David, 277, 279, 282–84,
    288–90, 382
Lynne, Gillian, 207, 260

Macbeth (Shakespeare), 276, 402–11
MacFarlane, Seth, 394, 426
MacLachlan, Kyle, 280, 283–85, 289

MacMurray, Fred, 236
Madsen, Virginia, 280
Mallard (railway engine), 25
Malvern Theatre (England), 46
Mamas and the Papas, 334
Manchester Library Theatre
    Company, 23, 167, 193–94,
    195–201
Mandela, Nelson, 91–93
Mane, Tyler, 387
Mangold, James, 427, 428
Manners, Janet, 196
The Man with the Golden Helmet
    (School of Rembrandt van
    Rijn), 54
Marat/Sade (play), 241
Mark Taper Forum, Music Center
    (Los Angeles), 235
Marlowe, Christopher, 240
Marlowe, Raymond, 271
Marsden, James, 386
Marsh, Matthew, 302
Marvel Comics, 383. *see also X-Men
    movies*
The Master Builder (Ibsen), 272,
    390–91
Matalas, Terry, 435–36
Mathias, Sean, 397, 400, 421
May, Mathilda, 291
May, Val, 208
McCartney, Paul, 214–15, 216, 400
McDowell, Malcolm, 223–25
McFadden, Gates, 319, 322, 328,
    338–39, 436
McKellen, Ian
    "aura" of, 90
    "Gogo and Didi Do NYC" social
        media campaign, 424–25
    on *Macbeth* (Shakespeare),
        403–4
    Stewart's friendship with, 397–
        401
    on Stewart's *TNG* hiring, 315

McKellen, Ian (*cont.*)
Stewart's wedding to Ozell
officiated by, 419–22
on unions, 163
in *Waiting for Godot* (Beckett),
47
in *X-Men*, 386
McMillan, Kenneth, 280
mentors. *see* Dormand, Cecil;
Heard, Daphne; Ross, Duncan;
Shelley, Raphael "Rudi"; Wynn
Owen, Ruth
Merchant, Stephen, 395, 396–97,
427
The Merchant of Venice
(Shakespeare), 56–58, 74,
204–7, 209–13, 418
Merivale, John, 175, 179, 183,
187–88
Method acting, 126
Metro-Goldwyn-Mayer (MGM)
Studios, 235
Mexico
Dune filmed in, 277, 279–90
Old Vic World Tour in, 190–92
Stewart and Ozell in, 415
Michelson, Bill, 416–18, 420
Michelson, Judy, 416–18, 420
Michelson, Sunny Ozell. *see* Ozell,
Sunny
Middlemass, Frank, 185, 190, 193,
206
Middleton, Thomas, 233
Midnight Express (movie), 285
A Midsummer Night's Dream
(Shakespeare), 191, 241, 242,
249–55, 257–60
Miller, Arthur, 366, 388–89
Mirfield (Northern England)
Labour Exchange
(unemployment), 149
lifestyle in, 1–3, 5–13
Mirfield Reporter, 82–83, 87–96

Mirfield Secondary Modern
School, 53–58, 59–61, 68–72,
80–81, 82
prejudice encountered in, 174
Stewart family's move to, 16
Stewart's visits, after starting
professional acting, 153–54,
170–71
theaters and drama societies,
45–47, 60, 79–81, 94–96, 99
Mirren, Helen, 238, 242, 244, 245
Montague, Bruce, 176, 182, 184, 186,
190
Moore, Bill, 149, 195
Moore, K. V., 150, 157, 159
Moore, Mary Tyler, 366
Moore, Ronald D., 353, 378
Moore, William, 147
Morris, Douglas ("Mugless Doris"),
169–70, 175–76, 180–81, 186
Moxon, Leslie, 182
Moynihan, Daniel, 220
Much Ado About Nothing
(Shakespeare), 238–41
Mulaney, John, 394
Muldaur, Diana, 339
Music Center (Los Angeles), 235,
238, 322
Myers, Mike, 393, 394
Mytholmroyd residential drama
course (1953), 59–67, 90, 99,
100, 105

National Theatre (London), 156,
238, 272, 298–301
Nederlander Theatre (New York),
251
Neil (Stewart's niece's husband), 441
Nettheim, David, 189
Neuss, Wendy, 381–82, 390–91
Neville, John, 132–33, 372
Newman, Paul, 253
Newton, Isaac, 371, 372

New York Post, 360
New York Times, 252–53, 416
Nicholas Nickleby (Dickens), 234, 362
Nichols, Nichelle, 338
Nickodell (Los Angeles bar), 328–29
Nimoy, Leonard, 306, 317, 355, 425
No Exit (Sartre), 76, 100–101
No Man's Land (Pinter), 400–401, 419, 424
North and South (TV miniseries), 273
Nottingham Playhouse, 146
Nunn, Trevor
  Goodbody at RSC and, 267, 268
  Lady Jane (movie) directed by, 266
  RSC direction/artistic direction by, 233, 238–40, 261, 262, 267, 277, 278, 403

Occupations (Griffiths), 267–68
Old Vic School. *see* Bristol Old Vic Theatre School
Old Vic Theatre Company (Bristol)
  Old Vic School and, 46, 145–49
  Stewart's application to (1961), 193
  Stewart's performances with (1965), 208–9, 213–16
  Theatre Royal location of, 114–15
Old Vic Theatre (London). *see also* Old Vic World Tour
  A Christmas Carol (Dickens) at, 360–61, 364–67
  Stewart's early exposure to, 132–33
Old Vic World Tour, 173–94. *see also* Leigh, Vivien
  in Australia, 181–88
  in Buenos Aires, 192
  company, 174–77
  Duel of Angels, 170, 175, 176, 182
  Lady of the Camellias, 170, 176, 179–80, 182, 184

  living arrangements, 173–74, 177, 179, 184–85
  London rehearsals and preparation, 173, 174, 177–78, 180–81
  in Mexico, 190–92
  in New Zealand, 189, 190
  Stewart hired for, 19, 169–71
  tour's end, 22–23, 193–94
  Twelfth Night, 170, 176, 182–83, 185, 191
  U.S. travel and, 190–91
Oliver Twist (Dickens), 204
Olivier, Lady. *see* Leigh, Vivien
Olivier, Laurence, 91, 99, 123, 170, 238
Olivier Award, 367
O'Neill, Eugene, 268–71
On the Waterfront (movie), 40–41, 123, 126, 273
Original Tommy's (Los Angeles), 236–37
Osborne, John, 299
Ost, Geoffrey, 129, 158, 160–61, 169, 181, 193, 196
Other Place (RSC experimental theater), 266–68
O'Toole, Peter, 147, 398
Overnight Lows (Ozell), 432
Owen, Alun, 201
Ozell, Sunny (Stewart's third wife)
  in Berlin, 54
  brother-in-law's passing and, 440–42
  home life of, 205, 393, 434–35
  Kirk Douglas meeting and, 350
  Lloyd's friendship with Stewart and, 240–41
  music career of, 410, 432
  in New York City, 237
  social media publicity by, 423–26
  (*see also* social media)
  on *Star Trek: Picard* plans, 437

Ozell, Sunny (*cont.*)
  on Stewart's accent, 76
  Stewart's age difference from, 423
  on Stewart's childhood, 5, 7
  Stewart's early romance with,
    407–19
  on Stewart's pottery, 55
  Stewart's Sonnets (Shakespeare)
    and, 432–33
  Stewart's wedding ceremonies
    with, 419–22
  in Stratford-upon-Avon, 162

Page, Anthony, 272
Palling, Mr. (Labour Party
  candidate), 32
Pankow, John, 377
Paquin, Anna, 387
Parachute Regiment (British Army),
  4–5, 25
Paramount Pictures. *see also*
  individual Star Trek *entries*
  actors' trailers, 320
  Gore's visit to, 141
  on Stewart in *A Christmas Carol*
    (Dickens), 364
  Stewart's first visit to, 305–6,
    308–12
  TNG and threats to cancel,
    335–36
  TNG early syndication, 329–30
paranormal experiences
  mother's death and, 294
  in Silver Lake (Los Angeles)
    home, 351–53
  Stewart's "aura," 90
Park, Ray, 387
Parker, Alan, 285
Parkin, Barry, 86, 88, 95–96, 102,
  111, 153
The Pawnbroker (movie), 275
peach incident, 31
Pettiward, Stella, 73

Phillips, Michelle, 334
Phillips, Robin, 118–19, 124,
  146–48, 242, 261–62
Phillips, Siân, 276, 280, 285
Picard character
  Borg and, 339, 378–79
  in "Chain of Command" (*TNG*
    Season Six), 373
  as Dixon Hill character, 334
  as Kamin on planet Kataan,
    355–56
  Kirk with, in *Star Trek Generations*
    (movie), 376
  "Picard maneuver," 330
  Picard movie plans, 438
  Roddenberry legacy and, 354
  romance storylines, 340–41
  in *Star Trek: Picard* (TV series),
    428–31, 435–37
  Stewart's intended final scene for,
    437
  Stewart's interpretation of,
    322–24
Pickard, Mary, 161, 170
Pickles, Charlie, 86–87, 92–93, 94,
  95, 96
Pill, Alison, 432
Piller, Michael, 355
Pine, Chris, 428
Pinter, Harold, 116, 142, 222, 299,
  400–401, 419, 424
Police (rock band), 286
Pomerance, Jill, 166–67, 170
Porter, Eric, 238
potato incident, 164–66
Pour Lucrèce (Giraudoux), 170
Preston, Carrie, 377
Previn, André, 366
Priestley, J. B., 105
Prior, Father (Community of the
  Resurrection), 91
Prochnow, Jürgen, 280, 283, 284,
  285

Public Theater (New York), 388
Pulp (rock band), 159
Punch magazine, 82, 86

"quadruple take" social media post,
    419–20
Quarry Theatre (Mirfield), 45–47
Quigley, Godfrey, 228
Quinn, Patricia, 276

Railsback, Steve, 291
Reagan, Ronald, 371
Rebel Without a Cause (movie), 311
received pronunciation (RP), 75–76
Redford, Robert, 253
Redgrave, Lynn, 46
Reed, Oliver, 299
Rees, Roger, 234, 362–64, 366, 367
Reeves, Saskia, 302
Refuge (domestic violence
    organization), 37
Reiner, Rob, 319
The Reluctant Debutante (play),
    162
Rembrandt van Rijn, School of, 54
The Revenger's Tragedy (Middleton),
    233–34
The Rhythm of the Saints (Simon),
    411
Richard III (Shakespeare), 191
Richardson, Ian, 233, 241, 242, 244,
    377
Richardson, Ralph, 91
The Ride Down Mt. Morgan (Miller),
    388–89
Roberts, Julia, 382
Robert (Stewart's nephew), 440
Roddenberry, Gene
    death of, 354
    Stewart's *TNG* hiring and, 304,
        305–8
    TNG and Beverly Crusher
        character, 338
    TNG and Original Series concept
        of, 333
    TNG Season One, 317, 322–23,
        329, 330
Rodenburg, Patsy, 74
Rodes, David, 298, 303–4, 306–8,
    312–13, 318, 357, 373
Rodway, Norman, 228, 250, 269,
    270, 271
Rogers, Paul, 132, 218, 220, 222
Romeo and Juliet (Shakespeare),
    132–33
Romijn, Rebecca, 387
Rose, Margot, 356
Ross, Duncan "Bill"
    fear of failure advice by, 144–45
    Old Vic School director roles of,
        100–101, 116–17, 120, 126,
        127, 143, 146, 148
Rover (Stewart family's pet), 8
Royal Academy of Dramatic Art
    (London), 168
Royal Shakespeare Company (RSC),
    217–30, 231–47, 257–72
    Goodbody and Other Place
        experimental theater,
        266–68
    London locations of, 217–18,
        277, 289–90 (*see also* Aldwych
        Theatre (London))
    Los Angeles shows, 235–38, 240,
        268, 322
    McKellen and, 315
    New York shows, 249–55
    Nunn appointed artistic director,
        238
    on-stage incidents, 224, 226–27,
        246
    patrons of, 231–32
    "performing" vs. Method acting
        at, 126
    prestige of, 156
    Rees and, 362

Royal Shakespeare Company (RSC) (*cont.*)
  RSC "club" (Dirty Duck/Black Swan), 228
  stage makeup for, 140
  Stewart's audition with, 209–13
  Stewart's early ambition for, 195, 198–200
  Stewart's early lead roles with, 257–60, 266–68
  Stewart's in Associate Actors Group of, 229–30
  Stewart's tenure at, 231, 232, 295–98
  Stratford location of, 217–18, 231–32
  Wynn Owen and, 75
Royal Shakespeare Company (RSC), performances
  Coriolanus, 260, 261, 267
  Doctor Faustus (Marlowe), 240
  Hamlet, 225–27, 268
  Hedda Gabler (Ibsen), 268
  Henry IV, Parts 1 and 2, 218–23, 277–78, 288–90
  Henry V, 213, 223–25
  The Iceman Cometh (O'Neill), 268–71
  The Investigation (Weiss), 241–42
  Julius Caesar, 262–66
  King John, 266–68
  King Lear, 238–39
  Macbeth, 403
  Marat/Sade, 241
  The Merchant of Venice, 57, 418
  A Midsummer Night's Dream, 241, 242, 257–60
  Much Ado About Nothing, 238–41
  Nicholas Nickleby (Dickens), 234, 362
  Occupations (Griffiths) at Other Place, 267–68
  The Revenger's Tragedy (Middleton), 233–34
  The Taming of the Shrew, 233–38
  Troilus and Cressida, 261
  The Two Gentlemen of Verona, 119, 242–47, 257, 261–62
  The Winter's Tale, 295–98, 439
  As You Like It, 233–38, 281
Rudnick, Paul, 185, 374
Ruehl, Mercedes, 388
Rushdie, Salman, 370
Ryan, Jeri, 435

Sainsbury, Susie, 414
Saint, Eva Marie, 273
Saint Joan (Shaw), 205–7
Sally (daughter of Wynn Owen), 73
Salote (queen of Tonga), 189
Salt-N-Pepa, 394
"sandwich scene" (*Macbeth*, Shakespeare), 406–7
Sarah (Sheffield landlord), 166
Sartre, Jean-Paul, 76, 100–101, 105
Saturday Night at the Crown (play), 157–58
Saturday Night Live (TV show), 393–94
Scarborough, Adrian, 426
Scase, David, 193–94, 196, 197, 200, 203–4
Schoenfeld, Gerald, 388, 389
Scott, Dougray, 386
Scott, Ridley, 272
Semley, Roy, 74, 115, 119, 120
Shaffer, Peter, 116, 238, 298–301, 314
Shakespeare, William
  burial place of, 415
  Stewart on writing of, 399
  Stewart's early Shakespeare training, 74–76, 117, 195, 199
  Stewart's teaching about, 240, 298, 303–4, 313
Shakespeare, William, works of
  Coriolanus, 260, 261, 267
  Hamlet, 208–9, 213, 225–27, 268

Henry IV, as Picard character inspiration, 322

Henry IV, Parts 1 and 2, 213, 218–23, 277–78, 288–90

Henry V, 167, 194, 199, 210–13, 223–25, 353

Julius Caesar, 262–66

King John, 266–68

King Lear, 238–39

Macbeth, 276, 402–11

The Merchant of Venice, 56–58, 74, 204–7, 209–13, 418

A Midsummer Night's Dream, 191, 241, 242, 249–55, 257–60

Much Ado About Nothing, 238–41

Richard III, 191

Romeo and Juliet, 132–33

Sonnets, 432–33

The Taming of the Shrew, RSC, 233–38

The Tempest, 377, 395–97

Troilus and Cressida, 261

Twelfth Night, 170, 176, 182–83, 185, 191, 194, 198

The Two Gentlemen of Verona, 119, 242–47, 257, 261–62

The Winter's Tale, 295–98, 439

As You Like It, RSC, 233–38, 281

Shakespeare in the Park (New York), 377

Sharp, Timm, 426

Shatner, William, 159, 306, 317, 324, 333, 376

Shaw, George Bernard, 86, 116, 146–47, 205–6

Sheffield Playhouse (Yorkshire, England), 158–70
  acting training at, 162–63
  British Actors' Equity Association and, 163–64
  company members, 161–62
  Ost's direction at, 158, 160–61, 169

stage makeup for, 141

Stewart's departure from, 169–71

Stewart's hiring by, 106, 128–29, 158–60, 193, 196

Stewart's homes and social life while working at, 164–68

Shelley, Raphael "Rudi," 63–64, 116–18, 127–29

Shelmerdine, Guy, 163

Sheridan, Richard Brinsley, 146

The Shewing-Up of Blanco Posnet (Shaw), 146–47

Shimerman, Armin, 333

Shubert Organization, 300, 303, 388–89

Sim, Alastair, 91

Simon, Paul, 411

Simpson, N. F., 142

Sinatra, Frank, 369

Singer, Bryan, 383, 385, 386–88

Sir Nigel Gresley (railway engine), 24

Sirtis, Marina, 319, 329, 331, 342, 435

"The Skaters' Waltz" (Waldteufel), 117–18

Smiling Pizza (New York City), 237

Smith, Paul, 285

social media
  "Empire State! #gogodididonyc @TwoPlaysInRep" campaign, 424–26
  Ozell's publicity talent for, 423–26
  Patrick Stewart's Cowboy Classic (fake album), 424
  pizza "slice" in New York City, 237
  "quadruple take," 419–20
  Sonnets (Shakespeare), 432–33

Solness, Halvard, 272

Sondheim, Stephen, 46

Soni, Karan, 426

Sonnets (Shakespeare), 432–33

South Africa, Mirfield clergyman and, 91–93

Spiner, Brent
  acting by, 371, 375
  Data character of, 328
  Picard movie plans, 438
  on *Star Trek: Picard*, 435, 436
  TNG final episode, 380
  TNG hiring of, 319
  TNG Season One, 320, 321, 325,
    326, 329
  TNG Season Three, 342, 343, 345,
    353
  TNG Season Five with Spock, 355
squirrels
  Cheryl the Squirrel, 434–35
  squirrel incident (1947), 29–30,
    433, 435
stage career. *see* Stewart, Patrick,
    stage career
Stanislavski, Konstantin, 126
Stanton, Barry, 254
Starr, Ringo, 215
Star Trek (Original Series)
  costumes, 333
  "The Naked Time" (episode), 329
  "Space, the final frontier" (*Star
    Trek* opening voice over), 324
  Stewart's lack of knowledge about,
    305, 317–18
  TNG cameos of actors from, 325
  Uhura character, 338
Star Trek: Deep Space Nine (TV
    series), 333, 348
Star Trek: The Next Generation
    (movies), 375–81
  First Contact, 376, 378–81
  Insurrection, 380
  Nemesis, 380–81, 429
  Star Trek Generations, 225, 376
Star Trek: The Next Generation
    (TV series), 317–32, 333–48.
    see also audience, fans, and
    publicity; Picard character
  artifact of, 320

Berman as producer-in-chief, 359
Beverly Crusher character, 338–39
Borg, 339, 378–79
camaraderie and antics, 126–27,
    129, 320–21, 325–29, 337, 342
cameos and reunion on *Picard*,
    430, 435–37
"Captain's Log" voice-overs, 324,
    381
celebrity guests and guest
    appearances, 209, 371–73
conventions, 321, 331–32
Data character, 328
"Engage," 439
Enterprise bridge scenes, 327
Ferengi alien species, 333
Guinan character, 338
impact of *Star Trek* franchise and,
    369–70
"line must be drawn h'yah!," 379–80
"Make it so," 439
"Number One," 342
Q character, 324, 375
Roddenberry's death and, 354
Season One, 333–35, 370
Season Two, 335–40, 371
Season Three, 339–48, 353–56,
    370–71
Seasons Five and Six as pinnacle
    of, 372–73
Season Seven, 360, 374
Stewart's audition and hiring, 304,
    305–16
Stewart's contract for, 314–15,
    337, 374
Stewart's preparation and routines,
    315, 317–23, 337
Tasha Yar character, 333
time travel themes, 18
Vash character, 341–43, 348
Vulcans and United Federation of
    Planets, 378
Worf character, 327–28, 354, 394

Star Trek: The Next Generation (TV series), episodes
"All Good Things . . ." (Season Seven), 375
"The Best of Both Worlds" (Season Three), 353–54
"The Big Goodbye" (Season One), 334
"Captain's Holiday" (Season Three), 341–43
"Chain of Command" and Cardassians (Season Six), 209, 372–73
"Code of Honor" (Season One), 370
"The Defector" (Season Three), 353
"Descent, Part 1" (Season Six), 371–72
"Encounter at Farpoint" (show pilot), 324–25, 329–30, 369, 375, 439
"The Inner Light" (Season Three), 355–56
"The Last Outpost" (Season One), 333
"Manhunt" (Season Two), 371
"The Naked Now" (Season One), 329–30
"The Offspring" (Season Three), 370–71
"11001001" and Bynars (Season One), 370
"Redemption, Part 1" (Season Four), 371
Spock in "Unification" (Season Five), 354–55
"We'll Always Have Paris" (Season One), 334
Star Trek: Picard (TV series), 428–31, 435–37
Star Trek: Voyager (TV series), 435

Starz, 426, 431
Steele, Tommy, 228
Steiger, Rod, 41, 123–24, 273–75
Steinbeck, John, 10, 86
Stevenson, Robert Louis, 154
Stewart, Alfred "Alf" (father)
  death of, 294–95
  drinking and violent behavior of, 30–38, 111–12, 297
  early biographical information, 17–23
  early family home life of, 8, 11–12
  food preferences of, 42
  Geoffrey's early childhood and, 15–17
  leadership qualities and military service of, 4–5, 15, 16, 70–71, 324, 405
  "Pat" nickname of, 4
  return to civilian life by, 26–27, 364
  son's education and, 72, 96, 102–3, 114, 138, 149
  son's journalism job and, 82–83, 85
  son's stage career success witnessed by, 293–95
  Towngate council house of, 109–10, 295
Stewart, Daniel Freedom (son)
  childhood of, 201, 231, 240, 247, 250, 268, 280
  A Christmas Carol (Dickens) and, 359–60, 364
  education of, 335
  mother-in-law of, 420
  name of, 15
  parents' divorce and, 335, 339, 346, 351, 442
  as *Star Trek* fan, 305, 317–18
  on *TNG*, 356
Stewart, Geoffrey (brother). *see* Barrowclough, Geoffrey

Stewart, Gladys Barrowclough
(mother)
acting by, 79–80
death of, 293
Geoffrey's birth and early life,
14–17
husband's return to civilian life, 26
husband's violent behavior, 30–38,
111–12, 297
Mirfield (Northern England)
lifestyle of, 4, 12–13
mother-in-law of, 19
on son's "aura," 90
son's birth, 3–4
son's education and, 66, 96, 102–3,
107, 114, 138, 149, 151
son's inspiration from, 324
son's journalism job and, 83
son's stage career success
witnessed by, 293–95
squirrel incident and, 29
textile work of, 2, 31, 41
Towngate council house of,
109–10, 295
Stewart, Mary (paternal
grandmother), 14, 18–23, 171
Stewart, Patrick. see also audience,
fans, and publicity; Royal
Shakespeare Company; Star
Trek: The Next Generation
(movies); Star Trek: The
Next Generation (TV series);
individual names of family
members
acting as main purpose in life, 3–4
acting income, 150, 170, 212,
314
acting preparedness, 219–20
age and aging, 423, 442–43
appreciation for career success,
41, 54
career disappointment, National
Theatre, 238

cars and gearhead interest of, 39,
40, 113, 201, 214–15, 337
classical music fan, 53, 183, 201,
286, 322, 381
comedy of, 237, 393–97, 419–20,
424–26, 431
confidence, 168, 195, 196
domestic violence awareness as
cause of, 37
drinking by, 205–7, 407–8
father's qualities/tendencies
recognized in, 70–71, 265–66,
324, 405
fear of failure, 49–52, 144–45
first-class travel to Dune set,
280–82
first on-screen kiss, 291
first trip outside England, 138–39
knighthood ceremony, 295,
412–15
Lloyd's friendship with, 239–41
McKellen's friendship with,
397–401
name of, 4, 17, 174
paranormal experiences of, 90–91,
294, 351–53
physical description, 85–86, 103,
128, 136–37, 193, 289, 308–9,
311, 405
political views of, 141–42, 156,
163–64, 371
pottery collection of, 55
"poverty mentality" of, 321,
336–37
social media presence (see social
media)
sports interest, 52, 112, 226–27,
305, 319, 416–17
Transcendental Meditation
practiced by, 290
"We are not here to have fun"
incident, 127, 129, 326, 426,
428

Stewart, Patrick, accolades and
reviews
A Christmas Carol (Dickens), 360,
365–67
Dewsbury and District Reporter on
Stewart, 171
disappointments about, 103
Julius Caesar at RSC, 266
A Midsummer Night's Dream, RSC
white-box production, New
York, 252–53
Stewart Hall (Mirfield Secondary
Modern School), 53
Yonadab (Shaffer), 300
Stewart, Patrick, acting training. *see
also* language and voice
amateur dramatics ("am-drams"),
60, 80–81, 94–96
Brighouse Children's Theatre, 66
drama school planning, 81, 96–98
early age of, 60–61, 118
listening, 199–200
Method acting vs. "performing,"
126
movement training, 63–64,
128–29
Mytholmroyd residential drama
course (1953), 59–67, 90, 99,
100, 105
at Old Vic School, 99–104,
122–25 (*see also* Bristol Old Vic
Theatre School)
theater vs. film/TV, 123
voice/acting lessons with Ruth
Wynn Owen, 66–67, 72–78
vulnerability in acting, 125
West Riding County Major
Scholarship, 99, 104–7
Stewart, Patrick, early life, 59–83
birth of, 3–5
Bristol Old Vic Theatre School
preparation, 110–14 (*see also*
Bristol Old Vic Theatre School)

at Crowlees Boys' School, 45–52
at Lee Green Infants School, 32,
41–44
at Mirfield Secondary Modern
School, 53–58, 59–61, 68–72,
80–81, 82
non-acting jobs, 40, 85–96, 97–98,
102, 107, 110, 131, 133–36
non-acting jobs, in journalism,
82–83, 85–96
oldest brother of, 14–16, 26, 55,
294
parents' homes, 7–13, 16, 109–10
parents' marriage, 30–38, 111–12,
297
paternal family background,
17–23
reading preferences of, 10–11, 86
school bullying by/of, 30, 48,
51–52
twenty-first birthday celebration,
184
working-class lifestyle of family,
1–3, 5–13, 50–51, 137–38, 164
Yorkshire connection in
professional life, 106
Stewart, Patrick, film career. *see also
Star Trek: The Next Generation*
(movies); *X-Men* movies
Conspiracy Theory, 382
Dune, 277, 279–90
Hennessy, 41, 273–75
Jeffrey, 185, 374
Lifeforce, 290–91
Stewart, Patrick, homes and lodgings
in Brooklyn, 414, 424, 430, 432
childhood homes, 7–13, 16,
109–10
in London, 217, 232, 295
in Los Angeles, 235–36, 240, 318,
336–37, 340, 343, 344, 350–53,
432
in Manchester, 196–97

Stewart, Patrick, homes and lodgings (*cont.*)
  in Manhattan, 250
  Old Vic World Tour living arrangements, 173–74, 177, 179, 184–85
  in Oxfordshire, 440
  in Sheffield, 164–66
  in Warwickshire, 134–36, 217–18, 231, 243, 295
  in Yorkshire Dales, 113–14
Stewart, Patrick, journalism career
  at *Dewsbury and District Reporter,* 82–83, 85–87, 91–93
  at *Mirfield Reporter,* 88–90, 93–96
  obituary writing, 93–94
  quitting of, 94–96
  South Africa and Mirfield clergyman story, 91–93
Stewart, Patrick, romantic life
  extramarital affairs, 341–43, 345–48, 390–91
  marriage, first (*see* Falconer, Sheila)
  marriage, second, 381–82, 390–91
  marriage, third (*see* Ozell, Sunny)
  marriage breakdown and divorce from Falconer, 302, 335–36, 339–48, 349, 350, 391, 418
  as young adult, 119–22, 136–39, 148, 149, 159, 166–70, 196–99
  youthful romances, 6, 14, 40, 50, 88, 111
Stewart, Patrick, stage career, 293–304. *see also* Royal Shakespeare Company; theater acting and business
  Bristol Old Vic, 208–9, 213–16
  A Christmas Carol (Dickens), one-man show, 356–67 (*see also* *A Christmas Carol*)
  early acting interest of, 29–30, 38–41, 44, 52

early lead roles, 167, 295–303
early Shakespeare exposure, 56–58
Every Good Boy Deserves Favour (Stoppard), 386
first acting job after Old Vic School, 150–51
frightening experiences on stage, 46–47, 276
grandfather's acting career and, 20–23
Liverpool Playhouse, 193, 200–208
Manchester Library Theatre, 167, 193–94, 195–201
The Master Builder (Ibsen), 272, 390–91
The Merchant of Venice (Shakespeare), 418
No Man's Land (Pinter), 400–401, 419, 424
Old Vic World Tour, 169–71, 173–94 (*see also* Old Vic World Tour)
on-stage incidents, 202–4, 206–7, 246
parents' knowledge of success in, 293–95
The Ride Down Mt. Morgan (Miller), 388–89
RSC full-time employment ended, 295, 345–46
Sheffield repertory company, 158–70, 193, 196
The Tempest (Shakespeare), 377
Theatre Royal (Lincoln, England), 150–51, 153–59
traveling education program (US), 240, 298, 313
as UCLA visiting Shakespeare professor, 303–4
Waiting for Godot (Beckett), 47, 397–401, 424

Who's Afraid of Virginia Woolf?
(Albee), 301–3, 305, 388
The Winter's Tale (Shakespeare),
295–98, 439
Yonadab (Shaffer), 298–301
Stewart, Patrick, television career.
*see also Star Trek: The Next
Generation*
American Dad!, 394
Cannes TV convention (1988),
336
Extras, 394–97
Family Guy, 394
first TV set and, 232
I, Claudius (BBC), 276–77
North and South (miniseries), 273
Saturday Night Live, 393–94
Uber Eats (commercial), 163
Stewart, Pat (sister-in-law), 413, 414,
420, 440
Stewart, Sophie (daughter)
birth of, 231
education of, 335
in Mexico, 280
parents' divorce and, 335, 339–40,
343–46, 350, 356, 442
as *Star Trek* fan, 305, 317–18
on Yorkshire Dales home, 113
Stewart, Trevor (brother)
brother's knighting ceremony and,
413, 414
brother's *TNG* hiring and, 317,
440–42
brother's wedding to Ozell and,
420
brother's Yorkshire Dales home
and, 113
death of, 440–43
early life of, 9, 11–12, 14, 16, 25,
33–35, 38, 47, 49, 112
parents' deaths and, 293, 294
in Royal Air Force, 35
wedding of, 85

Stewart, William (paternal
grandfather), 18, 19–20, 22
Stiller, Ben, 395
Sting, 286, 400
Stirling, Jennifer, 202–3
Stockwell, Dean, 280
Stoppard, Tom, 386
Stratford-upon-Avon, RSC location
of, 217–18, 231–32. *see also*
Royal Shakespeare Company
Suzman, Janet, 196–99, 225, 238
Swander, Homer D. "Murph," 240,
313
Sydow, Max von, 280, 283, 284, 287

"tall poppy syndrome," 365
The Taming of the Shrew
(Shakespeare), 233–38
Tanner, John Sigismund, 11
Taplin, Terry, 254
Taylor, Elizabeth, 301
Taylor, Jeri, 355
Taylor, Paul, 367
"t'bottom field," 1–3
television career. *see* Stewart, Patrick,
television career
The Tempest (Shakespeare), 377,
395–97
Tennant, David, 226, 415
Teotihuacán, Mexico, 192
Thacker, David, 301, 303
Thatcher, Margaret, 156, 163
That Was the Week That Was (TV
show), 234
theater acting and business. *see
also* clothing and costumes;
language and voice
casting, 157
dress circle (theater seats), 114
film/TV acting vs. theater, 123
genre, absurdist theater, 142
genre, musicals, 207–8
hierarchy of personnel in, 175

theater acting and business (*cont.*)
  live theater as captivating, 132–33
  makeup, 140–41
  nonacting positions in, 121
  stage management work, 154–56
  "tall poppy syndrome," 365
theater career (*see* Stewart, Patrick,
    stage career)
  weekly and biweekly repertory,
    156–58
Theatre Royal (Bristol, England),
    114–15, 399. *see also* Old Vic
    Theatre Company (Bristol)
Theatre Royal (Lincoln, England),
    106, 150–51, 153–59
Theiss, William Ware, 330
Thesiger, Ernest, 128
Thomas, Charles "Charlie," 199, 200,
    210, 212
Thomas, Dylan, 46, 143
Thorndike, Sybil, 91
Tierney, Lawrence, 334, 342
Tilvern, Alan, 271
TNG. see Star Trek: The Next
    Generation (movies); *Star*
    Trek: The Next Generation (TV
    series)
Todd, Hallie, 370
"Tomorrow, and tomorrow, and
    tomorrow" soliloquy (*Macbeth,*
    Shakespeare), 402–3
Tony (Stewart's cousin), 53, 96–97
Tottenham Hotspur (football club,
    England), 319
Tourneur, Cyril, 233
trainspotting, 24–25
Transcendental Meditation (TM), 290
Treasure Island (Stevenson), 154
Troilus and Cressida (Shakespeare),
    261
Twelfth Night (Shakespeare), 170,
    176, 182–83, 185, 191, 194,
    198

The Two Gentlemen of Verona
    (Shakespeare), 119, 242–47,
    257, 261–62
Tyler, Gerald, 60, 62, 66, 99, 105, 107
Tyzack, Margaret, 276

Uber Eats (TV commercial), 163
UCLA, 298, 303–4, 312–13,
    358–59, 373
UC Santa Barbara, 358
Under Milk Wood (Thomas), 143–44
United Kingdom. *see* England

Vereen, Ben, 366

Wadsworth Theatre (UCLA),
    358–59
Waiting for Godot (Beckett), 47, 115,
    397–401, 424
Waldteufel, Émile, 117–18
Waller, David, 254
Wanamaker, Zoë, 205
Ward, Anthony, 404
Ward, Mr. (teacher), 45
Warehouse (Donmar Warehouse,
    London), 218
Warner, David, 208–9, 213, 226, 227,
    320, 327, 372–73
Weaver, Jacki, 426
Weaver, Sigourney, 374
Weber, Steven, 374
Weiss, Peter, 241
Wells, Dolly, 426
Westmore, Michael, 339, 342, 353,
    370, 379
West Riding County Council,
    Mytholmroyd residential drama
    course (1953), 59–67, 90, 99,
    100, 105
West Riding County Major
    Scholarship, 99, 104–7
Wheaton, Wil, 319, 321
Whitelaw, Billie, 302–3, 307

Who's Afraid of Virginia Woolf?
    (Albee), 301–3, 305, 388
Williams, Clifford, 218, 219
William (Stewart's uncle), 21–22
Wilsher, Barry, 398
Wilson, Henry, 82, 93, 95–96, 171
Wilson, Ruth, 380
Winslet, Kate, 395
The Winter's Tale (Shakespeare), 241,
    295–98
Wolfe, George C., 377
Wolfit, Donald, 91
Wood, Durinda, 339
Wood, John, 262–66
Woodard, Alfre, 379
Woodcock, Bruce, 38
Woodward, Joanne, 253
World Cup (1966), 226–27
World War II
    Anderson (air raid) shelters, 6–7
    postwar election, United Kingdom
        (1945), 32–33
    Stewart's father's service in, 4–5
    V-E celebration, 2
Wright, Nicholas, 185, 190
Writers Guild of America (WGA),
    335–37
Wynn Owen, Meg (Margaret
    Shuttleworth), 73–74
Wynn Owen, Ruth
    home of, 43, 76–78, 90

    at Royal Shakespeare Company,
        75
    on Stewart's "aura," 90
    Stewart's early training by, 64,
        66–67, 72–78, 93, 111, 115,
        117, 124, 127, 195, 199
    on Stewart's Old Vic Theatre
        School attendance, 99–100, 102

X-Men movies
    Charles Xavier (Professor X)
        character, 385–86, 393, 427–28
    Logan, 54, 427–28
    McKellen and, 315
    Stewart's hiring, 382–83, 385
    The Wolverine, 427
    X-Men (2000), 385–88, 397
    X-Men: The Last Stand (2006),
        397
    X2 (2003), 388

Yonadab (Shaffer)
    at National Theatre, 238, 298–301
    revival plans for, 300–301, 304,
        314
    Yorkshire Post (England), 93
    Young Vic Theatre (London),
        301

Zapata, Joy, 310, 311
Z-Cars (TV show), 146